The Texas Revolutionary Experience

Number Ten:
Texas A&M Southwestern Studies
ROBERT A. CALVERT and LARRY D. HILL
General Editors

For Lynn

The Texas Revolutionary Experience

A POLITICAL AND SOCIAL HISTORY
1835–1836

By Paul D. Lack

TEXAS A&M UNIVERSITY PRESS
COLLEGE STATION

The paper used in this book meets the minimum requirements
of the American National Standard for Permanence
of Paper for Printed Library Materials, Z39.48-1984.
Binding materials have been chosen for durability.

Library of Congress Cataloging-in-Publication Data

Lack, Paul D.
    The Texas revolutionary experience : a political and social
history, 1835–1836 / by Paul D. Lack.
        p. cm. — (Texas A&M southwestern studies ; no. 10)
    Includes bibliographical references.
    ISBN 0-89096-497-1 (cloth); 0-89096-721-0 (pbk.)
    1. Texas—History—Revolution, 1835–1836. I. Title. II. Series.
F390.L194   1992
976.4'03—dc20   91-23368
                                                              CIP

ISBN-13: 978-0-89096-721-8 (pbk.)

Contents

Tables

Maps

Acknowledgments

In the midst of preparing yet another book review during our graduate school days, a friend once casually remarked that he intended to write a book with a distinctive section of acknowledgments. His version would read something like: "I wish to thank no one because I did all the work on this book myself." This remark yielded a good laugh at the time, but the experience of completing a historical manuscript for publication reveals how far from the truth such an anti-acknowledgment would be.

Many deserve prominent mention for providing encouragement and opportunity. My wife Katha Lynn Lack, to whom this work is dedicated, supported my education and taught me a great deal about writing as my first editor. L. Tuffly Ellis as executive director of the Texas State Historical Association had the confidence to invite me to prepare a study of slavery and the Texas Revolution for the sesquicentennial edition of the *Southwestern Historical Quarterly,* a project that sparked my interest in this period. He also read and evaluated an early version of the introduction.

McMurry University provided a one-semester sabbatical that gave me a good start on the research. The East Texas Historical Association awarded an Ottis Lock research award that funded trips to Nacogdoches. I wish to thank Dr. James V. Reese of Stephen F. Austin University for calling my attention to this grant. My friends Richard Crowell and Dr. Gerald McDaniel offered transportation and companionship during research journeys to Austin.

Several scholars have read the manuscript at various stages and offered valuable suggestions: Dr. Arnoldo De León of Angelo State University critiqued the Tejano and Tory chapters and encouraged my participation in several conferences. Dr. Alwyn Barr of Texas Tech University suggested research opportunities, read the army chapters, and offered his astute appraisal of the concepts of this work. He has remained my teacher long after those formal duties ceased. The Rev. Dr. Fane Downs evaluated the chapter on Anglo Texans and as my most esteemed colleague shared her unique insights on the Texas experience. Dr. Ralph Wooster of Lamar University, in the capacity of reader for the press, examined the entire work and offered suggestions for improvement that I have followed as closely as possible.

Dr. Robert Calvert of Texas A&M University showed interest in the book and recommended it for the Southwestern Studies series for which he and Dr. Larry Hill serve as general editors. Calvert and Dr. Walter Buenger gave me the opportunity to prepare a chapter for the work they edited on Texas historiography and thereby helped to sharpen my perspective.

Adán Benavides of San Antonio gave timely and expert assistance on Spanish names. Ana Carolina Castillo-Crimm answered the call for maps with a unique combination of historical knowledge and cartographic skill. Whatever errors remain in the work after all this assistance are of course solely my own.

Many librarians and archivists also deserve special mention. Lynn Haggard and Joe Specht of the Jay-Rollins Library at McMurry University helped to locate works and obtain them on interlibrary loan. The archivists and assistants at the Barker Texas History Center and in the Special Collections division of the Steen Library at Stephen F. Austin University performed their duties with professional expertise. At the Texas State Archives Michael Green and the other archivists patiently helped me to understand finding aids and to dissect collections that were otherwise unyielding. All the staff at the Archives Division of the General Land Office, headed at the first of my research by Dr. Mike Hooks and more recently by Dr. Frank de la Teja, were likewise considerate in extending special advice.

Some persons unfortunately may have been inadvertently overlooked, but I cannot fail to acknowledge my debt to a few others. Pat Shackelford assisted in preparing the manuscript. My children, Spence and Brooke, showed tolerance for the intrusions in their lives of an author at work. Jim Hindman and Jo Ann Stiles helped by talking me through issues addressed by the book with patient interest. Others either cannot or wish not to be thanked here but know of my gratitude for their contributions.

Introduction

On February 13, 1836, the provisional government of Texas confronted crises from all directions. A Mexican army that dwarfed the irregular Texas forces in size, discipline, and military organization had crossed the Rio Grande and now marched northward. Still lacking a unified command, the Texans had divided their force, taking positions at Béxar and Goliad; then the army had splintered further, following different leaders who espoused a variety of strategic plans and quarrelled among themselves. None had indisputable legitimacy because the political establishment had never succeeded in asserting authority over the army.

Instead, the governor and Council, installed three months earlier by an indecisive convention known as the Consultation, had likewise surrendered to the forces of chaos. Accentuated by explosive personalities and an awkward constitutional arrangement, differences over the goal of the uprising had resulted in repeated conflicts and eventual impeachment of Gov. Henry Smith. He refused to yield to an acting governor appointed as a replacement; the membership of the Council soon withered away in despair. Fundamental issues that had divided the Texans since the beginning of the rebellion remained unresolved. Even the answer to the question of what the Texans were fighting for remained unresolved. The government would not declare independence until more than two weeks later, too late for word to reach the soon-to-be martyrs of the Alamo.

Having failed to respond to — much less resolve — these various signs of internal disharmony, the Council chose this thirteenth day of February to issue yet another proclamation. Its words announced what circumstances should have made obvious — that they were revolutionaries.

Perhaps more in hope than belief, it asserted that their revolutionary spirit could overcome all adversities: "teach the *Tyrant of Mexico* and his hirelings that *the sons* of the BRAVE PATRIOTS of '76 *are invincible in the cause of* FREEDOM *and the* RIGHTS OF MAN."[1] In part, this and other ideological statements sought merely to place the Texas cause within an Anglo-American tradition. The previous December a newspaper writer had asserted that "the history of the revolution of the United States furnishes abundant lessons" applicable to the current crisis. This usable past generally taught, in the words of the inaugural address of Interim President David G. Burnet on March 17, 1836, "the rectitude of our cause and [the] indestructible inheritance of gallantry which we derive from the illustrious conquerors of 1776." But others interpreted the Texas crusade in a less ethnocentric manner. Even before the armed conflict began, one writer styling himself "A True Mexican" prophesied that liberty would not easily be stamped out by Santa Anna: "the Sons of the free will have redress—*they will be free.*" "The free born sons of Texas," as a Brazoria resident toasted them, sought to identify with a revolutionary tradition as old as the ancient Hebrews.[2]

Outside supporters appealed for aid from all persons of liberal opinion, especially from Americans who could identify with the recent struggles for freedom in Hungary, Greece, and Poland. Typically, a meeting in Mobile, Alabama, advertised for attendance by: "'The friends of Texas and of humanity, the descendants of heroes and patriots, all those who truly love the cause of civil and religious liberty, all who can sympathize in the wrongs and sufferings of their fellow beings.'"[3]

During the uncertainties of their struggle Texans looked also to a future brightened by the triumph of the revolutionary spirit. In late November, 1835, Haden Edwards expressed hope that the land would become a "Haven of Liberty and independence."[4] This attitude infected some even before they reached Texas soil. From near Natchitoches a volunteer fated to die at the Alamo wrote to his brother to explain "the reason for our pushing on . . . it is a Master one" involving feelings of "an instinctive horror" of tyranny and a love of republicanism: "The cause of Philanthropy, or Humanity, of Liberty and human happiness through the world called loudly in every man who can to aid Texas." Besides, he added in an equally revealing aside, "if we succeed, the Country is ours, it is immense in extent and fertile in its soil."[5]

Perhaps in part because of the duality of motives suggested by this patriot's statement, the Texas cause has never gained much credence as a revolutionary phenomenon. Nevertheless, as one scholar recently observed, Texas historians continue "grandiloquently" to term it a "revolution."[6] The process of disparaging revolutionary qualities began with the earliest accounts. Those critical of Texas viewed the war as a product of counterrevolutionary attitudes and activities. The most influential of these interpretations, *The War in Texas,* published by Benjamin Lundy in 1837, reflected views of critics in both the United States and Mexico.

Lundy's suspicions regarding the conflict proceeded from a decade-old career as an anti-slavery editor and from recent visits in Nacogdoches, Brazoria, Béxar, and other Mexican provinces. Lundy wrote to refute the popular idea that "the inhabitants of Texas were engaged in a legitimate contest for the maintenance of the sacred principles of Liberty, and the natural, inalienable Rights of Man." His historical narrative developed the theme that southern-born colonists had evaded Mexican emancipation measures, finally moving toward a goal of separate statehood to establish slavery on a firm constitutional basis. When foiled in their efforts, a "vast combination" of Texas slaveholders, supported by land-jobbers, slave-breeders and dealers and their political lackeys in the United States, implemented a "treasonable" scheme to divide Texas from Mexico. In Lundy's view the Texas rhetoric of liberty only covered up individual greed and sin. The conflict, he wrote, derived from "motives of personal aggrandizement, avaricious adventure, and unlimited, enduring oppression."[7]

A few foreign observers such as Frederic Leclerc wrote flatteringly that the spirit of the French Revolution effused the Texas rebellion;[8] but most of those who defended the Texans in this early war of words made no real attempt to rescue their reputations as genuine revolutionaries. Lundy's most stinging charge—that the leaders of the revolt were conspirators—seemed best defended by emphasizing their respectable and conservative qualities. From the first, many exponents of the Texas cause had never been comfortable with a revolutionary label. "'The character of the struggle in which Texas is engaged is now clearly developed," Stephen F. Austin explained to the new provisional government in early December, 1835, "it is one of self-preservation.'" Using this evidence, the earliest writers in the partisan debate thus could appropriate a self-generated image of the Texans as cautious defenders of the status quo.

Chester Newell published a *History of the Revolution in Texas* in 1838, based, he claimed, on interviews with its leaders and on examination of official documents. In his account Mexico—with its history of "intestine collisions" including violence, insurrection, usurpation, and revolution — had sparked the conflict with Texas by succumbing to despotism in 1835. Until then the Texans had been, though "jealous of their rights," loyal and "obedient to law." He praised their "forbearance" and orderly resistance to earlier "unconstitutional" Mexican provocations. "Disposed to peace" despite "the revolutionary state of the interior of the Republic," Texas sought independence only in response to the "utter anarchy" that existed once the despot Santa Anna had overthrown the constitution. Moderate, "pacific" acts to obtain "good order and constitutional regularity" had all been exhausted before the Texans reluctantly took up arms in defense of their "constitutional rights." Later nineteenth-century historians wrote better documented and more complete accounts, often adopting the term "Texas Revolution" and even the adjective "revolutionary" to describe the epoch but still emphasizing its conservatism.[10]

Twentieth-century scholars brought different and clearer perspectives, somewhat less partisanship, and more sophisticated and thorough research to the study of this era. Nevertheless, few gave much credence to the presence of revolutionary dimensions. One persistent school of thought emphasized a variety of conspiracy theories involving land speculators or grasping politicians.[11] Modern scholarship continued to concentrate primarily on the causes of the struggle rather than on its internal character, due partly to the dominance of Eugene C. Barker. This greatest of Texas historians focused on Austin, whose historic significance declined after the beginning of hostilities. Thus, Barker's work dealt primarily with background topics.

Self-consciously "scientific" in methodology, he claimed to have purged his work of the easy stereotypes of previous accounts in order to emphasize fundamental historical forces. The westward movement of the United States produced Anglo-American settlement of Texas. This process led in turn to an incompatible marriage of divergent cultures ("racial inheritances," to use Barker's terminology) which sincere leaders on both sides struggled unsuccessfully to reconcile. Chronic political instability in Mexico sparked the rupture by frustrating those who had sought reconciliation and by threatening to overturn the earlier pattern of compromise and salutary neglect. Barker described specific long-standing annoyances — differences of tradition on religion, slavery, immigration, judicial and political arrangements — that disturbed relations between Mexico and Texas. However "exasperating and persistent" these issues proved to be, the absence of "mutual understanding" between the two peoples made revolt inevitable. Therefore, Mexican authorities rejected Texas statehood, the only possible solution, and unwittingly brought on the conflict by measures designed to defend the province.[12]

Barker noted general similarities between his subject and the American revolution, but he emphasized the uniqueness of the Texas case because "racial feeling" dominated: "The Texans saw themselves in danger of becoming the alien subjects of a people to whom they deliberately believed themselves morally, intellectually, and politically superior."[13] In Barker's account, then, the Texas Revolution held even more obvious conservative credentials. Its prudent leader reluctantly embraced armed resistance only after exhausting passive measures; the essential quality of the movement was an effort to preserve or even restore a traditional culture.

Superior by far to anything that had been done before in terms of quality of research, clarity of interpretations, and lucidity of writing, Barker's work dominated the scholarship on this period. Other contributors generally reaffirmed his theories. Samuel H. Lowrie's *Culture Conflict in Texas,* though different in scholarly style, reflected Barker's hypothesis. Carlos E. Castañeda's sweeping narrative displayed greater sensitivity in evaluating both Mexican and Texan behavior, but his work basically followed the interpretive pattern established by Barker.[14]

Historians of the last forty years occasionally noted what one described as the "cross currents of revolution"[15] present in the independence struggle; yet none fully addressed the revolutionary experience in Texas. The single most important scholar of the subject, William C. Binkley, edited the correspondence of the Texas Revolution and wrote a succinct account that analyzed its background and the war period as well.

Binkley recognized the need for "considerations of the role which revolutions have played in making the present what it is," but he argued that this task awaited more scholarship on the nature of revolution. His narrative reiterated Barker's understanding of the causes of the revolt, more strongly emphasizing economic issues and the centralist-federalist dispute as precipitating factors. In this way Binkley also depicted the Texans as conservative defenders of the existing arrangement of government and cast Santa Anna's centralists as the aggressors. Nevertheless, Binkley observed some revolutionary dimensions of the Texas struggle. Noting that conservatism predominated at the outset, he suggested the existence of party divisions regarding how fast and far to push the break with Mexico and over the purpose of the movement. Binkley showed that events unfolded rapidly in a complicated and directionless manner, with resulting conflict among the Texans. Efforts at establishing a legitimate government initially failed and contributed to the confusion within the unruly Texas armies. In fact, wrote Binkley, "the progress of the revolution seemed to evoke almost continuous internal strife." In general, he saw this episode as "a logical extension" of the revolutionary struggles for independence in the New World, but he concluded candidly: "The one thing which can be suggested with assurance is that the last word concerning the meaning or significance of the Texas Revolution has not yet been said."[16]

Many words have indeed been said since Binkley's study appeared in 1952, but his invitation for further study has been accepted by surprisingly few. The editor of the ten-volume *Papers of the Texas Revolution* became so chagrined by this paucity of scholarship as to disparage the historical profession in general. In Mexican historiography, too, according to a 1978 analysis, the years 1824–36 were a "neglected period" for those writing in both Spanish and English.[17] A notable recent exception is David J. Weber's *The Mexican Frontier, 1821–1846*, which provides needed perspective. This work demonstrates that the northern provinces of Mexico developed along similar lines out of common historical forces. Mexico's long struggle for independence initiated a period of strife and change. Ruinous separatist and class-oriented revolts in Texas in the 1810s and subsequent Spanish efforts at reform raised expectations of local autonomy and other liberal ideals. Upheaval in the interior accelerated the decline of the presidial system, the church, and other traditional means of authority at the same time that a vigorous Anglo-American culture also entered the region and pulled it toward another orbit. Political, economic, military, and cultural changes throughout the frontier divided it from central Mexico prior to the mid-1830s, when rebellions arose in California, New Mexico, and Sonora as well as Texas. Weber cogently analyzes Texas independence as part of an evolutionary process common to the region, and thus, his view also suggested its non-revolutionary character. In fact, such radical features as class conflict occurred most dramatically in the revolts of New Mexico in 1837. The Texas event was but one of many successful rebellions in the borderlands, a "simple and rather conservative political revolt," he states elsewhere.[18]

No recent scholar has reexamined the Texas Revolution in a detailed fashion. Although the emergence of Mexican-American consciousness has been a constructive historiographical force, challenging the racism that undergirded earlier views, the focus has been on background and causation issues. Other works, both popular and scholarly, have centered on military topics. The sesquicentennial celebration raised awareness, stimulated scholarship, and prompted considerable demythologizing; nevertheless, most of this is specialized, and the collective result still provides but piecemeal coverage.[19] Scholarship has barely touched on the question of the revolutionary dimensions of the Texas Revolution, and the present study is the first systematic attempt to analyze the event in detail as political and social history.[20]

The continuing search for the character of the Texas Revolution might appropriately start with a clear understanding of what is meant by the term "revolution." Even casual observation suggests that this is no simple task. When President Ronald Reagan, an avowed conservative, called for a "second American Revolution" in his 1985 state of the union address, he joined the growing ranks of those who have appropriated the word for the purpose of emphasis only. Historians and other social scientists also use "revolution" loosely and without common agreement as to its meaning, in part simply reflecting the absence of overall ideological consensus. However frustrating this rhetorical imprecision may be, the state of scholarship on the nature of revolution has advanced considerably and suggests several helpful lines of inquiry.[21]

First, any effort to interpret a particular upheaval as conforming to a formula derived from observing other revolutions will be forced, artificial, and misleading. Historically, revolutions have been complex phenomena following no precise recipe but rather having diverse ingredients mixed together in a variety of ways. Nevertheless, historian Crane Brinton and others who searched for what he called a sociology of revolution have identified processes frequently experienced in revolutionary settings.

Second, by some definitions, the Texas movement for independence, despite the trauma it released, could never be considered revolutionary. Mark N. Hagopian and like-minded scholars have restricted their list of true revolutions to profound, epoch-making, globally significant crises identifiable by ideological contributions or reverberations of class conflict.[22] The Texas Revolution had significance in several different contexts, some of which have been exaggerated by Texas chauvinists.[23] But this event produced no new ideology and imparted no worldwide revolutionary contagion, even though other parts of the Mexican frontier did soon experiment with armed revolt.

Hagopian distinguishes revolutions from lesser events such as coups d'état, peasant or aristocratic revolts, mob, nativist, or Millenarianist risings, and regional separatist movements. The secession phenomenon seems particularly applicable to the Texas case. Regional revolts occurred most often when ethnic and other cultural configurations provided a geographical area with an identity different from that of the rest of the nation. Often efforts at "standardization" or centralization precipitated a crisis by threatening to overwhelm the section, which usually sought autonomy before resorting to violent resistance. In turn, armed revolt occasioned reprisals by national authorities. These secession efforts, whether they ended in success or failure, often stopped short of becoming revolutionary, even in cases where protracted and bloody wars of independence occurred. However, some of these conflicts developed into revolutions. This especially took place when the central government sought to promote internal conflict—along ideological, class, or ethnic lines—in order to quell the regional rebellion. If these cleavages were profound enough, they led to revolution even after a region achieved autonomy and began to struggle with problems of new nationhood. Thus, secession movements often became more profoundly revolutionary than their creators intended.[24] In fact, one of the more consistent themes in the scholarship of revolution is that movements tend to get out of hand and develop imperatives of their own.[25]

Another instructive model for the Texas Revolution is European historian Arno Mayer's concept of "pre-emptive counterrevolutions." In this view, avowed conservatives initiated this kind of revolt in the name of thwarting the triumph of forces that threatened to transform the status quo. One recent overview of the American Civil War cast the southern movement for independence as one of these preventive efforts. Several years ago Emory Thomas explained how the Confederacy evolved into revolutionary experience from conservative origins and intentions.[26]

Despite their many insights, neither historians nor social scientists have developed an inclusive or widely adopted definition of revolution. The following composite one makes no pretense at supplying this need, but it does at least indicate some major characteristics to be considered in this volume: the term revolution describes a sudden, severe change that abolishes or substantially reorders the political system in terms of structure, functions, and personnel. To succeed it must have leaders willing to use violence or other forceful methods commonly believed to be extraconstitutional. A genuine revolution results in internal conflicts which affect wealth and social status.[27]

Comparative studies also suggest that certain tensions and processes characterized revolutionary situations. Brinton identified discernable stages: the emergence of armed conflict, rule by moderates who prove incapable of stemming the radical tide, extremism including a Reign of Terror and Virtue, and a Thermidor period of reaction and convalescence. Several critics have pointed out that this model relies excessively on the French Revolution and has less applicability to the English, American, and Russian experiences that are described in his *Anatomy*. Investigations of other revolutions not considered by Brinton also indicate the possibility of less rigid patterns. Moderates sometimes succeeded in limiting the pace of change and degree of upheaval; the radicals, too, have frequently extended the life of their "phase" of the revolution.[28]

Without posing an alternate mechanistic model, recent scholars show that some features of revolutions have been repeated often enough to warrant the attention of those who seek to understand the revolutionary experience. Leaders of revolutionary movements commonly adopted or developed ideologies designed to appeal to a broad spectrum of the population. Their ideas frequently emphasized links with the past in order to establish a cultural identity and thereby gain a degree of legitimacy. After much experimentation and even competition among various notions, an ideology emerged that appealed to popular passions, often by using the themes of progress, nationalism, secularism, and democracy.

Successful ideologies were applied to mobilize as well as arouse action by encouraging participation in what appear to be (and may actually be) spontaneous institutions. Local committees, or whatever these popular bodies may be called, carried the revolution only so far before yielding some of their functions to a central authority. Even if the revolution originated in protest against this kind of "tyranny," circumstances often dictated a greatly expanded centralization. Revolutionary governments intruded in people's daily lives with economic controls, new legal initiatives, and other unprecedented demands. Levels of violence varied, depending on the degree of involvement by foreign powers and the relative security of the new authorities, but revolutionary regimes often conducted purges of both counter- and ultra-revolutionaries.

Another issue confronting those in power, and one that frequently led to the decline of more moderate factions, concerned management of the military. The army posed an especially significant problem when its members fancied the application of democratic methods to its organization. Usually imbued with more revolutionary and nationalist zeal than any other element in society, the army commonly provided an instrument for radical takeover. Revolutions seldom have succeeded without sacrificing democracy for discipline in the military.

Most scholars agree that true revolutions brought about conflict in society as well as on the battlefield. However, these movements originally appealed to a cross-section of the population. At some point heterogeneous support vanished as ancient or crisis-generated divisions became more powerful. These conflicts have taken the form of geographic, class, ethnic, racial, or other status struggles; normally, they resulted in shifts in power, property, and prestige. Radical elements all seemed to confront decays in enthusiasm, and though a period of reaction may have been forestalled, the gains in the direction of freedom never triumphed so completely as many revolutionaries earlier envisioned.[29]

The Texas Revolution reflected processes and characteristics common to those described above, even though its leaders labored in an environment that retarded revolutionary behavior. Texans entered into their quarrel with Mexico as an individualistic, fragmented people, divided from one community to another by rivalries for land and other jealousies, bothered by ethnic and racial tensions, and devoid of consensus about the meaning of political changes in Mexico. As a result, the Texas cause originally proclaimed the moderate intention of statehood in the Mexican confederacy and officially became a movement for independence only when confronted with the clear impossibility of achieving the original goal. Eventually, leaders of the Texas Revolution created an ideology based not only on liberal political theories but also on appeals to ethnic awareness and to latent nationalistic aspirations. Propagandists seldom failed to remark that "we are Anglo Americans" with a special destiny of political and economic progress. The initial activities of the struggle centered in committees of safety created by communities throughout Texas. Basing their authority on electoral and democratic principles, these bodies served a multitude of functions, including investigation, information-gathering and dissemination, vigilante-style justice, fund and troop raising, and creation of a central government. Reflecting their localized origins and leadership, the committees seldom worked in complete harmony; some attempted to slow rather than hasten the revolutionary process or objected to submitting to the "tyranny" of a new national government.

Thus, the pursuit of unity and the creation of a forceful government proved elusive. Provisional authorities displayed much internal disharmony and inopportunely collapsed so completely as to endanger the entire movement. Those who gathered in the "Consultation" hastily created a government structure that proved sorely inadequate, particularly in delineating the lines of authority between governor and Council. Austin and other established leaders, placed in positions where they could not easily direct the movement, frequently found themselves suspected of inadequate zeal. Those who emerged on top—for example, Governor Smith—displayed intemperate qualities, omnipresent suspicion of "internal enemies," and competing visions of how the doctrines of liberty should be applied. The Council's impeachment of Smith led to a crisis of confidence and an unhealthy diversion from pressing affairs of state. When another set of leaders assumed the helm at the Convention of March, 1836, they did so not only supported by more precise written guidelines but also armed with greater emergency powers. Subsequently, Interim President David G. Burnet issued decrees to provide a shroud of legality for such practices as martial law and other violations of civil liberties, impressment of materials and labor, military conscription, and enrollment of a "regular" army.

This last measure had been urged by Gen. Sam Houston for months as a remedy to the problems that all commanders had experienced with their troops. Self-consciously organized into "volunteer" units, recruits generally displayed great reluctance in accepting any authority, even though most of their officers had been chosen in a democratic fashion. The soldiers habitually insisted on voting on everything from their leaders to matters of tactics or strategy to politics (many proclaimed their right to elect members of national representative bodies). Almost from the first the army had pressed hard for independence and for offensive operations and had grumbled ominously about government corruption that seemed to keep them under-provisioned. When Houston finally placed himself at the army's head, he seemed to have little choice but to retreat because of inadequate discipline. Under the whip of necessity this situation improved, but the army retained something of its ungovernable quality even after San Jacinto when it intervened in the release of Santa Anna and threatened to stage a coup d'état.

A sizable body of Tories rallied to the side of the Mexican centralists, and the war stimulated other divisions. Social conflict of immense variety also occurred in the Texas Revolution. Mexican policy, which for years had threatened to abolish slavery and which was based on a belief that blacks were on the brink of rebellion, now called for these people to claim their freedom. In 1835 and again in 1836 local authorities announced the outbreak of slave insurrections. Blacks who lived in or near war zones especially availed themselves of the opportunity of escaping from their owners to the security provided by the invading forces.

Another form of struggle also grew out of the ethnic diversity of Texas. Even though they fought on the side of independence in proportions equal to the Anglos, Mexican Texans found themselves suspected of conservatism at best and disloyalty at worst. One Anglo correspondent warned Governor Smith (probably unnecessarily, because the chief executive had splendid credentials for bigotry) of "our most formidable foe — our internal enemy — Mexican tory party of the country."[30] Their private property seemed to be expropriated most frequently by military confiscators during the war and, after its conclusion, by those using extralegal pressures. Other social conflicts occurred because of the unsettled nature of the times. Widespread bitterness at property confiscation and losses occasioned by military failure weakened support for the Revolution. Women, children, and others who fled Mexican forces in the Runaway Scrape saw themselves as victims; men who joined in this panic to protect their families and property often came under criticism for shirking their military duties. For the masses of Texans the Revolution was a time of dislocation and grief which even the eventual outcome of battle did not heal.

The Texas Revolution also reflected tensions over the distribution of property and power. East Texans had been dissatisfied for years because of failures to grant them clear land titles; elsewhere, some of the initial reluctance to fly to arms against the centralists had occurred because of suspicions that land speculators had sparked the controversy and intended to deprive the people of the public domain. The provisional government had willy-nilly entered the field of property distribution by disallowing land transactions during the war and by promising rewards to those who entered military service. Political authority also shifted during and after the Revolution. New local oligarchies emerged to dominate their communities, and on the national scene men with the best credentials of wartime service replaced those who had held power in the Mexican years or who had temporized during the independence struggle.

The pages that follow elaborate on all these subjects in an effort to understand the Texas revolutionary experience. The emphasis is on a degree of disorder, upheaval, and conflict that has been largely unrecognized and unrecorded in a systematic way. The concluding chapter attempts to explain how these revolutionary qualities ebbed and persisted during the next decade as Texas became a more placid, if never quite staid, society. The experiences of the years 1835–36 left a new nation burdened by political upheaval, social disorder, and ethnic bitterness that helped to define the Texas identity for the future.

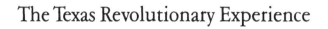

The Texas Revolutionary Experience

1. Background to the Revolution

Like other upheavals of its kind, the Texas Revolution had a very discordant development characterized by false starts and internal dissent. Therefore, in terms of background to the events of 1835–36, two important questions must be addressed: (1) what forces caused the conflict between Texas and Mexico—why did such a movement occur at all? and (2) what factors restrained the rebellion and divided the Texans, leading to the hesitant, lurching qualities that characterized their efforts?

The people of Texas had received much from the government of Mexico and had not been badly treated. The sparsely settled region on its northeastern frontier presented the new Republic (independent in 1821 after a decade of debilitating struggle against Spain) with a serious dilemma. At its outset as a nation Mexico suffered from a weakened economy, population decline, and political uncertainty. With its resources thereby limited, how could Mexico rule the land of Texas, which shared a border with the expansive people and government of the United States? Influenced by the fact that emigrants from the United States had already begun to settle in Texas, Mexico invited colonization and sought to regulate it. Colonists received land for small fees, often paid to Anglo-American "empresarios" like Stephen F. Austin and Green DeWitt, who recruited them and sometimes provided assistance in the settlement process.

Historians have emphasized the issue of cultural conflict, but in practice Mexico did not demand that Anglo settlers be substantially Hispanicized. The Mexican Constitution of 1824, in some ways even more loosely federalistic than that of the United States, allowed considerable local autonomy. Business in areas where most Anglos lived could be carried on in English without hindrance. The requirement that emigrants adopt the official state religion was ignored, and the people became "catholic" in quite a different sense than the law provided. Farmers and merchants pursued their callings, normally with little interference from Mexican authorities. Seldom has the ruling hand been felt so lightly as in Texas in the period 1821–35. Yet, certain chronic disputes between Mexico and its northeastern province created an undercurrent of tension, mutual suspicion, and frustration that developed alongside the growth of Anglo American influence in Texas. Barker described these issues as "dull, organic aches" in the relations between Mexico and Texas.[1]

Disagreements on the matter of racial bondage proved to be a perpetual source of irritation. Antislavery ideology had triumphed in Mexico as part of the revolutionary ethos that accompanied the movement for independence. By contrast, the Anglo Texans had emigrated largely from the southern United States where intellectual reactionaries defended the peculiar institution. In Texas the colonists circumspectly argued in favor of slavery on the practical grounds that progress depended on forced labor. To a large extent debate on slavery occurred within a nation-state framework, as a matter of principle versus interest. Throughout the 1820s local authorities in Texas blunted repeated but indecisive antislavery measures.

Anglo leaders either muted the impact of these laws or simply ignored them, in particular by persuading the legislature to sanction a bogus "contract" system allowing imports of bound labor. This subterfuge received a jolt on September 15, 1829, with the promulgation of a general emancipation decree by President Vicente Guerrero, but local officials once again gained an exemption for Texas. Henceforth the barrage of antislavery measures lessened, yet the status of the institution remained in doubt. When the legislature in 1832 established a ten-year limitation on the length of labor contracts, Anglo Texas colonists launched a movement for separate statehood. These repeated clashes resulted in something of a stalemate — slavery survived amidst a sense of uncertainty. Masters bought, hired, and sold workers with little regard for the law, but Mexican policy had the effect of slowing the pace of immigration, perpetuating labor shortages, and retarding growth.[2]

Many antislavery actions occurred as part of a larger effort to regulate immigration into Texas; on this issue Mexican and Anglo interests also clashed fundamentally. Congress in 1824 had enacted a measure which, except for restrictions on the size of individual grants and on their location near foreign or coastal territory, allowed nearly open immigration under the direction of state governments. Coahuila, the state authority over Texas, created the empresario system the next year, making land available to individuals in enticingly large plots at virtually no cost. These measures, together with a depression and a more restrictive land policy in the United States, resulted in an unexpectedly large movement into the areas claimed by Austin and the other Texas colonizers. Many more emigrants continued simply to cross the Sabine into Mexico and occupy land without benefit of government sanction. The pace of population growth caused a quick reconsideration of the liberal land policy. Leaders also became apprehensive in response to U.S. diplomatic designs on Texas and to stirrings of rebellion against Mexican authority.

By the end of the 1820s Mexico sought to reverse its policy and to bring Texas more nearly into the orbit of the nation. The far-reaching plan of Gen. Manuel Mier y Terán envisioned expanding Mexican military presence, attracting colonists from the interior of Mexico and Europe rather than the United States, and establishing a better trade pattern. His program achieved only partial implementation. The law of April 6, 1830, by which Congress banned all immigration from the United States to the bordering provinces of Mexico, proved to be unenforceable and did much to worsen relations between Texas and the central government. Anglo-American immigrants continued to seep in illegally, and two of the empresarios gained temporary exemptions, so the North American presence hardly declined. Anglo settlers greatly resented the law and sought by petition and other forms of political activism to have it repealed. These efforts increased Mexican suspicion that Texas had become disloyal. Nevertheless, in November, 1833, Congress reopened the nation's borders to residents of the United States, effective in May of the next year. On the matter of immigration, as on slavery, Anglo Texans had challenged the power and the will of Mexico and found it weak.[3]

Inadequate government machinery frustrated the correction of other problems. The fact that Mexico had no means of enforcing tariffs or other measures pleased Texas free traders, but the effort to establish customs houses in the 1830 resulted in explosive controversies without appreciably adding to Mexican authority. By the mid-1830s little coastal trade had developed between Texas and other Mexican ports, with the result that, in the words of historian David J. Weber, "the government failed to integrate Texas into the national economy."[4] The impetus for judiciary reform came from Anglo settlers who found the Mexican system alien, cumbersome, and subject to excessive appeals to distant courts. They received relief with an April, 1834, law that made justice more Anglicized and localized for the Texans.[5] On these as on the other controversies, the colonists had blocked efforts to augment the power of the central government and agitated successfully for policies congenial with their own civilization. The Anglo colonists venerated the 1824 constitution because localized and limited government protected their way of life.

Despite triumphs resulting from pressure tactics, the Texans' methods had unfavorable results as well; increasingly, Mexico viewed the province as dangerously ungovernable. Recurrent demands for further reform increased Mexican suspicion of this dynamic, distant region. Persons of varying shades of political opinion resented the Texans' turbulent behavior, disrespectful attitude toward colonial policy, continued identification with the United States, and aggressive tactics.[6]

Whether malcontents and "adventurers" really dominated the Texas scene, as many observers believed, some fiery spirits did take control at certain times. What Barker called the "popular disturbances" of 1832 in fact amounted to armed rebellion. The incidents at Anáhuac (a fort above Galveston Bay) in part resulted from an awkward constitutional arrangement: this military town came directly under the authority of the national government, which had always denied colonization in the coastal area. The land claims of the nearby community of Liberty emanated from the state government of Coahuila and Texas. Tensions grew in 1831. National officials sent more soldiers to Anáhuac, began to issue titles that conflicted with those of agents of the state, and enforced import duties as well. Unaccustomed to paying taxes in any form, many Texans hated the new collection policy and regarded its enforcers, Col. Juan Davis Bradburn and George Fisher (stationed at Brazoria), as arbitrary military despots.

Mier y Terán had appointed these officials in an effort to implement the law of April 6, 1830. From his fort at Anáhuac the tactless Bradburn quarrelled with settlers and state officials over the major issues that divided Texas and Mexico. He disputed the power of state officials to establish civil government in this area, and he harbored runaway slaves in a manner that seemed likely to spread discontent. Fisher's enforcement of tariffs appeared equally arbitrary to Brazoria merchants and consumers. In late 1831 they clashed with his troops in defying payment of import taxes.

Throughout the year 1832 rumors of a planned attack by civilian volunteers confronted Bradburn, but local compromisers averted violence for a time. Citizen soldiers and leaders from Liberty, Brazoria, and San Felipe finally converged on Anáhuac and clashed with some of Bradburn's forces, themselves divided on political issues. The Mexican commander fled to Louisiana and then back to Mexico. Compromisers managed to avoid Mexican retaliation by sending out the Turtle Bayou Resolutions, presenting the revolt as part of the nation's restoration of federalism.[7] Although this coincidental political upheaval in Mexico had helped prevent a complete rupture in 1832 in Texas, the events at Anáhuac had great significance. The centralist effort to establish firmer machinery of national control had been defied, and those who led the resistance no doubt gained in confidence as a result.

Since Texas had narrowly averted a full-scale armed conflict with Mexico over these incidents, moderate Stephen F. Austin reacted without enthusiasm to the proposal for a convention in the fall of 1832. Fearing that such a gathering would involve only Anglo participation he preferred to accomplish reform goals by a more cautious policy of petitioning or by gaining the support of existing political officialdom in Texas. Mexico, he knew, regarded unauthorized meetings as revolutionary. Unable to dissuade the popular leaders, Austin met with the people's representatives when they congregated in San Felipe in October and again in April, 1833. Their proposals included changes in immigration, judicial, and other political policies that eventually were passed by national or state governments. But the conventions also favored separate statehood for Texas and Coahuila, an idea that even previously sympathetic Mexican officials regarded as a dangerous step toward secession and eventual independence. The delegates went so far as to draw up a Texas state constitution. This cause provoked suspicion among some Hispanic residents in Béxar and Goliad and left those communities divided; but Austin believed that failure to grant the colonists' demand would lead to war. The fact that separate statehood had become largely an Anglo movement hurt Austin's chances during his mission to the political authorities in Mexico. They eventually imprisoned him when he, in exasperation, advised Texas to forge ahead without the approval of the central authorities.[8]

By 1832–33 the Texans had become both impatient with what they regarded as the nation's constant political turmoil and contemptuous of Mexican power. Nevertheless, they remained quieter in 1834, in deference to Austin's lobbying efforts on their behalf at the national capital. The state government once again responded to their agitations with further concessions; Texas in 1834 gained more representatives in the legislature, an additional political department headquartered in San Felipe, more municipalities, and several judicial reforms.[9] Writing retrospectively after Texas has won its independence, Austin concluded that during the previous decade "'the country was placed . . . upon a volcano, subject to be ruined by popular excitement on the one hand or by the jealousy of the Mexicans on the other.'" But during his 1834 sojourn in Mexico the people overwhelmingly followed his conservative advice. Further, many other pacifying factors had emerged: immigration had been legally renewed, the state government seemed benign, localism prevailed in politics, and a cholera epidemic discouraged controversy. The region hummed with economic activity rather than political agitation.[10]

For two years after the April, 1833, convention controversies ebbed, relations seemed to improve between Mexico and Texas, and a mood of optimism prevailed among the colonists. Citing the repeal of the law of April 6, 1830, and other favorable measures, one observer in February, 1834, explained: "The people generally appear to be satisfied with what has been done for the present [and] are willing to defer the state question. They consider their pro[s]pects truly chearing." Slightly over a year later this attitude had been bolstered by continued hopes for statehood and rapid immigration from the U. S. Many no doubt concurred with Thomas H. Borden, who suggested that this turn of affairs could be credited to the Texans' resistance to unfavorable Mexican policies: "Our political affares are more settled than they have been for some time past." Though "it is uncertain yet whether our fights here in 1832 have been a benefit or not," Borden admitted that "one thing is certain that it increased there jealousies, but it also done this good it showed them our spunk and what we could do if we were a mind."[11] In retrospect, it is clear that by 1835 an explosive and perhaps inevitable clash had been brewed. Mexico wearied of Texans' perpetual recalcitrance and ongoing insistence on more concessions, while the Texans believed that their resistance had been successful and had developed an agenda of additional demands.

At the same time several aspects of the Texas scene restrained the potential for conflict with Mexico. An overriding factor was the character of the people, whose rampant individualism and political lethargy distressed those who emphasized the need for cooperation and activism. In 1834 John A. Wharton wrote despairingly about the apathy that caused his newspaper to fail, leaving Texas without a free press

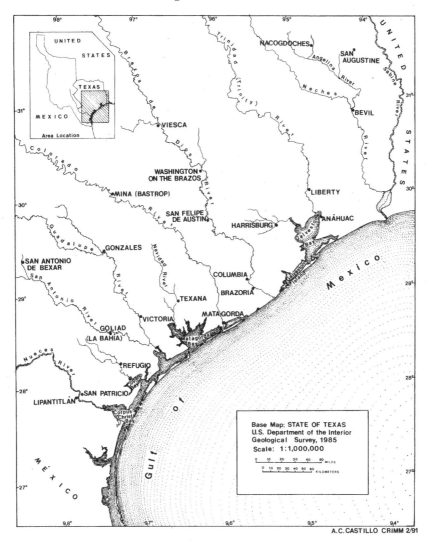

Map 1.   Principal Communities of Texas, 1835–36

and subject to misinformation, demagoguery, and tyranny. Others used this languid quality to reassure Mexican officials of the continued loyalty of the province. In an 1834 address designed to facilitate the release of Austin, R. M. Williamson (president of the San Felipe Ayuntamiento) insisted that the people "are not of a revolutionary disposition."[12]

The empresario himself wrote back to encourage a "dead calm" in Texas, only to fear that he had succeeded too well when words of concern and support dwindled to virtually nothing. Though Austin confined himself to pleading for unity and condemning divisions among the people, others occasionally attempted to explain the causes of the self-oriented and non-cooperative attitude that prevailed. Rival empresario Sterling C. Robertson noted in October, 1835, that "Texas is divided into small municipalities unconnected by any bond of union except their common danger."[13]

A different sort of geographic determinism occurred to an anonymous writer who visited the new Republic in 1837. He, too, observed the "backwardness" of the Texas settlers in engaging in "revolutionary measures" in 1835 and attributed it to their character: a favorable climate and natural abundance resulted in an ease of living and indolence. For this reason the people were complacent; they responded slowly to the political crisis, convinced themselves that "the justice of Mexico" would prevail, and resorted to arms belatedly under an actual invasion. Following the defeat of Mexico, according to his observations, the people "relapsed into their former unconcerned mode of life and seem to take but little interest in the affairs of government."[14]

The question of a national or regional "character" always proves to be a formidable and elusive subject, but a few scholars have attempted to understand the Texans of the 1830s. Invariably the high degree of individualism receives prominent attention, and some historians have also adopted modified geographical explanations for this quality, emphasizing the early Texas environment and the frontier experience. Mark Nackman has suggested that the emigrants of this period brought with them an enhanced dislike of social restraints. He noted that Texas attracted a large number of persons who were propelled out of the United States by business failures, brushes with the law, family disputes, and other misfortunes. They sought sanctuary from the law, new adventure, and a chance to begin again. To many, these ephemeral ambitions all translated into one tangible goal: land, the symbol and means of freedom. Benefitting from the generous Mexican policy, Texans had acquired as a result even more personal independence. They did not intend to surrender either the land or the independence. Many others, especially in east Texas, settled without acquiring titles and lived virtually free of any government, content not to stir the waters of discord.[15]

Whether Texas attracted immigrants who by character were predisposed to intense individualism, their experience on the frontier of Mexico nurtured this quality. Texas society imposed remarkably few constraints on personal freedom. Throughout the period of heavy Anglo migration, the Mexican Constitution of 1824 provided the northern provinces with a liberal framework of government, including representative institutions based on electoral principles and a high degree of free speech. Some Texans chafed at their union in statehood with Coahuila and expressed frustration about the political upheavals that beset Mexico, but in practice government fell mostly under their local sway. Settler J. P. Cole expressed the common disgust at Mexican politics to a prospective immigrant but quickly added, "upon the score of Local Government we get along very well[.] there is such an ident[it]y of Interest here that the will of the people form a government." Even though he was writing on the eve of war, Cole considered Texas "to be perfectly safe and while this is the case (and belev it will not be otherwise) we have nothing to fear."[16]

The federalist system in fact brought little more than a shadow of government over Texas. Political chiefs residing in Béxar, backed by only a token military force, naturally had difficulty enforcing their will in scattered settlements to the east. Mostly, they tended to defend regional needs and perspectives to outside authorities; the creation of additional departments of Nacogdoches in 1831 and Brazos in 1834 furthered government responsiveness to local interests. Municipal politics (with twenty-two municipalities in 1835 ruled by elected ayuntamientos) also remained close to the people; confronted by huge geographic dimensions, they were as a result very limited in authority. In the words of scholar Carlos E. Castañeda: "Left much to themselves, the colonists ran their own affairs" according to their traditions and needs.[17]

Localized and weak government did concern some Texans because it crippled the judicial system. Texas communities employed no salaried law enforcers, and in many instances elected officials had difficulty obtaining what Henry Smith called "enough public spirit" to conduct a formal trial of those who by chance got arrested. This ex-alcalde lectured his former constituents on the "duties incumbent upon us as members of the society," but still found the citizens unwilling to pay any of the taxes levied by the ayuntamiento for judicial purposes. That the government might compel collection seems to have occurred to no one. Though they sometimes complained about the cumbersome legal system, most settlers actually seemed content with the vigilante justice that by the mid-1830s had already become a Texas tradition.[18]

Austin and other reformers advocated the extension of a measure of government control over the economy, believing that commercial regulations might improve ports and lessen the unfavorable balance of trade. In practice the efforts of Mexico to collect import duties in Texas faltered, and its largely self-sufficient majority continued to have nearly complete economic freedom.[19] Progressive-minded citizens recognized also a need for developing certain beneficial social institutions. Several tuition-supported private academies sprang up in various communities late in the history of Mexican Texas; these included some female-operated boarding schools that survived more than one or two terms. Nevertheless, education remained largely the private function of the family.

Religion existed in a state of flux and variety. Despite maintaining an officially favored status, the Roman Catholic Church had undergone considerable decline as a result of Mexico's independence. The triumph of liberal ideology, secularization, an end to government aid, and the inability to recruit Spanish Franciscans sapped the vitality from the mission system by the 1820s. Even the traditional religious centers, Goliad and Béxar, underwent religious decline; the area where most Anglos lived, including Nacogdoches, which also had a sizable Mexican community, remained without services for all but a few years. Thus, Texas had the practice if not an official theory of toleration. This situation emboldened Protestant activity in the early 1830s, despite Austin's continued concern that "fanatical" preachers might provoke the attention of Mexican authorities. The few Anglo missionaries active in Texas did not establish institutionalized churches, despite the appearance of Sunday schools and camp meetings. Many settlers expressed dismay about the absence of piety and morality due to the weakness of formal religion. Conventional minds considered Texas to have a distinctly irreligious climate of opinion. "They are a most ungodly people," wrote diarist William F. Gray.[20] Remarkably few institutions existed to develop group consciousness and cohesion. Though certainly not a static society, Texas on the eve of its revolution remained a land of unfettered personal freedom and intense individualism.

The unpoliticized character of many Texans and their habit of placing individual concerns over the needs of society were qualities that first impeded the growth of revolutionary zeal and later undermined political and military efforts. Various internal divisions in Texas also existed, further segmenting the people and threatening the development of revolutionary unity. Racial and ethnic diversity increased the potential for internal discord. By the mid-1830s slaves, concentrated on river bottom plantations near the coast, comprised over ten percent of the total Texas population. Their numbers had grown dramatically in recent years, due partly to a widely condemned but flourishing traffic in "African" imports. Beginning in the early spring of 1833 one boat-load after another of Africans (totalling four documented cases in the next eighteen months) came by way of Cuba and landed near Galveston Bay for distribution to labor-hungry planters. These unaccultur-ated bondsmen increased the volatility of a black population whom some Mexican investigators considered already on the verge of revolt. In 1834 Juan N. Almonte circumspectly informed Texas blacks of their freedom under the law; Mier y Terán had earlier advised against aboli-tion, suggesting that the threat of insurrection would restrain Texas secessionism.[21]

Possessed of intense racial consciousness, the Anglo settlers also gen-erally viewed Mexican Texans with considerable suspicion and aliena-tion. Friction between the two groups did not constantly occur. In-deed, their leaders often cooperated, and immigrants from the United States generally accepted the need for restraint while Texas remained Mexican territory. Most importantly, in the words of an 1835 descrip-tion, "the Mexican population is Entirely sepperateed from the N. American people in Texas." The Anglo author of this remark considered segregation indispensable because "the manners habits & Genious of the two people are so widely different." The Tejanos, numbering only about four thousand on the eve of the Revolution, had already become a distinct minority in the province as a whole. However, most of them resided in the city of Béxar or on the large ranches in that vast depart-ment, where they formed a majority and still elected their own to posi-tions of local leadership.

The few Tejanos, or native Mexicans, in the Austin colony worked primarily for wages rather than as landowners; however, in two other places they competed for property and power with non-Hispanic col-onists. Nacogdoches had a sizable Tejano community of around six hundred persons who until 1834 dominated or at least shared political offices. Their recent minority status had accelerated ethnic tensions; both they and the North Americans feared being cheated as the govern-ment began settling the conflicting land claims of eastern Texas. These arose because many families had failed to secure written titles, some new settlers simply squatted in unoccupied areas without worrying about the law, and various empresarios squabbled, fought, and specu-lated in land, altogether leading to a situation of hopeless chaos. Increasingly, the Tejanos of the Nacogdoches area voted as a bloc and otherwise retreated into a separate community, and seething animosities lay close to the surface in this region.[22]

To the south and west of Austin's grant lay another area with complex and competing land claims and a variety of ethnic divisions. Victoria had been founded as a colonial center by Tamaulipas rancher Martín de León, whose grant of 1824 unfortunately provided very indistinct boundaries. This fact became critical when territory to the north, west, and south came into the hands of other empresarios; the situation brought what Castañeda has described as "suspicion, distrust, and hatred" among the various residents. Nevertheless, the De León colony attracted over one hundred Mexican families by 1835. These regional tensions accentuated the Anglo Texans' predisposition toward viewing the fate of Texas in racial terms. Even the previously restrained Austin burst out in 1836 that the war represented a contest between the barbarism of a "mongrel Spanish-Indian and negro race, against civilization and the Anglo-American race."[23]

Cultural dissimilarities also divided other colonists in southwestern Texas. Two sets of Irish empresarios attempted to settle the region. James Power and James Hewetson received grants near the coast between the San Antonio and Nueces rivers in 1826. Some of their settlers persevered through a discouraging start and congregated on lands formerly held by Refugio missions; a number of Tejano residents continued to ranch and farm in this neighborhood. Other Irish colonists also competed for this territory, establishing their claims on the contracts of empresarios John McMullen and James McGloin. Even those who moved southward to the town of San Patricio, founded in 1830, inhabited territory claimed by Power and Hewetson. Several of these settlers possessed an enhanced loyalty to Mexico because of their religion. Other Tejanos in the region based their real property rights on prior occupancy, on the De León grant, or on privileges recognized by the ayuntamiento of Goliad. As a whole, the entire southwestern coastal area had explosive potential.[24]

Even without the ethnic element, disputes over land rights created powerful animosities. To the east of Austin's colony confusion also prevailed. Lorenzo de Zavala, David G. Burnet, and Joseph Vehlein, having all failed to settle the number of families required by the terms of their contracts, disposed of their grants to the Galveston Bay and Texas Land Company as if they actually owned the substantial territory. The speculative company in turn sold scrip to immigrants who believed they had acquired acceptable title to the land. Other colonists failed to gain Mexican deeds because their claims were for land in the foreign boundary zone adjacent to the United States and by law forbidden to settlement. The upper Brazos also came under dispute between rival empresarios. Sterling C. Robertson struggled against the potent partnership of Stephen F. Austin and Samuel M. Williams, who attempted to invalidate Robertson's grant on grounds of insufficient settlement and to avoid other Mexican restrictions in a new claim of their own.[25] These controversies all involved more than a few speculators; the colonists themselves stood to gain or lose their land depending on the outcome of these imperial-sized schemes.

Political partisanship also contributed to the spirit of disharmony. These divisions had only a small ideological content; both "war" and "peace" parties favored greater autonomy for Texas and differed mainly on the best means to achieve that goal. The more conservative of these groups tended to oppose violent methods and to emphasize loyalty to Mexico, thus becoming the "peace" party and also being branded as "Tories." Those favoring more forceful action (hence the term "war" party) often found themselves characterized as tax-evading merchants, land- or job-schemers, and hard-drinking, boastful adventurers. Length of residence played a role in determining factional identification, with more recent arrivals tending toward the "war" party. Leadership loyalties also seem to have been at the core of these disputes; William and John Wharton headed the faction that generally opposed Stephen F. Austin and his "peace party." Subleaders and positions shifted back and forth so frequently that faction is a better term for them than party. Nevertheless, these conflicts generated genuine ill will, and partisan feelings had the effect of elevating the level of internal bitterness. After attending a meeting that dissolved into "confusion" because of war and peace party conflicts, one veteran of Georgia politics concluded in disgust, "the people knew nothing. . . . they are damned stupid and easily ruled by Demagogues and factions."[26]

Rampant individualism, political disunity, and serious social divisions—these characteristics limited Texas' revolutionary potential. In 1834 few apparently allowed their contentment to be stirred by the warnings of the newspaper *Advocate of the People's Rights,* which editorialized on the dangers of unpreparedness. According to this account, too many placed faith in past victories over small Mexican garrisons or counted on assistance from the United States. The journalist feared that "the young and enthusiastic" might rashly plunge into war and then, having no property to protect, would flee to the United States. How, he asked, could Texas win such a contest "with an unorganized population of a few thousand, without even provisions enough at this moment to raise the present crop, without arms, without money, without able commanders, and without a disciplined soldiery?" The fighting would undoubtedly occur on Texas soil and might well become a struggle like that of Mexico against Spain, lasting for years with devastating effects. Even those who took these warnings seriously probably saw little point to them. The editor urged his fellow "North Americans" not "to submit to oppression," but who had the means to prepare the people for the worst?[27] In this fashion the Anglo Texans eased through the year 1834 and into 1835 hoping for more signs of progress or, at the least, preservation of the status quo.

2. The Coming of the Revolution
1835

From the early months of the year through September, 1835, Texas charted a spasmodic course toward revolution. The province reacted slowly to the triumph of centralism in Mexico and the resulting overthrow of the Coahuila and Texas state government in Monclova. Although a few warned of the dangers these political changes posed for Texas, leaders either failed to emerge or to stir the masses out of their accustomed routines. Efforts in May and June to aid the unpopular state government proved unsuccessful, and it collapsed in the face of punitive measures by centralist authorities. In late June some of the hot-blooded from San Felipe and Harrisburg took up arms against a Mexican outpost at the perennial troublespot of Anáhuac, but spokesmen for peace in other communities repudiated the use of force and sought to initiate conciliatory moves. Committees of safety emerged slowly and without a consensus as to the direction Texas should take — some fostered revolutionary attitudes while others sought to establish an accord with Mexico. This absence of unanimity led to a call for a popular convention to resolve the differences; however, the cautious-minded objected to this measure as a potentially provocative step. Not until mid-August did the different factions, bolstered by reliable reports of the impending military escalation in Texas by Mexico, coalesce behind a "Consultation" called for mid-October.

In short, the Texas reaction to the advent of a centralist government in Mexico was anything but forceful, wise, uniform, or confident. To a considerable degree this sputtering response resulted from ignorance regarding the meaning of the latest changes in the Mexican government. In fact, the political order in the interior underwent a fundamental change in 1834, but neither the direction nor the profundity of this shift was clear from the Texans' frontier perspective. Even Austin and other observers closer to the scene confessed bewilderment or misinterpreted events. The conservative movement designed to unify Mexico behind a dominant central government began its ascent under a former liberal, Antonio López de Santa Anna, whose prior record and initial actions favored some of the reforms that benefitted Texas interests in 1834. His drive toward centralism began slowly following the ouster of Gómez Farías in the spring of 1834. Not until nearly a year later did the pattern of uprooting state and local power become clear. At the end of March, 1835, the centralists ordered crippling reductions in state militias, and just over a month later a new Congress abrogated the 1824 constitution. In October this body passed further measures that rendered the state governments subservient.[1]

Though eventually many outlying regions opposed these innovations under the banner of federalism, only Zacatecas and Coahuila (the state which included Texas) defended their state rights in 1835. Santa Anna suppressed these revolts with ease; Coahuila managed but a token display of resistance because it had become mired in related upheaval of its own. Rival state governments at Monclova and Saltillo competed for power in 1834, with the latter faction supporting the new central government of Mexico. In the spring of 1835 this contest became personified in a struggle between federalist Governor Agustín Viesca of the Monclova government and Santa Anna's brother-in-law, Martín Perfecto de Cos, who had been dispatched with troops to support the Saltillo claims and to compel obedience to the centralist order. Despite having mostly federalist sympathies, Texans generally stood aside in disgust and confusion as their state government descended into chaos. A proposal to organize a separate provisional state government gained little support; meanwhile, Texas representatives remained busily involved in the Monclova legislature. Some significant measures came out of its hasty and crisis-filled sessions, including several that seemed to benefit the Texas delegates personally. The most controversial of these provided large land grants to individuals who raised troops to fight on the side of the state.[2]

Proponents of this law defended it as the only means by which the bankrupt Coahuila and Texas government could defend itself against Santa Anna's military tyranny. Critics quickly arose to denounce the plan as mere speculative corruption. The average Texan reacted to these developments with a mixture of befuddlement and passivity. In addition to contributing to the inherent lethargy in Texas, political events in early 1835 also added to internal divisions in the province. The new state land policy cast aspersion on Austin's business partner, Samuel M. Williams, as well as on fellow legislators John Durst and James Grant, who had made down payments on property near the source of the Trinity River that had previously been granted to another empresario. Disappointed land barons Thomas J. Chambers and Benjamin Fort Smith, who had expected to bid on this real estate on a competitive basis, quickly published denunciations of their rivals' "Mammoth Speculation." Others who apparently benefitted from the Monclova legislative schemes included Francis W. Johnson, Robert Peebles, Green DeWitt, Thomas F. McKinney, Spencer H. Jack, and Mosely Baker, all of whom had played leadership roles in Texas. Williams also obtained legislative endorsement of his and Austin's claims to the territory they disputed with Sterling C. Robertson, thus adding that clan to those who opposed the state government. The Coahuila governor had also come to dislike Texas for the disrespectful and obstinate behavior of its delegates and had plans to govern it more effectively.[3]

Defense of the Viesca government thus enjoyed hardly any innate popular appeal. Instead, as Castañeda explained, the land speculation episode created doubts about Coahuilan denunciations of Santa Anna, "dulled the perception of the colonists, [and] delayed concerted action."[4] Some historians maintain that the movement of Mexican troops into Texas aimed primarily at arresting corrupt legislator-speculators and became an occupation force only when the guilty parties received sanctuary.[5] Actually, Mexican attitudes toward Texas had already hardened before the province harbored these fugitives.

Past Texas behavior had already worked on the minds of the officials who served in the province in 1835—they came prepared to find and combat rebellion and soon saw much cause for alarm. One of the first letters from Domingo de Ugartechea, the military commandant in Béxar, expressed concern that Austin's colonists were giving away untitled land to all comers from the United States. Cos received reports that 250 families had settled in the Nacogdoches department during a one-month period early in 1835; officials who paid attention to the Texas newspaper no doubt read the boast that 1,500 immigrants had landed on the Brazos in the first five months of the year. Cos heard that the native Mexicans in both the Departments of Brazos and Nacogdoches had been forced to submit to the power of "strangers," since elective offices went altogether to the "transgressors" from North America.[6] Customs and other officials among the Anglo colonists complained of disrespect for the power of Mexico as shown by scorn for its small military detachments in Texas. Antonio Tenorio, the commander who drew Anáhuac, resented the insubordinate attitudes displayed by the colonists. From his Béxar post Ugartechea reported back to Tenorio that similar sentiments existed elsewhere, too: "Nothing is heard but God damn St. Anna. God damn Ugartechea."[7]

As early as April 9, 1835, the Anáhuac commander informed his superiors that inadequate numbers prevented him from enforcing import duties or providing self-defense "in case of an outbreak for which I am looking from one moment to another." Without additional men and arms to compel respect, he predicted an Anglo effort to "wrestle" the frontier territory from Mexico. Three days earlier Cos, in Saltillo, had already written his superior, minister of war José María Tornel, that Texas would demand the attention of the central government before long; he advised that at least one battalion of six hundred men be dispatched. Tornel replied in late April that soon after the Zacatecas revolt was ended, a large number of troops "will be sent to Texas to settle the business there definitely." This satisfied Cos, who wrote back to the war minister that these measures would let "those ungrateful strangers know that the Govno. has sufficient power to repress them" and that they must "march from the country if they do not want to submit themselves to its laws."[8]

Cos communicated the news of this pending build-up, but until they had the necessary force at hand, the centralist authorities in Texas confined their militance to their private correspondence. Their inactivity helped defuse charges in circulars written by Monclova federalists, who warned that the Santanistas intended to establish military despotism.[9] The Texans, however surly in demeanor toward Mexican soldiers, reacted warily to pleas from Coahuila. They sponsored no organized movement in support of the Viesca government or the federalist system before the middle of May. Mexican officials continued cagily to bide their time. Plans for decisive military actions in Texas remained secret, and Cos recommended on April 6 that the impact of troop movement into the province be deflected with the guise of guarding the frontier. On May 12 he followed this plan in a public announcement praising Texas colonists "who, from inclination as well as interest, have always remained faithful to the Supreme Government"; he urged the loyal majority to avoid seductive advances by self-seeking rebels. Only briefly did Cos allude to the coming of Mexican troops as Indian fighters.[10]

This charade—with the Texans uneasy but not in arms and the Mexican authorities preparing for but postponing hostilities—continued to be played with only ominous interruptions until early summer. Even those inclined toward rebellion plotted in ignorance of Santa Anna's military plans for Texas. William Barrett Travis believed that "it is utterly impossible in the nature of things that two people so diametrically opposed in everything can be amalgamated." Yet, Travis doubted that Mexico would bring on a conflict. "The rumor of troops coming to Texas in great numbers must be false. Nothing has been heard of it here . . . Such a measure," he concluded, "would kindle a flame in Texas that would burn in twain the slender cords that connect us to the ill fated Mexican confederation."[11]

The rumor he mentioned emanated from representatives to the Monclova legislature. In early May Samuel M. Williams and Francis W. Johnson reported that the Santa Anna party intended a complete destruction of the existing political and social order in Texas. Both urged Texas to dispatch forces to assist the state government. Johnson instructed his correspondent and "all friends" to stimulate "the boys to act promptly."[12] Counter-rumors of land fraud and a long-standing repugnance for the Coahuila government dogged the efforts to rescue it from the centralists. Those who distrusted these firebrand accounts of impending doom used newspapers and other means of communication to prevent premature action. As late as the end of June some correspondents maintained that Mexican troop movements aimed only at arresting those who had "hoodwinked" the Viesca administration.[13]

With one exception Texas communities refused the pleas for aid from the state government, and this lone incident resulted in disaster for the federalists. At noon May 16 about one hundred militiamen under the command of Juan N. Seguín marched and rode from Béxar toward Monclova. Centralist military commandant Ugartechea responded that afternoon by ordering Political Chief Angel Navarro to recall this force. A contest of nerves and diplomacy then ensued. Initially, Navarro refused to back down, maintaining that the militia would obey only state authorities. Ugartechea described himself as "anxious . . . to remain within the bounds of moderation," in a note penned at 11:00 that night, and he postponed sending an expedition to intercept the Béxar militia. Navarro soon bowed to his impulse of preventing bloodshed, but neither he nor the military commandant made timely decisions. Ugartechea dispatched forty troops the next morning while the political authorities were wavering; by the time Navarro acted, it appeared to be too late to avoid bloodshed. After consulting with the local town council, he made a belated decision to give in and so directed the militiamen to return by a route chosen to avoid a clash with Ugartechea's soldiers. A public meeting of about seventy citizens mirrored the attitude of their chief. It resolved at first to attack the regular troops but then yielded when older heads advised peace and patience. All but a party of twenty-five of the militia returned to Béxar on May 17. Navarro wrote a letter of explanation and apology to state officials, defending his course on the basis of unpreparedness, absence of outside support, and the threat of retaliation by centralist reinforcements.[14]

The Béxar chief had little need to apologize, for the Coahuila government demonstrated only timid vacillation during this time of crisis. Viesca procrastinated but soon capitulated before the superior force of the centralists; on May 20 he issued an order dissolving all the militia that were gathering in his defense. Seguín's small command had no choice but to withdraw soon after arriving in Monclova, its leader being "disgusted with the weakness of the Executive, who had given up the struggle."[15] The events of mid and late May proved to be a turning point for Texas; henceforth, rallying support for the deposed state government became difficult. Béxar turned into a centralist stronghold, with Navarro won over to that side, although the citizens of the district held divided loyalties. Still, after May resistance to the Santa Anna regime came mostly from regions dominated by Anglo colonists.

One final attempt to garner support for the state government occurred in June, 1835, as a result of Viesca's decision to move his headquarters to Texas. The reports that arrived in central Texas emphasized a continued state of confusion in Coahuila and noted the rise of a military faction that threatened local interests. The San Felipe Ayuntamiento began to meet and urge preparedness; more importantly, on June 21 Political Chief of the Brazos Department J. B. Miller issued a circular calling on the public to organize and march to the governor's rescue. This proclamation presented the political conflict as a struggle of constitutional republicanism against militarism and appealed for action to end "the anarchy which now prevails."[16] The next day a public meeting in San Felipe listened to more inflammatory rhetoric from its chairman, R. M. Williamson. Labelling the land speculator theory a myth, he urged people to face the fact that "you are in the midst of a revolution, that threatens your destruction." Williamson invoked all the specters that haunted Anglo Texans. The Santanistas "are coming to compel you into obedience to the new form of Government, . . . to give up your arms, . . . to have your country garrisoned, . . . to liberate your slaves, . . . to submit to the imperial rule of the aristocracy, to pay tithes and adoration to the clergy." He appealed to the self-interest of those who had failed to acquire land titles and he also resurrected the image of forefathers who had first unfurled the banner of freedom on American soil, promising the support of worldwide liberal opinion.[17]

Texas did not enter militarily into the Coahuila conflict, partly because General Cos arrested Viesca in Monclova before he could leave for Texas. The federalist movement also met with stiff resistance from those who considered it a stalking horse for independence. The day following the gathering at San Felipe another meeting occurred in Columbia, led by John A. Wharton, William H. Jack, Branch T. Archer, and others thought to be in the war party. Those who convened listened to "a report and resolution Cut and dried in Caucus last night," as one critic saw the proceedings. Henry Austin, the author of this description, did more than complain. He engineered passage of amendments that defeated what he considered "an attempt . . . to involve us in an immediate Revolution." The resulting resolutions of the Columbia meeting thus recommended "union, concert, and moderation," delaying any real action until another session on June 28 and until the political chief could investigate the general public will. This postponement gave Henry Austin time to marshall supporters.[18]

In the interim the Brazoria *Texas Republican* attacked Miller's call for military organization as precipitous, and it reiterated the people's animosity toward the land-speculating phobia associated with the Monclova government. Even though the newspaper also warned of ominous centralist plans, including an imminent invasion of Texas by a large Mexican force, the meeting of June 28 continued to hedge and work at cross-purposes. It called for obedience to the law, denounced as foreigners those who sought war with the general government, and declared that the people "are the faithful and loyal citizens of Mexico." Other resolutions from Columbia reflected greater militance, calling for a provisional government in Texas to end "the reign of anarchy in the state" and creating a vigilance committee made up of both political factions. These actions moved the community toward a rebellious posture, in contrast to other measures designed to promote peace.

The only clear conclusion was that the people remained divided and uncertain.[19]

In the early summer of 1835 all Texas communities struggled with some disagreements among their residents, but a few areas faced more provocative crises. The coastal region chafed at tariff collection and other trade restrictions that were being enforced with renewed vigor for the first time since 1832. Residents of the Brazos valley felt particularly angry at the activities of the schooner *Montezuma*, which captured vessels engaged in trade on Galveston Bay and detained goods and passengers. Would-be radical leader William B. Travis in late May wrote that this controversy "aroused the indignation & resentment of the whole people" like no other issue he had seen in Texas. Officials in Mexico commonly regarded Texas resistance to the patrol ships as tantamount to rebellion.[20]

Once again the garrison at Anáhuac became the focal point. By May 1 Captain Tenorio had dispatched enough alarming reports of tensions with area citizens that his superior described the situation as desperate.[21] Tenorio's opponents adopted tactics that escalated steadily in a militant direction, beginning first with grumbling and unfulfilled threats. On May 5 the anti-taxation protesters met in Anáhuac and adopted a civil disobedience approach. Their memorial complained particularly of duties on necessary provisions and of unequal enforcement procedures, and the petitioners "resolved to pay no more." If these threats intended to provoke an immediate confrontation with the jittery post commander, they failed. Instead, they divided the local population. Almost a month later the ayuntamiento of nearby Liberty issued a public appeal defending the right of Mexico to collect revenues and condemning resistance as "unwise . . . illtimed . . . [and] criminal." Its message concluded with words of loyalty and peace: "the great body of the people of Texas are too sensible of their duty to themselves and allegiance to the Republic of Mexico, to be precipitously drawn into collission with its constitutional authorities."[22]

On June 4, three days after publication of the Liberty conservative document, certain self-styled "Citizens of Texas" met again and resolved to force the issue. They condemned the Anáhuac officials for harming innocent people by illegally collecting taxes and pledged themselves with "cool determination" to form a military company at Harrisburg and march against the military post. This group acted with less confidence than its rhetoric implied. Some of those who signed the pledge subsequently reneged, and the leader, Andrew Briscoe, proceeded with trickery rather than boldness. He lured Mexican officials into a scuffle on June 12 but failed to bring on a crisis, due to the calming influence of Judge William A. Duncan.

A bolder spirit finally brought this simmering situation to boil. Travis, along with several others who had signed the Harrisburg pledge, attended the proceedings at San Felipe on June 22. With the apparent compliance of Political Chief Miller, Travis put together a separate meeting where he recruited a company of militants. They promised to rendezvous on the San Jacinto river, march to Anáhuac, and disarm the military. A week later he fulfilled this threat and took the town, backed by a force of fifty men, two cannon, and a sloop from Harrisburg. Tenorio left the fort and, after a night in the woods, entered into negotiations with Travis, who left no doubt that the purpose of the expedition was resistance to the general government. On June 30 the garrison formally capitulated, turning over its arms to the rebels in exchange for a promise of safe conduct to the interior. In effect the Travis expedition had acted while the divided local residents debated. It thus by-passed the Liberty conservatives led by Judge Duncan and Alcalde John A. Williams, who were left to protest that these events had stripped duly elected civil authorities of their powers.[23]

The Anáhuac episode notwithstanding, altogether the events of late spring reveal the strength of the forces that restrained revolution. Inadequate politicization of the people, internal divisions, jealousies among would-be leaders, and a myriad of confusing loyalties left Texas still unprepared for revolt. The rebellion in Béxar had been stillborn. Only three other communities rose out of their lethargy in May and June — Brazoria, San Felipe, and the Liberty-Anáhuac area. In each of these places several wedges of division undermined even a semblance of unity and purpose. The land speculator controversy sparked suspicion of the San Felipe junta and its effort to direct military support to the Viesca government in Monclova. In the region of Brazoria preparedness deliberations succumbed to preexisting political quarrels, as J. F. Perry, Henry Austin, and other supporters of the absent empresario combated the Wharton faction. The resulting compromise resolutions of Columbia, which swore loyalty while preparing for rebellion, left the lower Brazos area in flux. Revolt finally broke out in Anáhuac but amidst ominous protest by nearby civil authorities.

The moves by Travis and the other radicals provoked a far different reaction among their fellow Texans than had been intended. During the month of July momentum seemed to shift away from revolution.

One participant retrospectively recalled: "We remained during the summer in that feverish and excited state that usually precedes some great convulsion, frequent public meetings were held & committees of Safety appointed in every part of Texas." He failed to point out that much of the "feverish" activity erupted from opponents of rebellion who sought reconciliation. Historians have noted what one called the "almost continuous internal strife" of the Revolution, but attributed it to leadership jealousies and ideological quarrels.[24] Actually, at this stage of the revolutionary process divisions took on essentially geographic dimensions.

Most of the initiative for resistance to centralism had occurred in the Brazos valley from San Felipe downward, in the Austin colony. When settlers in outlying regions spoke, they did so in protest against being led into rebellion against their will. The first group met on July 4 at Mina on the upper Colorado River and declared a determination "at all times [to] sustain the legal authorities in the exercise of their constitutional duties." Soothed by assurances of the pacific intentions of Mexico's current rulers, the citizens who convened at Mina again a few days later attacked the "misconduct" of "designing men" seeking to sow "disaffection to the General Government." This disgruntlement suggested that the committee of safety organized by the Mina meetings served to guard local interests, whether challenged by Mexico or by other Texans.[25]

The people of Gonzales, in the DeWitt colony, also condemned San Felipian rashness. But, much more unequivocally than in Mina, the Gonzales meeting went beyond an attack on those who sought to precipitate a crisis and declared acceptance of the Santa Anna regime. Its resolutions protested corruption in the state government, suggested modifications in customs policies to make them acceptable, expressed confidence in the president and General Congress, and opposed creation of a provisional government in Texas. The proceedings of this meeting also offered the refusal of the province to heed Viesca's call to arms as evidence of Texas loyalty "towards the Nation."[26]

To the southwest, in the communities of Victoria, Goliad, Refugio, and San Patricio, few public expressions of active resistance to centralism surfaced during the summer. Further, the constitutional officials demonstrated intentions of enforcing edicts handed down by Navarro and Ugartechea, the commander of the Goliad militia expressed loyalty and willingness to arrest dissidents, and the ayuntamiento denounced anyone who attempted to sow discord, resist the legal authorities, or otherwise provoke conflict. This proclamation ended with an appeal for the people to live quietly and to go about their labors.[27]

By mid-July the tide of reaction had backed up into the municipality of Columbia, which had previously hedged its position. On the eleventh the ayuntamiento criticized the rebellious, "uncautious and unreflecting" minority and joined in the attempt to restore "peace quiet harmony and concord." Soon this body proclaimed that "the citizens of this Jurisdiction hold themselves to be true, faithful, loyal, and unoffending Mexican citizens"; even the local committee of safety assured the people that they need not fear Mexican aggression but should adhere strictly "to the laws and constitution of the land." The voices of peace in Columbia included that of erstwhile radical John A. Wharton.[28] In San Felipe political activists either kept a sullen silence, confined their radical rhetoric to private correspondence, or sought a more moderate course.[29]

The would-be leaders of Texas operated in ignorance and confusion regarding the nature and meaning of events outside the province; in contrast, Mexican policy-makers had an abundance of accurate information. In Béxar Ugartechea received and passed on to Mexico reports from a variety of sources—proceedings of public meetings, opinions of governmental officials in the colony, advice and data from correspondents seeking to promote reconciliation. These accounts presented the Béxar commandant with a clear consensus, if not a completely uniform picture: the principal revolutionaries enjoyed minimal support; the preparedness efforts in Texas continued through July but without much success; the people had recovered from their rebellious lapse, and a majority sought peace but still hoped for long-term reforms like separate statehood; some fear of the general government existed, but the greatest continuing apprehension concerned the possibility of an invasion aimed at attacking the people and their property. As one correspondent wrote to Ugartechea, "the entrance of troops will alarm them and provoke them to revolution." The Béxar commandant in turn faithfully reported this aversion to Cos but on July 25 added an opinion that the troops "which the supreme Government" had previously determined to send to Texas "are now in my opinion very necessary." None of the officials wavered from their resolve of the previous spring—neglect and retreat from the exercise of power must end. The time to govern more firmly had arrived.[30]

Essentially, Texas had become a military problem for the military authorities of Mexico; their policy, as revealed in personal communications, centered around a troop build-up to enable them to arrest and punish individuals guilty of sedition. The commanders on the scene should remain on the defensive through the summer until sufficient forces arrived to command respect. Eventual military escalation would serve to demonstrate to all the inhabitants of Texas, in the words of War Minister Tornel, "that the Mexican Government has sufficient energy and power to force respect for the laws and enforce its rights in all its subdivisions."[31]

Both in private and public correspondence the Mexican officials denied that they intended any harm to the peaceful, loyal, and law-abiding citizens. However, as Cos warned the people on July 5, Mexico intended to use its "strong arm" to demand "subjection to the laws," and should conflict ensue, "the inevitable consequences of the war will bear upon the persons and property" of those who disturbed "the public order." For the next month and longer the sterner notes of this message faded as words of conciliation prevailed. Proclamations and letters to popularly elected bodies repeated assurances that law-abiding settlers had no cause to fear for their rights since the soldiers came only to prevent smuggling and to deal with the Indians. The propaganda of the central government also promoted divisions in Texas ranks by ascribing the entire quarrel to land speculators and to homeless, propertyless adventurers who could easily escape the ravages of war by fleeing back to the United States.[32]

Mexico sought to implement its policy through the machinery of the established government, which during the summer maintained its semblance of authority. Béxar Chief Navarro functioned in a manner that generally satisfied superiors as to his loyalty; his reports likewise emphasized the predominance of tranquility, order, and obedience among the citizens of his department. In contrast, an atmosphere of mutual distrust characterized the relationship between the Anglo political chiefs of Brazos and Nacogdoches and the military spokesmen for the government of Mexico. Cos and Ugartechea repeated their public reassurances to these officials and ordered them to arrest the Texas delegates to the Coahuila legislature, the leaders of the Anáhuac expedition, and such opponents of the centralist government as Lorenzo de Zavala. Fulfillment of these policing responsibilities would help prove that Texas stood loyally with the nation, according to these instructions. These communications never mentioned that military escalation had also become part of Mexico's plans.[33]

Like their constituents the chiefs operated in a shroud of incomplete information and incompatible objectives, resulting in numerous inconsistencies. J. B. Miller, of Brazos, had urged armed support for the Viesca government and had complied with the planning of the Anáhuac expedition. In early July he supported the preparedness strategy of the Columbia committee of safety, not only verbally but also by attempting to organize militia units. But at this same time he began to cooperate with the movement for conciliation, reversing his previous militant orders and calling for public tranquility. On July 19, pleading ill health he resigned as political chief, a symbol of his region's inability to plot a coherent course of either rebellion or accommodation.[34] He selected his own successor, former Regidor of San Felipe Wylie Martin, who had also been involved in earlier resistance to the centralists but disavowed that path while functioning as political chief. Martin dutifully ordered the return of arms captured from Tenorio and the arrest of those sought by Ugartechea, though he procrastinated and failed actually to implement those policies. The acting chief advised Ugartechea of the people's desire to avoid conflict and their willingness to support the government. One correspondent sympathetic to these goals asserted on July 25 that by Martin's "influence in a good degree has peace been restored."[35]

Around four hundred miles of territory insulated the Department of Nacogdoches from the command stationed at Béxar. Political Chief Henry Rueg followed generally the same pattern as those who held his position in the Brazos department. In July he issued messages in English and Spanish warning of the hostility of the general government and urging organization of the masses to defend their rights and property; however, the Nacogdoches Ayuntamiento found excuses to avoid activating the militia. Rueg's stand occasioned a reprimand from Ugartechea, who received letters of protest from loyal public officials in the department. Cos also wrote, in English and in no uncertain terms, "you will employ your best exertions to calm the general excitement and to prevent any subversive measure" or be treated like a traitor. By the end of the month Rueg had lapsed into a position of non-commitment by using the excuse of distance. In August he reported improved prospects of peace to the ayuntamientos and urged on them a continued policy of unity and non-violence.[36]

While geography allowed Rueg and his constituents the luxury of following rather than leading, the department contained serious internal splits that also encouraged caution. The Tejano population opposed overt resistance that could lead to independence, and local Tejano officials wrote to state authorities protesting against being by-passed by Rueg's efforts to organize the militia. Late in the summer Nacogdoches *Síndico Procurador* Antonio Menchaca [also Manchaca] informed the Governor that Anglos had taken the law into their own hands to oppose Santa Anna and planned to "disarm all the Mexicans so that they cannot help defend the Government." The letter concluded with a plea for outside protection of "the Mexican citizens who love their Country," but throughout the summer months centralist officials could only promise that treason would eventually be punished and order restored.[37] The strength of the Liberty loyalists also served to restrain those in the Department of Nacogdoches who favored bold anti-government policies.

Throughout Texas between mid-July and mid-August the established political machinery of both appointed and elected officials, apparently reflecting more than leading the popular will, beat a retreat from the path of rebellion. These days became quite trying for those who attempted to lead the revolution. As early as July 6 Travis admitted that even in San Felipe there "seems to be some dissention" on the Anáhuac attack, and that "offensive measures seem to be abandoned by the people." A few weeks later he published a newspaper item requesting "a suspension of public opinion" regarding his role in that episode; soon he admitted that the "peace party" had gained the ascendancy. He acknowledged that more formal means of consolidating popular support had to be created before the period of backsliding and waiting could be ended.[38]

Travis withstood much public criticism, but hardly alone. Briscoe and Williams also felt compelled to write public defenses. Citizens meetings in mid-July in Harrisburg and parts of the Nacogdoches department suffered from lethargic attendance, an absence of unity, unwieldy or cross-purposeful resolutions, and poor coordination. Efforts to organize militia companies had failed. By July 25 an advocate of accommodation in San Felipe could proclaim with confidence, "all here is in a train for peace, the war and [speculating] parties are entirely put down."[39]

Actually, the struggle for conciliation reached its zenith in late July. Several questions had to be answered before a platform for peace could be achieved. Would Texans submit to taxation, centralized government, and an expanded Mexican military presence in order to avoid war? Could existing institutions generate sufficient public support and simultaneously establish coherent programs that worked for peace? Those who asked these kinds of questions sought answers in a general council called for August 1 by Political Chief Miller at the urging of the Columbia Ayuntamiento. Municipalities of the Brazos department chose delegates "to consult and advise on the most prudent and proper measures to be adopted in the present state of the Country," as the Mina alcalde described the purpose of the meeting. The proposed council dissolved without a single accomplishment. Representatives from only four of the seven municipalities showed up; acting Chief Martin met with them only to deliver a message that he had no agenda for the gathering, which he then dismissed.[40]

The nonevent of August 1 was one of several developments that helped shift momentum again toward resistance. It contributed to waning public confidence in the established government—from the beginning of the crisis the political chiefs had adopted such zigzag courses that neither side placed much faith in them. This collapse also left Mexico with enfeebled means of influencing public opinion and of enforcing its own will in the Anglo-dominated regions of Texas. The unresolved issues that had been directed to the aborted council still pressed for solution. Although many Texans had renounced violence and affirmed a conditional loyalty to Mexico, neither the government nor the people carried out the demand to arrest the designated leaders of rebellion. All observers acknowledged that the military build-up which Mexico had in fact resolved on would provoke further opposition in the colonies. When news of the dreaded coming of these reinforcements began to reach the Brazos department in early August, the messages condemned the behavior of these "Cutthroats" in their relationships with civilians. These reports stimulated a new series of public meetings,[41] growing out of the previously established committees of safety. By mid-August many of their leaders sensed a more moderate strategy—of calling a convention to work for peace while preparing for a possible conflict—that appealed to a sufficiently broad spectrum of public opinion.

The idea of a convention originated with a conservative faction. In early July the Mina committee of safety recommended such a gathering to combat the "rash and precipitate measures" of the San Felipe junta. Those who pushed for it believed that a convention could express the pacific will of the majority, clear up the confusion sowed by "Demagogues," and otherwise help restore tranquility. Though endorsed by the Columbia Ayuntamiento and by a popular meeting in San Felipe, support for the proposed gathering grew slowly for the rest of the month. Some conservatives, dubbed by their opponents as the submission party, feared a convention as a revolutionary step that would alarm the otherwise quiescent authorities in Mexico.[42]

A second, moderate group favored the convention technique, believing it to be legal rather than provocative, useful as a means of checking the aggressions of the radicals, and necessary in order to ascertain and then follow the majority will. The moderates also thought that they had the support of most of the people who wanted, in the words of one spokesman, "to keep pease as long as (hands off) and when our rights and privileges are invaded to kick like mules all feet at once."[43] The more radical faction, or "war party," asserted in words and deeds that political events in the interior had dissolved the relationship between Mexico and Texas. Soon they, too, advocated a convention predicated on cautious goals: it could end the "evils of petty feuds and factions," and might restore "order, peace, and confidence."[44]

Until mid-August the movement grew only slowly. A Columbia meeting on July 30 dissolved without issuing a call, and according to a newspaper account, "great dissatisfaction prevails." The convention campaign, bolstered by alarm at the arrival of Mexican reinforcements and the failure of the Brazos chief's council meeting, began to spread rapidly in the second week of August. Travis finally joined the Whartons as radicals endorsed the convention. A Brazoria public meeting on August 9 recommended procedures to insure appropriate representation of the people through a policy of instructing the delegates, a step believed necessary to quell fears of party manipulation. On August 15 this movement spread to other communities; a Columbia meeting, supported by a petition of 135 other citizens who had been unable to attend the gathering, empowered the committee of safety to organize a "consultation." The newspaper exaggerated in claiming "unanimity" in the district, but some, at least, held back for fear that other districts would refuse to cooperate.[45]

Except for poor communications, these skeptics would have been quickly proven wrong. San Augustine and Nacogdoches residents also gathered on August 15 in response to the promptings of emissaries from San Felipe. In spite of continued divisions in Nacogdoches, the public meeting adopted a series of fiery resolutions that asserted revolutionary political theory, blasted Mexican military aggression and violations of liberty, threatened slackers and "Tories," and approved the call for a convention. When the conservative council refused to hold the necessary elections, the committee of safety simply reconvened and moved forward with the process.[46]

Other communities followed suit. San Felipe, which according to Travis "is unanimous for a grand council of all Texas," for once dispelled its jealousy enough to follow Columbia's lead. A public meeting of August 26 resolved its support for "a consultation of the people of Texas." Even the cautious Liberty district fell into step when its citizens met on August 30, although its convoluted resolutions continued to reflect a desire to live peacefully in the Mexican nation. The Mina municipality, which had initiated the drive for a convention in early July, could hardly withhold approval. Altogether this support represented about as much unity as Texas could hope to muster. The Columbia committee finished setting the stage by issuing a plan with dates and other procedures for the selection of delegates and instructions to gather on 15 October.[47]

At the end of August Travis spread the good news to several correspondents. He wrote with typical partisanship and exaggeration, proclaiming that the radicals had resumed control. "Although the Mexican or Tory party made a tremendous effort to put us down, principle had triumphed over prejudice, passion, cowardice and knavery," he boasted to a fellow Anáhuac conspirator. The expected arrival of additional Mexican troops boosted his optimism even further: "The people are becoming united, more & more every day I think in a month more, there will be no division at all."[48]

Other events in September added to this growing sense of purpose and organization. News of Austin's release from Mexican imprisonment meant that he was no longer being held hostage to the good behavior of Texas, thus freeing his reluctant supporters to join in the revolutionary movement. Apparently sensitized to the cause of freedom by his recent experience in and out of Mexican jails, the great empresario returned to the province without his former dedication to loyalty and restraint. From New Orleans in late August he had written friends and relatives of his candid opinion "that Texas shall be effectually, and fully, *Americanized. Texas must be a slave country. It is no longer a matter of doubt. . . .* A gentle breeze shakes off a ripe peach. Can it be supposed that the violent political convulsions of Mexico will not shake off Texas as soon as it is ripe enough to fall[?]" Despite these convictions, before he surveyed the Texas scene for himself Austin continued to think in terms of prudent and defensive policies. He placed great hope on a sizable immigration from the United States to complete the ripening process.[49]

His experiences in Texas quickly convinced Austin to abandon a timetable of postponement. Although a few correspondents still intoned the old dirge of disunity, personality clashes, and "sectional feeling," most presented news of cooperation and determination both within and among the various communities of Texas.[50] The Brazoria committee welcomed Austin warmly and provided him a public forum from which on September 8 he endorsed the consultation and other steps that were already in motion. Austin echoed other leaders in expressing hope that the convention would overcome internal conflicts of "personalities, or divisions, or excitements, or passion, or violence" that had traditionally plagued Texas, and he urged associates to follow his example of setting aside past party or personality divisions in the effort "to unite so many discordant materials."[51] Henry Austin and others in the empresario's faction quickly asserted that Stephen F. Austin's return "unites all parties." Moses Austin Bryan attributed even more charismatic qualities to his uncle: "they hail him as the Savior as they think he and he alone can unite the people in the present perilous state of things." Historians have generally repeated this exaggerated and partisan view of Austin's significance; in fact, no leader emerged during the Revolution who really checked the tendency to divide and nearly crumble from within. Nevertheless, Austin did help solidify support for the course on which Texas had set during his long absence.[52]

News of Mexican military advances in September also contributed to the growing alarm and determination to resist. Although a few Mexican authorities continued to issue calming reassurances, trustworthy evidence to the contrary also came to Anglo Texas. From Béxar would-be peacemakers wrote of their failure: Ugartechea personally intended to undertake the arrest of those who had been charged by the authorities, and nothing could prevent a clash except utter submission. Conservative Edward Gritten wrote on September 8 that "they intend to regulate the affairs of Texas by force whether or not the obnoxious individuals be given up." Ten days later James W. Fannin reported that two vessels laden with Mexican troops had landed at Copano and that a clash appeared imminent.[53]

In the midst of these unifying developments the existing committees of correspondence continued to assert themselves. Atypically harmonious meetings at San Felipe on September 12 and 13 led the way by reaffirming previous plans for a consultation and by asserting revolutionary doctrine. This body resolved that it had "full and unlimited power, to organize a local Government, under the constitution of 1824." Travis, who had been denied a leadership position on the committee, nevertheless reacted ebulliently. "The tories are routed, horse and foot," he exclaimed. The San Felipe committee also fulfilled a communications and propaganda function. Its broadside of September 18 announced the coming of Mexican reinforcements whose "real object is to destroy and break up the foreign settlements in Texas." Thus, it advised, further efforts at conciliation "are hopeless . . . nothing but the RUIN of Texas can be expected from any such measures. . . . War is our only recourse."[54]

Other vigilance committees also swung into action. Mina continued to experience some discord among its members, but the meetings in Brazoria and Columbia successfully arranged for elections of delegates and initiated establishment of militia or volunteer corps to "hold themselves in readiness as minute men." New groups also appeared and demonstrated a willingness to join in the revolutionary mood. The San Augustine committee resolved to grant the consultation "unlimited powers," while the Matagordans repeated all the measures previously enacted in San Felipe and Columbia. Even in regions where revolutionary organizations had not been formed, individuals reported the existence of resolve and unity.[55] Before the end of September measures of military preparedness had been taken in San Felipe, Columbia, Brazoria, Matagorda, Harrisburg, and Nacogdoches, as well as in Gonzales, where the initial clash of arms occurred.[56]

By the time the Texas Revolution became an armed conflict, its leaders had also developed an ideology designed to rally the masses to the cause. The strong reaction against rebellious actions and ideas that occurred in July demonstrated the power of appeals to peace, order, law, and constitutional duty. Henceforth, revolutionary propaganda appropriated much of this conservative doctrine, rather than simply emphasizing the struggle for liberty. Although many wrote of freedom and the rights of man, and some even established a link between the struggles of Texas and those of the Greeks and Poles, most placed the tag "revolutionary" on Mexico and gave it responsibility for initiating the conflict. The nation, according to this mode of thought, fell frequently victim to rebellion, leading to perpetual "confusion and disorder." This maze of chaos in Mexican politics destroyed all legitimate authority; the republic first struggled under "no government at all" before succumbing to the "military despotism" of usurper Santa Anna. The twin monsters of anarchy and dictatorship then threatened to engulf Texas, precipitating the crisis faced by its citizens in the summer of 1835.[57]

In this context the ideologists of the Texas Revolution evoked a familiar natural rights political philosophy: events in the interior had dissolved the social compact, leaving Texans in a state of nature and free to choose from a number of political arrangements. At the time the fighting began in early October, the free-born Texans had not yet decided on a new form of government. Most rejected further relationship with the centralist government, whose emergence, in their theory, severed the constitution and broke the rightful contract. Whether to invoke the right to create a new political system and deal with Mexico as a foreign power had become a matter of expediency. The convention called by the sovereign people for October could declare independence or seek to re-establish the federalist system under the constitution of 1824. Those who developed a political doctrine for Texas in 1835 repeatedly appealed to the spirit of '76, but they emphasized the conservative similarities between their movement and the American Revolution. From this perspective the Texans fought for republicanism against despotism and for liberty against oppression, but they entered the battle for "not Partisan war but Constitutional war, as did our forefathers."[58]

In newspapers, broadsides, and published addresses to the people, the authors of the ideology of the Texas Revolution repeatedly emphasized the defensive characteristics of their cause. Anarchy had come about not due to the actions of Texans but as a result of revolution in Mexico and the imprudent policies of that nation's illegitimate government. The northern province remained faithful to its constitutional duties. Military misrule, they emphasized, now marched toward Texas in the form of a brutal army (variously estimated at from three thousand to sixteen thousand) that had already whetted its appetite for plunder in Zacatecas and Coahuila. In the words of William H. Jack in early August, Texas would be the next victim sacrificed on the "bloody altar . . . of petty tyrants." Stephen F. Austin wrote simply, "our all is at stake."[59]

Others foretold in graphic detail the ruinous policies that the Mexican soldiers would enact. Horatio Allsberry claimed to base his August 28 circular on personal observation in Monterrey. The "thousands" of troops coming to Texas, he wrote, would establish customs houses, overturn land titles, "burn the houses and drive from the country" many citizens, and "put their slaves free and let them loose upon their families." Throughout the summer doomsayers had warned of black insurrection and other horrifying consequences of the military build-up, but in late August and September their words carried greater authority. For example, the broadside of James H. C. Miller explained that his previous efforts at cooperation with the Mexican authorities had failed due to their deception. Now he understood "that many of the dangers, once supposed to be fanciful, are too real; that the government are contemplating and actually fitting up a formidable invasion of the rights and properties of Texas; that the ruin of her commerce, the emancipation of her slaves, the abolition of the system of colonization, the prostration of her local militia and other oppressive measures are within her scheme, all ruinous to the interests of the country." He ended with an apology for his inadequate foresight and error in believing in the "good faith of the government."[60]

With the support of these pronouncements by knowledgeable, trustworthy, and cautious observers, more radical spokesmen could afford to add fire to the doctrine. Committee of safety chairman Branch T. Archer informed the people of Columbia jurisdiction in late September that *"War* is upon us. . . . let us take the field. We call upon you . . . in the name of every thing that is dear. . . . You will be fighting for your wives and children, your homes and firesides, for your country, for liberty," and for your sufferings in conquering the "wilderness."[61] The ideology of the Texas cause had thus been refined into a powerful creed, depicting a struggle for constitutional order and for hallowed, familiar political principles and against a direct, personal threat to life, family, property, racial hegemony, past sacrifices, and future well-being. Texas entered the military phase of its revolution with little more than an army of promises. Yet, it had overcome the individualism, apathy, localism, and other divisions that hampered the movement from the first. Its leaders placed high faith in the Consultation that they had created to continue the struggle against these old forces of internal discord, the army of invasion from Mexico, and other challenges that war itself would inevitably create.

3. The Consultation

OCTOBER–NOVEMBER, 1835

Texas entered the military phase of its struggle with Mexico in a mood of confidence, a new attitude following months of hesitation and internal squabbling. Basking in the unaccustomed comfort of this sense of unity, soon-to-be commanding general Stephen F. Austin most eloquently described it. "There is now but one spirit, one mind, one object — to drive the military out of Texas and organize a government for this country," he wrote to the Matagorda committee of safety on October 2, 1835. Austin believed that the "common purpose" had enough strength to carry the country through until its political and military tasks could be accomplished.[1] His optimism remained two weeks later when he assured another committee that "the enthusiasm increases daily," as evidenced by the disappearance of party emotions. Austin hoped that partisanship could be restrained by the common goals that had emerged — armed resistance to centralism, a provisional government, and step-by-step movement to independence. The latter measure (confined still to private correspondence) had only recently become part of his official creed, and he apparently believed that it removed a source of contention between his followers and their more ardent opponents.[2]

Other observers shared Austin's evaluation of the pervasive public consensus and its significance. Newspapers praised "Texas Patriotism" that "prevails among all classes," including the ladies, "bless their souls," who appeared willing to volunteer themselves for military service and mere boys who did so without parental approval. The *Texas Republi-*

can maintained that the war would be ended without fighting if Santa Anna could but witness the enthusiasm; while others may have doubted this wishful thinking, the general conclusion was widespread. "Such united spirits cannot fail of success," wrote the head of the first provisional government to the residents of east Texas. Only a few in the early fall even appeared to doubt whether this unity would survive on its own momentum. Branch T. Archer advised the people of the Columbia jurisdiction to punish as traitors any who questioned the necessity or justice of armed conflict, but most Texans had no stomach for revolutionary coercion.[3]

Initial military triumph contributed to the optimism that swept Texas in the fall of 1835. Enough Texas volunteers rallied to Gonzales on October 2 to turn back the centralist force from Béxar in an engagement that conjured storied images of Lexington and Concord. A week later another set of fresh recruits forced the surrender of the Mexican garrison at Goliad. Decisive victory against the forces that General Cos had massed at Béxar proved more elusive. The Texans won another battle at Concepción near the end of October, but after that Cos allowed the Texans to choose between an offensive or a siege. Despite their advantage in numbers (negated partially by the constant coming and going of the volunteers), several Texas army leaders urged caution. Impatience spawned criticism of the siege, and debate wrenched the loosely organized army. Prolonged inactivity before Béxar created problems of supply and morale so serious that the troops almost dissolved before their leaders rallied them to storm the town on December 5. After five days of bitter house-to-house street fighting, Cos capitulated.[4]

It required only a few weeks of military and political experience to crush the idealism of early October. According to Barker, after about a month of attempting to lead the discordant elements that comprised the "Army of the People," Austin adopted a metaphor of tragedy to express his feelings. "The character of the struggle in which Texas is engaged . . . is one of life or death, 'to be or not to be,'" he informed the political leadership. Although he went on to refer to the war of extermination with which Mexico threatened Texas, Austin might more incisively have alluded to the Hamlet-like internal disorders and suicidal tendencies that beset the youthful revolution. By mid-December Gov. Henry Smith wrote repeatedly not of a sense of purpose guiding the people but of "restless, disorganizing spirits."[5]

Although disunity arose from many sources, the burden of resolving conflict rested in the political realm. Several leaders recognized the problem of creating a competent and efficient authority, but Lorenzo de Zavala most fully described the challenge that confronted Texas. He had risen to political prominence amidst the turbulence that carried over from Mexican independence, and his perspective sharpened with diplomatic service in France. Though he had only recently cast his lot with the Texans, the Mexican liberal understood far better than they the vicissitudes of revolution.

In a letter to Austin, Zavala expressed without great confidence a hope that the recently-returned empresario could hold Texas together. Zavala candidly explained the source of past difficulties and disturbing prospects: "although there is individual patriotism there is no unified patriotism. . . . They will defend their private rights until death; but still they do not realize the necessity for cooperation." He feared that the Consultation, unable to arrive at a true consensus, would either declare a premature independence or would merely draft some reports and adjourn, leaving Texas in "its present anarchy." For the movement to be successful, Zavala believed, the people had to understand the necessity of establishing a revolutionary government and of giving it real authority, but he despaired of accomplishing this "among a people where there are no public powers and where each citizen is a king like unto Adam."[6]

Ensuing events demonstrated the wisdom of Zavala's evaluation. Over the next five months three political bodies appeared — an inappropriately named "Permanent Council" in October, the long-awaited Consultation in early November, and a provisional government made up of a governor and General Council in the middle of that month. Each effort failed, sending Texas into a political chaos that threatened to destroy the revolt by the time Santa Anna's reinforcements arrived in February.

Local committees of safety continued to function in early October in many of the far-flung districts, from Matagorda in the southwest to San Felipe in the center to Liberty, Nacogdoches, San Augustine, and Sabine in east Texas. They attempted to fill some of the political void left by the absence of a single authority, corresponding with each other on matters of information and ideology, raising funds, soldiers, and arms on a voluntary basis, and attempting to heal the wounds of the past within their communities. These bodies also lent support to the movement to create a legitimate government and encouraged popular acceptance of the council when military events delayed the Consultation planned for mid-October.[7]

Buoyed by the spirit of unity of October and the success of the Texas volunteers in their initial battles at Gonzales and Goliad, the decision to postpone organizing a government came easily. An expected quick victory against the remaining Mexican forces in Béxar would then allow the political work to be accomplished in a leisurely manner. Various committees of safety representatives who joined together in early October, including San Felipe's Gail Borden, saw through the excessive optimism and believed in the necessity of creating an interim "standing authority."[8] This movement struggled with several initial problems. Something of a challenge arose from a competing body. Delegates-elect of the Consultation and officers chosen by companies of volunteers gathered at Gonzales on October 10 to organize the army; they proceeded to instruct the delegates who might gather for the Consultation scheduled to meet on October 15 to present themselves for military service instead. Should a quorum materialize, the Gonzales meeting still urged the delegates to "suspend all action" until November 1. This "Counsel of War" chose Austin as commander in chief, thereby pre-empting military control from being exercised by the council assembling at San Felipe. The Gonzales resolutions cast aspersions on the patriotism of those who remained away from the army and doubt on the legitimacy of any political group that formed before November.[9]

Those who pressed ahead with organizing the Permanent Council in San Felipe had difficulty finding a sufficient number of suitably-credentialed representatives. Its membership ranged from a handful to a total of twenty, but fewer than that served at any one time. Over half the active delegates came from three municipalities—Liberty, Harrisburg, and Viesca—and only seven districts had representation. Despite the council's appeals, no participants arrived from Columbia, Mina, or any of the western municipalities. Four served despite not having been elected; among these, Isaac Batterson, of Harrisburg, and William Pettus, of San Felipe, had been active in committees of safety. Contrastingly, most of the delegates who served on the council in October had not been heard from during the earlier movement, either for conflict or reconciliation. This short-lived governing body thus operated under a shadow of uncertainty regarding its claim as a gathering authorized by the people.[10]

From its initial actions on October 9 the council conducted itself in a hesitant manner. This demeanor existed because of a number of factors besides the weak credentials of its membership. Although the situation called for balance rather than boldness, the council teetered between disastrous inaction and failure caused by popular reaction to perceived excesses. Furthermore, the council functioned in subservience to the power of the army, whose members largely repudiated outside authority and whose head continued to have stronger political than military instincts.

In some respects, the council served merely as Austin's political surrogate. Before the body formally organized, its leader, R. R. Royall, attempted to recruit members based on the idea that "Col. Austin's absence renders it especially necessary" to have a political authority in San Felipe. Royall subsequently kept the commanding general informed and sought his advice or even consent; Austin responded with answers that seemed more like orders than mere opinions. A letter from the council head on October 14 reveals this deferential attitude: "please take into consideration," Royall asked Austin, "the Situation of this Council whose powers will cease when the convention goes into operation." The president requested that the general arrange for the council's continuation as a kind of administrative arm of the government.[11] This interim body gained a bit more legitimacy on the sixteenth when thirty-one delegates of the Consultation assembled at San Felipe and empowered the council until the new convention date of November 1. However, membership grew thin after mid-October, and those who stayed on continued to be plagued by self-doubt. On the twenty-first Royall dutifully explained to Austin the "delicacy" of issues that the government confronted: "necessity" seemed to compel taxation and other measures, but "the People of our country . . . would not likely recognize the Council in such acts of Responsibility."[12]

The Permanent Council seemed confident only as a propaganda and advisory agency. Royall issued appeals to several audiences. He called on committees of safety to raise men and materiel. Twice he directed messages "to the Citizens of the United States of North America," explaining the origins and justice of the Texas cause, appealing for philanthropy, and seeking manpower. Despite having no official power to do so, Royall made an unqualified pledge "to Compensate each Adventurer" who volunteered from the United States with a plot of the ample land of Texas.[13] The council also issued two circulars to the general public. The first of these, issued on October 18, informed the people concerning recent events and explained the origin of its authority. It ended with an attempt to arouse non-participants, presenting the conflict as a direct threat to individual life and property and urging the people to "lay aside party feeling and sectional prejudice." Another address came five days later, repeating these familiar themes. This time the council also added threats to its persuasions: "The Army flush with Victory will remember you. The present generation may brand you with Infamy. Posterity will remember it towards your children. He who does not now protect Texas—Texas will not Protect hereafter. . . . Punishment and Disgrace alone for those who are secretly or silently its enemies."[14]

The council functioned more tentatively on matters that required actions rather than words. It reported rumors of treasonous activity to Austin rather than undertaking investigation and repression itself. "In times like these when we are surrounded by Warr, . . . military rules must Prevail in some Extent till otherwise Provided," Royall rationalized to the commander.[15] Likewise, the council authorized the army to impress arms and other supplies from those unwilling to give their property to the cause, but the interim government itself shied away from using direct methods of obtaining provisions. It eventually turned to issuing drafts and borrowing money, but the council stopped short of levying the tariffs that Zavala suggested.[16]

Royall exaggerated in reporting, "we have taken upon us in the present times (Pregnant as they are with Emergencies) some Responsibilities." Except on the question of land sales, the council confined itself to issuing statements, making recommendations, and approving the army's measures in its own behalf. The council's single bold action, closing land offices until the end of the war, occurred on October 27 under intense military pressure. Many of the volunteers feared that speculators would grab the best land while the patriots remained in the field; they insisted that the government prevent this fraud. Officials and prospective landowners immediately protested the land policy as unconstitutional. When this interim government ceased its meager functions on November 1, it did so amidst a din of criticism and charges that the council had become as abusive toward individual rights as the military usurpers of Mexico.[17]

The passing of the Permanent Council went largely unnoticed. By November 1 delegates of the long-awaited Consultation had gathered in sufficient numbers in San Felipe to preserve continuity and provide political solutions in the name of the sovereign people. Those who deliberated for the next two weeks still could not claim to be completely representative—none came from the war zone districts of Béxar, Goliad, Refugio, Victoria, or San Patricio, and less than half the elected delegates attended from Bevil, Mina, and Matagorda, leaving those municipalities underrepresented.

This troublesome situation occurred because of military pressure; at least half of the absent members stayed to defend their homes or submitted to the sentiment of the army and remained with their units in the field. An arrangement whereby some delegates left the army for the Consultation while staff officers and a few others remained in the military service had been worked out by Houston, Austin, and Archer to stem a threatened mass walkout by the soldiers. Until then, in the words of one of the commander's aides, the issue nearly became "the means of disbanding the army as I heard most every one say that he would return [home] if the members of the convention left."[18] Nevertheless, fifty-eight of the ninety-eight credentialed delegates attended the Consultation; most participated for the entire two-week session. Nonattendance evened out the ideological and factional balance by reducing Austin's influence. Not only did he remain with the besieging army, but at least ten of the absent delegates had strong affiliations with the Texas commander.[19]

Most of the representatives to the Consultation recognized each other by name, if not by sight, because a majority had been elected to public office, usually repeatedly, before that November. Twenty of the fifty-eight delegates had been active in public meetings and committees of safety in 1835, including the chair of the group in San Felipe (R. M. Williamson), Harrisburg (John W. Moore), San Augustine (Jacob Garrett), Gonzales (William S. Fisher), Mina (Don Carlos Barrett), and Columbia (Branch T. Archer). An even larger number, twenty-four, had occupied positions of influence during the tensions between Texas and Mexico that led to conventions in 1832 and 1833.[20]

In other respects, too, the Consultation delegates came from the established leadership of Texas. Some historians have echoed the arguments of Mexican officials of the summer of 1835 that revolutionary activity emerged from "turbulent characters," men whom Cos described as "without country, morality, or any employment." According to this critical view, the revolutionaries had nothing to lose by duping honest old-time colonists into revolution.[21] While the matter of character and morality may defy precise measurement, the background of the delegates as either established settlers or transients can be established. Land and other colonial records reveal that the Consultation delegates had resided in Texas in excess of seven years, on the average;

Table 1. Texas Revolution Activists:
Age and Residence Characteristics

Event/Activity	No.	Age	Residence
Anáhuac pledgers	65 (25)	35	7.84 years
Committee of Safety	93 (55)	40	9.14
Consultation delegates	98 (96)	38	7.05

NOTE: The figures in parentheses represent the number identified in terms of biographical details; figures for age are the median, while figures for length of residence are the mean.

more had lived in the province for ten years or longer than had emigrated in the three years prior to the 1835 convention. The representatives were reasonably mature in age as well as length of residence, the average delegate being over thirty-eight years old.[22]

Of all the distinguishable groups involved in the struggles of 1835 — those who by signing pledges identified themselves with the Anáhuac conflict, activists in vigilance and safety committees, and the Consultation delegates — only the Anáhuac pledgers bore any resemblance to the rootless profile. In fact, this group also contained many long-term settlers; those whose length of residence can be established had been in Texas for nearly eight years prior to their rebellious episode. But forty of the sixty-five (or over sixty percent) who signed these pledges in June 1835 do not appear in extant records, suggesting that a majority of them had either been in Texas a short time or failed to establish a recognized land claim. By contrast, all but two of the ninety-eight credentialed Consultation delegates can be identified in terms of length of residence. Further, the Anáhuac activists seem to have eschewed politics as a means of redressing their grievances; scarcely any of them had held prior elective office. The trend toward entrusting power to the established leadership had begun before the November Consultation; experienced, established leaders dominated the officers of public meetings and membership of the committees of the summer and early fall. Even excluding those eventually elected to the Consultation, the committee of safety activists included six former alcaldes, eight delegates to the earlier conventions, and two former members of the Coahuila and Texas legislature. This group also had solid credentials in terms of their long residence in Texas. Clearly, the traditional ruling elite had quickly reclaimed its dominant position in the wake of the Anáhuac upheaval.[23]

In choosing Consultation delegates the public rejected the familiar

leaders in only one respect — those identified with the land speculation scandals in the state legislature and those who had gone too far
toward conciliation with Mexico fell from popular grace. The influence
of the Monclova "speculators" declined long before November; most
defended their reputations or simply kept a low profile in order to avoid
contaminating the resistance movement with the image of a self-serving
leadership. Not until late summer did a few of them — business partners Samuel M. Williams and Thomas F. McKinney and their lawyer,
Spencer H. Jack — even step forward to endorse the convention. McKinney and Ben F. Smith campaigned for election to the Consultation in
the Columbia jurisdiction but fell far short of victory, despite McKinney's fervently aired charges of irregularities at the polls. Smith and
ex-legislator James Grant subsequently claimed seats as representatives
from Goliad, but both remained at their army posts and did not attend the political gathering. The absence of these formerly influential
leaders may also have reduced Austin's influence, since many of them
had been his close allies. Ironically, the same result occurred because
other Austin supporters had lost popular influence due to their commitment to peace and reconciliation with Mexico. The empresario's
cousin Henry Austin, brother-in-law James F. Perry, and their friends
in the McNeil family all lost in the bitterly contested Columbia elections; the rival Wharton faction succeeded by depicting itself as the
"People's Ticket" and the Austin supporters as "Gentleman candidates."[24] Other prominent local politicians also did not reach the Consultation, including military and political chiefs Peter Ellis Bean and
Henry Rueg, of Nacogdoches, and J. B. Miller, of Brazos, Liberty Judge
William Duncan, who led the reaction against Travis's Anáhuac adventure, and Asa Brigham, head of the Columbia Ayuntamiento that passed
peace resolutions in July. Officers of the public meetings at Mina and
Gonzales had also expressed loyalty toward Mexico that month and
likewise failed to retain their positions of leadership.[25]

The delegates who congregated at San Felipe came mostly from the
previous summer's moderate movement that sought a course between
submission and revolution.[26] Yet, this consensus was extremely fragile.
It had been forged with difficulty as advocates of war and peace com-
promised their positions in the quest for unity while postponing real
resolution of "all our jarring discords and discontents" until the Consultation.[27] Although the coming of armed conflict in October settled
one issue, the delegates still faced the difficult task of reconciling divergent views that, previously pushed into the background, would in-

evitably resurface as they debated the purpose of the war, the power and structure of government, and the virtues of different leaders. Furthermore, given their roots in the old political establishment, the members brought with them scores of old personal jealousies, regional suspicions, and factional quarrels which threatened to undermine their otherwise homogenous characteristics. Even though William H. Wharton remained at the military front, his brother John and friend Henry Smith attended to direct those who resented the Austin clique, headed at the Consultation by Don Carlos Barrett. Neither the Wharton nor Austin faction (each with about one-third of the delegates) could dominate, giving the unaligned ones the balance of power.[28]

In terms of policy, distinctions between the two groups often crumbled, but partisan positions did exist. Barrett continued to favor a war to preserve the 1824 constitution, a stance which necessitated cooperation with Mexican federalists in or out of Texas. The Austin faction hoped that this policy might end the war without forcing recruitment of many United States volunteers, whose land bounties would erode the claims of the established empresarios. The Wharton-Smith line of thought grew out of more overtly anti-Mexican attitudes and sought an immediate declaration of independence and other thorough policies, including establishment of a large regular army and repression of internal enemies of the Revolution.

The Wharton faction gained the initial advantage, but only by being the first to move toward compromise. One of its members, Branch T. Archer, of Columbia, won the privilege of presiding over the assembly. His initial address urged the delegates "to divest yourselves of all party feelings, to discard every selfish motive, and look alone to the true interest of your country." Sam Houston, allied with that same faction, also lent his magnetic oratory to the effort "to harmonize the feelings of the people and to produce unanimity of sentiment," as Gail Borden described it. "He made the best speech . . . I have ever heard," this observer continued, "I believe he has the interest of the country at heart."[29] Given this captivating effect on an Austin supporter like Borden, Houston's presence undoubtedly had influence on some of the political novices who made up the non-factional group at the Consultation. The efforts of Archer, Houston, and other conciliators like J. W. Robinson and Lorenzo de Zavala moved the members into the spirit of give and take but, of course, did not obliterate partisanship. The balanced make-up of the Consultation resulted in expediential rather than forceful policies: most major decisions either passed as compromises or had to be followed by concessions to the other faction in order to prevent the body's collapse.[30]

Even the fundamental question of the extent of the body's authority divided the delegates. Some agreed with the San Augustine committee of safety in urging that this meeting of the people's representatives "be vested with unlimited powers, to be governed entirely by circumstances, [and] . . . to act with energy and decision." More conservative voices, such as Borden's *Telegraph and Texas Register,* insisted that the gathering had originally been created to investigate, counsel, and recommend to the people (thus a meeting to consult together rather than a convention with sovereign power) and denied that it could assume legislative functions. In this restrictive view the Consultation should organize a limited civil government to protect property and person but act with "extreme caution, prudence, and moderation." Bold policies— even "one imprudent measure"—might lead to the "ruin" of Texas.[31]

Those who urged these limitations on the Consultation obviously hoped to prevent it from becoming an instrument of revolution. The delegates simply chose to by-pass the controversy about the extent of their power and moved obliquely to address that issue as they debated the purpose of the war. For a few days they continued to hedge by producing a new batch of rhetoric praising patriotic gallantry in the battle for human rights "against a malicious demagogue and his blood thirsty demons." But the time had passed when a torrent of words would suffice as an explanation of the Texas cause; the body could not move ahead until it had defined more specific goals. Wharton's resolution for a committee "to make a Declaration setting forth to the world, the cause that compelled us to take up arms, and the objects for which we fight" passed after an animated debate on November 4, the first full day with a quorum. He chaired the group, but Archer appointed to at least half its seats conservatives who with Austin still opposed independence. The committee deliberated for three days without approving a document; meanwhile, the delegates impatiently began discussing the issue on the floor, though Borden reported that "good feeling" remained "the order of the day."[32]

Williamson and Barrett both presented drafts of declarations in favor of continuing the struggle in the name of the federal Constitution of 1824, with the latter making an explicit appeal for participation in the war by "our fellow citizens" in Mexico and the department of Béxar. Pragmatic arguments supported their position; the advocates of this view still maintained that Mexican liberals would rally to support Texas once it dispelled the impression that independence had already been declared. Thus, with a timely, conservative proclamation and auxiliary support for Gen. Antonio Mexía's expedition against the centralists, the Consultation might divert battle from Texas soil and win an easy victory almost without fighting.[33]

In the third day of its own debate and with the committee still deadlocked, the Consultation itself voted on the question of "a provisional government upon the principles of the Constitution of 1824." By a margin of 33–14 it endorsed this concept as the basis for the declaration, and the committee obliged with a document, approved and signed by convention members the following day, November 7. Yet, in its final form the declaration reflected the illogic of compromise rather than an outright victory for the Austin-Barrett faction. It affirmed the contract theory of government based on the philosophy of natural rights, including by implication that of revolution. In this view the usurper Santa Anna had already "dissolved the social compact" and surrendered any legitimate authority over Texas, which rightfully could create "an independent government. . . . but [the people] will continue faithful to the Mexican government, as long as that nation is governed by the Constitution."[34]

While the declaration did stop short of proclaiming formal separation, it asserted only a most qualified loyalty to the Mexican republic. Basically, it offered Mexico a last chance to overthrow centralism as a condition for Texas to rejoin the old federalist union. Historian David Weber regards the November 7 declaration as "disingenuous" because it declared loyalty to a nonexistent government; however, in the context of the debate of the day, the document may also be described as simply indecisive. Certainly, it did not satisfy Austin, who soon wrote to the provisional government bemoaning the Consultation's policy for having failed to stem the growing unity of all Mexico against Texas. Austin urged new officials to come to "some resolution of a decisive character."[35]

Having hedged on the issue of purpose, the Consultation attempted to move more quickly in establishing a government, only to find that its previous irresolution continued to haunt the deliberations. Henry Smith, who chaired the committee working on a plan for a provisional government, gained its approval of a document that included an implicit declaration of independence. Article I copied much of the preamble of the U.S. Constitution (hardly appropriate for a provisional structure); the second article of this draft declared Texas a "sovereign state," free of any bond with Coahuila, and "governed by her own laws and decrees."[36] After being outvoted in the Smith-led committee, Barrett on November 9 maneuvered the issue back to a full meeting of the Consultation, which turned the question over to a new, smaller committee made up entirely of his supporters. Its version, purged of the two objectionable clauses and adding an oath of office supporting "the republican principles of the constitution of Mexico of 1824," underwent scrutiny and amendment by the committee of the whole before winning final approval as the "Organic Law" on the thirteenth.

But the victory of Barrett's conservatives was hardly complete; this final fine-tuning process generally added sterner, more clearly revolutionary features. On November 11 Houston successfully moved a provision that abolished the old office of political chief. The delegates also added a clause "That all persons who leave the country in its present crisis, with a view to avoid a participancy in its present struggle . . . shall forfeit . . . any lands they may hold or have claim to." These provisions passed in part because even Austin had come to share the more forceful attitude. On November 5 he wrote in confidence to the Consultation from his headquarters near Béxar that he had changed his opinion on many issues: "Every effort will be made to destroy us — we are therefore fully justified in resorting to every means of defense. . . . under the circumstances there must be no half way measures on our side — no hesitation or scruples."[37]

Despite this growing sense of resolution, the Organic Law itself reflected the spirit of compromise, balance, and hesitation. It established an executive along with a General Council, made up of a representative from each municipality chosen by his delegation, to "assist" the governor. Its members had no legislative authority unless "in their opinion the emergency of the country requires" it; the document enumerated the powers of the body, including that of levying import duties but no other taxes. The constitution gave the governor "full and ample" executive authority, made him head of the military forces, and provided that the council could grant him "all other powers which may be thought necessary." It also provided for judiciary and treasury departments and allowed for expansion of governmental authority in order to implement the policies of the Consultation.

Structurally, the Organic Law suffered from an unsound political concept in assuming an unrealistic level of cooperation between the governor and the council. Their relationship resembled that of an executive and cabinet, except that neither had appointive or other means of influencing the other; rather than proposing a system of checks and balances, this provisional constitution mandated that the two branches share the same powers and work together.[38] The Consultation's choice of Henry Smith as governor over Stephen F. Austin by a 30–22 vote, perhaps part of a bargain to offset Barrett's constitutional victory, practically assured a future of discord. Smith had always displayed flamboyant, controversial, and partisan tendencies as a politician. The delegations chose a council of balanced factional make-up; however, it included Barrett and would soon change composition and become overwhelmingly opposed to the Wharton-Smith camp.[39]

Another fatal tendency of the Consultation was its deferential attitude toward the army in the field. It designed a land policy to reassure the soldiers who feared that while they sacrificed, the speculators would carry off the spoils. In three separate articles the Organic Law nullified the "fraudulent" grants made by the last state legislature, reaffirmed the benefits of earlier emigration policies to citizens who had not yet received their land, and ended all transactions "during the agitated and unsettled state of the country." The Consultation had earlier provided for an unspecified amount of land for each volunteer as well as their monthly pay and reimbursement for losses of personal possessions.[40] These policies could be defended as both just and necessary, but yielding to the soldiers on the matter of authority over military affairs demonstrated the weakness of the Consultation and laid the basis for future disaster. The Wharton-Smith faction pushed for a regular army, disciplined by conventional military rules and subject to oversight by the civil government. Warning ominously that "without discipline" "your armies will be mobs . . . [and] can achieve nothing," President Archer urged the Consultation to resolve this problem. On November 13 along with the Organic Law the body passed a sweeping measure concerning the military. It provided for militia organization but, more importantly, also created a regular army of men enlisting for two years or the duration, commanded by a major general (to which Houston achieved unanimous election), "subject to the orders of the Governor and Council," and governed by U.S. army regulations.[41]

The real issue still remained. Would the Consultation attempt to assert its will over the existing bodies of troops? Barrett's committee advised against such a procedure, arguing that the military companies predated the Consultation. Since "their movements have hitherto been regulated by officers of their own choice, no obligation can be imposed on them to submit to the control of the provisional government." This army could be advised, supplied, and compensated by the civil authorities, but the soldiers would continue to rule themselves. Lest any rumors of resentment develop among the volunteers, Lt. Governor-elect James W. Robinson explained the policy explicitly. Regarding "the Army of the people now in the field," he wrote to Capt. Thomas J. Rusk, "Gen. Houston will not be authorized to command them, unless it is their wish fully expressed."[42]

Thus, Texas had two military forces: a regular army on paper, with discipline, a single commander, and civil direction but no soldiers; and another consisting of several hundred volunteers who showed but a minimum of respect to any authority, submitted occasionally to an officer of their own choosing, and constantly debated such matters as whether, when, or where to fight. One delegate proposed an extreme solution of furloughing the entire army until emergency required recruitment of another force, presumably regular, but the house refused to consider this resolution on November 14, the day of its adjournment.[43] On the matter of the army, as on all other issues that came before the Consultation, policies of postponement and compromise had been adopted to prevent the proceedings from coming apart. In the three months that followed, the new government succumbed to these inherited problems, sending Texas into anarchy.

4. Into Anarchy
NOVEMBER, 1835, TO FEBRUARY, 1836

The provisional government established by the Consultation had responsibility for ruling Texas at a crucial time, from mid-November, 1835, through February, 1836. It soon had advantages not available to earlier authorities. The military conflict in and around Béxar ended on December 10 after five days of bitter fighting in the town. The results of this engagement left the region free of Mexican forces for nearly three months, ample time to concentrate military command, organize and drill soldiers, and lay plans for the future. The lull in fighting also presented an opportunity for the government to establish itself, address some of the issues left unresolved by its parent convention, and gain a measure of respect from the people. Instead, despite widespread recognition that, in Austin's words, "the country must have organization, and that immediately,"[1] affairs steadily deteriorated into political and military chaos.

This situation came about for a variety of reasons. The democratic and antimilitaristic ideology of the Texas revolution appears to have made the people more reluctant than ever to surrender any of their personal autonomy. Old factional splits still dogged efforts to gain governmental legitimacy, and divisions between various interest groups fueled clashes along economic and class lines. Those who attempted to lead Texas struggled with problems carried over from the indecisive Consultation, and they did so from within an unwieldy governmental structure. The governor and the General Council, rather than resolving these issues, became badly estranged. They enacted few significant measures, implemented even fewer, and often tacitly delegated responsibilities to other entities. The two branches eventually concentrated most of their flagging energies on assailing each other as the government dissolved into anarchy.

For all his shortcomings — unforgiving partisanship, an uncontrolled temper, grating and bombastic language, unreflective disposition, and other excesses — Governor Smith as least recognized the depth of the crisis facing Texas and the revolutionary policies it demanded. Two days after he took office Smith bluntly advised the council, "You have to call system from chaos; to start the wheels of government, clogged and impeded as they are by conflicting interests, and by discordant materials." He urged support for the army in the field, rewards to lure new recruits, additional measures for defense, and policies to raise revenue. The council passed tariff, post office, and other bills that he considered minor; it also attempted to make its authority felt among the people by sending commissioners into the different municipalities to administer oaths of loyalty to the new government. But generally, the council took a cautious, bureaucratic approach to its task, refusing in any way to coerce obedience from the people or the military bodies that had sprung up from volunteer ranks. In mid-December Smith urged the "Legislative Council" to act boldly in the wake of the fall of Béxar: "It is now time for the Government to bring every thing under its own proper control, and pursue the organic system in place of confusion, or desultory warfare."[2]

In practice the provisional government generally followed the easier path, as revealed by its response to a most serious need, provisioning the army. The General Council relied on voluntary means of supply, appointing agents and contractors to perform this task or allowing commanders to impress their own equipment, food, and other necessities. Naturally, this approach led to scarcities and suffering among both civilians and troops, to an excessive burden on people in the war zones, to abuses by some impressing agents, and to disenchantment with the government by virtually all those affected.[3] Austin, Archer, and Wharton, the agents selected by the Consultation to represent Texas interests in the United States, raised a $250,000 loan in New Orleans in mid-January, but the goods derived from this source did not meet the pressing needs of the military between November and February.[4] The government's commissary failures certainly won no admiration from an army already disposed to resist the governor's desire to curb its autonomy.

Smith's first official action, an order to the commander of the army of the people, demonstrated a desire to exert civil control over the military; however, the council refused to follow his lead. On November 30 it expressly reiterated "determination not to interfere with the appointment of officers, or to direct the movements of the volunteer army, now in the field."[5] The council did pass ordinances to raise additional forces — as militia, regular army, and auxiliary volunteer corps — more responsive to government control. These efforts all failed, made worse by a debilitating quarrel with Major General Houston over the matter of responsibility. The council did eventually heed his recommendation to increase the land bounty for those who enlisted under him; other schemes were proposed to fill the regular army ranks, but no inducement seemed to work.[6]

The Texas armies became steadily more chaotic, splintering into ever smaller units governed only by unwritten rules of democracy. Following Cos's surrender, many Texans trudged home in weariness, hoping that the war was over. Other soldiers had made the long journey from the United States and hungered after more action. All those who attempted to command the volunteers agreed that activity in fact held the key to any possibility of discipline. Thus, even though the prudent course seemed to dictate settling into winter quarters, leaders arose proclaiming a new objective: on to Matamoros. Aggressive patriotism and plunder could both be satiated by this strategy, according to the prevailing view. At the end of the year Francis W. Johnson, who had led a wing of the Texas force in the assault of Béxar, took two hundred men from there to the Goliad area, which was to be the staging ground for the assault. Only about a hundred men stayed behind. Three commanders (empowered variously by votes of approval from the soldiers, Governor Smith, or the council) struggled to assume control over the fragmented volunteers for the ill-fated Matamoros expedition. A common hatred of some or all parts of the provisional government and a propensity for giving advice on political issues seemed to be the only link between the discordant military elements, which suffered the paralysis of irresolution throughout January and February, 1836.[7]

This military uncertainty expressed more than the problem of unruly soldiers and ambitious officers. The overall issue of war purpose — either for the federal constitution or outright independence — had not yet been settled. Several contentious factions pressed for their point of view. Such Mexican liberals as ex-Governor Viesca, his military aide Col. José María Gonzales, and General Mexía attempted to make common cause with Texas in behalf of the Constitution of 1824. They found hopeless division among the various authorities and widespread distrust expressed by rank and file Anglo Texans. Viesca first appeared at Goliad in November, expressed disappointment at the informal reception given by Texas forces, and soon made his way out of the province. Gonzales also complained of his treatment, even though the council furnished him with some financial support. On December 10 he published a call to arms in defense of federalism, aimed at besieged Mexican soldiers in Béxar who surrendered that day. The document attempted to reassure Mexicans everywhere of the sincerity of the Texan commitment to the 1824 constitution. The next day the council issued a similar appeal to "patriotic Mexicans . . . [to help] us sustain the federal compact."[8] Governor Smith and others assailed these moves as wasteful, fanciful, and unpatriotic. Austin, Barrett, and the conservatives meanwhile advocated monetary grants to Mexía's expedition to Tamaulipas, hoping that it might prompt renewed civil war in the interior and relieve the military pressure on Texas. Mexía arrived in Texas on December 3, experienced inhospitable and insulting treatment by "our exalted patriots," as Austin called the anti-Mexican elements, and returned to New Orleans a month later in disillusionment. Though the government did not openly abandon the federalist cause, even the council refused to make a financial commitment to the distrusted adventurer. By plotting Anglo-led campaigns against Matamoros, Texas moved willy-nilly toward a national war.[9]

The momentum of political decisions (or nondecisions) also carried Texas steadily toward independence. The council refused to take the final step, despite growing pressures from the Wharton-Smith faction, General Houston, some officials in east Texas, and large segments of the volunteers. Eventually, public meetings at Texana and Goliad voiced the demand for independence in uncompromising terms. The December 22 army-led declaration from the latter place caused particular consternation in the council because of attacks against the character of its members and resolutions that asserted Texas to be "a *free,* sovreign" state irrespective of any actions by the political body. The council sought to delay the movement for formal separation by pleading an absence of sovereign power and the need for open political debate; eventually, it authorized new elections for delegates to a convention scheduled for March 1. Thus, the council again took refuge in postponement, whereas the Whartons had demanded a January 15 convention date.[10] Political leaders also divided on the question of voting rights for delegate elections. The resolution conceded the suffrage to "all free white males," including "citizen volunteers" and "Mexicans, opposed to a central government," while Governor Smith favored confining the electoral privilege to Anglos.[11]

Under the influence of U.S. public opinion and his fellow commissioners Wharton and Archer, Stephen F. Austin in January also publicly endorsed the independence cause as a financial and diplomatic necessity. But in December, while in Texas between his military and foreign service posts, Austin articulated conservative ideas that demonstrated a connection between several interrelated political and economic conflicts. On the twenty-second he sent letters to members of the council graphically outlining the dangerous consequences of independence, a movement which he traced to fanatical demagogues. Austin wrote from Quintana while under the influence of a partisan friend, Thomas F. McKinney, who had recently warned that "if a stand is not taken against self dubed patriots all our labors in Texas are gone to the devil and me with it." In less intimate correspondence the merchant constructed more disinterested arguments. He explained to Col. Thomas J. Rusk that the stir for independence which appeared to be sweeping the entire coastal region had in fact been conjured up by Archer and John Wharton, whose appeals found support among naive U.S. volunteers but ran against the wishes of the people. McKinney wrote to provide assurance that public opinion was swinging against any precipitous movement. Intriguers like Wharton had become as "harmless as a snake with its teeth pulled out."[12]

Before his departure Austin wrote to relatives, old friends, prospective supporters, and the authorities in San Felipe, expressing some consistent themes and some ideas tailored to suit specific hopes or fears. The empresario warned his allies in San Felipe of a scenario that threatened the interests of "the farmers and substantial men of Texas": independence would force reliance on U.S. volunteers enrolled in a large regular army, result in a huge national debt, deter emigration of new settlers, and saddle the young nation with a government of power-hungry politicians. Those who plotted for independence knew "that there must then be a considerable standing army, which, in the hands of a few, would dispose of the old settlers and their interests as they thought proper." At the very least, failure to adhere to the 1824 constitution would unite Mexico, expand the conflict, and "compel the men of property in Texas to give up half or all" to support the greater war effort.[13] Austin also contacted Rusk, a recent emigrant to east Texas already enjoying a meteoric rise in influence. This appeal sought to rally "the honest part of the people" against "low intrigue[rs]" who pushed for independence to further their power. The empresario suggested that Texas declare statehood and provide troops to Mexican federalists on a pay-by-plunder basis as stopgap measures that would allow maximum flexibility, reduce costs, and keep the war at a distance. Austin also reiterated his other themes.[14] As a whole his advice favored suspicion, disharmony, and open factional conflict. Although he soon recanted some of these views, members of the Council continued to express them in both word and deed.[15]

Naturally, advocates of immediate independence, especially those with solid army connections, countered with barbs of their own, labelling their opponents as dishonest, undemocratic land speculators and "marauders upon human rights." Those who sought to reestablish the Constitution of 1824, according to Virginia volunteer John Sowers Brooks, were "actuated" by "their own aggrandizement. . . . Their influence with the prominent Mexicans enables them to govern the Colony as they desire." An east Texan argued for decisive action before clashes among "the Leading Men of Texas" ended with the formation of "a landed Aristocracy." Independence, if achieved by rapid military movements, would secure the public domain "for the General Good of the bone and Sinew of our Country the Actual Settlers."[16]

The Goliad declaration of December 22 provided the most complete statement of the independence ideology. It emphasized council ineptitude, hatred of Mexicans (including Texas "creoles"), the evils of deceitful, office-seeking speculators, and a kind of class rhetoric not uncommon in the Jacksonian era. Once Texas attained the "solid ground" of independence, the declaration continued, "a new; invigorating; & cherishing policy" would follow: "a policy extending equal; impartial; and indiscriminate protection to all — to the low, as well as the high, the humbly bred, & the well-born;— the poor, & the rich; the ignorant, and the educated; the simple, & the shrewd." In the minds of the Goliad radicals the Revolution had become "the work of political, or of moral renovation."[17]

The two above-described programs and ideologies manifested themselves also in a conflict within the provisional government. Governor Smith stood squarely with the faction that opposed cooperation with Mexicans, favored independence, and encouraged the establishment of a regular army. The council, which became steadily more partisan in make-up during December, held opposite views from Smith on each of these issues. Their quarrel frequently took on petty, personal, back-biting overtones, but significant divisions on real issues also lay behind the dispute.

Well before Governor Smith lashed out against the General Council in January, he had become an isolated political figure with little real power. The original council had a slight majority of the Austin-Barrett ilk, but by December changes in the composition of that body swung it decidedly toward this faction. Those who retired after November almost all came from the Wharton-Smith element or the ranks of those without strong partisan affiliations. In their place arrived James Kerr, John J. Linn, Randall Jones, and Juan A. Padilla, all Austin supporters, conservative empresario-types John McMullen and John Malone (a surrogate for James Power), and others with slight political experience who could no doubt be swayed by the preponderance of anti-Smith sentiment. The governor, given his natural taste for confrontation, had wielded the veto power from the first, but by December 13 the council routinely and unanimously overrode him and rejected all his appointments. His commitment to bringing volunteer forces under control of the civil government had alienated the military, headed in mid-December by Francis W. Johnson, another bitter opponent of Smith. As he surveyed the scene, the governor discovered himself alone and powerless.[18]

On December 17 Smith undertook a bold but doomed counterattack, calling a "Secret session" of the council where he presented charges against archenemy D. C. Barrett and ordered him suspended. The executive accused his opponent of crimes ranging from forgery and corruption in the North Carolina bar to counterfeiting and embezzlement in Texas, to "universal lying and deception." A week later the council asserted its exclusive power over judging official misconduct and making appointments, a constitutional position to which Smith only partly conceded.[19] But his ill-planned foray to regain part of his prerogative utterly failed and left him friendless, at least in San Felipe, and politically impotent. He expressed rage at this humiliating position in rambling letters that leave an impression of derangement. To his supporters Smith complained of ill health and, in an end-of-the-year letter to Houston, admitted to "confused" feelings. "It is truly discouraging to meet with so much opposition and of so violent and damning a character," he began, but later claimed, "I have no fears . . . though but a single individual I feel myself a host when intruded on by such scoundrels. . . . I have no time to give you information at present. . . . The friends of Hell are on the alert. I have to counteract them at every point. . . . I sleep but little"; however, nothing "can throw a damper on my spirits."[20] A week later to another correspondent he flayed again at corrupt intriguers, including the "mob, called an army," who harassed him. Though he always denied suffering "with the Hypo," Smith clearly functioned in an emotional wringer as Governor.[21]

According to his later, rationally phrased explanations, the governor intended his next action, a keenly severe message to the council on January 9, 1836, to shock and perhaps bluff his enemies out of their ruinously corrupt policies. Smith "sent them the Devil, in the shape of an address [because] nothing short of fire and brimstone would drive them," and the veto or other more sedate measures had already failed.[22] His charges contained words of vituperation in every line. The council seemed to "endeavor to ruin the country" by allowing "Judas" and other "scoundrels" to run its affairs. In defense of honesty, national good, and his "duty," Smith suspended the council, cut off further communication with its members, and assumed a position as commander-in-chief of the army and navy.[23]

The General Council responded almost immediately. Two days after receiving the governor's order it voted impeachment on the grounds of his violation of a sworn oath of office, perjury, slander against the council, assumption of "dictatorial powers," and misconduct "aimed at general disorganization." Even before it formally preferred charges, the council sent a committee to inform the governor of his suspension and defended its conduct in a public declaration. This swiftness confuted Smith, whose near apology and plea for "Christian charity," forbearance, and an effort to "harmonize" the two branches came quickly on January 12, too late to reverse the course of events.[24]

The council sought to promote an image of calm, caution, and legality, in contrast to what it described as the "mortifying" and extreme conduct of Smith. "The encroachment of Executive power," warned acting Governor Robinson, had subverted the high principles of most if not all historic revolutions. Smith's "lawless exercise" of power in the name of duty was reminiscent of "the tyrant's plea!!!" from the days of Alexander and Caesar to those of Napoleon and Santa Anna. Robinson promised to work for fiscal responsibility, military efficiency, social order, and protection of private property;[25] however, events of the week after January 13 resulted in a stand-off and further political paralysis. The "ex-governor," as now labelled by his enemies, considered impeachment invalid on the grounds that the Council contained representa-

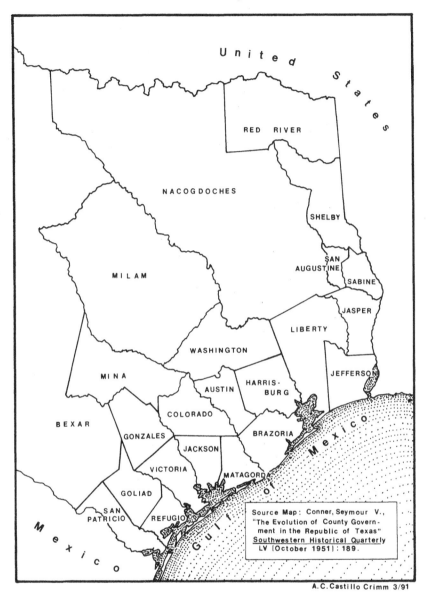

United States

RED RIVER

NACOGDOCHES

SHELBY

SAN AUGUSTINE

SABINE

MILAM

JASPER

LIBERTY

WASHINGTON

JEFFERSON

MINA

HARRIS-BURG

AUSTIN

COLORADO

BEXAR

Gulf of Mexico

GONZALES

BRAZORIA

JACKSON

VICTORIA

MATAGORDA

GOLIAD

SAN PATRICIO

REFUGIO

Mexico

Source Map: Conner, Seymour V., "The Evolution of County Government in the Republic of Texas" *Southwestern Historical Quarterly* LV [October 1951]: 189.

A.C. Castillo Crimm 3/91

Map 2.   Texas Counties, 1836

tives from too few jurisdictions. He refused to surrender official executive documents even when called on by a newly appointed marshall of Texas. The council ordered this official to enlist a citizens' posse to seize the disputed papers by force, but nine of the twelve men sum-- moned refused to act against Smith, who stubbornly held on to his title in anticipation of being acquitted by the March convention. The acting governor lost much of his tenuous credibility when, beginning January 18, the council on which he depended failed to produce a quorum.[26] Over a month before the appearance of Santa Anna, Texas surrendered to the impulses of anarchy.

Reaction to the governor-council split naturally varied according to political leanings. Like McKinney and Fannin, others who had felt Smith's venom favored impeachment and reported similar feelings among the people, even in the ex-governor's hometown of Columbia. From another coastal community former council member R. R. Royall painted a more realistic picture of divided sentiment: some of Smith's friends continued to support him; a majority now favored his removal; others accepted the ex-governor's charge that his enemies had fallen "under the Influence of Bribery corruption & c." The east Texas re- sponse came more slowly, but one politician found few who blamed the council and many who considered Smith's conduct "outrageous," while most "seemed indifferent and careless" about the whole affair.[27] Voices of unqualified support for the deposed governor came only from Béxar, where a joint citizen and soldiers meeting passed resolutions condemning impeachment as "anarchical," and criticizing the council for its Matamoros policy, corruption, and "tory" attitudes on indepen- dence.[28] The soldiers there and elsewhere lamented the political con- troversy which, in the words of Béxar commander J. C. Neill, "create distrust & alarm and at this critical period of our history." They be- lieved that the quarrels left Texas without a legitimate head. From ob- servations made on his journey between San Felipe and Béxar, Wil- liam B. Travis concluded that this despair had spread beyond the ranks of the military: "Our affairs are gloomy indeed. The people are cold and indifferent. They are worn down and exhausted with the war, and in consequence of dissensions between contending and rival chieftains, they have lost all confidence in their own government and officers."[29]

Their power crumbled further under the weight of adverse public reaction, but neither Smith nor Robinson proved willing to abandon his claim to authority or to set aside the ongoing quarrel. Both asserted their integrity and patriotism in letters to each other, public addresses, and communications to the Texas agents in the United States. Each deplored the disorganization, confusion, and other evils that arose out of their conflict, accused the other of swindling by receiving public funds, and warned of the dangers of disunity in the face of an impending invasion by Santa Anna. But their conduct still centered around a determination, as Smith wrote, "to first exterminate our internal enemies, who are far more to be dreaded than our external ones."[30] The executive claimants suffered from shrinking bases of authority. By the end of January only a tiny "advisory committee" of the council supported Robinson; Smith apparently attempted to persuade a body of troops to arrest his opponents and transport them to Béxar for military trial. With the failure of this plan, both sides busied themselves with preparing new charges against the other as they awaited vindication by the March convention.[31]

On February 12 the acting governor issued yet another proclamation, pleading for sufficient public restraint to carry his shaky government through the end of the month. He warned against supporting the suspended governor's effort to establish military rule. Robinson urged the people to reflect on the tendency of revolutions to lead, in turn, to anarchy, despotism, and a spirit of "desolating vengeance": "Destroy this Government, and what is the consequence? . . . Ambition will prompt the daring and unprincipled to seize upon the disorder of the times and a Robespierre may arise among you," leading to lawless plunder, riot, and murder. Robinson included an unrealistically solemn promise to reduce the enemies of the government to obedience, but his analysis accurately explained the origins of opposition. Recent events only added to popular revulsion. From the first, "many persons" of different parties "disputed the right of the General Consultation to establish the present form of Government." Poor organizational structure, "many imprudent measures," and (he could have added) an inability to enforce its decrees, all caused further "dissatisfaction."[32]

Opposition came from a variety of sources, its character depending on time, place, issue, and other circumstances. Since the Permanent Council, Consultation, and provisional government adhered to few clear lines of policy, they received some criticism from almost every angle. The hedging response to the question of independence, for example, satisfied few, whatever their point of view. Over the course of this period, growing popular alienation from the Texas political authorities reflected their overall failure. Sectional dimensions also contributed to the problems of government. Localism remained strong and weakened efforts to enforce decisions made in San Felipe or even to inaugurate the new officials sent out from there. Internal rivalries, political squabbles, and ethnic conflicts within different communities also complicated their responses to the revolution. At or near the front only the irregularly organized, independent-minded military units provided a semblance of authority. Disunity characterized this phase of the Revolution because no force had yet emerged strong enough to hold Texas together. In fact, regionalism functioned in a centrifugal manner — the power of the provisional government weakened in proportion to distance from the lower Brazos valley.

No area illustrates the tensions felt by the people during the fall and winter of 1835–36 better than the former Department of Nacogdoches. In the past the town had been the center of explosive conflicts with Mexican authorities that by 1835 had left many inhabitants wary of involvement. Several elements contended for local power during the Revolution, including leaders who had been appointed or elected under Mexican authority and officers of the committees of vigilance and safety that emerged in the summer. This latter faction contained many recent immigrants, often impatient with Hispanic institutions that they considered alien and backward. The town of Nacogdoches also had a sizable population of Tejanos who, though no longer in the majority or holding many offices, could not be ignored politically or militarily by the various other contenders for power. Reflecting these divisions and the fact that, as one official observed, "a majority of the inhabitants . . . have refused to take part in the revolution," Nacogdoches experienced early and particularly sharp internal conflicts. Public resolutions of mid-August threatened property confiscation against residents who refused cooperation with committee measures, which included statements dissolving the political connection with Mexico. These actions seemed especially threatening to the local Tejano population.[33]

Internal discord persisted, but power shifted with the outbreak of war in October. The most ardent revolutionaries, who had dominated the committees of safety, went westward in military or political service. This left local authority in the hands of more conservative leaders. The committee fell under the leadership of George A. Nixon, a member of the cautious ayuntamiento, and long-time speculator-adventurer Haden Edwards. These men, along with the military chief, Peter Ellis Bean, and the political chief, Henry Rueg, all silently abandoned their commitments to peace and evinced a willingness to cooperate with the new San Felipe government in procuring soldiers, arms, horses, supplies, and the support of local Mexicans. By late October representatives of the council, who had earlier found "much division" in Nacogdoches, reported more united, active support for the Texas cause, although alleged fear of Mexican-Indian collaboration kept down enlistments.[34] The ayuntamiento formally endorsed an armed struggle in defense of popular rights under the 1824 constitution and then, without actually disbanding, began to defer to the committee of safety. Throughout the fall this irregular but popularly elected body in an orderly manner raised funds by subscription (totalling $5,000) which it used along with notes of credit to purchase and distribute provisions of war. Former chief Rueg also gave the appearance of collaborating with the provisional authorities in securing the acquiescence of local Mexicans and otherwise promoting order, peace, and security.[35]

This apparently easy transition from divided loyalties and political conflict to unified cooperation and moderation broke down in late November with the arrival of officials dispatched by the provisional government. Only two men came to enforce the laws of the Consultation and the will of the governor and council. Judge John Forbes had been a member of the more radical faction that led the committee during the previous summer; S. H. Everitt, who represented the Bevil district earlier in November, drew the more difficult assignment of land commissioner with responsibility for taking over government archives and ending further transactions. He and other observers believed that Rueg, Nixon, and other local officials sought to use their influence to secure last-minute land claims for speculative purposes. In contrast, the political establishment in Nacogdoches claimed to represent the "whole community" in protesting the land office shutdown, even though such a measure had been supported by the committee of safety in October. Late in the year opponents of that policy contended that permitting sales of previously surveyed land would secure the possessions of local volunteers, raise needed money, and otherwise further the war effort.[36]

Some expressed early apprehension that "considerable excitement" would erupt over the land issue; this prophecy turned out to be an understatement. Everitt reported that powerful residents "are treating the Acts of the Consultation as if they were criminals at the bar trying to find flaws that they may evade them." His opponents used more direct means as well. A public meeting at Nacogdoches, while denying any intention of promoting discord, nevertheless challenged the justice of the land policy and the authority of the commissioners. Its chairman also wrote to the lieutenant governor, arguing that the people had not yet given their sovereign approval to a new, revolutionary government, and local officials accordingly refused to hand over the archives or surrender power to Everitt and Forbes.[37]

These events left the land commissioner and the judge feeling isolated at Nacogdoches, "kept in the dark" by the San Felipe authorities, and without funds, means of communicating with the people, or power of enforcement. Opposition to the provisional government land policy centered around the local economic as well as the political establishment. Wealthy entrepreneurs Haden Edwards, John A. Veatch, John K. Allen, and Henry Raguet all joined the movement of protest. The last-named of these darkly warned Houston that the land issue had dampened support for the Revolution "in this quarter for it is here frequently expressed that if we are to have a dictator let it be from Mexico and not of our own Countrymen. . . . really I am afraid [of] civil war in the East should several measures be tried to be carried into effect."[38]

While this group wrote threats, the entire machinery of government engaged in overt resistance. Political Chief Rueg, ayuntamiento officials Nixon, Radford Berry, and D. A. Hoffman all refused to turn over public documents and instead continued to execute their authority, including more transactions in land than ever before. They also attempted to secure support from local Tejanos who lived in sullen peace. According to Judge Forbes, these "late Mexican authorities emboldened by the support they receive . . . say that they know no provisional government and will not obey its ordinances and decrees." The Nacogdoches Committee of Safety, dominated by these same men and such other powerful figures as J. K. Allen, also ruled local affairs "in opposition to the Council." That committee in mid-December discussed methods of replacing the provisional government. An observer from the Sabine municipality found the anti-council faction still openly "Belching Fury against the Acts of the General Council" on January 9. Forbes continued his impotent perseverance through that month, despite a physical assault against him that he blamed on the committee; he held on in "this pest house of Corruption" only to help direct the campaign of candidates friendly to the government in the race for delegates to the March convention.[39]

The provisional government provided no actual support for its beleaguered Nacogdoches officials, other than to reaffirm the Consultation land policy. The council explained the necessity of closing the land offices in a resolution passed in early December; after Christmas the governor alerted the Council to the state of crisis that existed in east Texas and recommended "some kind of effort" to enforce decrees. Yet, he stopped short of endorsing the use of military force, which he recognized might be required to implement the land policy. Forbes, who had been recruiting militiamen since November, enlisted volunteer companies sworn by oath of allegiance to serve the government of Texas "against all her enemies whatsoever." He never dared to use this force against his enemies, partly perhaps because the governor-council quarrel left him confused and even more bereft of local support.

The turmoil of the provisional government finally destroyed Forbes's position. On January 14 Acting Governor Robinson, to whom the judge had directed most of his pleas for aid, recommended instead that the council concede to the opposition and reopen land sales. Such an action would only have recognized reality, for local officials in Nacogdoches never surrendered their documents.[40] By the end of January Nacogdoches became quiescent but still in apparent disaffection, as all local governments, whatever their source of authority, virtually ceased activity. The spirit of turmoil and forces of anarchy had spread from San Felipe to the political center of east Texas.

Although one first-hand observer concluded that "San Augustine has Generally followed suit to Nacogdoches," none of the other municipalities in that department experienced as much internal discord. Committees of safety in San Augustine and the Sabine district controlled local politics with little dissent and repeatedly resolved their confidence in the Permanent Council, Consultation, and provisional government. Outsiders expressed some displeasure with the war contributions of this region, but politically it lined up solidly behind the Revolution, advocating property confiscation against those who impeded the war effort, favoring independence, and urging establishment of a regular army under supervision of a well organized government.[41]

The Liberty municipality once appeared more divided and "Tory" dominated than any other in Anglo Texas; however, by the late fall the most ardent loyalists had either fled or moderated their positions. Judge John A. Williams, of the ayuntamiento, who led the opposition to resistance in the summer, fulfilled his proclaimed intention to withdraw from politics. In his place new leaders blended their efforts with William Hardin and other former "Tories" in an effort to achieve moderate consensus. By early October a broad-based committee of safety exercised local political authority in areas ranging from Indian relations to raising war supplies to communications. It worked equally hard to disseminate information and doctrine that might appeal to all "worthy and patriotic citizens," including former advocates of peace. The committee asserted that all hope for an accord with Mexico had ended, but it opened "the door of conciliation" to former opponents of the revolution for one last chance to abandon opposition or neutrality. Soon "those who are not for us . . . will be dealt with according to the utmost rigors of military law," the committee warned. Slightly more than two weeks later this body reported to the Consultation a unanimous concurrence in "the good cause" in Liberty.[42]

This portrait of harmony differed considerably from reports on this region that reached officials in San Felipe. R. R. Royall informed Commander Austin on October 16 that Williams had raised fifty-eight men to secure the area for a Mexican invasion, causing near panic among citizens who feared "to leave their homes lest their families be destroyed" by civil war. Weighty discussions ensued in the council regarding this alleged treason, but they resulted only in a resolution to report the matter to the military. Austin, in turn, expressed skepticism about the extent of this disaffection and advised a policy of watchful waiting. This potentially explosive matter died out without further action; despite all the militant talk about repression of dissent, high Tory Williams continued to reside in Liberty as late as March, 1836.[43] Between October and March residents of this municipality carried on their lives in relative isolation. They engaged in the slave trade and other forms of commerce without paying duties, expressing ignorance of even major political developments of the provisional government.[44]

No such isolation protected southwestern Texas, which suffered under scattered governmental authority, divided loyalties, and military occupation. Even Matagorda municipality underwent considerable disorder, despite being outside the war zone during the winter of 1835–36. At the beginning of hostilities many zealous volunteers came from this area, but others opposed local defense efforts or refused to leave their prospering businesses for military service. Council-appointed Judge Charles Willson failed to unify the populace. Though a veteran of both the Consultation and local committee of safety, the judge found himself in conflict with Matagorda vigilantes who appropriated property from a shipwrecked *Hannah Elizabeth*. Like other officials of the provisional government Willson struggled for power against the local committee, a situation made worse by inadequate communication from the council. As a result, as he explained on Christmas eve, no authority existed to suppress the piracy and other forms of "villainy" endemic to the Colorado River coastal region.[45]

Farther west — in the area up from the Gulf of Mexico, between the Guadalupe and Nueces river systems and encompassing the towns of

Victoria, San Patricio, and the old mission communities of Goliad and Refugio—the war came in early fall, destroyed the already weak civil government, and brought to power a variety of contentious military forces. Since the summer of 1835 residents of this region felt the brunt of being caught in the middle. There the Mexican army build-up coincided with a growing movement for peace in Anglo areas, leaving property owners fearful of army expropriation and resentful of abandonment by other Texans. Replacement of local officials by the orders of Béxar Political Chief Navarro in September heightened the sense of instability.

The governments that met in San Felipe in the fall and winter had little authority over the people living between Victoria and San Patricio. Although the General Council reaffirmed the power of the old ayuntamiento officials as judges, only the military forces exercised actual control after their victory at Goliad on October 9. Jealousies and disputes among the various military units garrisoned there, coupled with the soldiers' general refusal to show allegiance to outside political authorities, perpetuated the pattern of disorder.[46] Philip Dimitt, the longest-tenured of the commanders of the forces operating out of the Goliad fort, struggled to restrain long-standing tensions among the ethnically diverse people of the area. Furthermore, this region was the center of Tory activity, and the army had difficulty distinguishing between disloyal behavior and actions taken by the people in self-defense. The troops at the fort also harbored strong anti-Mexican attitudes that contributed to local disaffection toward the Texas cause.

Dimitt proceeded in a straightforward manner that seemed ruthless to his detractors but completely necessary to his supporters. Although his extensive problems clearly justified some blunt measures, Dimitt's tactlessness added to the unpopularity of his regime. For example, he distrusted the loyalty of the "creole troops," even those under Victorian politicians Juan A. Padilla and Plácido Benavides who had participated in the successful engagement on October 9. Dimitt dispatched these forces to Austin and refused to accept additional Mexican soldiers, thus surrendering the possibility of gaining the confidence of local residents. Those who took up the march to Goliad had pledged "to give the population of that town protection against military domination," but this intention soon dissolved into bitter irony. With not only his but other armies pleading for additional provisions, Dimitt instituted harsh appropriations of private property, eliciting complaints about broken promises of protection.[47]

Austin had given early advice to the Goliad commander to "spare no pains to inform area residents of the Texas commitment to federalist principles and get them to pronounce for the same Cause." Instead, Dimitt ignored and thus alienated the existing civil authorities; he communicated to the people through orders rather than appeals for cooperation. When the Goliad garrison finally issued a public proclamation in late December, it derided Mexican ignorance and pronounced in favor of independence. The commander gave consideration to the importance of protecting the people, but he did so by abrogating civil rights and proceeding without regard to their political sensitivities. These harsh procedures seemed necessary from a military perspective, because the soldiers of the fort confronted armed opposition throughout their days of occupation. A few companies of centralist soldiers remained in the area and won the support of some of the Irish settlers of San Patricio, which became a center of Tory resistance.[48]

Another problem confronted Dimitt in the person of the ex-governor of Coahuila and Texas, Agustín Viesca, who escaped from prison and arrived in Goliad on November 11. Trouble immediately erupted over protocol. The ex-governor and his supporters complained of rude treatment by Dimitt, who claimed to have been courteous and to have offended the arrogant Viesca only by refusing to recognize his continued right to the gubernatorial office. This incident led to a mutiny inside the fort, aided by Dmitt's discontented opponents in the community. Both the insubordinate soldiers and civilians disliked the commander's thorough policies and his commitment to independence. Dimitt responded with what he described as "unhesitating firmness," arresting the rebellious soldiers and placing the entire "environs" under martial law. His decree spelled out his position in uncompromising terms: "All persons manifesting an opposition dangerous to the cause espoused by the People of Texas—All who opposes, or threaten to oppose, the observance of order, of discipline, and subordination; or who endeavor to excite discontent within the Fortress, or within the Town, will be regarded as public enemies, arrested as such, and dealt with accordingly." The proclamation also created a passport system and explicitly placed civil authority under military edict.[49]

The alcalde's and Dimitt's military opponents both turned for support to his supposed superior, army commander Stephen F. Austin. Thomas G. Western asserted, "we have experienced from the present Commandant nothing but tyranny and oppression[.] neither the persons or their property are safe[.] they are neither Secure from the external nor internal foe." He asked "whether we are subject to Civil, or to military power and what we are fighting for, whether to establish Despotism or the liberties and rights of man and of Texas under the Constitution of 1824." Austin ordered a replacement for Dimitt, but the soldiers of the fortress refused to accept the change and sent the Béxar commander a lecture on their democratic prerogatives.[50]

This episode suggested that what little authority existed in the Goliad region rested with the turbulent forces that occupied the old fortress. Political opposition was widespread but quiescent after the Viesca episode. At the end of the year a few citizens met at Texana, petitioning the provisional government to protect the loyal native Mexicans of the region. The General Council instead authorized expeditions against Matamoros that used Goliad as a staging ground. The new troops plundered more property, arrested civilians, and undermined the power of commander Dimitt, the sole, albeit unpopular, voice of authority. Thus, the southwestern region also dissolved into anarchy in January, 1836, but there many people had grimly determined to support the centralist forces should they return.[51]

Up river from Goliad the largest town and traditional political headquarters, Béxar, remained in the hands of Ugartechea and Cos from the beginning of hostilities until early December. Reports from spies, civilians, and military observers almost unanimously agreed that the town's inhabitants sympathized with the "American" cause because of their federalist principles. The townspeople also became discontented with their treatment by the occupying centralist forces. The anticipated harmony of relations between Texas and local authorities did not develop after Cos's December 10 capitulation, once again largely due to political failure by the provisional government. The Texas army of occupation enjoyed virtual autonomy, and many of its members held Béxareños partially to blame for the bitter street fighting that characterized the last days of hostilities. The ranks of the resentful included new commander Francis W. Johnson, who made no attempt to reestablish local government or otherwise to court popular favor. J. C. Neill, assuming command from Johnson at the end of the year, immediately divested himself of civil authority and restored a traditional form of civilian rule. This new spirit of cooperation did not survive Neill's departure in early February, and serious issues still divided the army and the people. The size of the occupational force shrank steadily, but its proindependence militance increased; conflicts with local government returned, leaving understandable doubts among the Tejanos regarding the status of their defense, the purpose of the war, and the possibility that hostilities would once again return to ravage their economy.[52]

With virtually all areas other than San Felipe drifting off in apathy, bitter silence, political conflict, or armed revolt, the center could not hold. Even before the provisional government dissolved itself into chaos, serious opposition arose to it in Austin's colonies. Protests here concerned many of the same questions — land policy, taxation, inadequate support for the volunteers, and allegedly self-interested appointments. As one Austin correspondent concluded on this latter issue, government procedure "proves to my mind the old adage that give Men power and they will help themselves." Most of the malcontents proposed peaceful methods of change, such as advancing the March convention so as to replace the governor and General Council at an earlier date.[53] But others plotted an irregular overthrow of the provisional government. Smith on November 25 had warned the council of a "deep laid and preconcerted plan . . . to overthrow our newly formed Govt" by elements that favored a return to the old system "of intrigue, bribery, and speculation." He recommended a treason bill making it criminal to assail "the existing authorities, either by waging war making threats, or in any wise menacing" the government. "Some rigid course should be pursued," he concluded, "for I warn you that troubles are ahead."[54]

Given the governor's addiction to exaggerated and inflammatory rhetoric, the council not surprisingly ignored his message. However, events during the week before Christmas came close to fulfilling his prophecy. Only sketchy details remain of this revolt, since the government naturally wished to give it as little publicity as possible. What one observer described as a "Mexican faction" of disaffected politicians called a "disorganizing meeting" in San Felipe on December 19. Its leaders — Mosely Baker, Wylie Martin, and William Pettus — had all lost influence with the coming of the Revolution. Austin regarded this incident as "a paragraph in the long chapter of evils" resulting from the last, controversial Monclova legislature. Opponents of the Texas government apparently argued that it had lost legitimacy by moving too far toward independence and away from the 1824 constitution. The meeting failed to arouse much sentiment for its organizers, as speeches by Houston and others successfully countered the address of Baker, who then suffered the ignominy of being hissed down and "like a pitiful Hound puppy crouched and slunk off," as Smith described it. The disorganizers, "abusing" members of the council and swearing that it "should never meet in session again," raised a mob by throwing out the grog shops; however, their tactic failed. The crisis soon cooled down, but some officials had been frightened enough that they favored moving the seat of government to a more congenial place like Washington, where the people "say that you shall be guarded against mobs if you come."[55]

Houston also attributed the incident to land speculators who hoped to gain from continued affiliation with Mexico, but he admitted that "many honest and clever men do not accord altogether" with the direction recently taken by Texas politics. During the next week members of the council received further warnings, purportedly based on reliable firsthand information, that behind the current "death like stillness" lurked another threat of rebellion. One of these claimed that the mob leaders had subsequently been active, travelling through the country "organizing their bands to make a desperate effort for your overthrow" on New Year's Day. This plot supposedly included plans to assassinate Houston and D. C. Barrett. On January 2 the general wrote the other intended victim from Washington: "There was no *fuss* here, on yesterday, and I trust you had none in San Felipe, for if so our Country, will be ruined. . . . Dissention will destroy Texas."[56] He correctly saw the result, if not the form, of the internal conflict that paralyzed the government. When the governor and council a few days later turned their animus against each other, the latter body again expressed fears of a coup, this time one directed by Houston.[57]

The general of course lacked the power to carry out this blow, and the government by February, 1836, had virtually disintegrated of its own weight. The fate of the mob leaders and other opponents of the course of the Texas Revolution further illustrates governmental impotence. Martin continued to oppose independence but raised a military company in time to bedevil Houston again on the eve of the San Jacinto battle. Pettus and Baker, like many who had led the "peace" movement of the previous summer, still enjoyed full freedom of movement. One of this group, T. J. Chambers, even received an appointment with the exalted title Major General of Reserves to raise volunteers in the United States.[58] Certainly, the Texas government failed to command the kind of respect that comes from fear.

By February the crippled provisional government collapsed under the weight of its own failures and the waning of public support. Members of the Council continued to stay away despite appeals and orders from the acting governor. Its fragment, an "advisory committee" which shrank on occasion from four to two members, confined itself to preparing impeachment documents against the still recalcitrant Smith. Secretary E. M. Pease on February 8 wrote candidly to an absent councilman, "we have not had a government since you left [in late January] and [have] no prospects of one" before the March convention.[59] Many worried about the resulting state of military unpreparedness: armies had melted away, commanders flayed at each other and dissipated their energies on the Matamoros madness, and civilians refused to volunteer despite the imminence of a formidable invasion. Even those who believed that the public would rally worried that it might be too late. Officials republished the militia law and issued pleas, scoldings, and warnings, but they could not enforce the draft, and hardly anyone enlisted. Those who did found no organization functioning to supply their basic needs for arms, food, and clothing. The council turned again to Houston, one of its leading critics, but the prospects for recruiting a regular army by that date had become an even more distant dream.[60]

An editorialist for the San Felipe *Telegraph* identified the source of Texas's problems: "We understand that some are not willing, under the present government, to do any duty. . . . That our government is bad, all acknowledge, and no one will deny."[61] In September Zavala had called for a government with "force, wisdom, and public support," and Austin optimistically wrote of the "one spirit" that promised just such an accomplishment. But by mid-December Henry Smith encountered "restless, disorganizing spirits" that soon led to a complete collapse amidst widespread public opposition and political conflict. In 1836 the fate of the Revolution rested with a disorderly army and a new convention, charged still with the formidable tasks of rescuing Texas from invasion, controlling internal upheaval, and establishing a semblance of unity.

5. The Convention
MARCH, 1836

From early January, 1836, forces of division and disorder ruled Texas. The provisional government formed in November, 1835, dissolved into chaos within two months. Bitter disputes on fundamental issues of independence and management of a democratic army resulted in a quarrel between governor and General Council that left both sides claiming power but neither able to exercise it. Discord also reigned in the military sphere as the Texas armies split into ever-smaller contending units or otherwise eroded, despite growing anticipation of an invasion from Mexico directed by President Santa Anna. Different partisan opinions assigned blame in a variety of ways; some, like Henry Austin, cursed all the "unprincipled demagogues in civil & military offices."[1]

Opinions varied as to the purpose of the upcoming convention. Some favored establishing a firm government; others were sensitive to preserving constitutional liberties and property. All looked for answers from the meeting scheduled for March 1 at the town of Washington. Well over a month before that, government virtually halted. Members of the council stayed at home, awaiting the meeting of those chosen by the sovereign voices of the people. Amidst all the doubts and dissension a common feeling, wary rather than optimistic, seemed to prevail. Former Consultation delegate R. R. Royall described the mood of crisis: "I sincerely hope," he wrote to Sam Houston, that "the Convention will remedy the existing evils and calm the Public since if not Texas must be lost."[2]

Before any such body could meet to bring about a greater sense of order and direction, delegates had to be elected. This democratic process frequently demonstrated the potential for stimulating continued disorder, a problem not envisioned by the council on December 10 when it had adopted "A Resolution for calling a Convention." This document waxed romantic with natural rights doctrines of freedom, equality, and the sovereign power of the people to check abuses of power-hungry rulers who might violate the social compact.[3] In contrast, accounts of the actual balloting on February 1 often emphasized themes of conflict and fears of popular excess.

The elections frequently reflected local political traditions and power arrangements and thus followed no uniform pattern. In Mina, which returned empresario Sterling C. Robertson and his recently arrived nephew, George C. Childress, the pollings occurred without controversy or even an alternate slate of candidates. Contrastingly, one of the hopefuls in the Jasper district reported two weeks before the voting date that "Politics Run high here. We have almost as many Candidates in the field as we have Inhabitants in the Jurisdiction." Where issues rather than personalities predominated, the question of independence received the most attention, but open debate did not necessarily occur. In the Jackson municipality, for example, a citizens' meeting in January ascertained and solidified sentiment in favor of this measure, precluding further public debate during the selection of delegates. Such an overweening consensus did not exist in other areas—in both the Brazoria and Austin districts partisan politics had thrived in the immediate past and continued to characterize the February 1 delegate elections. There, two distinct "tickets" emerged, though the voters did not all cast straight "party" ballots. At San Felipe in particular, with the newspaper giving them a forum, the candidates publicized their positions, either in favor of a Declaration of Independence or of "adhering to the Constitution of 1824." Yet, each slate qualified its stance, and the referendum in the Austin municipality yielded inconsistent results. Two of those who opposed immediate independence, Thomas Barnett and Randall Jones, won easily, but proindependence candidate Charles B. Stewart edged out Patrick C. Jack for the third seat. Perhaps many voters agreed with the anonymous author of a letter to the editor, who argued that it was "better to elect men of judgment and capacity, honourable and trustworthy" and rely on their integrity.[4]

The apparent deference to established leaders in some municipalities did not carry over into others. In some places a strong commitment to direct democracy prevailed, and the electorate selected candidates with clear public stands on the independence issue. Furthermore, emotional clashes frequently occurred, especially concerning voting rights. The suffrage issue centered on the status of two groups, Tejanos and recent arrivals from the United States in the army. The procedures for voting, spelled out by a council resolution which gained final approval on December 13, had attempted to head off such controversies. It enfranchised Tejanos "opposed to a Central Government" and empowered volunteers to participate through proxy procedures for candidates in their home districts.

Even then these rules had been controversial; Governor Smith had vetoed the measure out of opposition to Tejano enfranchisement, and some politicians had questioned whether the suffrage properly extended to U.S. volunteers. Changes occurred over the next two months that made these eligibility issues even more important. The army's composition changed fundamentally as Texas settlers left the service for home and the ranks swelled with what the *Telegraph and Texas Register* described as young, ardent U.S. recruits. According to the newspaper, these men "cannot be acquainted either with the state of the country or the character and pretensions of the candidates." Though the political situation still required "prudence," in the journal's opinion, the volunteers overwhelmingly favored immediate independence. Thus the *Telegraph* argued that giving them "the privilege of voting" was "impolitic and inexpedient" until they had fulfilled a "short residence" requirement.[5] The paper could have added that the geographic concentration of the troops gave them a decisive voice in the local balance of power.

The exact nature of the soldiers' role in the elections varied with the dynamics of specific local situations, but three consistent patterns emerged. First, members of the army participated, irrespective of the length of their residence in Texas. Second, they invariably supported candidates who made an unequivocal stand for independence, including often men from their own ranks. Third, controversies usually swirled around the votes of the soldiers. For instance, an election dispute at Matagorda, centering on dual voting by troops who had been discharged and were on their way back to the United States, was finally resolved on the floor of the Convention. At Goliad the volunteers quickly became familiar with Texas political developments, set up an election, and selected two of their own members as delegates.

This process either excluded or overwhelmed the Hispanic residents of this old mission area, but the local population offered more successful resistance in the empresario-dominated regions. At San Patricio election judges turned away many volunteers who sought to vote, a procedure that resulted in the selection of local land baron John McMullen until the Convention reversed the results. A similar problem confronted those stationed at Refugio, where officials declared the soldiers to be "an improper interference & calculated to deprive them of their representation," as the memorial of the volunteers explained. There the troops refused to be denied since they claimed "Texas as our adopted country" and considered "the elective franchise the dearest privilege of freemen and particularly in this important crisis." The volunteers observed the need for both independence and "a Government which we anxiously hope will restore order out of confusion & chaos." They avoided a clash with local politicians by holding a separate election which chose two enlisted men who later gained seats in the gathering at Washington.[6]

A changing social ideology accompanied the rising influence of U.S. volunteers, as during December and January the Texas Revolution became more openly anti-Mexican. Earlier, the expression of ethnic prejudice had been restrained by political prudence—many had expected anticentralist uprisings in the interior which might keep the war out of Texas. When this hope failed, Anglos began to express both open hostility toward Tejanos and a belief that fundamental cultural-political differences dictated the need for independence. In the words of resolutions adopted by a meeting in Texana, "the great mass of people" in Mexico had been so "deluded" by an "ignorant and Biggoted Priesthood" that they were "incapable of appreciating or even comprehending the Blessings of free institutions." The experience of war also stimulated tensions between Anglo and Mexican Texans. According to a political tract issued by Convention candidate Thomas H. Borden, of San Felipe, a majority of Béxar citizens had engaged in disloyal conduct by refusing to volunteer during the recent siege; Mexicans in general Borden regarded as "ignorant, bigoted, and superstitious."[7]

Clearly, strong feelings of bias existed throughout Texas, but cultural controversies in the February 1 elections did not occur uniformly because Hispanics predominated in only a few areas. Where numbers and tradition gave them influence (especially in Béxar and Nacogdoches) schisms and clashes characterized the political process.

Preliminary election preparations in Béxar had all the makings of a serious confrontation. The soldiers stationed there, according to several reports, unanimously advocated independence. Some zealots in the ranks favored extreme measures to offset the activities of what one volunteer described as the "speculative, disorganizing, tory party" that sought to rule the upcoming Convention. These alarmists spoke of the "crisis" posed by the "internal" enemies of Texas who in Béxar planned to deny the vote to those stationed there by requiring prior citizenship in the municipality. The troops asserted that the Consultation had made citizens of those engaged in military service but that no means existed for them to vote except in the Béxar district. Furthermore, they wanted actual army representatives in the Convention to correct past policies of negligence toward the military. The soldiers certainly believed, in the carefully chosen words of their memorial, that even though the local Mexicans "have the best intentions, [they] are yet unable, from differences of language & habits, to represent the Anglo American and Army interest."[8]

By late January garrison commander J. C. Neill and other officers had worked out a compromise with the Béxareños for which he sought the Governor's support. The Tejanos, upon taking an oath of allegiance to the provisional government, would hold one election for the four Béxar delegates, while the soldiers sought to have two of their own representatives also accepted at the Convention. Without gaining prior approval for this procedure, the officers carried it through anyway, as the only means available to prevent what they called a "breach in the good understanding which has so happily existed between the Citizens and our garrison."[9] Two "staunch Independence men [who] damn any others than such," as an admirer described Samuel B. Maverick and Jesse B. Badgett, received virtually unanimous support from their fellow soldiers. Similarly, citizen ballots went overwhelmingly to four local residents, though four soldiers gained a handful of votes in the regular election. By the means of this dual election Béxar escaped the violent potential of the crisis; however, this solution dissatisfied some volunteers. Disappointed at not having captured four places for soldier representatives, Amos Pollard retrospectively concluded that "Mexican policy perfectly hood-winked head-quarters" with the two delegation plan, and he warned "that if they vote against *independence* they will have to be very careful on returning here."[10]

Similar tensions in Nacogdoches did not stop short with a mere threat of force. Ethnic conflict, competing economic interests, emotional manipulation, leadership clashes, and other expressions of dissension had wrenched this highly politicized community throughout the course of the Revolution. To no one's surprise an atmosphere of intense excitement prevailed in late January as the candidates, numbering as many as twenty by one estimate, heatedly prepared for the February 1 contest. To some extent past controversies on government land policies continued as the basis for local factions, particularly since land commissioner John Forbes attempted to build support for Acting Governor Robinson and his allies in the delegates contest. The commissioner stayed on at Nacogdoches even in the face of threatened assaults because of his desire to influence the election outcome, but some new personalities also made their presence felt. Thomas J. Rusk and Robert Potter gained substantial popularity and support from contending groups and ideologies, though the latter also quickly acquired a reputation for double-dealing. Visitor William F. Gray soon concluded that Potter "can only float in troubled water"; if so, this North Carolinian had found a comfortable environment in east Texas.[11]

As in the Austin district, candidates at Nacogdoches openly declared their positions on the question of "absolute and complete independence." Here, too, the Béxar pattern of Tejano-army conflict also appeared, with these two elements enlisted by the closely divided factions in order to swing the contest. On February 1 an excited but peaceful atmosphere at first prevailed. The harangues of candidates stirred the usual shouts of support or objection until an election judge turned back Sidney Sherman's company of about forty Kentucky volunteers who attempted to exercise the usual prerogative of instant Texas citizenship. In response the officer advanced his soldiers, with weapons primed, toward the Stone House election quarters and threatened, as one observer explained, to "fight it out" with the judges. Colonel Sherman "swore with an oath that he had come to Texas to fight for it and had as soon commence in the town of Nacogdoches as elsewhere."[12]

The Tejanos reportedly made military preparations of their own before the harassed election official retreated to the democratic response of holding a vote on whether the troops should vote. The constitutionalists carried this issue, denying the suffrage to the Kentuckians by a margin of about thirty. This outcome, made more galling by derisive celebrations and by charges that women dressed as men had cast ballots, enraged the volunteers. Some of them gave hints of firing into the ranks of the citizens, but several speakers lectured the soldiers on republicanism, law, and free elections. Gray took pride on the effectiveness of his speech in stilling anger, but other voices carried the day. Robert Potter, who had previously been identified with the more conservative constitutionalist party, now exhorted the Kentuckians to persevere in their struggle for suffrage rights. Through the apparent intervention of Rusk the judges subsequently relented, and the U.S. recruits, after some hesitation, did cast ballots. That the armed volunteers "frequently marched to and fro, with drum and fife," as Gray wrote, cannot but have influenced the decision to enfranchise them.[13]

The outcome of the election, like the events of the day, was mixed and confusing. Gray initially identified all the winners as constitutionalists, but returns from other parts of the district eventually moved Potter from fifth to fourth place and thus to a seat in the Convention. Rusk, who had been a fiery activist in revolutionary vigilance committees, received the most votes. The other places went to John S. Roberts and Charles S. Taylor, both of whom had been involved in clashes with the Mexican government for more than five years but who took seriously their pledged support of the 1824 constitution, at least to the point of expressing reluctance to sign the Declaration of Independence a month later.[14]

The Kentucky volunteers departed the day after the election, but the bitter emotions of the political contest did not go with them. The speechmaking and toasting that accompanied this departure sparked a renewal of the Allen-Potter feud, with Rusk again stepping in as peacemaker. Gray observed with atypical understatement, "It is manifest that much ill blood exists in this little community." The threatening mood brought on by the election controversies did not dissipate quickly. A week later in another part of the municipality rumors again surfaced among the constitutionalists that Judge Forbes, who had supported losing candidates, intended to set aside the outcome on the basis of irregularities. This threat once again aroused the victorious faction and made them "indignant." The confusion and upheaval of the Nacogdoches district may have puzzled an outside observer like Gray, but of one conclusion he expressed no doubt: "We are in the midst of a revolution."[15]

Events in this east Texas municipality demonstrated that the quarrels of the past had not died but in fact received impetus from the contests for delegate seats. Yet, political divisions even in Nacogdoches were not cleanly drawn and elsewhere were not made at all. Instead, a growing consensus emerged in the February elections, one that sought to repudiate preexisting conflicts in the name of unified support for the common cause. Many leaders attempted to encourage factional reconciliation. From New Orleans Stephen F. Austin wrote to announce that a spirit of patriotism had overcome his past disagreements with the

Whartons. He now renounced the partisanship that he had espoused in December, asserting: "without union and harmony, our country is lost. . . . If substantial and deliberate men are elected to the convention, and violent demagogues are permitted to stay at home, we will go right." "My greatest anxiety," he explained, "arises from the fear that your internal discords may prove to be more dangerous, to your final success than the power of your Enemies."[16]

As the Convention approached, the impetus for unity also gathered momentum because of a vague awareness of military crisis. The size of the Texas army grew with the arrival of more recruits from the United States, but expansion in numbers only exacerbated organizational problems. Although the governor and council in December and January had both attempted to unify the Texas forces, political divisions in the military made the situation worse. Too few were stationed in Béxar to defend the place, and their potential declined further as the command struggle between James Bowie and William B. Travis divided the force. Near Goliad elections by the soldiers had placed James W. Fannin in command, but two units refused to accept his authority and headed south as if to attack Matamoros. Between February 6 and 13 both Travis and Fannin sent word eastward of rumored Mexican advances into Texas. In fact, by the end of the second week of the month General José de Urrea was on the way to Goliad and Santa Anna himself commanded a forced march toward Béxar. The obvious response by Texas military leaders—concentration of their forces—failed despite the efforts of James Bonham, an emissary from Travis to Fannin. It took no great astuteness to recognize that irresolution and disunity left Texans ill prepared to face military dangers.

The executive claimants continued their divisive behavior but could not undercut the growing consensus favoring unity. Deposed Governor Henry Smith acknowledged that the "difficulty and confusion" with which he had contended grew out of "party strife." For solution he sought to continue the struggle until the righteous cause triumphed: "This country can never prosper until a few of that baneful faction are immolated on the altar of their own perfidy. The convention will, I hope, afford the grand corrective." He found little support for this position; friends replied that excessive party feeling had already damaged the country. Smith's replacement, Acting Governor Robinson, believed in early March that "the spirit of party rages to an unprecedent height" but conceded that these divisions had unfortunate consequences.[17]

In fact, despite the hopes or observations of the two governors, partisan clashes reached a nadir by convention-time, as evidenced by the two men's treatment at the hands of that body. Neither had been elected as a delegate, and both awaited recognition in vain. Instead, the delegates coolly refused to reopen the impeachment issue, informed the claimants that their powers ended with the opening of the new, sovereign body, and demanded that state documents be turned over. As one observer later recalled, "very different feelings" from the previous "discord" dominated the March Convention. He characterized this new sentiment as "a disposition to consign to oblivion all past criminations and unitedly to go forward in building up the common interest."[18]

Rejection of the embarrassing past came easily to the delegates because they literally were new and different men. Only thirteen of the fifty-nine who attended the Convention had been part of the Consultation of the previous November; just seven had participated in the deliberations of the General Council since then, and they were among the least active in partisan politics. Those notably absent from the Convention included Austin (in the United States on a diplomatic mission) and his most prominent factional leaders, D. C. Barrett, R. M. Williamson, Wylie Martin, and R. R. Royall, as well as counterpart W. H. Wharton (also engaged in diplomacy), his brother John, or others like Henry Millard who had led their group. Only seven of the delegates were veterans of the 1832 or 1833 conventions. Three of their number and eight others had held various offices during the period of Mexican rule, their positions ranging in importance from member of the local ayuntamiento, to alcalde, on up to a congressman (José Antonio Navarro), and former provincial governor (Lorenzo de Zavala). Previous involvement in revolutionary organizations also did not distinguish the delegates, as fewer than twenty percent were on record as participating in the committees of safety of 1835.[19]

A large part of the contrasting group profile between these delegates and those who served at the Consultation resulted from the fact that they represented different Texas communities. This development occurred because of several factors. First, the General Council's December resolution setting forth the organization of the Convention assigned smaller numbers of representatives to certain voting districts than had attended the Consultation: the municipalities of San Augustine, Harrisburg, and Gonzales all received four fewer and Milam (Viesca) three fewer places than in November. Nonattendance further reduced the representation of San Augustine and San Felipe de Austin by one delegate each. Second, the Convention chose to seat more men from certain districts than the council had prescribed, giving Red River (Pecan Point) and Refugio a total of five extra representatives. In part this procedure validated the special supplemental elections of the volunteers. Third, several communities that had gone unrepresented at the Consultation did send delegates to the Convention. As a result of all these different arrangements, an extreme shift of geographic origins distinguished the March from the November meeting: about a third (nineteen) of the Convention delegates came from extreme east or west Texas districts which had not been present at the Consultation. As a whole, western and eastern Texas gained eleven and five more delegates respectively, while the central region had fourteen fewer.[20]

In other characteristics, too, this March body was composed of new and distinctive leaders. Their average age (37.4) made them younger by two years than those who had previously led the Texas cause. More (13) were in their twenties than forties (10) or fifties (8). Furthermore, most of the delegates had only brief experience with Texas affairs, although José Antonio Navarro and José Francisco Ruiz provided the Convention with the distinction of two who were native born. On the average, the representatives had resided in Texas for about four years, more than two years less than their Consultation counterparts. Almost a fourth had emigrated during the last year; 42 percent had been in Texas for two years or less. These recent arrivals included some who became leading figures in the Convention and during the months that followed under the ad interim government. They included George C. Childress, David P. Thomas, Bailey Hardeman, and Samuel P. Carson, all of whom had six months or less of Texas residence when the delegates convened on March 1. Potter, Zavala, and Rusk had preceded these other newcomers by a year or less.[21]

Military rather than political experience had attracted the voters to many of these delegates. Over 40 percent of them (twenty-four) had answered the call to arms in the struggle against the forces of centralism. Most had served in the Béxar siege and assault, several with distinction. Sam Maverick escaped from the clutches of General Cos, who had arrested him in October, in time to help direct the Texas troops as they attacked the town. Andrew Briscoe, John S. Roberts, James G. Swisher, Rusk, and Thomas all rose to officer status, either due to their roles in raising companies or because they had been entrusted with rank by the votes of the volunteers. Matthew "Old Paint" Caldwell earned the title "Paul Revere of the Texas Revolution" for spreading the alarm in time to raise Texas resistance at Gonzales on October 2. Ten of the delegates came to Washington as a direct result of votes from fellow soldiers anxious to have spokesmen for their perspective. Even some of those whose advanced ages excused them from the service had familial ties to the military. Both Collin McKinney (aged sixty-four) and Elijah Stepp (aged fifty-two) had sons in the army; one of the McKinneys had been killed at Béxar in December.[22]

Military events had clearly worked a powerful revolution in the attitudes of the voters, as evidenced by the changing composition of certain key delegations. The electorate in the Nacogdoches, Austin, Matagorda, and Mina districts removed men who had been conservative defenders of the 1824 constitution, replacing them with Rusk, Roberts, Hardeman, Robert M. Coleman, Charles B. Stewart, J. W. Bunton, and T. J. Gazley, all veterans. Altogether, those who through their own or a relative's armed service and/or who had been sent by the votes of soldiers totalled twenty-eight of the delegates, only two short of a majority at the Convention. No wonder, as Gray observed, "the military interest has a great ascendancy in this body. It is necessary to conciliate the military and scarcely anything that they can ask for will be refused."[23]

Other factors complemented the overweening army influence. Five delegates, including President Richard Ellis, came from the "Pecan Point" or Red River district, which many considered U.S. territory (Arkansas). These representatives had no ties with Mexico at all but, rather, harbored a powerful incentive to bring about independence and annexation in order to protect their property claims. All these characteristics — comparative youth and recent emigration, freedom from commitment to past policies, and experience in the military struggle — made the delegates aptly qualified to carry the Revolution to its more radical conclusion.

These characteristics meant that the outcome of the first issue to confront the Convention, whether to adopt a declaration of independence, was virtually a foregone conclusion. Although a few delegates came into the meeting having pledged to support Mexico's Constitution of 1824, they recognized the overwhelming strength of the pro-independence forces and seldom made even a token show of resistance.[24] In fact, sentiment for independence had been growing since the end of the Consultation; the movement had been turned back in December with difficulty and only on the rationale that the provisional government lacked the power to take such action. The council had considered but rejected a resolution to make the February 1 elections a direct referendum on independence; nevertheless, its call for a convention rested on the theory of the right of revolution.[25]

Support for independence had become so widespread that many observers simply equated that result with the opening of the Convention. By January even conservatives like Austin and Robinson had begun to rally support for it. The *Telegraph and Texas Register* also swung into line. For some time it and other organs of propaganda had emphasized analogies between the Texas situation and the American Revolution. This logic naturally led toward a Texas declaration: Mexico, like Britain, had imposed unjust policies, attempted to implement military rule, and abrogated the constitution, leaving conservative-minded colonists with no choice but first to fight to preserve the status quo and then to form a separate nation.

The racial element made the final step even easier for the Texans than for the English colonists. Whereas the early colonists' forefathers had broken away from a people of "kindred blood, language, and institutions," wrote *Jefferson* to the newspaper, "we separate from a people one half of whom are the most depraved of the different races of Indians, different in color, pursuits and character."[26]

Santa Anna's long-rumored advance transformed the issue irrevocably into an Anglo defense of property and freedom against Mexican religious and military despotism. Circumstances that had earlier dictated repression of anti-Mexican views had been altered by military and political developments. By 1836 the conflict had become a race war. Liberalism's collapse in the interior and the Tejanos' refusal to rally en masse to the Texas standard, wrote Houston, broke all remaining ties with the Mexican nation and allowed him to express a long unstated conviction: "the vigor of the descendants of the north [will never] mix with the phlegm of the indolent Mexicans, no matter how long we may live among them. Two different tribes on the same hunting ground will never get along together." David G. Burnet explained to Henry Clay that independence arose out of "the utter dissimilarity of character between the two people," the Mexicans being "a mongrel race of degenerate Spaniards and Indians more depraved than they." This view he described as "the predominant feeling in Texas." Certainly that attitude prevailed in the army, whose power resolved any remaining doubts of the politicians regarding the necessity of independence.[27]

On the basis of only a few weeks' experience in Texas affairs, delegate George C. Childress, who apparently went to the Convention with a declaration of independence already prepared, agreed with the opinions of these other leaders. He considered Mexicans "a semicivilized set, unfit to be free and incapable of self-government" and expressed the view that defense of the 1824 constitution "was but a mere *pretence* from the beginning." This interpretation certainly underestimated past support for Mexican federalism, but events at the Convention seemed to confirm his view. The delegates approved the document submitted by a committee of five (including Childress) on the first day after the body organized, without debate and in proceedings that required less than an hour.[28]

Some of the views that Childress expressed privately also found their way into this declaration, including the unfitness of Mexicans by character for a democratic system; however, its statement of grievances continued to insist that Texas constitutionalism was sincere rather than a sham. According to this formal explanation, Texas had prepared loyal remonstrances, only to receive repression in return. Mexico had "contemptuously rejected" needed reforms, had incarcerated or attempted to arrest Austin and other Texas citizens, had attacked local commerce, and had even encouraged Indian attacks. Succumbing to perpetual military revolutions, Mexico had exported its despotism to Texas in the form first of commandants who attempted to seize the people's arms as a preliminary to oppression and then as a full-scale "war of extermination." These policies altogether amounted to a dissolution of the compact of government — Mexican "malfeasance and abdication" resulted in "anarchy," so that "civil society is dissolved into its original elements." The Texans alone among citizens of Mexico took up arms to defend the constitution, so that "self-preservation" now required separation; the Declaration of Independence as adopted on March 2, ended by resolving that all connections with Mexico had ceased as the people of Texas instituted a "free sovereign, and independent republic."[29]

On March 3 the convention took up the matter of constructing a government for this new nation. That evening Gray noted with surprise that "the Convention has so far got on harmoniously." This spirit of consensus never fully dissipated, despite flarings of personality disputes, and factional lines remained less well developed or less significant than they had been at the Consultation. Nor did a single figure emerge to dominate debate or manipulate votes behind the scenes. Houston evoked the strongest charismatic appeal, but some delegates objected to the nightly drinking contests involving him, Rusk, and others. Furthermore, with his appointment as commander in chief the famous Tennessee "Raven" departed from Washington on March 6. Potter, Carson, Childress, Zavala, Navarro, and presiding officer Ellis all brought substantial political and even constitutional experience from outside of Texas to the Convention; however, each displayed some liability — partisanship, naked self-interest, unfamiliarity with Texas affairs, ethnic background — which prevented him from gaining the confidence of sufficient representatives to dominate the proceedings. Several other delegates also had legal or political training, but none came forward to seize the role of "Father" of the Texas Constitution. President Ellis, who sometimes stepped down from the chair to engage in debate, gained more of a reputation for partisanship than statesmanship. Other leaders like Edward Conrad appeared interested only in the land for veterans or some other special interest matter.[30]

The delegates seemed pleased at the weakness of party lines and only vaguely aware of the mediocre quality of leadership at the Convention, but the specter of war distracted their attention from the work at hand. Travis's urgent letter appealing for help at the Alamo, which they strongly suspected could not be answered, arrived on March 6. From that time forward a sense of military urgency harried the deliberations, several times threatening to cause adjournment before any government had been established.

Amidst this sense of danger the delegates struggled for two weeks after the adoption of independence to construct a suitable political framework. Their work appeared to drag rather than progress, as a committee labored for five days to correct the awkward passages of the first constitutional draft on March 7. These problems as well as some substantive issues continued to delay completion; the delegates considered a draft on the twelfth but resubmitted the document to committee and barely managed to approve the revision five days later, after several had already taken their leave from the body. Even in the instrument's final version some controversies — about land for veterans and loan provisions, for example — had been resolved by resolutions rather than by constitution article or were left to the interim government's discretion.[31]

The Convention's struggles and shortcomings in constructing a constitution resulted from the press of time and inadequacies of talent rather than from crippling conflicts of ideological or party alignments. Nor did the delegates suffer from any constraints on the scope of their deliberations, since they understood themselves "to be clothed with ample, unlimited or plenary powers, as to the form of government to be adopted," provided that they submitted the completed document for popular ratification. Despite this broad charge the Texas Constitution reflected very little experimentation; instead, it reproduced the basic features of the U.S. system, modified but slightly by some of the democratic innovations incorporated into many state governments during the first third of the nineteenth century and by the Spanish-Mexican legal tradition.[32]

In both structure — separation of powers into three branches, including a bicameral legislature — and scope of enumerated authority, the Texas Constitution varied scarcely at all from its model. The few minor changes were primarily designed to limit government and keep it close to the people: these included shorter terms of office (one year for representatives, three years for senators and the president), nonconsecutive terms for the executive, and a provision prohibiting the president from taking the field in command of troops without congressional authorization. Some reforms did find expression in the Constitution. It made establishment of "a general system of education" a "duty" of Congress, provided that all elections should be by ballot, established proportional representation for the House on the basis of white population only (in contrast to the systems that protected the slaveowners' oligarchy in states like South Carolina), and rigorously separated church and state by denying national office to any "minister of the gospel." Motions to lower the voting age to eighteen, either generally or for those youths engaged in military service in the war for independence, failed to gain adoption.

The Constitution contained a specific Declaration of Rights, also derived mostly from the U.S. document in ideas, if not exact language. Their Jeffersonian-Jacksonian inheritance likewise influenced the Texans' definition of rights. The last enumerated of these disallowed monopolies as "contrary to the genius of a free government" and prohibited laws of primogeniture or entail. In final form the document also provided an absolute abolition of imprisonment for debt, though the efforts of Rusk and others to qualify this provision occasioned what Gray described as "a very pretty debate" four days before the Convention closed.[33]

Several features of the republic's framework of government suggest the importance of more radical features of their heritage or of their revolutionary circumstance. The first two provisions of the Declaration of Rights set forth a social compact theory of government, in which all authority derived from the people. Though delegating considerable power, all citizens retained "equal rights" and the privilege to "alter their government," thus implicitly acknowledging the right of revolution. The authors of the Texas Constitution also recognized that their wartime leaders might have to resort to some extraordinary measures. Therefore, they omitted the third amendment from the U.S. Constitution, which outlawed quartering of troops in private residences. In addition, the Texas document authorized public impressment of property and services, provided that the government obtained consent or made "just compensation." For those who shirked their responsibility to the Revolution, the Constitution allowed even sterner medicine. According to Article VI, Section 8: "All persons who shall leave the country for the purpose of evading a participation in the present struggle, or shall refuse to participate in it, or shall give aid or assistance to the present enemy, shall forfeit all rights of citizenship, and such lands as they may hold in the republic." The journal of the Convention recorded no debate or opposition to the measure, but the delegates did worry about abuses of this power, in that the bill of rights contained a provision for the subordination of military to civil authority.[34]

These revolutionary features of the Constitution and its enumeration of human rights did not make the cause a thoroughly humanitarian one. The Texas conflict was also racial in nature, and the Convention adopted several proslavery and discriminatory enactments. These included a slave code to assure the chattel status of blacks currently held in bondage under bogus contracts and denial of equal rights to free blacks by giving citizenship to whites only. Prohibition of the international slave trade was enacted for diplomatic reasons — to counteract the hostilities of vigilant U.S. abolitionists.[35]

No member of the Convention rose in disagreement with the proslavery enactments, but the other most important property issue — land — occasioned vigorous debate and nearly irreconcilable splits. After watching their deliberations for ten days, Gray observed that the delegates "seem afraid to approach" the land question. Their hesitation occurred in part because of confusing and complex past policies. At one point Edward Conrad, a newcomer to Texas who zealously represented the army position on these matters, proposed a resolution to create a committee to investigate land records. This apparently useful suggestion failed adoption due to its impracticality, and actually several of those involved in the debate had little real need for clarification. Those knowledgeable or experienced on land policies included Mexican congressman Navarro, empresarios Zavala, Robertson, and Power; Nacogdoches land commissioners George W. Smyth and Charles S. Taylor;

and to a lesser degree the various settlers who had held some office under Mexican rule. At the top of this list stood an expert, S. H. Everitt, who had been sent to east Texas by the provisional government to close the land offices. Those with a solid grounding in land policies comprised over a third of the Convention.[36]

The land issue did have confusing features, but the real reason that it bedeviled the Convention had more to do with its controversial potential. Even a disinterested observer might have had difficulty devising a just policy that balanced the competing if not conflicting claims of native inhabitants, settlers, army volunteers, and colonizers (who had helped to spur population growth and hence economic improvement). In Texas in 1836 hardly anyone could be classified as disinterested when it came to these policies.

Further complicating this matter were the fraudulent or at least abusive activities of several empresarios. Zavala and a future president, Burnet, had been among those who illegally assigned their contracts to a company which in turn sold scrip and generated spin-off disputes. Other gamblers had taken advantage of the distracted condition of revolutionary Mexico in 1834 and 1835 to exchange money for huge land grants from the state government. Additional disputes concerned the policy of ending further land transactions, adopted first in October, 1835, in order to prevent the dispersal of premium tracts while citizen-soldiers were away at war. Nacogdoches delegate Taylor had been one of those who defiantly issued titles after that date. Other commissioners had appeared to comply while actually using a predating subterfuge. As a consequence, an omnipresent spirit of suspicion surrounded all land policies. The label "land speculator" was with varying degrees of accuracy widely applied to powerful or ambitious politicians; those who sought to defend themselves against this charge could with equal justice label their opponents as "demagogues."[37]

This explosive situation made for procrastination at the Convention: every constitutional proposal on land introduced between the opening and last day went down to defeat, onto the table, or to committee. Nevertheless, these resolutions (presented on March 3, 8, and 10) in amended form became Section 10 of the constitution when on March 17 the delegates accepted the report of a committee formed three days earlier. Even with some concessions made to large property holders, the land policy represented a triumph of democratic and patriotic impulses.

Potter, labelled alternately a speculator and a demagogue, and Everitt, also representing an east Texas constituency, pushed hardest for the basic features of the policy. Two groups — settlers and army volunteers — benefitted most. All residents were to receive the land which they had been promised as an incentive to emigrate. The Constitution validated surveys (for a league and labor per family) made prior to the closing of the land offices (in November, 1835). The provision did not require recipients to live on this land, but in the case of future title disputes it gave preference to "the actual settler and occupant of the soil." Further, aliens could not hold land in Texas except by direct legislation of a future Congress or through inheritance from a Texan. Veterans of the war for independence also received special constitutional protection. The land provision approved the past policy of closing land offices and kept those agencies out of operation for the duration; not until Congress gave authorization by establishing a land office could any additional claims be legally processed.

Although some of the delegates undoubtedly opposed aspects of the land measure, disagreement centered on the construction of the statement regarding large and allegedly illegal grants. In final form the land section of the Constitution invalidated three sets of claims: (1) those made to or on behalf of John T. Mason (a New York speculator and agent) by the Coahuila legislature in 1834; (2) grants enacted by this same body on March 14, 1835; and (3) eleven-league holdings located within twenty leagues of the U.S.-Texas border in contravention of Mexico's general colonization laws. These antispeculator provisions triumphed in a more limited form because they were surrounded by less pejorative language than the initial measure introduced by Potter on March 8. The major content change made by the Convention was to substitute these specific invalidations for his sweeping proposal to abolish any and all claims exceeding eleven leagues or a league and labor to individuals. The final outcome represented a more moderate policy, especially with respect to the holdings of men like Austin who had done so much to populate Texas; but either through oversight or by purposeful manipulation it also failed to repudiate certain large grants made under other Coahuila laws in 1835. Certainly the delegates had little time for last-minute refinements, as they adopted the Constitution while in a state of panic.[38]

The delegates' haste may also have doomed the effort to provide constitutional guarantees of land bounties to all those who served in the war. Conrad failed to make such a proposal until three days before adjournment. Almost literally at the last minute he succeeded in bringing his motion off the table and having it enacted as a resolution. It provided for rewards of 320 to 1280 acres, in increments of 320 acres as the amount of service lengthened.[39]

Many other policies emanated from this March body besides the Declaration of Independence and the Constitution, for the Convention served also as an emergency government. In this role it confronted a serious crisis. The imminence of renewed hostilities exacerbated several problems inherited from the previous authorities; but the new government commanded hardly any of the structures necessary to translate its will into action. Acting Governor Robinson acknowledged these past failures in a letter of March 4 which went on to outline the tasks of governing. He urged "your honorable body, so to organize, constitute and remodel the provisional Government, as to restore harmony, promote union, provide for the common defense and general welfare; and that the public interest may not be prejudiced or injured by the present unhappy state of dissention and disunion."[40] In short, the Convention had to do no less than direct a revolution.

However hesitant, divided, or confused the delegates acted on some issues, they did recognize the need to assert their power over military affairs in a manner that previous politicians had avoided. First, the Convention created the office of commander in chief of all Texas land forces, regardless of their origin or previous state of independence from external control. The preamble to this March 4 resolution began, "Whereas we are in a state of revolution, . . . the emergency of the present crisis" required the establishment of an office of major general with authority to organize the army and subordinate all units to his will.[41] The Convention also acknowledged that past reliance on voluntary methods had failed to fill the Texas ranks. Although the provisional government in February attempted to call up the citizen militia, even (as Robinson wrote to Houston) "by draft if we must," it had neither the statutory nor the actual power to force widespread compliance. Where successful, these efforts had depended on the will of ad hoc political bodies. For example, in San Felipe de Austin the work of organizing was done by what the newspaper called a "standing committee, appointed by the citizens of this place [on February 27], in the absence of any [other] authority to act in the present emergency."[42]

On March 12 the Convention enacted an ordinance to bring uniformity to the heretofore spasmodic methods of enrollment. The basic premise of this militia law—"it is the bounden duty of every man who asks of the country protection of his person and property, to stand forth in such a crisis in its defence"—meant that all able-bodied men (except Indians and slaves) between ages seventeen and fifty were "subject" to military service. Officials would be appointed to conduct registration in each district; two-thirds of those on this list, chosen by a rotating lottery method, would be called to duty by the chief executive at any one time. The law also provided for punitive measures against those who failed either to muster out or hire a substitute. It threatened courts-martial for shirkers and deserters, with penalty set at loss of citizenship and forfeiture of half the guilty individual's property. Only a few political officials received exemptions; even commissioned officers not in the field had to face conscription.[43]

The question of the role of Mexican Texans posed a serious dilemma. Members of the Convention, prodded by ravings in the letters of Travis as he attacked the disloyalty of the Béxareños, generally acknowledged that the conflict had become a race war. Distrusting the Tejanos on the one hand, the delegates seemed unwilling to exempt them from service on the other. The solution, establishment of "separate corps" for what Potter called "white men" and "natives," at first applied to Béxar, Refugio, San Patricio, and Nacogdoches. In the end the delegates adopted this procedure for only the last-named of these municipalities, leaving the draft status unclear for the Tejano population in the western region. The same day the conscription law passed, the Convention appointed enrollment officers to "organize and draft the militia."[44]

The delegates also applied the doctrine of forced contribution to the matter of supplying its military. An embattled Travis wrote the Convention from the Alamo to urge policies of revolutionary expropriation against Mexican Texans, whom he considered "public enemies." The political leaders at the time made no formal move to this end, but they did begin to authorize impressment from those who refused to sell on the public credit. The Convention urged restraint in regard to possible distress which might be caused to citizens, but it left no doubt that the success of the Revolution and its armies took priority over the rights of individual property holders. On the other hand, by mid-March the government also began to acknowledge its responsibilities for the welfare of individuals dislocated by the war by providing them with food and other necessities.[45]

The Convention of March 1–17, 1836, not only bowed to the directions being taken by the Revolution but also added to its momentum. Thus the essential actions transpired—declaring independence and drafting a constitution — and the delegates moved toward establishing an authority with sufficient force to give the cause a chance to triumph. What remained to be seen was whether the interim government that the Convention created could successfully direct the Revolution during a time of prolonged crisis.

6. The Interim Government
MARCH–SEPTEMBER, 1836

Toward the end of their deliberations Convention delegates began to express concern about the need for government after their adjournment. Asa Brigham proposed that law and order be protected by nominating "three discreet and judicious persons" in each county to "form a body politic" and to serve as unpaid police for the course of the war. Whether on pragmatic or ideological grounds, the delegates rejected this revolutionary procedure in favor of a more practical and tradition-respecting policy. The Constitution provided that all existing laws "not inconsistent" with the document as well as current judges and other civil officials should remain in power until repealed or replaced by new elections. Until that time Texas was to be led by an ad interim national government. This body was to consist of a president and vice president, chosen by the Convention, "invested with the same powers" set forth in the Constitution, and holding office until their successors were duly elected. An ordinance adopted on March 16 fleshed out the constitutional provision. Boasting a verbal "calmness unruffled" that belied the truly agitated emotions of the hour, the delegates reiterated the "full, ample, and plenary powers" of this temporary government. This measure also broadened the executive with five additional offices to form a full cabinet, decisions to be made by a majority vote. Its financial and diplomatic functions were specifically endorsed.[1]

Accounts of the elections to fill these posts differed widely in describing the process. Acid-tongued William F. Gray believed that he witnessed much electioneering and notorious lusting after power. David G.

Burnet, not a delegate himself but chosen as interim president, later insisted that he had merely "consented to be a candidate." He had intellectual and character credentials, being known as intelligent and honest, but Burnet's political liabilities made his choice somewhat surprising. In particular, he had not been a zealous revolutionary, having failed to attend the Consultation, being only a late convert to the cause of independence, having the taint of a speculator-empresario background, and lacking a power base in the army. Future events would also prove him to be a quarrelsome, if not irascible, person and a poor politician. Burnet's seven-vote margin of victory occurred undoubtedly in part because his opponent, Samuel P. Carson, had resided in Texas for only a few months, making him a newcomer even by the standards of this mobile society.

The loser, who became secretary of state, had not only political experience superior to any other delegate, but also a well-deserved reputation for hot-headedness. His political service had begun at age twenty-two in the North Carolina Senate, had continued in the U.S. House of Representatives, and had been interrupted only when he killed a man in a duel. His career had recovered from an unpopular association with the Nullifiers of South Carolina, but Carson came to Texas, perhaps having learned about it from his association with land dealer John T. Mason. Clearly, Burnet must have appeared as the more prudent candidate, and the goals of conservatism and balance also dictated the choice of Zavala as vice president (unopposed). Rusk defeated Potter for secretary of war, with the delegates then selecting the controversial loser in this contest as secretary of the navy. Remaining cabinet posts went to the army: veteran David Thomas became attorney general, and Bailey Hardeman consented to undertake the impossible burdens of the Texas treasury.[2]

In March and April most of the tasks facing these officials were problems inherited from the Convention. The matter of past loans from the United States had literally been dodged by the delegates and then passed on to the "Executive Government." When the issue first arose on March 7 some members criticized the terms of the arrangement and then had it referred to committee, or "smuggled out of sight," as the disgusted Gray wrote. This group's report emphasized the emergency circumstances of the loan that accounted for any disadvantageous terms and urged that earlier commitments be "unhesitatingly ratified." Again the Convention postponed action until the last two days when, amidst a crisis atmosphere, it passed the problem on to the cabinet.

By March 17 the dispersing delegates realized that any repudiation of past loans would irreparably damage the shaky credit of the new Republic of Texas. Subsequently, the government continued to express hesitation about endorsing past credit arrangements, but by late May Burnet gave the Texas agent in New Orleans authorization to pledge a half million acres of the public domain in order to raise more funds.[3]

The cabinet never really had the opportunity of functioning as a unit, as military collapse and near-unanimous hysteria soon gripped all of Texas. Houston had arrived at Gonzales on March 11. He learned immediately of the fate of the Alamo, ordered Fannin to retreat, and moved his own troops eastward on the thirteenth. While this Texas commander fretted, Urrea acted. His army defeated the units it confronted at San Patricio and Refugio, moved against the bulk of the Texas forces stymied by uncertainty at Goliad, and forced their surrender at Coleto on March 20. Houston, having crossed the Colorado River on the seventeenth, learned of this defeat a week later and continued to retreat, helpless to avert the massacre of Fannin's army on March 28. Fearing that his ill-trained set of volunteers might be good for but one decisive battle, the Texas general resisted pressure to stand and fight. An engagement did not occur on the Brazos, which the army of both Houston and his pursuer Santa Anna crossed between April 11–13. Lacking confidence that the Texans could stem the invasion, the people fled pell-mell eastwardly in the "Runaway Scrape."

During this month of panic after the Convention hastily adjourned, the executive officers moved first from Washington to Harrisburg and then on April 19 to Galveston Island. Individual members of the cabinet divided time between public duties and responsibilities of caring for family; Rusk and Thomas rejoined the army during April. Even with new or acting membership, the interim government managed to conduct only minimal business from mid-April to mid-May. Yet, despite its near chaotic character, the cabinet in either collective or individual capacity attempted to carry out the revolutionary policies of conscription, impressment, and punishment of disloyalists or shirkers that had been inaugurated by the Convention.

Burnet began the task of implementing a revolution by force on a very inauspicious note. His first official act was to publish a grandiose inaugural address filled with sentimentalized appeals for common sacrifice: "Let us . . . lay our heads, our hearts, and our hands together; and, like a band of brothers, feeling one interest and one affection, look with a single eye, and press forward with a single zeal."[4] Within a week of this faltering start, Burnet abandoned bombast and started to institute the forcible policies outlined by the Convention.

A March 25 order explained that crisis required unity of action and military participation. Unfortunately, he proclaimed, past "experience has demonstrated" that under "ordinary operation of the law" many "unworthy" Texans would continue to "rest quietly at home" while their noble neighbors or volunteers from the U.S. did the fighting. Yet, the laggards would also "expect to partake of the ultimate benefit" of the "struggle." In the name of the executive government, Burnet declared Texas and all its inhabitants to be under martial law. Existing political divisions became military districts, under the authority of a three-man, cabinet-appointed vigilance committee. These bodies were authorized to impress personal property for public use, conduct a military census, and enroll companies of militia. The order made it clear that any eligible citizen who refused to join would be treated as a deserter "liable to the pains and penalties of the military laws." Committees also had to undertake the care of suffering families through use of public provisions, including those acquired by press agents. That same day the president named and gave directions to militia enrollment officials in ten municipalities east of the Colorado River.[5]

During the last week of March and first week of April Burnet issued further proclamations, less specific and more rhetorical, designed to encourage compliance with these coercive policies. He used appeals to patriotism, words of shame, calls for revenge, and threats of reprisal. From army headquarters on the Brazos on April 13 Secretary of War Rusk reiterated all these literary devices. Secretary of Navy Potter gave orders on the coastal region to fulfill the impressment and conscription policies of the government, believing also that "in the present crisis men who are not *willing* must be *compelled*, to defend the Country."[6]

These messages and commands had some effect. Houston's army grew substantially (and also contracted constantly), despite the public mood of panic and the unpopularity of retreat; though the ranks held more volunteers than draftees. In early April officials at the local level, at least in some jurisdictions, compiled lists of those who had fled "without standing their draft," as the San Felipe supervisor described it.[7] At Harrisburg fifty or sixty troops enrolled in accordance with militia procedures. Nevertheless, Acting Secretary of War David Thomas reported to the commander in chief, "it is very difficult to enforce the late militia law, owing to the dispersed situation of the inhabitants of the country." He urged Houston to prepare accurate muster rolls, complete with the soldiers' home municipalities, as well as lists of deserters. This information "would greatly facilitate this department [in] forcing the people out" and in punishing those who shirked their duty.[8]

Thomas also indicated that the cabinet currently lacked an effective means of enforcing the militia policies ordained by the Convention and Burnet. This weakness occurred because the military emergency left too little time for the government to establish district committee or enrollment officials in accordance with its militia laws. Failure to secure publication of the Constitution meant also that the public could not easily abide by rules they did not know.

Developments in Nacogdoches reveal the failure of militarization at the local level, even in deep east Texas where Mexican troop movements did not carry. Acting on behalf of the self-appointed vigilance committee, Alcalde David A. Hoffman, not the appointed official empowered to take charge by the March 12 militia act, ordered all citizens to turn out on the nineteenth and submit to the draft. The plans for conscription somehow went awry, and Burnet's appointment of S. R. Peck as the municipality's enrollment officer the next week had no apparent impact. Rather, as a group of Nacogdoches leaders wrote on April 11, "there is no organization of the Physical force of this community, and we are without a head. The people, therefore, have assumed powers which belong to them" by reestablishing the committee of vigilance and safety. This group sought the services of an outsider to be "military commandant of this district." Nacogdoches had reverted back to the localism that had bedeviled the Revolution from the outset.[9] Other east Texas municipalities experienced more overt resistance to the new order. Shelby officials not only failed to comply with the militia ordinance but continued to conduct property and other transactions, to the despair of patriotic citizens, including Convention delegate Sydney O. Penington. He considered their actions to be "official Robery," made worse since they fled the country during the time of panic.[10]

In March and April the interim government implemented its impressment policy in a similarly spasmodic manner. Field officers either using written authorization or citing the law of necessity seized goods and animals in an irregular way that naturally stirred resentment. As the front arrived in central and southern Texas, a few inhabitants dared to express sympathy with the cause of Mexico; others began to hedge their loyalties, lost respect for a government that had been felled so often by disorder, placed the welfare of families above duty to the new nation, or fled out of simple cowardice.[11] Regardless of the legitimacy of these motives, the authorities had to respond to real and apparent examples of disloyal behavior. During the heat of passion from mid-March through mid-May, considerable sentiment favored the constitutionally imposed punishment of traitors and shirkers, including expropriation of property and deprivation of other citizenship privileges.

In this period the government investigated, ordered arrests, and actually took physical possession of a handful of suspected Texas Tories. All of these were accused of treason, meaning spying or giving other overt support to the enemy, rather than failing to stand for the draft. Yet most of the accused Tories managed to flee the country or otherwise wriggle out of long-term internment. Those actually arrested received something less than draconian treatment, but sentiment did exist among certain officials both for extending the label of treason to "Texians that will not turn out to defend their Rights," as Henry Millard wrote, and for increasing the severity of punishments. Convention delegate James Gaines advised the president "to march our [Tory] Enemies in the front of battle" as a form of punitive deterrence to continued opposition. Sterling C. Robertson urged General Rusk in May to direct the victorious Texas army against the people of the country who had failed to turn out, driving them completely out of the land.[12]

In more restrained but firm language General Houston and President Burnet sent out general orders to the public and specific directives to government officials, spreading the word of their intention to enforce provisions for forfeiture of land and citizenship against those who abandoned the country in the military crisis. The chief executive attempted to give substance to this threat by instructing officials and ferrymen to make reports of those who defiantly crossed the Sabine. Actually, Burnet had little stomach for the use of force against those who had been overtaken by panic and self-interest. He acted to restrain zealots from punishing anyone unless "guilty of some overt act of treason." He believed that the fates of all others should be left to the civil law courts during a calmer future time of peace rather than being subjected to military courts-martial. Statesmanlike in some respects, this lenient attitude also contributed to the continued absence of respect with which Texans viewed their government. In late May Robertson wrote that the people of San Augustine would refuse to submit themselves to the newest conscription effort. He urged rigorous enforcement of the confiscation law as well as a vengeful display of force to gain adherence to the government will.[13]

Instead of heeding this advice, Burnet pursued no coherent policy, especially in regard to the application of force to command popular obedience to his edicts. As a result, the government did too little to spread its revolutionary authority but enough to alienate the less zealous. It ultimately succeeded only in losing the respect of almost everyone. The cabinet's militia policy clearly reveals this half-hearted tendency. During late May and early June, in the relative peace that followed the San Jacinto battle, Burnet did nothing to implement conscription. In fact, his conflict with the army over military and diplomatic matters made the president reluctant to increase its size and influence. Then on June 20, in the face of rumors of another Mexican invasion of Texas, he decreed a reenforcement of the militia order. Burnet privately expressed doubts about whether the people would obey the draft call. Local leaders soon reported the absence of sufficient unity in their communities to meet the expected military emergency. On July 8 Secretary of War Mirabeau B. Lamar, who took office in May following acting Secretary Thomas's untimely death, admitted a widespread "indisposition" to obey the militia call and his own impotence when it came to enforcement. Continued warnings of property expropriation by Houston rang like empty threats because the government had done nothing heretofore to punish disobedience.[14]

The interim authorities carried out the matter of impressment with similar lack of coherence. Individual agents seized goods irregularly, prompting abundant complaints of "indiscriminate" and unjust attacks on private property, as Houston termed them. Burnet responded by repudiating all confiscations except those ordered by the army commander, but abuses continued, with a corresponding decline of respect for the government. Even its humane efforts to feed the helpless civilians who took refuge on Galveston Island led to charges of favoritism, waste, and corruption. In mid-June Robertson reported that the response to government shortcomings in east Texas had become a vicious cycle. Abuses by the excessive number of press masters, especially in confiscating animals required for farming, not only alienated the people but gave them a popular excuse to avoid the draft. Potential draftees argued that they had to stay home to protect their families from being stripped of all means of support by government agents. In the Sabine district powerful men also opposed conscription on the basis of constitutionality; the absence of reprisals against them encouraged others to take up positions of similar resistance.[15]

Essentially, the problems of the cabinet stemmed from its half-hearted allegiance to revolutionary policies. A minor incident from the late summer reveals Burnet's equivocal attitude. Attempting to persuade another official to reverse an alleged abuse by a "Muster Master," the president wrote, "This professes to be a government of laws not of force—let the laws prevail."[16] In contrast, more ardent leaders like Rusk displayed impatience with endless discussions of "abstract principles of Government." The repeated process whereby "politicks are to be discussed plans adopted and abandoned confusion and laughing introduced" dismayed the general and, he argued, endangered the country. Rusk favored imposition of martial law, enforcement of the militia laws, adoption of extraordinary measures to supply the army, renewed attacks against Mexico, and other policies that would produce what he called "System and order" in Texas. The indecisions of the cabinet reminded him of the errors of the previous provisional government. Why, he asked, had its leaders failed to learn "that the people of Texas are restless under the restraint of Government and particularly one which had come into power from the exigency of the times?" Only vigorous activity designed to promote a sense of security would gain popular respect for the interim rulers, in Rusk's opinion.[17]

Other politicians noted past susceptibility to civil disorder and worried about the future. An experienced leader, William H. Wharton wrote from the United States that the Texas cause was likely to triumph, but he expressed fear of "some great dissension and anarchy among the Texians themselves." A friend urged Secretary of War Lamar to remain in public office, believing that the breakdown of government and excited public mood was "a consequence [of] revolutions" rather than a peculiar disability of the new Republic.[18]

Besides a lethargic character, other factors also weakened support for the executive authority. Houston led a war of words against the government for its alleged panic in March and April. He and other critics charged that the hasty departure from Washington by Convention delegates beginning on March 16 and of cabinet members in the next few days had stimulated the Runaway Scrape. Others criticized politicians for setting a poor example by fleeing rather than serving in the army. Burnet and Carson in particular rankled at these implications of cowardice and launched a series of attacks against the commander for his strategy of retreat, which they held responsible for the desperate flight of Texans through the "Sabine Shute."[19]

These army-government tensions did not dissolve, even in the wake of the victory of April 21. The cabinet remained fragmented for nearly a month after the battle. Vice President Zavala soon joined secretaries of war and treasury Lamar and Hardeman at San Jacinto (Attorney General Thomas had been killed), but the president's long absence prevented regular conduct of business and, according to Rusk, caused missed military opportunities. Burnet, in turn, blamed his enemies in the service for tardily communicating news of the triumph over Santa Anna, but he admitted on May 23 that the interim government had hitherto been "embarrassed on all hands and perplexed with many difficulties." These included, according to Thomas F. McKinney, somnolent leadership. He derided "our sleeping President" for dozing through meetings and concluded, "My God what a burlesque on Government."[20]

When the cabinet finally did function, its policies aroused continued dissatisfaction from the army and new opposition as well. The chief issue concerned disposition of the captured Mexican commander. According to Burnet's later apologia (supported by Zavala's account), crucial military-diplomatic decisions had been made before the president arrived and subsequently dealt with Santa Anna. The Mexican general, by a battlefield armistice negotiated with Houston and Rusk, ordered a retreat of the invasion forces south of the Rio Grande in exchange for his personal safety. Other provisions, alternately affirmed and repudiated by various cabinet members and by Santa Anna, were not formally stated until May 14 in the Treaty of Velasco. In final form it called for prisoner exchanges, return of captured property, and (secretly) release of Santa Anna, who promised to obtain official recognition of Texas independence. Burnet defended this secret provision as the highest statesmanship — by a single stroke the new republic could secure its nationhood through diplomacy rather than costly war. "Santa Anna dead is no more than Tom, Dick or Harry dead, but, living, he may avail Texas much," argued the president.[21]

However advantageous as foreign policy, the plan to free the hated captive attracted widespread scorn. As Burnet described the public attitude, "a wild and intractable spirit of revenge is abroad among the people, it pervades all classes, . . . overlooks all claims of public faith, and all considerations of public policy." Many, in fact, did favor execution of Santa Anna, either summarily or by court martial, while others urged holding him until Mexico fulfilled completely all of the Velasco agreements. Citizens freely expressed these views both in correspondence and in publicly adopted resolutions, and many of their communications contained open or thinly veiled threats. A citizens' group from Austin and Harrisburg municipalities warned that it would be "Hazerdious [*sic*] for the government to act against the known wishes of their constituents"; a similar meeting in San Augustine suggested that the executive government abandon its diplomacy as "impolitic . . . tending directly to produce general dissatisfaction and consequent disorder and confusion throughout the Republic."[22]

Though most of these expressions came too late to reverse cabinet policy, the same sentiment prevailed in the temporary seat of government, Velasco. News that the government had on June 1 transferred the enemy leader to a ship in preparation for his release in Mexico aroused public wrath. Crowds gathered during the next two days to express the opinion, as one correspondent wrote "that the government shall comply with the wishes of a so large a majority." Burnet refused to capitulate to the proponents of direct democracy, even when threatened with violence. Others in the cabinet who attempted to speak before public demonstrators had their voices drowned by the clamor of the opposition, emboldened on June 3 with armed support in the form of volunteers who debarked from New Orleans. Only a known critic of government diplomacy, Secretary of War Lamar, gained the attention of the crowd. He offered no solace to the advocates of forcible reversal of the despised policy. "Mobs must not intimidate the government," Lamar reputedly said, "We want no French Revolution in Texas!"[23]

The head of the War Department warned against military domination of civil authority, but his words failed to stem the determination of the troops. On June 4 a body of soldiers seized Santa Anna from shipboard, placing him under military arrest for the remainder of the summer. This act cooled the furor somewhat, but the issue of his appropriate punishment continued to divide Texas opinion. On one occasion alarm resurfaced with rumors of a plot to free the prisoner. Only a few dared to continue advocating the release of Santa Anna as a matter of foreign policy.[24]

These events had lasting consequences in undermining the authority of the government. Actually, the issue had already badly divided the cabinet even before it became a matter of public conflict in June. Both Lamar and Potter, the secretaries over the military departments, opposed the secret provisions of the Velasco treaty, as did W. H. Jack, who became secretary of state in late May. With three members in dissent, a potentially tie-breaking voice devolved on the president, though the question apparently did not come to a re-vote after its May 14 adoption. The events of early June undid the already shaky confidence of the ad interim cabinet. Led by Vice President Zavala, several members argued, as Burnet recalled their position, that the government should yield its authority "to the people, the fountain of all political power" in the aftermath of the Santa Anna crisis. The president successfully opposed such an act, which he believed would "throw Texas into irretrievable anarchy and confusion," but the cabinet virtually broke up anyway.[25]

Zavala did submit his resignation, "'taking into consideration that the present Government of Texas has lost the moral confidence of the People and is therefore no longer able to carry into effect their measures.'" The president refused to accept any wholesale resignations, but the vice president ceased to be a working member of the cabinet, left Velasco on June 11, and became a critic of its head. According to Zavala, the president had failed to heed the proper advice on methods of organizing a working administration: "'Poor Burnet believed that composing notes and letters himself like an office clerk, would suffice very well.'"[26]

Even earlier, jealousies among the various heads had split the cabinet internally. Some expressed resentment of the rapid rise of the newer Texans in the body. Rumors flew that Zavala intended to use his position in the Texas government merely as a stepping stone to a coup in Mexico. Few politicians could stand any long-term association with the dispirited cabinet, derided by a female settler as "perhaps the most imbecile body that ever sat judgment on the fate of a nation." Thirteen different men held the five posts below the president and vice president during the interim government's seven month existence, and two offices became permanently vacant by the end of May. These frequent changes and reductions naturally confused and alienated the people, many of whom received only rumors or fragmentary news of the turmoil in government. However steadfastly Burnet had resisted formal dissolution, the shock of having its foreign policy overturned by popular rebellion had weakened the interim government irrevocably. On June 6 a supporter who sought a place gave the following analysis: "The cabinet is weak. No popularity or confidence — & altogether occupy a pitiful position both in eyes of friends & enemies."[27]

The President continued to discharge the functions of his office even though, he later admitted, the government had been "shorn . . . of all moral and physical power" and retained only "a semblance of authority." Burnet held on for over three more months in the face of still more upheavals in what he once called "this very excitable country." Conflict with the army did not end with the Santa Anna affair. Though the president attempted several measures to control the military branch, including limiting the number of new volunteers from the United States and nominating the popular Lamar as major general and commander in chief, various circumstances undermined the plans. An anticipated invasion caused renewed recruitment, and the army, in a show of democratic solidarity, steadfastly rejected Lamar. Burnet's initiatives subsequently backlashed as the army asserted its practical independence from his authority. The president stubbornly continued to lash out against the "base and unprincipled character" and "malignant influence" of his military opponents aligned with Gen. Thomas J. Green; this recalcitrance led a group of army extremists to attempt a coup in mid-July.[28]

Although saved from forcible loss of office by military moderates and civilian supporters, President Burnet never attained much prestige or influence. Even those who favored some of the cabinet's policies, as did Stephen F. Austin on his return in late June, refused to place unqualified confidence in the shattered government. Others libelled it relentlessly and without fear of retribution; a common opinion held that the people allowed Burnet to complete his term only out of anxiety about the diplomatic repercussions of further turmoil.[29] Although independence and military success destroyed some of the earlier factional issues, what E. M. Pease described as "violent" party feeling reasserted itself in the summer of 1836. Many jealousies centered around the contest for power between older and newer Texans; this division involved economic interest, as some settlers expressed reservations about sharing the vast domain of the Texas Republic with those who had come to fight. The old political war cries of "patriots" against "speculators" also began to be heard again.[30]

By early summer most Texans admitted that, despite some military success, the political situation had returned to the chaos of February. At the end of May former cabinet member James Collinsworth expressed concern about the "deplorable condition" and "unsettled state of the country." Sam Houston spent much of his convalescent time giving advice on how to snuff out the "domestic broils" that beset Texas in the absence of effective civil government. He concluded reluctantly that avoiding "disturbances at home" depended on voluntary restraints rather than the influence of any constitutional authority.[31]

Other prominent politicians also began to seek solutions to the internal problems of Texas. Zavala favored union with the United States so that "the stability of our government will be assured. . . . I believe it will be very difficult for Texas to march alone among the other independent nations." In early June a public meeting in Nacogdoches achieved rare unanimity in endorsing annexation. Certainly, the political upheavals of that month did nothing to increase confidence in Texas's capacity for orderly self-rule. A few days after his return Austin began to argue for surrendering independence to save the country "from the further evils of war, or of internal dissention."[32]

Those who held office took additional steps to rescue the new nation from political disorder. Lamar, riled at his rejection by the votes of the volunteers, wrote the president of "the high & absolute necessity of Convening a Congress. Nothing else can save the Country from dreadful disorganization and anarchy." Very soon after receiving this letter (on July 23) Burnet proclaimed elections for September to ratify the Constitution and elect another government. Many Texans once more began to look for salvation from this upcoming exercise in democracy, much as during the previous winter they had expressed faith in the process that afterward dissolved in a shambles. Rusk was among those who saw a new congress as a panacea. He hoped it would "settle all matters and that peace and quiet will prevail throughout the Country united we are safe divided we are yet in danger of losing our liberty."[33]

The upheaval endured by the early Texas government moved both its leaders and other observers to place its experiences in a revolutionary perspective. Though in some places Burnet wrote of the Texas Revolution as if it were unique, he also acknowledged that "the birth of a nation is usually painful, convulsive and protracted." Of course, he continued to argue that unfettered adoption of cabinet policies would have eased some of these pangs. Other less partisan observers took comfort from revolutionary analogies. The *Telegraph* reminded its readers that "tumultuous movements" had also at times threatened the American Revolution, which had triumphed through popular perseverance.[34] In the United States T. J. Chambers defended the reputation of Texas by making similar comparisons. He had to answer the disparaging analysis penned by volunteers who returned home disenchanted by their Texas sojourn. Two of these co-authored a public letter which attacked both the leadership and people of the new republic. This document charged that the Texans were incapable of sustaining a liberal but orderly system: "They are careless of the form of Government under which they live, if [it] will tolerate licentiousness and disorder." Accordingly, the people lived by their instinct for plunder while "there is really no organized Government in the country — no laws administered — no Judiciary — a perpetual struggle going on between the Civil and Military Departments — and neither having the confidence of the people or being worthy of it." "Considering the newness of the country and its revolutionary condition," Chambers replied, "there is much less division of opinion and party-spirit than have been found in every other country in the same situation." That the United States had triumphed in its revolution despite strong Tory opposition, he reasoned, meant that Texas, too, would be able to unite in successful pursuit of liberty. Whether optimistic or gloomy, few Texans in the late summer doubted that they were experiencing the travail of revolution.[35]

7. The Texas Army of the People
ORGANIZATION AND MAKE-UP

For many Texans military participation represented the essential feature of their experience in the Texas Revolution. Furthermore, the army held a dominant place in politics from the day that hostilities called it into being. Both these roles call for a description of army organization and composition. Such analysis requires considerable detail, for the armies that took the field in the war against Mexico had little continuity in membership, leadership, or structural style. Volunteers filled the ranks and demonstrated a militia-like tendency to turn out during crises but then dismiss themselves at apparent lull times to care for the needs of farms and families. Recruits from the United States appeared by land or sea, sometimes in previously organized units but also singly or in irregular groups. They displayed considerable wanderlust, served short-term or unspecified enlistments, and frequently returned home in a whimsical fashion.

Military setbacks contributed to this discontinuity, as entire units succumbed to the sequence of defeats that culminated in March, 1836, at San Antonio and Goliad. Driven in part by the quest for glory and by similar ambitions, a multitude of would-be leaders competed for the support of government and of men, further lending to the disorganization. The Texas armies achieved little in the way of military structure, failing to subscribe to company or regimental uniformity in size or rank and lacking even a regular system of numbering.

Circumstances of birth helped to mold the organization of the Texas army. The rhetoric that called it into being brimmed with expressions of freedom. In an October, 1835, recruitment broadside William H. Wharton urged everyone to join in the glorious fight for home, country, "immortal renoun," and "the great principle of human liberty." Leaders envisioned a force comprised not of conscripts or "the menial slaves of a Despotic Tyrant" who served the enemy but of men animated by the same spirit of freedom that had governed their revolutionary forefathers. Therefore, the circular of the San Felipe committee chose its words deliberately in naming the men who gathered in Gonzales: they were "the ARMY OF THE PEOPLE."[1] The leaders had in mind a mass turnout from all parts of Texas, a force that would offset by numbers and zeal any deficiencies in training. These politicians hedged their reliance on a populist army by seeking recruits from outside Texas, but early volunteers from the United States also took pains to disassociate themselves from mere mercenary impulses. In the words of one letter of introduction they were "actuated by a love of freedom, and generous Sympathy for the Oppressed." These soldiers invariably expressed an identification with the glorious struggle for liberty embodied in the Texas cause.[2] The army that emerged from these two elements, though initially adequate in size, never achieved genuine structural cohesion, and the turnout after December, 1835, proved disappointing indeed.

Imbued with this strong sense of individual rights and freedom, the men who served in the earliest Texas army built it on a democratic framework. Though they sometimes gathered in response to calls issued by political bodies, the volunteers formed themselves into separate units to which they swore allegiance. One such gathering of men at Guadalupe Victoria on October 9 created a social compact in which they resolved to protect their fellow citizens "against military domination" and pledged to uphold the agreement with "our lives, our property, and our sacred honour." This and less formally established companies all followed the principle of electing their own officers. Even these associations, which seemed insufficient to those familiar with military discipline, promoted some semblance of order, in contrast to those who preferred to wander into and out of camp without making any attachment whatsoever.[3]

During the second week of October the Texas recruits coalesced into two forces. The 49 men who joined at Victoria on the ninth marched to Goliad under the command of George M. Collinsworth. Enough gathered to compel surrender of the Mexican fort; for the rest of the year the Texas garrison there numbered between 40 and 120. This provided minimal strength at best, because the fort had responsibility for securing the entire region of the lower Guadalupe, San Antonio, and Nueces rivers, including a small centralist unit at Lipantitlán. Further, the men frequently followed their impulse to be nearer the presumed scene of action to the north at Béxar and moved back and forth between the commands at the two locations.[4]

The force that orginated at Gonzales, where 160 had gathered to see the first shots fired on October 2, gradually meandered its way toward Béxar and attracted most of the Texas volunteers that fall. As one veteran later recalled, "recruits were constantly arriving, singly and in squads, each squad being duly officered. . . . we soon had more officers than men," causing some to accept demotions as the informal units grew into companies.[5] Organization grew from the bottom up. Company representatives formed a council or board of war, but the men refused to allow that body to select a commander in chief. Acrimonious political wrangling by the different units, each with a favorite son, threatened to disrupt the army before an October 11 election; the recruits finally accepted the prevailing view that Stephen F. Austin was the only figure with prestigious, unifying, and statesmanlike qualities. He was chosen unanimously, thus temporarily quelling the divisive potential inherent in military democracy.[6]

The commander attempted to create a greater degree of military regularity in the Army of the People. His first order, issued on election day, emphasized the need for obedience, a theme which he reiterated and specified in general orders on October 14 as the men camped on their march to Béxar. His regulations attempted to curb the individualist temperament of the citizen-soldiers both in terms of disorderly behavior and antipathy toward formal organization: "every volunteer in the army who may not yet have attached himself to any company shall enroll himself in some one where he may bear his fair proportion of duty."[7] Despite Austin's effort, virtually every observer at the front predicted a self-dissolution of the forces, a fate averted not by the commander's leadership so much as the men's reaffirmation of their pledges to stay in the ranks despite the frustrations of the loosely conducted siege. Critics disagreed about strategy, necessary troop strength, and other matters of military policy, but all seemed to concur with Thomas J. Rusk's conclusion that the army needed "something like organization."[8]

The seriousness of the problem is illustrated by the fact that by the time Rusk made this comment some progress had been made toward achieving a recognizable structure. The army had not been fully organized when it straggled into the outskirts of Béxar between October 21 and 24, but by November, 1835, two divisions had been formed. One, initially led by Col. John H. Moore (replaced by the election of Edward Burleson in early November), consisted of eight companies; the other, headed by Col. James Bowie, had half that number. Two scouting companies led by Juan Seguín and William B. Travis served directly under Austin, who retained the prerogative at least to name an adjutant and other aides. At the time of the long-delayed storming of the town on December 5, according to historian Alwyn Barr, the Texas forces consisted of two divisions, led by colonels Ben Milam and Francis W. Johnson, of seven and eight companies respectively, with eleven other companies remaining in reserve or on scouting detail.

Nevertheless, the existence of these units does not demonstrate that disorganization was ever fully overcome. Rather, as the variation in its size indicates, the army remained a managerial nightmare. Numbers fluctuated daily as new recruits, including two companies totalling 118 men from New Orleans, barely managed to replace the dissatisfied ones who volunteered themselves to go home. Austin estimated his forces at 450 on both October 21 and November 4, with 150 having been lost to desertion during that interval. Barr's estimates place the Texas force at about 450 in late October, 600 in early and 800 in mid-November, and then down to 700 at the end of the month. The action in the attack on the town originally involved 400 Texas participants with an equal number in reserve, some of whom entered the fighting after the first day. A total of about 1,000 men served in the siege and storming of Béxar.[9]

The nature of this army and its role cannot be fully understood without reference to its make-up. With the exception of recent work by Barr, most scholars for years have set forth their judgments about the size and composition of the army — in terms of whether "old settlers" or U.S. recruits predominated, for example — without having sufficient data to make definitive statements. The tables below derive from a more systematic approach. In order to determine the characteristics of the army, extant muster rolls and other sources were used to compile a comprehensive enumeration of those who enrolled and their date and place of service. This procedure, it should be noted, is not without problems: it understates the number of Tejano soldiers because few lists of those who served in the companies of Seguín or other commanders have survived (see Chapter 11 for an extended discussion of Tejano service); it also slights those non-Texans who may not have remained in the Republic to establish their land claims. This latter factor is important because most of the biographical details derive from documents filed in land-related records. These unavoidable deficiencies make the statistics less than definitively accurate, but the numbers are reliable for establishing patterns of participation.[10] The result of this research is a set of group profiles of the army at various stages.

The origins and background of the 1835 army, as illustrated by Table 2, demonstrates that the goal of establishing an "Army of the People" was achieved. Its numbers were clearly adequate to confront and defeat the enemy—counting all places of service, over 1,300 men rushed to arms in October and November. Further, all but 150–200 of them were Texas residents prior to the outbreak of hostilities. Analysis of the personal characteristics of the army suggests that the war attracted widespread participation. Prospects of wartime adventure may have fired the imaginations of youth, but the average age of 31 indicates that the more mature also served in substantial numbers. Similarly, married men comprised half the army in 1835, and the volunteers had well-established Texas roots, the average date of emigration being 1830 (1832 even when the U.S. volunteers are included). Like most Anglo Texans of this period, the bulk of the recruits (over three-fourths) hailed from the southern part of the United States; however, those of northern or foreign birth turned out in ratios commensurate with their numbers in Texas. Most importantly (given the strength of intra-Texas regionalism) virtually every municipality produced a sizable contingent of the army. The most populated region, the area governed after 1834 as the Department of Brazos (made up of all of Austin's colonies as well as areas disputed between him and Robertson and that of DeWitt), provided slightly over half of the volunteers. The heavily Hispanic and partially occupied municipality of Béxar generated a fair share of the force, while an impressive number of the recruits (over one-third) came from the Department of Nacogdoches, in far east Texas, well removed and thus geographically buffered from the hostilities. In short, the volunteers of 1835 represented a cross-section of the people of Texas.[11]

If the turnout satisfied Texas leaders, the organizational inadequacies of the army prompted widespread concern. The situation at Goliad in the fall of 1835 revealed acute challenges to the authority of both garrison commanders and any outside leader. Benjamin Fort Smith had succeeded George Collinsworth in command and attempted to operate the fort under the authority of his friend, commander-in-chief Austin, who had ordered its soldiers to remain there in a defensive position. Most of the volunteers preferred the presumed scene of ac-

Table 2. The Army of Texas, 1835: A Profile
(Total No. 1,300)

	Mean	*Median*		*Single*	*Married*
AGE (235)	31.3	31	MARITAL STATUS (742)	50%	50%

BIRTHPLACE (261)	*Total*	*Texas Residents*	*U.S. Volunteers*
Upper South	42%	47%	21%
Lower South	31	31	31
Northern U.S.	15	14	21
Foreign	12	8	27

LENGTH OF TEXAS RESIDENCE (673)

	Date of emigration	*No.*	*%*
11 + years	(before 1825)	94	14
6–10 years	(1825–1829)	108	16
1–5 years	(1830–1834)	222	33
0–1 year	(Jan.–Oct. 1835)	62	9
unknown	(before May 2, 1835)	45	7
U.S. vol.	(after Oct. 1, 1835)	142	21

ORIGIN (820)

Department	*County*	*No.*	*%*
Brazos		420	51
	Austin	65	
	Brazoria	75	
	Colorado	15	
	Gonzales	41	
	Harrisburg	22	
	Jackson	19	
	Matagorda	57	
	Milam	34	
	Mina	37	
	Washington	55	
Béxar		124	15
	Béxar	71	
	Goliad	13	
	Refugio	22	
	San Patricio	8	
	Victoria	10	
Nacogdoches		276	34
	Jasper	35	
	Jefferson	23	
	Liberty	37	
	Nacogdoches	63	
	Red River	6	
	Sabine	21	
	San Augustine	57	
	Shelby	34	

tion, and a sizable group took off for Béxar on October 14 in defiance of the Austin-Smith directives. This split led to a company dissolution and reorganization that included Smith's resignation. His explanation urged Austin to "take warning by this mishap you are not upon a bed of roses—and if you are compeled to stay long at a place; rely upon it, your men will desert you—There is nothing but their honor to govern them—this is in many cases but a cobweb." The fragment that remained in Goliad seemed at first free of dissent, according to newly elected commander Philip Dimitt, but this sense of concert failed to survive the month. On October 29 three officers and three privates mustered themselves out of the detachment and set out for Béxar, "in open contempt" of an Austin order on obedience and desertion that Dimitt read to them. Two weeks later another faction mutinied over the cool reception their commander gave to Coahuila and Texas Governor Viesca, which led the firm Dimitt to declare martial law and in turn generated citizenry protest about his usurpation.[12]

Austin responded by ordering Collinsworth to replace Dimitt, a decision that precipitated an end to any pretense of authority of the "commander in chief" over the Goliad fortress. His action violated the democratic sensibilities of the men, who had elected their garrison commander but had no voice in Austin's selection. In a letter and resolution they lectured the general on their liberties and denied his right to remove their chosen leader. Austin seemed to regard them "like servile dependents," apparently based on the "anti-republican and revolting doctrine, of subjecting them to the unwelcome & unwise, nay, the antipatriotic and despotic command" of one who did not share their vision. The soldiers regarded the General's policy as "tyranny." They refused to "tamely submit . . . to the authority of the Usurper. It is against this that we took the field"; and the volunteers warned ominously, "against . . . the imposition of degradations like this . . . we are ready to fight again." Though in the military, they continued to function as "American freemen . . . [who] can never surrender but with life, the right, to elect, and elect freely, our immediate commander."[13]

Even before receiving this lecture, Austin's frustrations at dealing with the individualistic and democratic precepts of the Army of the People and the ego needs of its various officers led him to advocate both personal and structural changes in the military. On November 3 he wrote to the Consultation "earnestly and pressingly" urging it to establish a regular army under the command of "a Military man of known and tried Talents." Ten days later that political body adopted both aspects of the general's recommendation. Its ordinance creating a regular army established a structure clearly designed to curb the populistic excesses of the existing volunteer forces. The authority of the commander of the new army emanated from the government — he would be appointed by the Consultation, commissioned by the governor, and "subject to the orders of the Governor and Council." The ranks would be filled with men assembled in each municipality by recruitment officers. Though the soldiers retained the right of electing company commanders, the army as a whole was to be "governed by the rules, regulations, and discipline" of its United States counterpart. The day following passage of this military measure, Governor Smith communicated formally the appointment of the regular army major generalship to Houston, charging him to "require all officers and soldiers under your command to be obedient to your orders."[14]

Establishment of the regular army had no immediate impact, because the Consultation refused to clash with the existing volunteer forces. Instead, it resolved that "no obligation can be imposed on them to submit" to outside control and promised to redouble efforts to supply these soldiers. Though the government attempted to assert some judicial power and sought to commission popularly elected officers, Lt. Gov. James W. Robinson also reiterated the assurance that "the General Council do not wish to impose any person upon the army [as Commander], not agreeable to them."[15]

Political officials continued to recognize, in the words of a November 28 report of a committee on the army in the field, "that a great deal of prudence is necessary to keep the army together." This situation frustrated Houston. Officers continued to urge him to facilitate organization of the regular army, and he in turn advised some dramatic steps to accomplish that goal. The major general favored retreating from Béxar and furloughing all but a small body of the men in the hope that a new, disciplined force could be recruited under his command. He also lectured politicians on the failure to appoint enrollment officers, helping to further the quarrel between Smith and the council but having no beneficial results. The fundamental fact that retarded establishment of the regular army was the unwillingness of prospective soldiers to submit to its longer enlistment (two years or for the duration) and sterner discipline. Even more lavish rewards of land bounty failed to attract either Texans or volunteers from the United States. The latter group, as one of their officers explained to Houston, preferred him as a leader but "on no consideration will enter into any service connected with the Regular Army, the name of which is a perfect Bugbear to them."[16]

Plans for other kinds of military organization — militia, cavalry and ranger units, auxiliary volunteer corps, and army of the reserve to be recruited in the United States — remained unimplemented or incomplete in 1835. Texas military fortunes rested in the hands of the raw, poorly drilled, virtually unmanageable Army of the People. Governor Smith echoed the true sentiments of many others when he caustically described it as a "mob"; however, many also acknowledged the capacity of this force for hard fighting. Its long-postponed assault against Béxar on December 5 triumphed five days later. But this victory in arms precipitated an organizational disaster as the tenuously bound units resolved themselves into increasingly smaller factions with quarrelsome leadership. These disorders proved ruinous when Mexico renewed its attacks some three months later.[17]

The initial political failure to assert control over the army weakened efforts to establish unified command between December, 1835, and the following March. Governmental chaos during this period then doomed any prospect for greater unity and in effect stimulated further splintering, as officers claiming authorization from either the governor or the council competed for manpower, provisions, and leadership of campaigns.

The council responded to the Béxar victory on a hopeful note: its December 15 resolution of congratulations endorsed the granting of furloughs to "Citizen Soldiers" and promised to fill their places with a freshly recruited regular army and an auxiliary volunteer corps from the United States. The furloughs merely acknowledged a military reality, since General Burleson had already been granting discharges to all who bothered to ask. During the next two months the government did little to bring order to the ranks of the U.S. volunteers who made up the bulk of the Texas army (see Table 3 below). The council did appoint commissioners to administer oaths to the new enlistees, whereby they swore "true allegiance to the provisional Government of Texas" and obedience to the orders of the governor and appointed officers.[18]

But no financial support or real system of regularity characterized the enrollment process. On the journey to his diplomatic mission in late December, Austin encountered two hundred volunteers at Velasco who had not been "provided for [or] employed." Many recruits wandered around the countryside "on our *own hook*," as one recalled, and failed to receive anything but conflicting advice even when they made personal contact with the governor and the council. Houston discovered rampant discontent among these men who, having been left unorganized and without provisions, had established themselves as what he disparagingly called "Independent Volunteers."[19] By the end of December the government had lost the opportunity to create a more regularized military establishment.

Left thus to their own devices and urged on by the ambitions of prospective leaders, the members of the army continued to assert their democratic spirit. An election in mid-December had replaced Edward J. Burleson with Francis W. Johnson, a brigade commander during the assault. The new general became an immediate figure of controversy. Critics labelled him a usurper and political schemer who obstructed all initiatives that did not serve his interests. Nevertheless, company commanders on Christmas eve polled their men and found them unwilling to give up the right to elect officers or to join in the regular army. They also explicitly reiterated that "in no case, do we consider ourselves subject to variations or any infringement of our privileges" established at the time they had volunteered. A disappointed Houston supporter wrote him that "for fear you would be elected Commander of the Volunteer army," Johnson's supporters had prevented that specific issue from coming to a vote.[20]

All this politicking split the garrison at Béxar. On December 30 Johnson took two-thirds of the three hundred men and the bulk of all available draft animals and supplies and marched southward to begin an expedition against Matamoros. J. C. Neill, the new head of the Béxar command, managed to keep a force together despite chronic shortages of food or pay until he resigned in mid-February on a plea of family illness. He named William B. Travis to assume command, who in turn deferred to the men's democratic notions and ordered an election. Those who had not previously sworn to serve under Travis then voted unanimously for James Bowie, who promptly set off on a "roaring drunk" and overturned the existing civil authority by military force. In protest and in defense of his company command Travis moved it out of town to the Medina River.[21] In a space of slightly over two months after the storming of the city, the Béxar forces had voted themselves into three separate, disputing units. Further splits also occurred among those who congregated in the Goliad-Refugio area.

Ironically, the Matamoros campaign, which contributed much to this divisiveness, had been promoted as a remedy for just such a fate. Prevailing wisdom maintained that the secret to successful employment of volunteer forces lay in keeping them active. The political divisions between the governor and the council dashed any prospect of a united expedition. Johnson first obtained council consent, but it failed to provide him with unrestricted authority, even authorizing James W. Fannin to lead an auxiliary force to the same destination and at one time considering the concentration of all these troops under Houston, an opponent of the whole project. Houston favored a more defensive strategy and chafed at the machinations of "self created officers" and the fact that he still had no army to lead. Governor Smith, likewise objecting to Johnson and Fannin while also smarting over his conflict with the council, dispatched the commander of the regular forces to the Goliad area to "rob them of the army."[22]

By the time Houston arrived (January 17) at the staging point of Goliad, irreparable chaos prevailed. Johnson had earlier without success attempted to replace fortress commander Dimitt; on January 9 a group of volunteers under Johnson's assistant, James Grant, summarily seized the unit's *caballada*. Houston's oratorical skills succeeded in removing all but sixty to seventy men from Johnson and Grant but failed to stem the "Matamoras [*sic*] rage." In late January about the only area of agreement among the contending elements was acknowledgment that disorganization and confusion continued to prevail. The troops also sought to gain reassurances that their rights under the volunteer system would continue to be protected. Houston considered Johnson, Grant, and Fannin all guilty of insubordination, but the council, which suspected the major general because he had sided with Governor Smith, in turn countermanded some of Houston's orders.[23]

Observing the situation from Columbia, George W. Poe wrote to Houston in early February: "unless some measures are taken to reduce both officers & men to obedience . . . the whole will degenerate into 'Independent Volunteers.'" In fact, he but described the existing situation rather than some future prospect. On February 6 an officers meeting at Refugio to resolve the matter of command selected Fannin to lead the Matamoros expedition; Johnson and Grant declined to accede and set off toward Mexico on their own. Acting Governor Robinson wrote to Houston, who had gone east to parlay with the Indians, urging the "speedy organization" of the regular army and assuring him that "all is harmonious" in the Goliad–Refugio–San Patricio region. Such a conclusion ignored the damaging consequences of the month-long upheaval. As one historian observed, "while Fannin to some extent *led* his men, he never *commanded* them."[24] The tragic fate of this army can be traced to a large extent to organizational chaos, which in turn stemmed from both political upheaval and democratically-inspired military procedure.

Unlike in their earlier engagements, Texas armies now suffered from distinct numerical inferiority, for the militant behavior of the Texas people reached its pinnacle in the fall of 1835. Table 3, below, reveals that only slightly more than nine hundred men served in the units stationed at or near Béxar and Goliad, the centers of activity between January and March, 1836. These figures include all who reported for duty of any length at these places during that period. At no time did the Texas forces total that number. Once again, men frequently came and went — sometimes as a result of illness, reassignment to recruitment, or similar responsibilities, but some also were simply A.W.O.L. They also changed companies, volunteered for special duty, or returned home out of frustration with political wrangling and inadequate supply. Therefore, the Texas army could not muster many more than six hundred men when hostilities recommenced in late February, and then the fighting unfolded so rapidly that additional volunteers did not augment the numbers by more than about one hundred at the scenes of action.

Despite some shifting from one garrison to the other, the armies at Goliad and Béxar remained reasonably separate. Although most of the volunteers returned home after the capture of the city or left in late December and early January to participate in the projected Matamoros expedition, at least 86 recruits from the United States either stayed in San Antonio or reported there in early 1836. A total of 245 saw duty for commanders Neill, Bowie, and Travis between January and March, counting those who retired with the first-named of these in early February and those dispatched as messengers and scouts after Santa Anna began the siege. Seventy-two of these were veterans of the 1835 siege and storming of the city. Among the Texans, residents of the Béxar department and Gonzales municipality, in other words those living near the hostilities, predominated.[25]

The volunteers who concentrated in the Goliad–Refugio–San Patricio area functioned under a number of leaders, but for the sake of convenience the force is generally known as Fannin's command. A total of 672 men saw service under him between January and the final demolition of this army at the Goliad massacre in late March, 1836.[26] Though the soldiers transferred at their own or officer's initiatives, the individual companies generally had clear identities. Three units, made up mostly of U.S. recruits from New Orleans who had participated in the Béxar siege, marched south to this location in early January in anticipation of the campaign against Matamoros. A battalion of four companies from Georgia had arrived in the region mostly in late December. Seven other companies also hailed from the United States. Two large ones came from Alabama (arriving in early and mid-January) and two large companies from Kentucky (arriving in late December). One company consisted of stragglers from the ill-fated Tampico expedition out of New Orleans, and two smaller ones of various origins were formed in Texas from volunteers who had no other affiliation. These companies expanded only slightly with Texas volunteers, 41 residents joining the 503 U.S. recruits already enrolled. Dimitt's command largely broke up with the arrival of other commanders claiming more troops and authority over the region, but four predominantly Texas companies (comprised of 76 residents and 27 who arrived after the commencement of hostilities) also served in Fannin's command. Another 25 in various companies cannot be identified as to place of origin.[27]

Analysis of Table 3 provides abundant evidence of the distinctive character of the army that enrolled in the area of Béxar and Goliad between January and March, 1836, in comparison to that of 1835. Just as virtually every class and locale in Texas had supplied volunteers in the fall, so did Texans of varied conditions stay away from the army during the winter. Many settlers no doubt eased their minds with the knowledge that a large number of U.S. recruits who had come in the fall stayed on at the front and that other units raised there also joined them. Well over three-fourths of the nine-hundred-plus soldiers who defended Texas during this period had emigrated after October, 1835. Roots in place and property or responsibilities of family did not bind many of these men. Compared as a group to the earlier army these volunteers were younger by four years, the average age being about 27, and nearly two-thirds of them were single.

Only about one-fourth as many Texans participated as had in the fall, and they came almost exclusively from the most exposed, western region rather than from all parts of Texas as had been the case previously. Fifty-seven percent of the Texas volunteers hailed from the Department of Béxar or the western districts of the Brazos department (Gonzales, Matagorda, and Jackson), even though these areas contained only a small proportion of the total population. Conversely, the Department of Nacogdoches and the eastern (Washington and Harrisburg) and frontier (Milam and Mina) districts of the Department of Brazos produced

Table 3. The Army of Goliad and the Alamo: A Profile
(Total No. 917)

	Mean	*Median*		*Single*	*Married*
AGE (216)	27.9	27	MARITAL STATUS (214)	64%	36%

BIRTHPLACE (204)	*Total*	*Texas Residents*	*U.S. Volunteers*
Upper South	37%	35%	39%
Lower South	23	22	24
Northern U.S.	18	20	16
Foreign	22	23	21

LENGTH OF TEXAS RESIDENCE (793)

	Date of emigration	*No.*	*%*
11 + years	(before 1825)	29	4
6–10 years	(1825–1829)	35	4
1–5 years	(1830–1834)	55	7
0–1 year	(Jan.–Oct. 1835)	20	3
unknown	(before May 2, 1835)	38	5
U.S. vol.	(after Oct. 1, 1835)	616	78

ORIGIN (259)

Department	*County*	*No.*	*%*
Brazos		154	59
	Austin	21	
	Brazoria	18	
	Colorado	1	
	Gonzales	53	
	Harrisburg	3	
	Jackson	6	
	Matagorda	30	
	Milam	6	
	Mina	7	
	Washington	9	
Béxar		59	23
	Béxar	25	
	Goliad	4	
	Refugio	9	
	San Patricio	16	
	Victoria	5	
Nacogdoches		46	18
	Jasper	5	
	Jefferson	0	
	Liberty	10	
	Nacogdoches	17	
	Red River	0	
	Sabine	1	
	San Augustine	8	
	Shelby	5	

but small numbers of winter soldiers. Northern U. S., Texas, and foreign-born recruits represented nearly half of this number, another reflection of their recent-emigrant/western Texas origins. Evidently, the people of Texas became overconfident in their initial victories and quickly weary of war; many began to act the parts of sunshine patriots who placed concerns of self, family, and locale above country in the early days of 1836.[28]

Even before confidence gave way to panic and before the extent of the losses at the Alamo and Goliad became evident, new initiatives emerged in the area of army organization. The structural weaknesses of the past and the sense of crisis with the approach of Santa Anna created a new attitude among politicians. Two days after the Convention declared independence, it resolved to assert unequivocal control over all Texas forces. Recognizing "that there should be an Superior head or Commander in Chief and degrees of Subordination defined established and strictly observed," the Convention placed Maj. Gen. Sam Houston over "all the land forces of the Texian army both regulars, volunteers & militia." The resolution further endowed him "with all the rights privileges & powers due to a commander in chief in the U[.] States of America."[25]

On March 12 the delegates established a militia system that incorporated principles of conscription. Those chosen by a lottery in each district had to muster into the service or hire a substitute; failure to comply was punishable by loss of citizenship and property. First the Convention and then the new cabinet appointed officers to "organize and draft the militia," and some communities, through municipal officials or vigilance committees, independently instituted enrollment procedures. Both the Colorado and Nacogdoches jurisdictions on local initiative recruited conscripted militias before the national law took effect.[30]

With the people in what Acting Secretary of War David Thomas delicately called "a dispersed situation," it proved impossible to enforce the militia law in March and April. Nevertheless, officials compiled muster rolls and lists of those who had shirked military duty to join in the Runaway Scrape, if for no reason other than to enforce the punitive features of the law at the end of the conflict. In proclamations and orders President Burnet, General Houston, and Secretary of War Rusk once again resorted to appeals for voluntary enrollment in the army. But none of their rhetorical devices—calls for vengeance of fallen martyrs, cries of desperation, appeals to patriotism or protection of home, family, and property, or threats of perpetual disgrace and legal retribution—filled the ranks to the satisfaction of its commander. As he prepared for battle on April 19, Houston wrote that "I have looked for reinforcements in vain." He went into action with an army of about nine hundred plus a camp guard, he estimated that a good turnout would have put four thousand men in service.[31]

In one of his proclamations Burnet had urged the gallant men of Texas first to volunteer and then to submit themselves to "subordination and discipline" in camp. Houston attempted to bring order to the unorganized men gathered at Gonzales in early March. He resorted to courts-martial (though he stayed the resulting executions) to accomplish this goal, and some observers expressed satisfaction at the degree of order in the army. Yet, not all the volunteers agreed to enroll in a specific unit, and Houston did not achieve regimental organization until perilously close to battle. Companies commanded by Mosely Baker and Wylie Martin received special assignments because of their leaders' dissension. Officers and men alike, distressed at the failure to stand and fight, gave thought to deposing its major general. Yet, he held the army tenuously together in what one admirer has described as a triumph of individual over mob will.[32]

The exact number of volunteers who served with Houston's army during the months of March and April cannot be calculated. The commander complained frequently about the problem of desertion—some estimates place the maximum strength of his army at 1,600. The figures traditionally cited indicate that only about 900 fought on the Texas side in the April 21 battle, with an additional 250 in the rear at Harrisburg suffering from illness, engaging in the baggage detail, or following disaffected leaders like Baker and Martin. The extant muster rolls and bounty or donation grants for service at San Jacinto (including those stationed at Harrisburg) places the army at 1,282 (see Table 4 below). Even accepting this number (larger than tradition by over 100), it remains true that the Texas forces would have been seriously outnumbered had they faced the massed Mexican army rather than the fragment under Santa Anna on April 20–21.[33] Furthermore, more detailed analysis in Tables 4–7 reveals that Houston was correct in believing that his army fell far short of the potential size that a full turnout from the people of Texas would have produced.

Scholars for years have misconstrued the character of the Texas army that fought at San Jacinto. Pioneering historian Eugene C. Barker acknowledged that the majority of Texans remained "pacific" rather than militant in behavior; however, he also concluded, "it really was the 'old settlers' who did, almost unaided, all the effective fighting," including "practically alone" winning the battle of San Jacinto.[34] In fact, however, the broadly representative group that turned out the previous fall did not return in the spring of 1836 as is evident in Tables 2 and 4. About the same number served under Houston as had enrolled in 1835. Slightly more than one-fifth of each army had come to Texas since October to fight in the war, a figure that could have been much larger had not so many of these men perished at the Alamo and Goliad. Otherwise, Houston's was not the same force that had volunteered in 1835, for the army that did battle in April possessed several distinctive characteristics.

The reverses of February and March had broken resistance in the west—men from the Department of Béxar died in the service, took flight in protection of their families, or made their private peace with the Mexican army. Only 5 percent of Houston's men came from that region, mostly serving with Col. Juan Seguín. Over two-thirds of the volunteers lived in the Department of the Brazos, as opposed to only half the previous fall. The western municipalities of this department, given their heavy losses during the previous month, supplied impressive numbers of soldiers, but most of them came from the area drained by the Brazos river—Brazoria, Austin, and Washington municipalities alone provided over a third of the Texans who served. Proportionately, the frontier districts like Mina and Milam also produced impressive turnouts. To a "redlander" like Houston the fact that fewer from San Augustine municipality served under him than had volunteered in the fall must have been especially galling. In fact, among east Texas areas only Nacogdoches exceeded its previous turnout. Harrisburg had another small contingent in the army, and the Jasper and Shelby districts fell far short of the numbers they provided in the 1835 campaigns. This geographic pattern suggests that personal and familial concerns often triumphed over patriotic impulses—Texans volunteered where the Mexican advance directly threatened their interests. In other places men waited warily at their homesites.

The composition of the Texas army reveals other significant patterns. Many families duplicated the behavior of the Klebergs, who lived about ten miles from San Felipe. After conferring, they decided that the father would join the women and children as they fled eastward, while the younger men went off to military duty. As a result of these kinds of decisions, the army was on the average only twenty-eight years old and was comprised primarily of single men (60 percent). Furthermore, those

Table 4. The Army of San Jacinto: A Profile
(Total No. 1,282)

	Mean	*Median*			*Single*	*Married*
AGE (360)	28.1	28	MARITAL STATUS (645)		60%	40%

BIRTHPLACE (467)	*Total*	*Texas Residents*	*U.S. Volunteers*
Upper South	45%	46%	43%
Lower South	25	26	22
Northern U.S.	19	19	18
Foreign	5 [Tex. 5%]	4 [Tex. 6%]	16

LENGTH OF TEXAS RESIDENCE (907)

	Date of emigration	*No.*	*%*
11 + years	(before 1825)	80	9
6–10 years	(1825–1829)	134	15
1–5 years	(1830–1834)	311	34
0–1 year	(Jan.–Oct. 1835)	151	17
unknown	(before May 2, 1835)	39	4
U.S. vol.	(after Oct. 1, 1835)	192	21

ORIGIN (852)

Department	*County*	*No.*	*%*
Brazos		572	67
	Austin	92	
	Brazoria	103	
	Colorado	26	
	Gonzales	34	
	Harrisburg	28	
	Jackson	16	
	Matagorda	25	
	Milam	57	
	Mina	79	
	Washington	112	
Béxar		45	5
	Béxar	31	
	Goliad	3	
	Refugio	3	
	San Patricio	4	
	Victoria	4	
Nacogdoches		235	28
	Jasper	8	
	Jefferson	23	
	Liberty	47	
	Nacogdoches	79	
	Red River	6	
	Sabine	19	
	San Augustine	43	
	Shelby	10	

who had been in Texas for a long period of time often looked after their well-developed property interests instead of volunteering. Rather than representing the "old settlers" that Barker saw as the core of the Texas forces, the soldiers of San Jacinto had shallow Texas roots. The median date of emigration of Houston's army was 1834, two years later than that of the recruits of the previous fall. Fully one-sixth of the army had emigrated to Texas between January and October of the previous year.[35]

In addition to those who joined Houston's army, over 600 other men served in March and April 1836 with companies that did not make it to the climactic battle (see Table 5). These included 47 in the Jasper Volunteers enrolled by veteran Capt. James Chesshire on March 23, a company of 53 from San Augustine raised by W. D. Ratliff in early April, 73 members of the Nacogdoches Mounted Volunteers led by Capt. James Smith with service beginning on April 11, a Mississippi unit of 24 led by John A. Quitman that arrived at Nacogdoches on April 12, and 20 in ranger or other frontier units commanded by Sterling C. Robertson, Silas Parker, and Byrd Lockhart. Most (406) of the soldiers received bounty warrants for military service in the spring of 1836 with no indication of their company or place of service; 128 of these cannot be identified by other biographical information either, making this group profile (in Table 5) less definitive than those compiled for the other army units.[36]

Of those whose origins are known, about one-third had just come to Texas from the United States. Recent emigrants also dominated the ranks in these otherwise varied units, the average date of emigration being 1834 for the Texans. Single men predominated (54 percent), but otherwise these miscellaneous spring recruits differed from those who enrolled under Houston. Many of their companies acted like home guards and were formed in the eastern part of the new nation, namely in Nacogdoches, San Augustine, and Liberty municipalities. Adding the number from Harrisburg to those from the Department of Nacogdoches, the east Texans formed the majority. The average age of thirty-four suggests also that these companies made up a kind of last line of defense, though it seems unlikely that they could have stemmed a Mexican invasion without a common leader or even location.

Further insight into popular behavior in regard to military service can be derived from analyzing the data in Tables 6 and 7. The first of these tabulations details the characteristics of the four hundred men who might be termed the superpatriots—veterans of 1835 service who

Table 5. Other Texas Soldiers, January to May, 1836: A Profile
(Total No. 623)

	Mean	Median		Single	Married
AGE (68)	34.9	34	MARITAL STATUS (272)	54%	46%

BIRTHPLACE (105)	Total	Texas Residents	U.S. Volunteers
Upper South	37%	54%	15%
Lower South	39	31	50
Northern U.S.	20	14	28
Foreign	4	2	7

LENGTH OF TEXAS RESIDENCE (359)

	Date of emigration	No.	%
11 + years	(before 1825)	24	7
6–10 years	(1825–1829)	40	11
1–5 years	(1830–1834)	99	28
0–1 year	(Jan.–Oct. 1835)	53	15
unknown	(before May 2, 1835)	33	9
U.S. vol.	(after Oct. 1, 1835)	110	31

ORIGIN (328)

Department	County	No.	%
Brazos		188	57
	Austin	35	
	Brazoria	17	
	Colorado	6	
	Gonzales	6	
	Harrisburg	31	
	Jackson	7	
	Matagorda	11	
	Milam	30	
	Mina	18	
	Washington	27	
Béxar		7	2
	Béxar	2	
	Goliad	0	
	Refugio	1	
	San Patricio	2	
	Victoria	2	
Nacogdoches		133	41
	Jasper	12	
	Jefferson	6	
	Liberty	21	
	Nacogdoches	35	
	Red River	5	
	Sabine	13	
	San Augustine	34	
	Shelby	7	

Table 6. Veterans in the Army of 1836: A Profile
(Total No. 398)

	Mean	Median		Single	Married
AGE (126)	29.9		MARITAL STATUS (189)	58%	42%

BIRTHPLACE (152)   *Total*

Upper South	72	(47%)
Lower South	38	(25%)
Northern U.S.	24	(16%)
Foreign	18	(12%)

LENGTH OF TEXAS RESIDENCE (322)

	Date of emigration	No.	%
11 + years	(before 1825)	34	11
6–10 years	(1825–1829)	39	12
1–5 years	(1830–1834)	108	34
0–1 year	(Jan.–Oct. 1835)	40	12
unknown	(before May 2, 1835)	16	5
U.S. vol.	(after Oct. 1, 1835)	85	26

ORIGIN (330)

Department	County	No.	%
Brazos		209	63
	Austin	38	
	Brazoria	39	
	Colorado	11	
	Gonzales	24	
	Harrisburg	10	
	Jackson	7	
	Matagorda	22	
	Milam	16	
	Mina	19	
	Washington	23	
Béxar		36	11
	Béxar	18	
	Goliad	4	
	Refugio	10	
	San Patricio	1	
	Victoria	3	
Nacogdoches		85	26
	Jasper	9	
	Jefferson	2	
	Liberty	12	
	Nacogdoches	27	
	Red River	2	
	Sabine	2	
	San Augustine	22	
	Shelby	9	

Table 7. The Army of 1835, Single Service: A Profile
(Total No. 902)

	Mean	*Median*			*Single*	*Married*
AGE (109)	33		MARITAL STATUS (553)		47%	53%

BIRTHPLACE (109)   *Total*

Upper South	38	(35%)
Lower South	43	(40%)
Northern U.S.	15	(14%)
Foreign	13	(12%)

LENGTH OF TEXAS RESIDENCE (351)

	Date of emigration	*No.*	*%*
11 + years	(before 1825)	60	17
6–10 years	(1825–1829)	69	20
1–5 years	(1830–1834)	114	32
0–1 year	(Jan.–Oct. 1835)	22	6
unknown	(before May 2, 1835)	29	8
U.S. vol.	(after Oct. 1, 1835)	57	16

ORIGIN (490)

Department	*County*	*No.*	*%*
Brazos		211	43
	Austin	27	
	Brazoria	36	
	Colorado	4	
	Gonzales	17	
	Harrisburg	12	
	Jackson	12	
	Matagorda	35	
	Milam	18	
	Mina	18	
	Washington	32	
Béxar		88	18
	Béxar	53	
	Goliad	9	
	Refugio	12	
	San Patricio	7	
	Victoria	7	
Nacogdoches		191	39
	Jasper	26	
	Jefferson	21	
	Liberty	25	
	Nacogdoches	36	
	Red River	4	
	Sabine	19	
	San Augustine	35	
	Shelby	25	

volunteered again, to fight at the Alamo, Goliad, or San Jacinto, or joined other companies in March and April, 1836. Table 7 reveals that over nine hundred men who had responded to the initial call to arms failed to reenroll in any of the units raised in the winter and spring of 1836. Compared to the veterans who avoided military service, those who reenrolled (Table 6) were more likely to be young and single, with shallower Texas roots (over one-fourth being U.S. volunteers) and origins primarily in the Department of the Brazos, the area colonized by Austin. Further, most veterans, well over two-thirds in fact, did not join for a second stint.[37] Believing, perhaps, that they had already done their duty while many Texans had shirked theirs, these men no doubt had little trouble with matters of conscience. Older by five years than those who served under Houston that spring, these veterans had more to protect in terms of families and properties acquired through a comparatively long stay in Texas, with the average tenure being over five years and with one-third of the group being residents for seven years or longer. Many of these vets hailed from east Texas and apparently planned not to enter the army again even if the war came to their doorsteps. This behavior may have seemed appropriate when they saw their roads filled that spring with central Texans running away rather than fighting for family, property, or country.

Table 8 provides composite data on the overall make-up of the army of the Texas Revolution. The figure 3,685 is an unduplicated total; that is, those who served on more than one battlefront are counted only once. This total number was not paltry for a new country with a total population of around 40,000; however, at least 40 percent of those enrolled whose origins can be ascertained had come as volunteers from the United States after the fighting began. That figure suggests that the combined municipalities of Texas produced just over 2,000 soldiers, or one recruit for every twenty residents. Further, these volunteers never demonstrated a willingness to join the regular army for a long enrollment or even to sacrifice their democratic structure to the imperative of unified military leadership. These factors meant that no single commander ever led into battle more than one-fourth of the total number of 3,685 who served the Texas cause. For a people of such fabled militance, the Texans turned out for army duty in this period of crisis at a low rate of participation, and their equally fabled sensibilities on matters of individual liberty hampered the establishment of an effective military organization. Otherwise, the turnout of U.S. and Texas volunteers combined might have been sufficient to offset any

Table 8. The Army of the Texas Revolution: A Composite Profile
(Total No. 3,685)

	Mean	Median			Single	Married
AGE (750)	29.4		MARITAL STATUS (1,659)		55%	45%

BIRTHPLACE (867)	Total	Texas Residents	U.S. Volunteers
Upper South	42%	46%	31%
Lower South	29	29	29
Northern U.S.	18	18	19
Foreign	11	7	22

LENGTH OF TEXAS RESIDENCE (2,399)

	Date of emigration	No.	%
11 + years	(before 1825)	197	8.2
6–10 years	(1825–1829)	277	11.5
1–5 years	(1830–1834)	579	24.1
0–1 year	(Jan.–Oct. 1835)	243	10.1
unknown	(before May 2, 1835)	139	5.8
U.S. vol.	(after Oct. 1, 1835)	964	40.2

ORIGIN (1910)

Department	County	No.	%
Brazos		1,105	57.8
	Austin	161	8.4
	Brazoria	174	9.1
	Colorado	37	1.9
	Gonzales	109	5.7
	Harrisburg	72	3.8
	Jackson	40	2.1
	Matagorda	100	5.2
	Milam	111	5.8
	Mina	121	6.3
	Washington	180	9.4
Béxar		199	10.4
	Béxar	111	5.8
	Goliad	16	.8
	Refugio	25	1.3
	San Patricio	29	1.5
	Victoria	18	.9
Nacogdoches		606	31.7
	Jasper	51	2.7
	Jefferson	50	2.6
	Liberty	103	5.4
	Nacogdoches	165	8.6
	Red River	15	.8
	Sabine	52	2.7
	San Augustine	120	6.3
	Shelby	50	2.6

disparity in centralist strength — Santa Anna brought around 6,000 troops in 1836.[38]

Houston's achievement in keeping his disputatious men together did not survive the battle of San Jacinto. As he had feared all along, the army suffered almost as much disruption from victory as it would have from defeat. Perhaps the general had no choice but to concede to mob spirit in allowing the men to divide the Mexican plunder among themselves. This "produced more disorganization amongst the men," according to his successor, Rusk. As the new commander recalled, the cabinet appointed him in the belief that he had the best chance to keep the army together. He accomplished this task "with the utmost difficulty" and not without some setbacks. About three-fourths of the group that fought on April 21 had been Texas citizen-soldiers on short-term or unspecified enlistments. They soon drifted off, leaving the army with about half its battlefield strength (or less than one-third of the 1,282 who received credit for San Jacinto service) by mid-May and its leader alarmed for fear of a Mexican counterattack.

During June the ranks filled again, primarily with additional U.S. volunteers, to between 1,300 and 1,700 in early July and perhaps as many as 2,500 in 53 companies over the next two months. Over 1,800 of that number (or nearly three-fourths) were men who had come to Texas since Santa Anna's defeat. These new arrivals had headstrong, ambitious leaders; one, Brig. Gen. Thomas J. Green, held rank equal to Rusk. Nevertheless, Green, for one, preferred a larger and unruly force to "this eternal discharging and disbanding."[39] To Rusk's advantage the army was concentrated rather than dispersed, and his disposition, which included what one veteran called an "easy familiarity with the privates," won the confidence of the men. A democratic style made Rusk popular but did not help his authority. Disorder frequently prevailed, and some companies functioned in an independent manner which he found galling.[40]

Rusk tolerated these unmilitary procedures but engaged in a running battle with the cabinet over its shortcomings, especially in the areas of communication, diplomacy, recruitment, and supply. On June 11 he wrote Burnet a stinging letter outlining these complaints and, further, charging him with failure to "produce System and order" in the military. The general and other zealots favored expanding the army through conscriptive methods. The president hesitated because of financial exigencies but also out of fear that a strong force posed dangers to the principles of liberal government. Under Burnet's leadership Texas had no consistent policy. In early June he ordered the recruitment agent in New Orleans to discourage discreetly any further embarkation to Texas of the U.S. volunteers assembled there. Then, in the face of an apparent renewal of hostilities with Mexico, Burnet recanted on demilitarization and even ordered the resumption of conscription on June 20. He expressed optimism concerning operation of the militia law, but its most notable effect was to bring a large number of substitutes into the army for the first time.[41]

Omnipresent tensions between the army and President Burnet ultimately came to focus on the ultimate issue — civilian control. On July 1 he attempted to rein in the military by appointing as major general the popular hero of San Jacinto, Mirabeau B. Lamar. Burnet naively believed that this maneuver would "meet with general satisfaction" among the soldiers, a hope that failed to reckon with the self-governing tradition of the Texas army. Officers and troops alike assembled to protest the appointment, not out of objection to Lamar per se but in response to Burnet's transparent effort to assert cabinet authority over them. Some proclaimed the constitutional theory that Houston could only be removed by the sovereign equivalent of the convention which named him. Maj. William P. Miller stated more forthrightly that the Lamar nomination was "contrary to the wishes of the army in full meeting assembled." General Green protested that this act would give the President "more power than the Kings of France & England."[42]

Lamar had delayed his departure to the Victoria headquarters for long enough that he knew of this unfavorable reaction, but some of his correspondence encouraged him to think that the protest meeting represented only a willful minority of the total army. This evidence, coupled with a faith in his own popularity, led Lamar to demand another assembling of the entire army. He spoke on his own exploits, promotion from the ranks, and desire to lead men again in battle. His oratory was rebutted by Rusk, Green, and Felix Huston. A polling took place on the question of whether to receive Lamar as commander in chief, with men moving bodily to one side or the other; he lost by an estimated vote of 179 to 1,500. Even so, the would-be major general apparently obtained Rusk's reluctant surrender of command of all but Green's brigade, which remained in what Lamar considered a state of "rebellion." He threatened courts-martial but then retired in the face of continued and overwhelming defiance, leaving Rusk still in command.[43]

The army of the summer of 1836 retained the same spirit of democracy and independence from civil government with which the Army of the People had begun the war the previous October. Further, it grew to an unprecedented size with centrality of location and a higher measure of united leadership than at any time in the war. This achievement occurred at precisely the time that Texas stood in the least need of such a force for its security. Instead, the army gained the power to pose a threat to civil order while also serving as a force for revolutionary action.

8. The Texas Army

A FORCE FOR REVOLUTION

The democratic but often chaotic nature of the Texas army produced two major behavioral characteristics: a penchant toward disorderly conduct, and a pattern of political activism. Both of these expressions made the army a force for revolution, contributing to the upheaval of the times and pushing the cause in more radical directions. The individualistic character and libertarian ethos resulted in massive discipline problems but also politicized the army. Considering themselves to be in some ways the truest embodiment of the sovereign people, the soldiers debated every political issue and generally resolved on the most advanced positions. The army thus placed itself in the forefront of the movement for independence, against the manipulations of wealthy speculators, in favor of chastising those it considered slackers (including most Tejanos), and, of course, for guarding the liberal distributions of land to veterans at the expense of large empresario accumulations.

The tendency toward disorderly conduct challenged army officers from the moment that recruits began to gather in October, 1835. General Austin's initial regulations emphasized the need for order. He explicitly prohibited "riotous conduct and noisy clamorous talk," backed by threats of courts martial and arbitrary punishment.[1] Similar pronouncements from subsequent leaders during the remainder of the war reveal a failure to compel obedience. Essentially, the Texas soldiers could not accept the premise that a war for freedom could require suppression of individual liberties. Instead, the volunteers maintained an antipathy for military regiment. As one stationed at Goliad wrote, "we have experienced from the present Comandant [Philip Dimitt] nothing but tyranny and oppression." This led the recruit to question "what we are fighting for, whether to establish Despotism or the liberties and rights of man?"[2]

One serious problem of control evolved from the tendency to extend the electoral principle of the democratic army organization. The possibility of promotion kindled political ambition. Among Austin's problems as commander, according to his nephew, was "aspiring men to deal with." Six months after his resignation, when he returned from a diplomatic mission, Austin still recalled that part of his experience as a general. Writing at a time that Mexico appeared ready to renew its offensive, the former commander urged his cousin in New Orleans to recruit a company but cautioned: "impress it on those who come . . . that they cannot be Generals, Colonels, Majors etc."[3]

Those with leadership aspirations had many issues to focus the attention of the troops, for the men generally expected to have a voice on everything, including tactics and strategy. The 1835 campaign against the centralists at Béxar became a mess of confusion because the military could not reach a consensus on whether to launch an assault on the city. After weeks of irresolution, on November 21 Austin believed he had a sufficient number committed to the attack that he "issued a positive order to storm at daylight [the next day], but on trial I found it impossible to get half the men willing for the measure, and it was abandoned from necessity." He went on to bemoan the inadequacies of the "volunteer sistem," which produced so many difficulties as to wear him out. He sought rest by returning to political assignment.[4]

The army also had a manic-depressive quality. Austin's successor, Edward Burleson, gave another order to attack in early December but cancelled it, apparently because a popular consensus still had not been achieved. The officers then voted to abandon the lines and retreat, but this decision led to what one participant described as a "mutiny." Instead of obeying orders, about half the army "marched out and declared their intention of storming the fort that night. Many of the officers made speeches against the project, friends begged and entreated others not to throw away their lives foolishly, &c &c — all was in vain." Some withdrew into a reserve force, but the remainder under Ben Milam launched an assault on December 5. Following their victory, the Texas troops even voted on the treaty that set forth the terms of the centralist capitulation on December 11.[5]

The democratic process regarding military tactics did not always lead to successful results. The aborted Matamoros expedition derived impetus from its popularity with the men but had only divisive consequences. The remnants of forces raised for this campaign gathered at Goliad under Fannin in February, 1836. They devoted much energy to debating strategy and discussing the demerits of their commander, which "caused a corresponding depression of his mind," in the words of one of the few survivors. With some men determined not to abandon the fort, Fannin fatally delayed making a decision. Even in the midst of a losing battle on the poorly selected ground at Coleto the possibility of a saving retreat was lost because the soldiers voted against abandoning the wounded. Having witnessed the malaise caused by this endless tactical debating in the ranks, Houston stubbornly and against tradition refused until the eve of battle to hold any councils of war. The men generally obeyed his orders to retreat, but amidst considerable "discontent in the lines," as the commander himself once candidly wrote. Many believed that the army would have dissolved rather than retreat beyond the San Jacinto, and the desire of the men to bring on an engagement entered into Houston's decision to stand and fight.[6]

On a great variety of issues the volunteers challenged the authority of their commanders—demands for improving discipline became the standard lament of virtually all who served as officers. But those in authority responded ineffectively, as they held position at the sufferance of their men. Although Houston issued blunt, threatening orders on the matter of discipline, those of other commanders had more of an apologetic tone. A general order of Stephen F. Austin, for example, began by explaining that "the interests of the Country the success of the Campaign and the Safety and Honor of the Army require that order and discipline should be observed so far as it is possible to do so." He ended with a disclaimer: "The Commander in Chief has no higher ambition than the interests of the Country."[7]

Politicians and officers alike proposed solutions to the disorderly character of the army. Consultation President Branch T. Archer recommended a military legal code; others sought improvement in the commander's staff. More insightful observers recognized that disciplinary problems derived from the character of the troops and structure of the military. These critics generally favored establishment of a regular army. Fannin held this opinion. In complete frustration he wrote to the acting governor in mid-February: "Stir up the people, but do not allow them to come into camp unless *organized*. I never wish to see an election in a camp where I am responsible in any manner."[8]

The soldiers' democratic attitude meant that obedience depended ultimately on the confidence that they placed in their officers. Authority required perpetual reaffirmation; for this reason, officers experienced frequent crises of command which they resolved by a variety of methods from altercations to patriotic appeals. Even Houston, made suddenly popular among the men as a result of the San Jacinto victory, acknowledged its post-battle mood of "dissatisfaction" and pled that it relinquish whatever ill will had been directed at him. As he departed from Texas to receive treatment for his wound, the major general asked the troops to "render obedience to the commands of their officers" as a necessary part of their soldierly duties. Houston's plea did not end the problem. In June an alarmed member of the Newport (Virginia) Rifle Company wrote to Rusk to explain that the men "will obey no command emanating from" their previously elected captain because he had lost their respect. The correspondent had attempted to take over but admitted, "I can enforce no discipline, no order." He held the captain partly to blame but acknowledged that the troops "have no disposition some of them to obey any orders."[9]

Contemporary observers confirmed the judgment that members of the Texas army by character made disorderly soldiers. A friend wrote Stephen F. Austin in early December that "I have heard with pleasure of Your return from Our Army, knowing as I do the materials of which the Army is composed, I mean the insubordination, and the impossibility of keeping up anything like discipline, in the absence of all Law." After a few days experience among the settlers who had formed themselves into an army at Goliad, another observer concluded that the Texans made uniquely insubordinate soldiers. He warned Houston that even previous experience with militia did not prepare him for the trials of leadership here: "I assure you such materials is not [present elsewhere] on earth."[10] Even their appearance celebrated this sense of personal independence. Generally, they lacked military demeanor. As one veteran described the soldiers, their clothing was of various colors, footwear was usually shoes or moccasins rather than boots (few wore socks), and headgear ranged from sombreros to coonskin caps to tall "beegum" hats." If armed, they arrived in camp bearing a variety of rifles and even shotguns.[11]

When the character of the volunteers came in for praise, such comments usually centered on their fighting qualities. Houston wrote, "No men are more patriotic or brave on God's earth, than what the boys of Texas are." This reputation stayed with the Texas citizen soldier for years, as reflected by the wry assessment reputed to Zachary Taylor: "On the day of battle I am glad to have Texas soldiers with me for they are brave and gallant, but I never want to see them before or afterwards, for they are too hard to control."[12]

Although the army gained large numbers of U.S. volunteers especially between December and March and again in the summer of 1836, changing composition did not dramatically alter its character. These wartime immigrants may have been somewhat more rowdy if only because they lacked responsibilities to family and restraints of property ownership in Texas. The people of Texas both welcomed and feared the U.S. recruits—their receptions varied with the fortunes of war. At times of crisis the emphasis was placed on the gallantry, chivalry, and nobility of their motives. "No sordid or mercenary considerations have induced them to leave their homes and share our fate," gushed Governor Smith in November, 1835. At times President Burnet reiterated this view, but he also privately expressed reservations about flooding "our country with an unprofitable tribe of needy adventurers." In the midst of postwar depression a resident of Columbia described the character of the U.S. volunteers in even more disparaging terms: "They were generally collected from the very dregs of cities and towns, where they had obtained a scanty living by pelf and petty gambling. They are the most miserable wretches that the world ever produced."[13]

Actually, the impressions of visitors, including the soldiers themselves, suggest that no single attribute characterized the U.S. volunteers. Some sought refuge from the law or had previous courts-martial. Others came attracted by the promise of revenge for their fallen countrymen or the prospect of wealth and a good climate. Often they were "animated," in the words of volunteer John S. Brooks, "by one spirit, defiance to tyrants—and our Watch word is 'Texas and Glory.' Our war cry is 'Liberty or Death.'" He expressed sympathy with the Texas cause as representing the struggle of the weak and oppressed. Yet, Brooks later wrote candidly, *"I am a soldier of fortune."*[14] Long-time resident Noah Smithwick also confirmed the polyglot nature of the army. It contained citizen soldiers who came in defense of their country, "another class" from the United States to aid their "countrymen," some motivated by love of adventure, and others "actuated by no higher principle than prospective plunder." In his view, the latter posed the greatest disciplinary problem and the Texas settlers the least, but in fact none of these groups meekly accepted the constraints of military life.[15]

Their commanders came to agree that activity served as the best antidote for the turbulent potential of the soldiers. R. R. Royall, after only a brief military experience, also expressed this opinion. He warned Houston that, regardless of whether the soldiers were "men of good fortune . . . they have interest in our cause for (self interest which with few exceptions Govern all mankind) fame or aggrandizement." Idleness invariably caused "disorder, disease and mutiny . . . but show them the way to fame and you may command them to the Canon's mouth."[16]

Unfortunately for its leaders, the Texas army, like all others, spent much time in various degrees of inactivity. During these lengthy periods the soldiers behaved in a boisterous and often disorderly manner. Observers at the time and since have disagreed in assigning blame for the insubordinate behavior of the Texas armies. Historian Harbert Davenport ascribed it to "the unwillingness, and inability, of the average frontiersman to subject himself to military command." This echoed the views of beleaguered commanders like Austin and Fannin who explained that dissension and disciplinary problems arose because the soldiers would not accept what the Goliad officer called "reasonable authority." President Burnet also argued that "intemperate and irrational" episodes arose inevitably in volunteer forces."[17]

This lament could be regarded as self-fulfilling prophecy, and indeed, critics of the Texas army blamed its disciplinary weaknesses on inadequate rules and organization by weak, popularity-seeking officers. Some leaders did in fact struggle harder than others to suppress the libertarian manners of volunteers. At Béxar J. C. Neill arrested and confined a soldier for refusal to obey orders, even though the culprit threatened violent resistance. Still, one historian regards Neill's army as having been in a virtual state of mutiny in January, 1836.[18]

Similar dynamics existed in the army led by Sam Houston in March and April, 1836. He repeatedly issued orders aimed at instilling subordination. While the army halted at the Brazos during its retreat, he even court-martialled a sentry who had left his post to gather wood. Houston went through a charade of preparing a grave and coffin and assembling a firing squad in front of the entire army before granting a last-second reprieve. The general took pride in having "under the most disadvantageous circumstances, kept an army together" without "even murmuring or insubordination." Others who viewed this force gave it and Houston lower marks for discipline. Aide George W. Hockley claimed that the men had been reduced to obedience, but four days before the battle of San Jacinto he still wrote of complete organization and discipline in the future tense. This letter was in part a reply to a scathing indictment written on April 9 by Maj. James Hazard Perry, who had been in the Texas service since November. He maintained that "these men are entirely without discipline" due to their poor leadership. The Texas forces resembled "an ordinary mob" more than an army. "Indeed," Perry went on, "in an Election riot in the United States I have seen the contending parties much better organized."[19]

One clearly debilitating feature of the Texas army was its irregularity of enlistment and propensity for desertion. The volunteers commonly made no commitment for a specific enlistment and considered themselves at liberty to depart as circumstances dictated. Concerns for family welfare and the failure of their commanders to employ them in actual *fighting* prompted many to return home. Often they "facetiously remarked," as one veteran of the Béxar siege recalled, that they were "going after that cannon" which the officers had deemed necessary for a successful assault. Subsequent to the engagement, most of the volunteers left with their officers' consent. Years later Ignacio Espinosa replied testily to an interrogation about why he had left the Texas service in December, 1835: "because we had joined as volunteers. Because we were all honorably discharged, we had performed the duties which we had volunteered [for,] to rid the Country from a Tyrants rule."[20]

The problem of desertion occurred less frequently among units recruited from the United States. These men had nothing in Texas to protect. However, the army raised in the spring of 1836 under Houston's command repeated the pattern of the earlier volunteer army. On March 15, only a few days after he arrived, the general reported twenty desertions. He asserted a determination to apprehend, try, and punish the guilty parties, not only to keep up military morale but to prevent spreading the panic. Nonetheless, battlefield reverses and Houston's resulting retreat led to a constant stream of departures from his army. Those who hesitated long enough to seek permission pled the necessity of caring for helpless families. The commander ordered out patrols to arrest deserters and to conscript those who avoided military service, and he issued appeals to remain in the service as the best means of protecting home and loved ones. These efforts failed to stem the tide — he lost hundreds to desertion during March and April.[21]

His replacement, General Rusk, expressed fear that the ranks had been so depleted as to endanger the security of the victorious army.

Though he frequently refuted the popular conclusion that the war had ended, Rusk wrote, "[my] expresses are drowned by the voice of deserters who cry peace peace." His plight was made worse by officers who discharged troops with the excuse that enlistments were up. Rusk estimated that one hundred had deserted by May 18, not counting those who "have served out their time and demand as a matter of right their discharges." He dealt more severely (through arrests, courts-martial, and threatened executions) with the problem of desertion once U.S. volunteers made up the bulk of his army in the summer of 1836.[22]

Those who stayed in the army generally displayed a spirit of freedom and personal indulgence against which their commanders struggled with inconsiderable success. Austin's earliest orders catalogued a number of prohibited activities which nevertheless continued under his leadership and his successors. "Promiscuous shooting," as historian Eugene C. Barker described it, headed the list. Some of the soldiers gave up this pastime in a serious but clumsy adaptation to military regimen, recalled a veteran of the siege, even though to do so was "uncongenial to their temperament and training." Another of these units, the New Orleans Greys, ignored roll call and spent their time riding and hunting "about as we pleased." These habits became so normal that Houston later cited the fact that no guns had been fired in his camp for two days as evidence of his success in bringing order to the army. However, in the last hours before battle on April 21 the men discharged weapons (so as to have fresh charges) in open defiance of the commander.[23]

Another custom that troubled the commanders was what Austin called "riotous conduct and noisy clamorous talk." A veteran of over two months of camp life described with pride the attitude of the Goliad defenders in early March. Despite dissension against Fannin, hard work in building fortifications, and inadequate food, "nothing can depress their ardour." "I have never seen such men as this army is composed of," he boasted, because, even after a day's labor, at night the camp rang with sounds of "the boys crowing, gobling, barking, laughing and singing." Their spirit sometimes erupted as rowdy behavior, especially during lax times. A Mexican prisoner wrote in amazement about a Galveston Island fist fight that turned into a general melee engulfing even the commanders. Later that summer the officers themselves initiated such fights, much to the diversion of the soldiers.[24]

While inactivity contributed to the potential for disorder, the Texans could also be demoralized by victory. Members of the assault on

Béxar plundered Mexican property and left the army for home with their booty before Christmas, 1835. At San Jacinto the victors killed prisoners in violation of Houston's orders, behaved in such a careless manner as almost to set fire to a supply of powder, and continued their revelry by searching for Santa Anna's treasury. Once found, they more or less insisted on an irregular division of the spoils of war; then they set out to redistribute the funds in the form of impromptu "gambling establishments" that Rusk had difficulty suppressing.[25]

The potential for excess increased substantially when the army found an opportunity to indulge its thirst for whiskey. Consumption of alcohol comprised such a regular part of camp routine that it attracted little comment except when it spilled over in the form of disorderly behavior. A new Illinois recruit had just joined John Shackelford's "Red Rover" company in the Goliad region when he saw a group of "tipsy" soldiers become embroiled in a "violent quarrel." The incident nearly became a knife-and-gun fight before the captain squelched it. Given this first impression, the soldier later expressed some surprise that the men actually possessed pleasant, rational demeanors under other circumstances. Some observers attributed most of the inebriated revelry to the "rabble" from the United States who landed in Texas in possession of ample supplies of whiskey and in a mood to raise hell. However, the potential for drunken excess was confined to no single classification. A celebrated incident occurred in Béxar in mid-February when James Bowie took command from J. C. Neill. The famous officer himself led his men in a general assault on local property and civil authority, including a jail delivery. When Judge Seguín objected, Bowie called for reinforcements from the Alamo. "They immediately paraded in the square, under arms, in a tumultuous and disorderly manner," according to the disgusted post adjutant, who attributed the episode to "Bowie, himself, and many of his men, being drunk."[26]

No single manifestation of disciplinary problems among Texas soldiers attracted more condemnation from the authorities than alcohol consumption. The army had been assembled only a few days before Austin began suggesting that whiskey be eliminated from its list of supplies. Soon he wrote to the civil government: "'In the name of Almighty God send no more ardent spirits to this camp—if any is on the road turn it back, or have the head knocked out.'" This plea became a refrain with many subsequent commanders, including the last of the revolutionary period, Thomas J. Rusk. Houston issued the most forthright orders on this matter, though some expressed incredulity because of the General's own notorious and prodigious thirst. Nevertheless, he forbade the presence of liquor within ten miles of camp and ordered the destruction of all spirits located in the path of his army. His unswerving position failed to win over the support of all his men. One officer accused the general of substituting opium for alcohol in his own habit. Among his subordinates, Capt. John Bird discovered a barrel of whiskey while on a scouting excursion and his company "staid with it to take care of it" in the carefully chosen words of one soldier. The problem existed away from the front as well. Though civil authority largely collapsed during the war, the Nacogdoches Ayuntamiento bestirred itself in February, 1836, to enact an ordinance forbidding the sale of ardent spirits to members of the army.[27]

Civilian complaints about disorderly soldier behavior concerned other matters in addition to alcoholic revelry. Until March of 1836 Anglo citizens usually encountered soldiers only as they travelled to the front. Often communities staged welcomes and other forms of celebration, but sometimes military-civilian relations took a less pleasant turn. The first publicized incident occurred at Gonzales in early November, 1835, when a company of troops from Ayish Bayou passed through on its way to Béxar. Populated largely by women and children since most of the physically fit men had left with the army, the town could put up little defense when transient soldiers formed themselves into a mob led by Charlton Thompson. The ruffians broke into all the houses and stole money, clothing, and any other valuables they wanted. They subjected women to insulting language and inflicted beatings on men who showed any signs of resistance. Dr. L. Smithers would have been killed for daring to occupy and presumably to protect the Dickerson household, had it not been for the last-minute intervention of one member of the company. Smithers and John Fisher, secretary of the ironically-named committee of safety of Gonzales, both wrote to Austin in protest. They concluded that the demoralization of the Ayish Bayou troops exceeded in ferocity anything that they had expected from Mexicans, "comanshee[s]," or even "Canebols."[28]

Complaints about this and perhaps other similar incidents reached San Felipe, where the *Telegraph* called for the government to establish "some plan to restrain the licentiousness of the troops, while not engaged in actual service." Yet, as the newspaper noted, the volunteers marched to the army prior to being organized; no governmental authority existed to provide "restraint" or "proper punishment," and they had to help themselves to food, fodder, and other provisions along their routes. These circumstances of soldiering in Texas clearly had some bearing on troop misconduct. In the case of the Gonzales episode both Houston and Archer urged that the accused receive bail and civilian trials because they were "gentlemen of good standing in society . . . highly respectable & patriotic."[29] The settlers who happened in the path of the Texas army in March and April, 1836, also bore the brunt of its marauding disposition, abuses of the impressment policy, and depredations by deserters or irregular forces.

Activities that the civilian point of view regarded as army excesses often derived from dire necessity as seen by the volunteers. Soldiers regularly suffering from commissary shortages were frequently left to their own devices. In desperation the government authorized impressment of whatever the army required. At first this policy seemed to work well enough. The troops rather gleefully rounded up whatever cattle and grain they needed, but by late October Bowie and Fannin complained that commodities had become scarce because farmers hid their goods. The two-week-old Texas army had discovered a version of Gresham's law — mere promises of future payment served as the worst kind of money in driving products off the market. The soldiers had begun complaining about shortages, these officers noted, and further concluded: "You know the materials we have — they will fight — and fight desperately, but must *Eat.*" Austin could only lamely advise Bowie and Fannin "to follow the Law of necessity." The Goliad garrison had somewhat better fortune in seizing a considerable cache of Mexican supplies. They shared some luxury items (coffee, sugar, and wine) with the Béxar besiegers but encountered difficulties of transportation.[30]

Left thus to provide for itself, the army managed to do so well enough to keep from falling completely apart, but it acquired a smoldering resentment of the politicians, regarding them as not only slackers but as inept and possibly corrupt. Not until November 9 did the Consultation vote to pay the volunteers a monthly allotment and expenses reimbursement, and this amounted to a pledge rather than an actual payment. The onset of winter weather in late November increased their suffering. On the twenty-sixth William H. Wharton added clothing to the standing list of shortages (coffee, flour, tobacco, and sugar). He warned that, "if not furnished as soon as possible, great and just dissatisfaction will ensue."[31] In other parts of Texas officers who attempted to supply their needs through appeals to public patriotism discovered widespread "indifference" among the masses. A contractor in mid-December wrote to the government that he had exhausted his own capital in purchasing provisions. By then the situation had worsened due to inflation and the refusal of farmers to sell "on the faith of the Country."[32]

From late December through February army morale continued to worsen. Winter weather, the belief that the war had been won, weariness with garrison duty, and the continued inadequacy of supplies combined to depress the volunteers and drive them homeward. The commissary crisis spread even to Goliad, where the military had previously been feeding both soldiers and civilians. At Béxar the troops entered their fourth month of service without pay or even new clothing. Colonel Neill described them as "almost naked" and dependent on the continued largess of local Mexican families for food.

The General Council responded with ludicrous resolutions empowering garrison commanders to appoint contractors to round up or otherwise procure supplies, a solution which Neill had recently denounced as unworkable because of the backlog of unpaid bills. To Dimitt, of Goliad, the government at least gave written authority to sell public property to raise funds. On January 20 a recent U.S. volunteer explained the predicament of the Texas soldier: "Every man in this country at this time has to go upon his own footing as the Government at present is unable to make any provisions for the Army." Others returned to their homes bearing even less flattering tales of neglect of army needs.[33] Failures of military supply certainly did not result from the absence of officer complaints, pleas, or threats. On January 27 Neill in Béxar wrote bluntly to Henry Smith that "We cannot be fed & clothed on paper pledges." One of his subordinates best summarized the army attitude: "no pay no clothes nor provisions[,] poor encouragement for patriotic men who had stood by their Country in the hour of trial."[34]

Most of those who persevered through the discontented winter and remained in the ranks up to March did not survive the battlefield failures of that month. The new volunteers who comprised Houston's army suffered the hardships of a difficult retreat across swollen rivers on rain-soaked, boggy roads. They endured outbreaks of measles and other diseases that arose from filthy makeshift camps. They also suffered from scanty provisions but complained somewhat less, largely because the soldiers impressed what they needed from settlers who fled before or with the army. The veterans in some instances bore their ragged and dirty appearances as symbols of honor.[35]

By May Texas began receiving shipments of supplies from agents in New Orleans. However, the government had difficulties of distribution complicated by the need to feed dependent civilians as well as soldiers. Further, the growth of the army in midsummer increased demands on these stores. President Burnet explicitly directed the officer with quartermaster responsibilities to observe "one general rule . . . that the army 'must' be sustained" prior to providing for the families, especially in regard to coffee and sugar: "The army cannot be kept together without an occasional supply of these articles." In early June the troops received some food but complained of shortages of clothing and shoes and an absence of pay.[36]

The resulting hardships convinced many soldiers that they suffered, as a large group of officers complained to Burnet, "while those who had ignobly fled before the enemy were rioting in the abundance of the public stores." This situation, in their opinion, owed its existence "entirely to the shameful inattention of the officers of the Government." Individuals and groups also directed similar communications to General Rusk and to the secretary of war in late June and mid-July, but most of the dissatisfaction focused against the president. Burnet continued to assert that he had done everything possible for the army, given the absence of funds, but he displayed little sensitivity for the feelings of the average volunteer. As he wrote to Lamar on July 8, "privations are incident to all Camps and the cheerful endurance of them, constitutes one of the peculiar glories of the military profession." A week later the quartermaster informed the government that a "Mutiny" might ensue should a long-expected cargo ship fail to reach Velasco soon.[37]

This attitude of pervasive dissatisfaction with living conditions helped to make the army highly politicized and lent a sharpness to its views. Generally, the soldiers held immoderate positions which they presented in strident tones. They basically resented everyone who failed to share in their peril and suffering, with politicians at the head of the list. This attitude preceded the government's failures of supply, for the very first "Army of the People" had adopted an antipolitician posture. The army had delayed the formation of the Consultation by refusing at first to part with those members who were elected to it. The Goliad volunteers had expressed an even more explicit antagonism toward those who sought political advancement rather than sharing in the military toils. On December 22 nearly one hundred men had signed a declaration which attacked "the busy aspirants for office, running from the field, to the Council Hall, and from this, back to the camp, seeking emolument not *service* — and swarming like hungry flies, around the body politic." This view blamed these "anti-patriotic" officials for retarding military and political progress.[38] The army also propounded a degree of class consciousness. Many volunteers felt the injustice of a system which recruited patriotic soldiers from the ranks of the poor while wealthier citizens remained safe and comfortable at home, developing or adding to their property.

Soldiers concerned themselves with the right of suffrage because they held decided opinions—usually on the more radical side—on all the major issues of the day. Different units frequently reflected the views of their commanders; therefore, the recruits did not share unanimous views on any subject. Nonetheless, certain lines of thought predominated. Initially, the army of the people at Béxar and Goliad endorsed pronouncements defining the struggle as a defense of the Constitution of 1824 of the Mexican Republic, the orthodox position at the time. Even then many of the Anglo Texas volunteers expressed a decided reluctance to enlist Mexican support for the Texas cause.[39] This attitude arose from both ethnic bias and also from a general waning of faith in the potential for aid from federalist elements in the interior. The Consultation's equivocation on the independence issue created dissatisfaction in some segments of the army and even engendered calls for a new convention in 1835. In light of the failure of that alternative, the Goliad garrison took the matter into its own hands by adopting a declaration on December 22. Brimming with antipolitician, anti-Mexican, antiaristocratic rhetoric, the document resolved that "the former Province & Department of Texas, is, and of right ought to be, a *free,* sovreign, & independent State," in defense of which the soldiers pledged their "lives, fortunes, & sacred honor." Officers like Johnson and Fannin continued to argue against independence, but the U.S. volunteers who numerically dominated the army in early 1836 advocated that cause almost unanimously.[40]

The newcomers soon acquired familiarity with the partisan and ideological disputes of Texas politics because the army to a certain extent resembled a debating society. On January 24, 1836, the soldiers of Béxar held a meeting to discuss the news from San Felipe. This gathering criticized the council for favoring land speculators, misappropriating funds intended for army support, and creating anarchy, all actions that adversely effected the interests of the military. Some soldiers intimated a willingness to restore Smith by force, but support for the deposed governor stopped short of violence. The position of the council received more sympathy with the army in the Goliad area, no doubt in part because of the influence of Fannin.[41] But mostly the volunteers on all fronts looked forward to the March Convention as the means of restoring political order, enacting independence, and fulfilling the promises of land grants to volunteers made by previous politicians. Given the military crisis and potential power of the army, the Convention in fact had little choice but to vote for all these measures.

Army political influence continued to expand following the battle of San Jacinto; by early summer the army's growing power and antagonism toward government policies, as expressed in the crisis regarding the fate of Santa Anna, led Burnet to a futile effort to establish greater civilian control in the form of a new commander, Mirabeau B. Lamar. The ensuing army rejection of this general not only confirmed its virtual independence but sparked an effort to overthrow the government. To the president and his supporters the Texas Revolution had become tragically ironic—a volunteer army of the people had defeated the tyrant Santa Anna only to raise the specter of its own military domination.

Several sources of discontent fed the army's animosity toward civilian authority; however, all these issues stemmed from a fundamental disagreement over the nature of the revolution and prosecution of the war. Like other armies of rebellion before them, the Texas force favored adoption of thorough military policies to gain an overwhelming triumph. By May many members of the Texas army, including its commander, had concluded that the cabinet purposely failed to supply soldiers properly in order to encourage reductions in military size and strength. The victims of this policy of willful neglect, in the words of a letter of protest composed by a large group of officers, were "citizen soldiers" who represented "the bone and sinew of the country." As true but exasperated patriots, the volunteers questioned the integrity of a government which remained shamefully inattentive to the necessities of war. The officers darkly warned that the present government seemed headed again toward anarchy, a fate which could be averted by a new Congress and other reforms or by "military rule." The protesters regarded the latter as an "unpleasant alternative" but threatened to adopt it in pursuit of "our most sacred rights."[42] General Rusk did not sign this document, but he nevertheless agreed with its principles and refused to suppress it. He felt dangerously ill-informed and hamstrung as a result of his reduced force, which had orders to desist from attacking the retreating Mexican army in order to chase Comanches instead. In his view the dangers to "liberal Government" posed by "a strong military force" had to be tolerated: "desperate cases require corresponding remedies." Victory and security had to be gained before delicate political matters could be resolved.[43]

The general and his men became more zealous when their march led them to La Bahia where they came across the grisly remains of the Goliad martyrs. Rusk conducted a burial ceremony in early June, delivering a eulogy that brought tears to the eyes of veteran soldiers. "In its conclusion," reported his aide de camp, "I observed several compress their lips and involuntar[ily] grasp their weapons more firmly as if the scenes of San Jacinto had not compensated [for] the brutal murder of their friends." Despite this inflammatory scene, Rusk did not consistently play the role of provocateur. For example, he attempted to dispel rumors that the government intended to renege on its promised land grants. This impression derived from the fact that Burnet and other conservatives wanted to limit the size of the army in order to keep the public domain in entrepreneurial hands. According to a rumor from Nacogdoches, the president preferred returning Texas to the Mexicans to turning it over to U.S. volunteers.[44]

Army-cabinet disagreements on measures to bring the Revolution to completion focused on one symbolic issue — the fate of Santa Anna. The soldiers' position was based on ignorance, passion, and wishful thinking — they knew little of the terms of the secret Treaty of Velasco of May 14, sought revenge for wartime atrocities, and (forgetting their own very real demoralization) argued that government restraints had prevented them from further routing the Mexican army in the month after San Jacinto. More rationally, Rusk and his men questioned the wisdom of freeing Santa Anna on the basis of a promise to obtain recognition of Texas independence and release of the prisoners in Mexican hands. Many volunteers favored giving the enemy general a cursory military trial followed by execution for war crimes. In a largely spontaneous action a group of recently debarked U.S. volunteers boarded the schooner *Invincible* and removed Santa Anna on June 4 before his imminent departure for Vera Cruz. The shaken captive then came under a military guard commanded by newly arrived Gen. Thomas J. Green.[45]

As Burnet argued, these events turned the issue into less a diplomatic than a constitutional crisis. He defended the patriotism and wisdom of government policy while pointing to the evil of military usurpation. Nevertheless, the president concluded in an address to the army, "we have yielded to your remonstrance because we hold the in-

ternal tranquility of Texas . . . as paramount to all other considerations."
In point of fact the government had no choice but to yield—the army
had the power and for a while, at least, the will to use it. The army's
rejection of Lamar signified its virtual independence from civilian control, as it had been at the beginning of the war.[46] The question then
became—would the army stop short of total political domination? Its
head, Rusk, shared the military discontent with government policies.
But he professed obedience to civil authority, avoided direct participation in the removal of Santa Anna, and accepted his replacement until
the soldiers refused to obey Lamar. As a leader of a democratic army,
Rusk had only limited authority and played the ambiguous role of a
bystander on occasion.

In mid-July smoldering military resentment flamed into a coup d'état
plot. On July 14 one E. L. R. Whelock, a soldier unknown personally
to the president but apparently a recently arrived U.S. volunteer, drew
up "Charges and Specifications preferred against David G. Burnet Esquire." These accused the executive of: first, "Usurpation" for functioning as president without benefit of an election by the sovereign
people; second, "Treason" for conducting "secret and clandestine" negotiations with the enemy and attempting to release "State Prisoner
St. Anna"; and third, "Sedition" for ridiculing the commander in chief,
discouraging enlistments, and corruptly misappropriating supplies. Col.
Henry Millard, claiming to act "under the orders of the comandr in
chief," on July 16 instructed Capt. Amasa Turner to arrest Burnet and
seize his public papers.[47]

According to the president's account, written some two weeks later,
"a violent Revolution has been attempted" to overthrow "Civil Authority . . . [and] create a Military Supremacy in the Government." He over-
came this coup by a combination of conciliation and resistance. Turner
acted as the prudent agent of compromise, rather than as the instrument of force; he presented Burnet with arrest orders and charges but
stopped short of confining him. This procedure and the emergence
of a pro-civilian party in Velasco allowed the executive to negotiate.
Initial army reports presented a victorious outcome. "The proceedings
of Col. Millard has had so far a most excellent effect," officer Alman-
zon Huston wrote to Rusk on the nineteenth: "The President has ac-
ceded to [Millard's] propositions and says he is desirous to do all in
his power for the army." The actual arrangement (made the previous
day) gave Rusk more authority over military movements while it allowed the cabinet to remain in existence. By mid-August each side rested

in the comforting assurance that it had emerged triumphant in the political contest, a mood encouraged by veteran political emissaries John A. Wharton and Branch T. Archer, who carried messages of accord from the seat of government to army headquarters.[48]

In fact, however, the attempted coup and resulting accommodation resolved none of the real conflicts between civilian officials and the army. Abrasive details like Burnet's order to revoke Millard's commission, which Rusk failed to implement, remained to irritate relations. Fundamentally, Burnet was left impotent, grasping at the formalities of authority while bitterly denouncing military usurpation. The army, from rank and file to the top, continued to be dangerously alienated and politicized. In late July reports circulated of plans for a summary execution of Santa Anna. Rusk still viewed himself as an innocent victim of cabinet slander and futilely articulated the case for a more thorough conduct of the war. According to this apparently widespread view the army had carried the brunt of the Revolution with far too little support from civil government or civilians. He advocated conscription of three thousand Texans to terminate the war with a total victory.[49]

Support for this approach grew, too, out of resentment of those who seemingly had sacrificed little. General of U.S. volunteers Thomas J. Green espoused this radical army position with the tone of a demagogue. In his view, the political contest had become one of a virtuous, self-sacrificing army against a Tory government representing the interests of "cowardly" shirkers and absentee rich. In the process, the cabinet and the "few miserable dogs" who supported it used the issue of military usurpation to detract attention from its policy of destroying the army and to protect the holdings of the "Land Mongers." While the soldiers in the field conducted the war in "defense of the poor men, women & children in this country," Green asked, "in Gods name where are the larger land holders? Why are they not fighting for their freedoms? Are they still in Bishops Hotel, Orleans drinking mint slings? . . . Is our blood to be spilt defending their immense estates," only to face their abusive cry of military tyranny? Even citizens who remained at home had fled the service at the earliest excuse or, worse, avoided military duty. These citizens often refused to supply their defenders except at the extortionate prices of "highway robbers." As Green saw the situation, the only patriots left in Texas were the recent immigrants comprising the majority of the soldiers.[50]

By late summer the Texas army had risen to its greatest strength, numbering about 2,500, and to its most alien composition, in that U.S. citizens outnumbered Texans by three to one. It had developed a radical ideology that distrusted all elements of society or government outside the military domain. The volunteers expressed dissatisfaction with their levels of sustenance, and they suspected that promises for pay and future land would likewise go awry. Some threatened to help themselves to the wealth of the country without regard for law. Should they have attempted to plunder, the government would have been unable to protect peace and order.[51] From this or some other wicked fate the people turned for deliverance to the September elections that would ratify the constitution and give the Republic new political leadership. In this contest, as well as in all previous political issues, the army would be an important force.

The army proved to be the most revolutionary body in the Texas Revolution. By pushing events toward more radical conclusions in the name of liberty, the military threatened free government in order to gain just rewards and provide the infant nation with security. In these positions and attitudes the Texas army joined, on a small scale, a long-established tradition of radical armies — the religiously zealous and populistic Roundheads of the English, the frequently mutinous volunteers of the American, and the supernationalistic and ruthlessly revolutionary of the French Revolutions. In each of these instances the democratic armies had been disciplined, chastened, or transformed by a dominant leader — a Cromwell, a Napoleon, or a Washington — but the Texas forces had met no master at the time Sam Houston won the presidency in the fall of 1836.

9. The Tories
OPPONENTS OF REVOLUTION AND INDEPENDENCE

Internal disagreement had threatened the Texas cause from the beginning. Regional disharmonies, personality clashes, contests for leadership, ethnic tensions, and other significant divisions undermined a unified response during the formative summer of 1835. Frequently, the more militant factions used the label Tory to discredit conservative elements; however, the arrival of war in October, 1835, healed many discords, if only temporarily. Texas propagandists de-emphasized the presence of procentralist sentiment in their effort to promote patriotism, a sense of unity, and outside support. Indeed, Tory behavior — defined strictly as giving aid and comfort to the centralist cause through military service or other voluntary support — characterized the response of a relatively small proportion of the total population. Nevertheless, suspicions of Toryism remained high because the revolutionary cause always stood in such a vulnerable position. The threat was real in that active support for the centralists existed mostly in the west — the war zone — where aid to the enemy could do the most damage, and in the east where the people suspected a vast Mexican-Indian stab-in-the-back conspiracy.

Military participation provides the surest way to measure the strength of genuine advocacy of the Revolution and thus to identify the areas of likely Tory sentiment, where volunteering was the weakest. In the fall of 1835 broad support for the war came from all sections of Texas but one — the lower valleys of the Guadalupe, San Antonio, and Nueces rivers. The four municipalities of this area provided just over fifty men to Texas armies, fewer than several single municipalities to the north and east. San Patricio, in particular, gave but few soldiers (eight), a reflection of both culture and geography.[1] Located on the southwestern edge of Texas settlement, removed from Anglo-American influences, this colony also stood in the shadow of the Mexican fort of Lipantitlán. Most of the Irish inhabitants of the region had emigrated there during the last five years and had avoided involvement in the political disputes between Texas and the government of Mexico. Their major public concern — over land titles — had just been resolved in their favor. They got along well with neighboring *rancheros* and *soldados* and felt strong religious ties to their adopted country.[2]

The San Patricians took no part in the events that led to war but could not remain immune from its influence. With the local government controlled by loyalists and a Mexican garrison in their midst, the residents had neither means nor opportunity to join in the rebellion in the first part of October. Nor did they have any apparent desire to revolt. By mid-month reports drifted north that "the people of St. Patricio have joined the military at the Nueces," though some suspected that this involvement reflected compulsion more than sympathy for the centralist cause. This charitable hypothesis dispelled quickly when two volunteers went to San Patricio seeking Irish support and found shackles awaiting them instead. Confronted with such evidence, Texas patriots increasingly expressed "doubt and distrust" about the behavior of Nueces river colonists, to quote Goliad commandant Philip Dimitt. His Mexican counterpart in Béxar concurred. Amidst growing Texas militance General Cos found support only from "the loyal Irishmen" of San Patricio.[3] A Texas expedition launched from Goliad against Fort Lipantitlán at the end of October dispelled any lingering doubts about the strength of pro-Mexican sentiment in the colony. Between fifteen and twenty civilians, including all members of the San Patricio Ayuntamiento, fought alongside the Mexican soldiers in a battle at the river on November 5. This loyalist contingent, which also included former alcalde William O'Docherty [O'Daugherty], suffered three casualties, including the serious wounds inflicted on current alcalde Henry Thomas.[4]

This engagement left San Patricio bitterly divided. Rebel forces claimed victory and also captured the fort, but they returned to Goliad almost immediately after installing a new local government which supported the 1824 constitution, at that time still a rallying cry for the rebellion. With the Mexican soldiers back in place at Lipantitlán, the settlers were left in the middle between political and military power. Some pro-Mexican settlers fled to Matamoros, but enough remained at their homes that in mid-November Dimitt expressed fear for those who had been "friendly, and well-disposed" toward the Texans. Being "too weak to oppose successful resistance, and unprovided with the means of retiring to less exposed settlements," they stood in danger of losing "life and liberty."[5] A "Remnant of patriots" remained in San Patricio despite threats of "venegeance" by the fortress commander, but they felt isolated and undersupplied. Potential volunteers and their families found bread unavailable "at any price." Many of the "Irish Partozans of Centralism," as described by the Goliad commander, stubbornly refused to abandon their beliefs or their homes. Susanah O'Daugherty boldly took over the leadership of the Tory cause from the deposed San Patricio authorities that included her ex-alcalde husband. Throughout the month of December the Mexican commander of the Lipantitlán garrison remained in communication with her and his other supporters in the town. Dimitt concluded from his reports that only another military expedition could unify the Irish community and remove the stain of pro-Mexican collaborationism. In San Patricio the Texas Revolution had assumed the form of a civil war, and even at the end of the year it remained out of step with the mood of the other Texas settlements.[6]

In early 1836 a muddled situation still prevailed there. Many stubbornly adhered to the Mexican side of the conflict; a few became converts to the rebellion while it could be defined in terms of defending the 1824 constitution, only to find that compromise ground vanishing by February. Amidst this atmosphere of confusion the settlers had to fend off attempts to confiscate their land and they also suffered from bushwhacking by their neighbors. A Texas troop build-up, intended to make their land a staging ground for a campaign against Matamoros, added to their problems and damaged their properties.

These developments strengthened Tory feelings; when Gen. José de Urrea's regiments arrived at the Nueces River in late February, he not only preempted the Texans' ill-organized advance but found substantial local support. Once again the Irish acted as informants and otherwise demonstrated enough pro-Mexican sentiment to convince some of their officers that Santa Anna's "war to the death" strategy was "stupid" and "ill-conceived" as José Enrique de la Peña described it. He argued that the entire region could have been courted into loyalism — the colonists in the Texas army either served under compulsion or "would have submitted" readily after their defeats if left to the influence of local Tories. Some of the Irish escaped the Goliad massacre because a priest successfully argued their loyalty to Mexico; de la Peña nevertheless believed that "several" loyal San Patricians perished in the execution.[7]

In all the municipalities in the western region of Texas a variety of factors influenced the choice of loyalties. Ethnicity certainly swayed the decision of many—the Irish and the Tejanos provided most of the recruits for the centralist cause. Nevertheless, blood and religious ties alone did not determine the difficult choice, as indicated by the fact that the neighboring Irish of the Power and Hewetson and Tejanos in the de León colonies held steadfastly to the Texas side. Local conditions in Refugio, especially a pattern of conflict with Tejanos over land titles, influenced these Irish colonists to serve in substantial numbers in the Texas army. None of them fought on the Mexican side. Similarly, matters of intensely localized scope such as leanings of established political leaders, strength of the centralist military power, and relationships with Anglo neighbors combined in various ways to influence Tejano behavior. Some fought on the Texas side, some on the Mexican; others sought a kind of vague neutrality, usually without success, in an effort to protect homes, families, and properties, or more simply, to survive.[8]

The exact magnitude of Tejano support for the centralist cause becomes blurred by the prejudices that raged during the war. Anglo Texans generally held disparaging views of persons of Mexican descent, stifled barely if at all by the strategic demands of the Texas cause, i.e., the need to moderate these attitudes to appeal for support from Mexican federalists. Thus, some Texas leaders published addresses urging cooperation on "'their Mexican neighbors,'" and sought cordial relationships between themselves and liberals from the interior who came to Texas seeking sanctuary or support.[9] The Mexican federalists also issued similar proclamations, but the goal of restraining Texas bigotry never fully succeeded, and relations with Viesca, Mexía, and Zavala all weakened as a result.[10]

By early December, with the hope for federalist aid from the interior growing dimmer, the Anglos' racial antagonisms achieved widespread expression. A report of the Consultation's Military Affairs Committee expressed the common view: "The Mexican people and the Anglo Americans in Texas never can be one and the same people. A civil compact can never bind together long people who differ so widely in their pursuits, their religion, their languages, and their ideas of civil liberty."[11] A speaker in San Augustine agreed that culture separated the two ethnic groups, that they were "primitively a different people" and that "strong prejudices" had actually increased over time.[12] Houston resorted to a bundle of mixed metaphors to emphasize the force of the racial antagonism: "Let us break off the live slab from the dying cactus that it may not dry up with the remainder; let us plant it anew that it may spring luxuriantly out of the fruitful savannah. Nor will the vigor of the descendants of the sturdy north ever mix with the phlegm of the indolent Mexicans, no matter how long we may live among them. Two different tribes on the same hunting ground will never get along together."[13] Governor Smith led the way in race-baiting and opposed cooperation with federalist leaders and enfranchisement of Tejanos.[14]

All of these politicians supported their anti-Mexican rhetoric with one argument: Tejanos were Tories. According to these charges, the Mexican Texans acted as spies. They wandered into and out of towns and military camps, retrieving information about political proceedings and military movements; others refused to provide material aid to the Texas cause; more than a few actually enlisted in the centralist army at Béxar, even joining it in retreat to the Rio Grande with a view to return in Santa Anna's army of conquest. "Most dangerous," wrote Houston, were those who fled "to their plantations on the banks of the forested rivers apparently to idly observe the war." They should not be allowed this malignant neutrality, he argued, for the times demanded enforcement of a primitive rule: "he who is not with us is against us."[15] These views, generally expressed by men who had spent their time away from the front and who lacked first-hand knowledge of Tejano behavior, defined loyalty in terms of ethnic origin. Given the strength and pervasiveness of these attitudes, it became virtually inevitable that military authorities would treat all Tejanos as enemies.

Soldier-civilian conflict developed very early in the war and became a key determinant of Tejano response. The Texas army that occupied Goliad after the capitulation of the centralist forces on October 9 consisted mainly of recruits from the Austin colonies. Military authorities, suspecting local Tejanos of Tory sympathies, attempted little recruitment from the heavily Mexican municipalities of Goliad and Victoria and dispatched most of these local volunteers to the Béxar siege. This situation made the Goliad command into an outside army of occupation and resulted in a state of tension and mutual suspicion.[16]

Impassioned charges and countercharges notwithstanding, the evidence suggests that the Tejanos of the lower San Antonio and Guadalupe river valleys (in the municipalities of Refugio, Goliad, and Victoria) responded in one of three ways and by no means adhered consistently to a single course of action. One faction, including virtually all of those in the de León colony, advocated the federalist cause against the centralists and volunteered in substantial numbers early in the war but not thereafter, because no Texas commander actively sought their services. Those Tejanos who remained politically active in the fall of 1835 advocated federalism but protested violations of civil liberty by the Texas military. Many residents fled the town of Goliad for the countryside, behavior that the local commander cited as evidence of their duplicity and Toryism.[17]

A second response by the Tejanos — an effort to guard self or family interests against the ravages of the military on both sides — paralleled the behavior of most Anglos. Prudence also encouraged a wait-and-see attitude. The army of General Cos had passed through in late September and early October. It made demands for assistance similar to those that would be issued by the Texans, with similar ill will resulting. The small garrison that he left capitulated on October 9 to a force of Texas volunteers. Many local residents apparently could see little to choose from, given the conduct of both sides, and took up residence on area ranches. In the mind of Texas commander Dimitt their flight proved Tory leanings, either active or tacit. The locals, he reported to Austin, "'had seen the brilliant equipment of General Cos . . . they had listened to his flattering and captivating speeches, they had attended his parties and tasted his wine.'"[18]

However inaccurately Dimitt and the other zealots judged the Tejano response in general, the centralist cause did generate some support in the region. Many of the residents were descended from former soldiers of the Goliad presidio and disliked the Anglo intrusion. Vicente de la Garza, a member of the most important Tory Tejano family, had urged a policy of Mexican arms build-up and force against recalcitrant Anglo colonists as early as April, 1835. The population of his ranch and ranches of other pro-centralists, like the Valdez family, swelled throughout the winter of 1835–36. Mexican Texans in this community also followed the lead of local politicians, who largely remained responsive to the prudent model and advice of the department's political chief, Angel Navarro. Fulfilling promises made to Cos, area residents served the Santanista cause in various ways. Juan Latano [Letona] of Copano pretended sympathy for the Texans but carried expresses for the centralists. Juan and Agustín Moya conducted guerrilla-style warfare in furnishing supplies, including the public *caballada,* to the garrison at Lipantitlán. A detachment of irregulars of this kind attacked a Texas expedition as it returned from this fortress to Goliad on November 10. The Tory force reportedly suffered twenty casualties.[19]

The preponderance of Texas power limited what procentralist Tejanos could contribute during the fall and winter. The Goliad-Refugio region lapsed into a genuine civil war. Mistrust prevailed on all sides, but local sympathies swung toward the centralists. By December and January only a few served the Texas cause willingly. Most fled their residences at La Bahía, the town near the Goliad fortress, and gathered at more isolated locations to shield themselves from contact with the growing Anglo-American forces that spread out haphazardly between Victoria, on the Guadalupe, and San Patricio, on the Nueces, in lieu of a unified command and purpose. Some of the local Mexicans, according to the memory of a U.S. recruit new to the area in January, "crossing the Rio Grande, had joined Santa Anna's forces" in preparation for a renewed campaign. J. C. Duval found many of the residents *"professedly* loyal to the Texans," but secretly plotting to aid the enemy. He never seemed to connect Tejano behavior to the treatment they received at the hands of the volunteers, who feasted on local corn and cattle, impressed horses, and went on drunken binges that terrorized the civilian population. In fact, area residents gave Duval's company a nickname — the Mustangs — in reference to its custom of kicking in the doors of their houses. The unit's military action before mid-February focused on raiding area ranches in search of Tories. One expedition resulted in the arrest of José Antonio Valdez, a priest, a member of a powerful local family, and one considered by Duval and others to be a "great scoundrel."[20]

These activities comprised part of a concerted antiguerrilla warfare program by Fannin. Though weak and generally vacillating, he had made up his mind about the sympathies of the local population. "There is more danger from these spies," he wrote to acting Governor Robinson, "than from twenty times the number of armed soldiers. I again tell you, we must not rely on Mexicans. It would be a fatal delusion."[21] If anything, the tactics of his forces strengthened the Tory cause among the Tejanos — the antiguerrilla tactics did too little to crush out opposition but quite enough to sway the uncommitted toward the centralists. The military situation changed dramatically in February, 1836, with the arrival of a major Mexican expedition under the capable command of Gen. José de Urrea. Before then the Tories had kept their eyes open and their defenses up against the more than five hundred Texas and U.S. volunteers who ranged over the broad region.

Leadership of the Tory cause came from the most influential Tejano families of the region. Despite the deportation of padre Valdez, brothers José María and Pedro Valdez remained in charge of the family ranch located in the forks of the San Antonio and Guadalupe rivers. The most renowned leader, thirty-four-year-old La Bahía native Carlos de la Garza, operated a ranch below the town on the San Antonio river. His establishment, including a store, church, houses, and outbuildings, occupied a key position on the Victoria-Refugio road. The ranch had supplied food and transportation to the Texans since November, 1835, albeit involuntarily. As late as February 20 Fannin impressed six horses there; however, the de la Garza place survived as a refuge for the uprooted and for Tories despite repeated Texas raids. Former Goliad alcalde Encarnación Vásquez joined ranchers Juan and Agustín Moya and others in preparation for actions against the Anglos. West of Goliad, Urrea relied on Guadalupe de los Santos to render aid between Refugio and San Patricio. Urrea also received scouting information from Jésus Cuéllar (nicknamed El Comanche) in the neighborhood of the Nueces River, though this ex-officer had turned coats so often as to earn the suspicion of both sides.[22]

These Tories aided Urrea's forces in several ways. Most Tejanos served in irregular capacities, but they provided Urrea with information obtained as spies or scouts, performed as advanced units for the main army, engaged in partisan warfare, and lent their knowledge of the countryside to round up stragglers from shattered Texas units. Active Tejano aid to the Mexican cause began prior to its February 27 victory at San Patricio. Urrea laid out his battle plans only after gaining "exact information as to the enemy" from Salvador Cuéllar (brother of El Comanche) as to current Texas strength and the probability of reinforcement. After his victory Urrea dispatched native Mexicans to watch the area roads for the anticipated approach of more enemy units. The Mexican commander quickly established communications with Tejanos living between San Patricio and Victoria. The resulting intelligence may explain why Urrea acted with such speed and confidence throughout his campaign in this region.[23]

Other Tejano Tories at this same time launched partisan warfare of their own. The timing of their actions indicates that they knew of the impending arrival of the invaders from Mexico. The day before the battle of San Patricio the few native inhabitants who remained in their homes at La Bahía left for neighboring ranches. On the same day that Johnson and Urrea clashed to the south, a Tejano force under Carlos de la Garza, known as the *Victoriana Guardes,* attacked the town of Refugio. These guerrillas appear to have been retaliating for assaults inflicted by Texans earlier in February. The partisans conducted a two- to three-day plundering of stores and Anglo houses and rounded up most of the available horses; however, they spared civilian lives except for an alleged plot to kill one Irish politician. As soon as the Tory attack ended, he set out for Goliad and pleaded successfully with Fannin for a military force to help the civilians evacuate.

Fannin dispatched a company under Capt. A. B. King to escort the families and later sent another unit to look for Tejano spies at nearby ranches. King gathered up a number of civilians, but before making it back to the fort he clashed with guerrillas (numbering two hundred by one estimate) near Refugio on March 10, took refuge in town, and requested reinforcements. These arrived on March 13 under Capt. William Ward. The partisans fought so stiffly against over two Texas companies (a total force of about 128) that King's men and the families barricaded themselves in the town's old mission church and with difficulty withstood the attacks of the besieging Tejanos. Ward's arrival temporarily broke the siege; but King imprudently set off on March 14 on a retaliatory burning-and-looting campaign against the ranch of Esteban López and other area guerrilla leaders, reportedly killing eight local Mexicans and plundering their gear. When King's company returned that evening, he confronted not only the partisans but the bulk of Urrea's army. A civilian company of thirty men led by rancher Guadalupe de los Santos served as the advanced unit of the Mexican army in the resulting engagements which broke up and dispersed both Texas companies.

The partisans made a considerable contribution. Their presence shielded Urrea, who in early March methodically dispatched Grant's forces at the Agua Dulce battle. More significantly, the threat of the Tejano irregulars caused Fannin to divide even further the already dispersed Texas forces which were defeated in detail by Urrea. Finally, the centralists seem to have fought without quarter, in part because of the emotions generated by their contact with Tejanos, who told Urrea "pitiful stories" of Texas army "thefts and abuses."[24]

Elsewhere the native Mexicans also contributed to the centralist cause, though their role differed from that of their allies in the Goliad-Refugio area. "The Tejanos of Béxar," as a recent account concludes, found themselves in 1835 "caught in the middle of a crisis that they had not created and could not control." This uncomfortable position worsened after September, as the town became first the scene of a military buildup by the centralists under Cos and then the focal point of the besieging and assaulting Texas forces between late October and December 10. As at Goliad, residents of the Béxar area responded to these events in one of three ways. Some sought a kind of neutrality; a second group (of about one hundred) followed the lead of Juan N. Seguín and enrolled in the federalist (Texas) forces; a third faction supported the centralists. These Tories, who elicited the verbal abuse of militantly anti-Mexican Texas leaders in the winter of 1835, have never been afforded serious historical analysis.[25]

A number of factors influenced residents of Béxar to support the centralist cause. The centralists generally appeared to be winning. Other Tejanos feared being overwhelmed by the swelling tide of Anglicization in Texas. Not a few Bexareños took up arms literally in defense of their homes when the besieging forces attacked the town in a house-to-house fashion beginning on December 5. Political and familial matters also played a considerable role. The centralist commander, in removing Erasmo Seguín from his office, helped to solidify that family's influence for the federalist side, and Cos also carried out forceful and threatening policies which led to some antagonism among locals. Nevertheless, Cos and later Santa Anna also handed out rewards of political honor and place that sealed the loyalty of some Bexareños. Although Juan Seguín assured Austin of the people's support, the masses did not follow any single leader.[26]

Even families split amidst the tensions of the war. José Antonio Navarro followed his business ties with the colonists, but his brother Angel, the political chief of Béxar, remained loyal to Mexico. Initially, he sought the role of arbitrator, but he consistently carried out the orders of the centralists after the commencement of hostilities. On October 14 Angel Navarro issued an address to the inhabitants of the department criticizing the rebellion as an attack on the national religion and on constitutional authority. Describing himself as the voice of "patriotism, reason and order," he attempted to persuade the people that the army under Cos had come to protect "our property on this frontier" against the assaults of enemy forces. Others in Béxar also "celebrated" the arrival of reinforcements from the interior as the best means of suppressing rebellion.[27]

The Mexican garrison already at Béxar under Gen. Domingo de

Ugartechea included a presidial cavalry company from the town. Made up of about ninety men, this force remained with the central government in October, even though Cos entertained some doubts as to the strength of its loyalty (and it, in fact, subsequently experienced some desertion). On October 14 the commandant addressed the troops at Béxar to warn them against heeding the pro-federalist pleas of rebellion by the colonists, whom Cos described as "enemies of the Republic." Though he also harbored anxiety about pro-Texas sentiment among the population — evident in his order to establish a pass system to control movement in and out of the town — the Mexican general found enough local support to warrant establishing a second military company of Bexareños. On October 17 Cos wrote to Angel Navarro that several citizens had come forward with promises to serve the government cause "against the rebellious colonists." Therefore, he ordered the chief to enroll these armed recruits into a company named "the volunteers of the Nation." Cos authorized Navarro to promise these recruits that they "will do battle with the citizens of the interior in this City only in case of an attack." Navarro promptly acted to establish this local militia company and on October 20 supplied the centralist commander with the names of its enlistees.[28]

The Texas forces arrived in the neighborhood in late October and made Béxar the focal point of military activity. For the six weeks beginning October 23 the people of the town and its immediate environs found themselves in the vortex of the conflict, and demands on them increased. Cos impressed eighty cargo mules and forty skilled "and trusted" drivers. In November he threatened to conscript violators of the pass system to work on the fortifications of the plaza. While the Mexican commander attempted to marshall support by force, Austin (his Texas counterpart) sought additional enlistments from the town through promises of amnesty and toleration.[29] This competition for local participation left everyone dissatisfied, for Bexareños remained divided in their sympathies throughout the siege and fought on both sides during the storming of the town. In addition to the presence of the two Tejano units in Cos's forces, the Texans clashed with Béxar residents in the ensuing house-by-house and often hand-to-hand combat. Some of the attackers shot and captured citizens who resisted; others allowed civilians to flee from the war zone. Hermann Ehrenberg was one of the soldiers who favored lenient treatment of the population in order to attract further Mexican support for the Texas cause.

Still, he concluded generally that "the citizens of San Antonio . . . had sided with Cos against us."[30]

Most of the veterans of the siege and storming of Béxar came away from this experience insisting that the people had behaved like Tories. Travis endorsed the claim of one Tejano who had been among those taking the Veramendi house on December 7, but he described this soldier as "one of the few Mexicans who rendered us essential service" and urged discrimination against "those who were against us or were neutral." Another veteran, Thomas H. Borden, likewise recalled these events with bitterness. In January, 1836, he offered the behavior of the Bexareños as proof of the illusion of gaining aid from Mexican liberals: "Witness the conduct of a majority of the citizens of Bejar, in our own state. Were they not asked to join the Volunteer army, in our first going to that place? Were we not answered by the rifle, as the death of Milam proves?"[31]

In the days after Cos surrendered on December 10, residents of the community remained disunited in loyalties and wary in behavior. Their earlier experience with these townspeople had not apparently left the centralists as disillusioned as it had the Texans. One historian of Santa Anna's decision to focus his offensive on San Antonio has suggested that the expectation of friendly cooperation from the residents influenced the general's strategic thinking. Most of the people in fact withdrew from partisan activity during the ensuing campaign for the Alamo, but the small number who sought involvement once more divided between Tory and rebel. Again, even families split apart — Enrique Esparza, of Béxar, participated in the assault while his brother Gregorio died defending the fortress. Those who favored Santa Anna gave aid in many forms. Béxar priest Manuel Menchaca conducted foraging raids against the Seguín and Flores ranches. In mid-February centralist spies kept Santa Anna informed of the status of Texas forces in town. Some Bexareños, according to historian Walter Lord, decided to collaborate after the invaders surrounded the Alamo. He names five Tejanos who, perhaps influenced by awareness of the increasingly Anglo-versus-Mexican character of the war, left the fortress after hostilities commenced. Further, one woman slipped away and gave Santa Anna details about the levels of the defenders' preparedness.[32]

Activities like these lent credence to the charges of anti-Mexican militants. Travis, whose powerful words of denunciation soon carried the added force of martyrdom, wrote on March 3 from the Alamo that with but three exceptions Béxar Mexicans had not joined in his defense. Therefore, he raged, "the citizens of this municipality are all our enemies; . . . those who have not joined us in this extremity, should be declared public enemies."[33] Political participation under the centralist order provides better evidence of the strength of Tory attitudes than does Travis's tirade. Santa Anna appointed Ramón Músquiz Gonzales to the post of political chief, and the malleable Francisco Antonio Ruiz became alcalde. In early April forty-nine citizens participated in elections that made José María Salinas alcalde and Salvador Flores síndico procurador.[34]

Though small in numbers, the few Tejanos who resided between Béxar and Nacogdoches 350 miles to the east fell under suspicion of disloyalty. In early December, 1835, the council levelled treason charges against Manuel Cárdenas, then residing in Brazoria. Specifically, his violations involved spying for the enemy, conveying large quantities of provisions to the opposing forces, and causing friends of the Texas cause to be arrested. A few Bexareños like María Francisca de los Reyes accompanied Santa Anna'a army as it advanced into the Anglo areas of settlement and attempted to provide some geographic guidance along the way. A settler whom Santa Anna described as "a Mexican" gave information on the whereabouts of leaders of the Revolution near Harrisburg. Regarding even those Tejanos who took flight before the Mexican army as potential enemies, Houston had at least one group placed under guard; but taken as a whole the Tejano population of central and southeast Texas was too small to pose a serious Tory threat.[35]

Outside of the Department of Béxar, only in Nacogdoches did Tejanos reside in sufficient numbers (about six hundred) to make their loyalties a serious issue. In east Texas they were viewed with suspicion from the onset of the dispute with Mexico. The situation differed substantially from that in the west. The Mexican Texan population lived mostly in and around the town of Nacogdoches but nevertheless became a minority in the early 1830s. When the movement of resistance to Santa Anna's government emerged in Nacogdoches in the summer of 1835, the Tejanos took no part in the rebellion. As a local Tory official reported to his superior, the "revolutionary plan" garnered less than overwhelming support, being viewed as "fatal to the generality of the inhabitants, and more particularly to the native Mexicans."[36]

The only question seemed to be whether the Tejanos would actually attempt to block the course of revolution or would acquiesce in a kind of nervous neutrality. Distance from a centralist military force militated against active Tory conduct, but the Nacogdoches Mexicans did have one source of potential power. Though Anglos had swept political offices before 1835, the captain of the local militia was ex-alcalde Vicente Córdova. From late August to November, 1835, he continued to make reports to the town alcalde. In general this correspondence told of chronic weaknesses of the militia: a shortage of guns and other supplies, refusal of some to fulfill their militia duty. However real these problems may have been, the issue still remained: would Captain Córdova attempt to involve the militia in the political contest? His opinions, as shown by the address to his company at the end of August, leaned toward defense of the government. He favored continuing the tradition of obedience to "the orders of our authorities" and "sustaining the laws" rather than heeding the voices of discontent. His rhetorical appeals—to God, law, tradition, tranquility, and preservation of property—all reflected mainstream conservative ideals.[37]

However strong these Tory leanings, Córdova's isolation from centralist support deprived him of a prudent course of action. Further, his position of adhering to the established order became awkward as other officials lined up behind the rebellion. In October the alcalde, on behalf of the political chief, ordered the militia company to attend a public rally. This meeting resolved that "we must sincerely solicit the ade of our Mexican fellow-citizens, who in this municipality (alone in Texas) have up to this time shown a disposition to remain silent" in the face of war against the centralists. Defensively, Córdova excused the poor attendance of and resignations from his "little company" and asked that its weak response be overlooked, but he did not make a clear political commitment.[38]

A kind of informal modus vivendi came about, with twenty-five Mexican militiamen becoming a permanent home guard to protect local families and their property and to preserve order. In essence, Córdova agreed not to resist the Revolution, whose leaders in turn did not insist on Tejano participation in the war against other Mexicans. By November rebel spokesmen expressed disappointment that the Nacogdoches Tejanos remained, as John Dor explained to Houston, "just as ever—[that is] to say unwilling to afford aid." Yet, fears of overt Tory behavior dwindled, even though the idea for the home guard did not fully materialize. Córdova, in fact, ordered his company to dissolve on November 10, in reaction to his perception of distrust on the part of the town alcalde and interference with his command.[39]

Events in early 1836 threatened the uneasy accommodation of the previous fall. Nacogdoches divided bitterly over the issue of independence. Citizens of Mexican descent once again entered into public affairs in opposition to revolutionary measures, once again failed, and passed into sullen discontent. The military crisis of March, generated by the fall of the Alamo and the eastward advance of Mexican forces, produced rumors of Nacogdoches Tejanos conspiring with Santa Anna and the Cherokees, and a full-blown panic erupted in mid-April.

The seeds of this incident had been sown much earlier. In early December, 1835, the Nacogdoches vigilance committee investigated "anticipated Indian difficulties" based on its "opinion that some disaffected citizens of this Country [unnamed] are and have for some time past been in Communication with the Indian Tribes." This group, in fact, received very specific testimony that Eusebio Cortines had gone to Chief Bowls with a commission from General Cos to activate a previous alliance. The vigilance committee attempted without clear success to dissuade the chief through a personal emissary, a brother of Cortines, and then took steps to insure "security " and assert control over suspicious or disorderly persons in Nacogdoches. The leaders of Texas took the threat of a Cherokee rebellion so seriously that General Houston spent February of 1836 in Indian diplomacy.[40]

An authoritative conclusion about this alleged conspiracy still cannot be established, and details of the nature of the supposed plot also vary. In most versions the uprising was intended to involve both Indians and the Tejanos of Nacogdoches, with a joint attack timed for the arrival of the regular Mexican army. Most accounts mention Santa Anna's emissary as Manuel Flores, who reportedly passed through east Texas and into Louisiana in late 1835 or early 1836. One document of unverifiable authenticity has Vicente Córdova previously communicating with Flores and indicating that the Nacogdoches leader also held a commission "to raise the Indians as auxiliaries to the National Army" of Mexico. Rumors of such a plot continued into the summer of 1836 and beyond — in fact, until Córdova actually did rebel against Texas authorities in 1838.[41]

These tensions nearly erupted in armed conflict during the week following April 9, 1836. On that day Alcalde David A. Hoffman issued a notice that abruptly terminated the unwritten understanding of Tejano neutrality. The Texas convention on March 12, in providing for military conscription, had specified that Nacogdoches Mexicans should be organized into a separate unit. Hoffman ordered "every Mexican Citizen liable to Militia duty" to "take up the line of March, to the headquarters of our army" or to move to Louisiana or west of the Brazos within ten days. "Any failing to comply with this order, . . . or in any manner corresponding with the Indians to the prejudice of our cause, shall be dealt with as enemies, and treated according to the usual custom in time of war."[42] The Tejanos did begin to form a new militia force under Córdova, but they made no effort to leave the vicinity and instead set up camp on the outskirts of town. Anglo-American volunteers also assembled from various places; when joined by U.S. recruits on their way to the front, they totalled between 220 and 250 men.

This gathering of manpower provided more confusion than security because initially "nothing like organization existed," as "Acting Comdt of this Municipality" R. A. Irion wrote to Houston. Indeed, with the people gripped by panic and the volunteers answering to no overall authority, but wanting to kill Mexicans, Nacogdoches became a tinder-box. On several occasions an explosion nearly did occur. Both groups engaged in what the other viewed as provocations. Although the authorities had, of course, ordered local Tejanos to arm themselves in preparation for war, the actual sight of them with guns in their hands frightened many civilians. Wild reports circulated, not only that a large enemy force had reached the vicinity but, as the head of the vigilance committee later recalled, "that the Mexicans of this Municipality were embodying themselves for the purpose of attacking the Americans." Consequently, Anglo recruits set out to disarm Tejanos, while civilians fled toward the Sabine in panic. These events in turn created alarm among Córdova's men, whom some estimates placed at an exaggerated three hundred strong. They feared that the evacuation would be followed by an attempt to burn the town, which they determined to prevent. On April 12 Córdova sent scouts toward Nacogdoches; this party "full of passion," as their commander wrote because of an impression that a conflagration had already begun, arrested and disarmed an American whom it apparently suspected of arson. Several other near clashes developed as Anglo soldiers inspected Córdova's camp, expecting to find either Mexican regulars or Tories in armed opposition.[43]

Prudence on both sides averted a major flare-up. Córdova and his opposites managed to negotiate their way first to a truce and then to an understanding. Maj. John A. Quitman, commander of a company of U.S. volunteers, rode into the Tejano camp but began by talking rather than fighting; this procedure averted a conflict even though it did not dispel suspicion. On behalf of the Anglo forces Irion engaged in correspondence with Córdova, each explaining his perspective on the incidents described above. On April 14 the Tejano pointed out that the actions of his men — in defense of the property of Nacogdoches, for example — gave proof of anything but treason. Further, he expressed willingness to follow Irion's directives (though not those of other commanders) and to explore ways of "reconciling our people." Nevertheless, Córdova made it clear that confiscated weapons had to be returned as evidence of faith. Otherwise, "if the Mexicans are thus to be treated and suspected — I beg it may be remembered that they have it in their power if they are so disposed to do much mischief."[44]

That same day Irion, having consulted with the other officers, accepted Córdova's terms, promising to return the improperly confiscated arms and offering to avoid additional discord through "mutual forbearance." In separate correspondence Irion asked the Tejano militia to come forward to protect the town. "It is not intended," he wrote in contrast to Hoffman's previous order, "that your duties will call you out of the municipality." Despite these efforts, other "unpleasant" incidents occurred on April 14, but Irion expressed his regret, attributed them to "reckless individuals," set up a conference between Córdova and all other officers for the sixteenth, and dispatched a personal representative to placate the Tejanos.[45] This meeting succeeded in maintaining an uneasy civil peace.

On April 17 both Irion and Henry Raguet (on behalf of the vigilance committee) wrote reviews of the situation to reassure General Houston. "This has been an affair of extremely delicate nature," according to the latter account, but it had been resolved sufficiently that 220 of the soldiers previously detained to defend Nacogdoches had been dispatched to the front that day. Irion's letter reached the same conclusions but provided additional details of the agreement with Córdova: "The Mexicans are organized and seen willing to do all they can in defence of the country against Indians [torn] who are pillaging." Yet, Irion added, the Nacogdoches Mexicans "will not fight their countrymen in the present instance." As to what the future would bring, he could but make an educated guess. "In case Santa Annas minions ever reach this quarter I believe the *main* part [of the area Tejanos] will pass the Sabine." The recipient of these letters did not share even that qualified confidence of their loyalty to Texas. In retrospect, Houston asserted that the enemy's strategy was "to cross the San Jacinto to unite with the Mexicans in Nacogdoches county, and incite the Indians to war." In the summer of 1836 he opposed any renewed attempt to enroll Tejanos in the army because of lack of confidence in their loyalty, but the general also advised continued prudence regarding a proposal to disarm them.[46]

Apart from these speculative fancies, the actual historical record reveals that the native Mexicans of east Texas did not rise in armed rebellion against the Texas cause, Anglo fears and provocations notwithstanding. However, neither can their behavior be described as reflecting genuine sympathy for the Revolution. At the very least, Nacogdoches Tejanos occupied a position of armed neutrality. They showed willingness to protect local property, including, of course, their own, against whatever threatened it. Yet, beyond that and a promise not to attack rebel forces, Córdova and his followers would not go. Further, they gave every indication of a will to fight rather than be enlisted on the side of rebellion, and they did not even promise to withhold aid from Santa Anna if his men arrived. By the "he who is not for us is against us" standards of the day, the Mexican Texans of Nacogdoches exhibited the traits of Tories, especially since the distance between armed neutrality and belligerency is such a short journey.

Among non-Hispanics in Texas, defense of family and of personal interests was a powerful if not dominant impulse in the spring of 1836. As a result, many Texans, perhaps even a majority, responded to the revolutionary crisis in ways that the militants considered less than patriotic; however, active opposition to the Texas cause seldom surfaced among Anglos. Many dodged military recruiters or attempted to protect their possessions from press gangs, but few engaged in actual Tory behavior, when that term is defined as joining the forces of or voluntarily giving aid and comfort to the Mexican army or even as challenging the political legitimacy of the Revolution. Instances of those kinds of opposition took place rarely and then in a highly individualized or localized manner.

As the Mexican army marched eastward into the region drained by the Colorado and Brazos rivers, it encountered many abandoned houses, few people at all, and only an occasional settler professing loyalty. Texas army officials explored a few cases of alleged pro-Mexican sympathy, as when Houston sought further information on a Fort Bend family rumored to "have openly declared, that they are determined to join the enemy at first possible opportunity." No arrests occurred, because the investigating officer concluded that this charge had been based on biased reports. In other instances settlers who had expressed intentions of making their private peace with the Mexicans fled when the invaders actually appeared. A few Texans did fall in with, or into the hands of, a Mexican force in March or April and expressed support for its cause. Often this represented fast-talking opportunism rather than genuine Toryism.[47]

At Brazoria others, described by Urrea as English, German, and American colonists, begged his protection under a claim of having resisted army enrollment and Houston's evacuation orders. Neither their number nor their true loyalties can be fully determined, nor can the authentic identity of one who surrendered under the name Dr. Benjamin Harrison. He reputedly sought to convince Brazorians not to resist the Mexicans. Pass in hand, "Harrison" then disappeared, leaving Urrea convinced that he had found a useful emissary and the Texans who knew of the episode doubting that the man was the true son of Old Tippecanoe as he claimed. Santa Anna as well as Urrea encountered small groups in the Brazos bottoms who passed on information as to the whereabouts of the Texas army, but this collaboration did not appear significant enough to warrant subsequent investigation, much less repression.[48]

When the Texas authorities did make arrests on charges of treason in this region, the Toryism often proved to be of the phantom variety. Several strong advocates of peace in the summer and fall had their earlier misjudgments thrown back at them in the form of suspicions of disloyalty. In fact, different visions of the Texas cause competed legitimately before the March 2 Declaration of Independence, and advocacy of peace before the war or of federalism in its early stages did not usually translate into loyalty to Mexico in the spring. These conservatives responded variously to the coming of hostilities. Some volunteered for military duty, while others of various opinions did not, but most accommodated their beliefs to the revolutionary political order. Dr. James H. C. Miller of Gonzales had probably gone too far in the loyalist direction to recant successfully, since he had urged the arrest of agitators like Travis. Miller quietly fled from Texas, as much from fear of retribution as out of political conviction. Edward Gritten, who had also worked for an accord between Mexico and Texas, probably wished he had done likewise. The commander in chief on March 29 ordered Gritten's detention, along with D. C. Barrett (who had prudently gone to New Orleans), for trial "as traitors and spies." Arrested at Harrisburg on April 2, Gritten denied that he had given military intelligence to the enemy and pointed out that he had continued to work for the Texas government as a translator even after he knew of these allegations. Earlier this onetime mediator had recanted his faith in Mexican restraint and identified himself with the Texas cause in several ways.[49]

Houston may have had a stronger basis for charging others with aiding the enemy in east Texas. Two categories of people there expressed by word or deed a meaningful form of pro-Mexican sentiment. First, several individuals, mainly former officeholders, refused to accept the new government of Texas. In late march President Burnet received word that former Coahuila and Texas legislator John Durst, who had lost favor in some quarters because of alleged land speculations in Monclova, along with "many of his disciples is proclaiming against our independence." His "Toryism," as described by one Convention delegate, involved continued adherence to the 1824 constitution and active opposition to conscription. Other former officials behaved with enough recalcitrance to elicit charges of Toryism and demands for repression.[50] A few judges and land officials in the Nacogdoches and Shelby municipalities refused to cease their operations or otherwise comply with the new political order. The men who held the two leading positions under Mexican rule in the Department of Nacogdoches took different paths of cautious noncompliance toward the Texas government. Political Chief Henry Rueg delivered his archives to the alcalde and moved to nearby Natchitoches, Louisiana, which provided a safer vantage point. Peter Ellis Bean, the military chief, played a more dangerous game. He seemed to lend support to the Texas cause in relation to area Indian affairs while in fact having secret communication with Santa Anna. Houston learned of these activities too late—his April 13 arrest orders failed to reach Nacogdoches in time to lead to the incarceration of the slippery Bean.[51]

Other charges of individual disloyalty by spying and spreading false rumors for the Mexicans also troubled Texas leaders in April, 1836; however, they may have taken some comfort in the knowledge that these Tories had few, if any, followers. Contrastingly, the Liberty-Anáhuac area contained quite a number of people of pro-Mexican disposition, but no one emerged to rally this opinion into a genuine movement. This neighborhood had been bitterly divided since the Bradburn disturbances of 1832, a political-military conflict rooted in the economics of competing land claims. In turn, these events took on dimensions of family feuding for which east Texas was becoming infamous. During the fall of 1835 the council had investigated reports that Judge John A. Williams was raising fifty-eight adherents to centralism, but this leader did not surface in 1836, and his followers also stayed underground. While some of the area's opponents of independence did submit to the Texas cause, past loyalty to Mexico, potential for personal gain, and animosities toward patriot neighbors combined to make the people of Liberty possible candidates for cooperation with the invading army in the spring of 1836.[52]

In spite of this potential, few of the residents came forward to render actual aid to the Mexican army, but they did attack the Texas cause with considerable verbal abuse. On April 18 at Cow Bayou, east of Anáhuac, William F. Gray listened to a woman express "wrath against the Texans for bringing on the war and its consequences." She waxed particularly "eloquent" against the recent convention. Yet, in conduct, if not in words, these folk tended to be wary. One of those who chased them down following the San Jacinto battle described the disaffected as "Americans . . . who stood on the fence ready to jump on the side that should prove victorious." Many of the accused beat a hasty retreat in the direction of the good graces of Texas authorities once the military outcome had been determined.[53]

Two kinds of action placed people under suspicion: in the Liberty area many did not flee in panic at the approach of the Mexican army, thus raising suspicions of a willingness to live under centralist rule, and a few engaged in friendly communication with Santa Anna. Accused Tory Hervey Whiting did both but later denied having ever violated his pro-Texas principles. Subsequently, an abundance of conflicting testimony came forth and left much in doubt, but some facts emerge clearly. Whiting avoided military service, pleading family duties and ill health and claiming to have hired a substitute. Neither did he join other residents as they fled to the sanctity of Galveston Island. By his version, he worked to secure the property of President Burnet until the Mexicans arrived, after which an ill wind kept him landlocked. Whiting had property staked in a Texas victory in that the government owed him over $2,000 for supplies he had furnished on credit. Nevertheless, when the Mexicans assumed control of the area, he voluntarily contacted them. Whiting spoke in a friendly way to both Almonte and Santa Anna, received assurances as to the security of his property, and gave his boat to the generals. Whiting argued that he neither provided nor received anything of value in this relationship, a conclusion with which both Texas courts and the informal judgment of his neighbors later concurred. Historians have disagreed about whether this conduct represented genuine Tory behavior; the evidence does show clearly a man who had attempted to hedge his fortunes.[54]

Whiting seems to have been a representative figure of those accused of Toryism in the Liberty district. A few turned over their houses to the invaders or attempted to curry their favor with small gifts. Benjamin Page, seen with Whiting on his April 18–19 visit to Santa Anna, later stood accused of carrying messages to other Tories on the Trinity River in an effort to find guides for a projected march to the Sabine. Certainly Santa Anna did not receive information of value from residents of this area. As historian Andrew Forest Muir observed, the commandant may even have been misled by them into a belief that the Texans would not fight.[55]

Actual armed support for the Mexicans also failed to materialize, albeit narrowly, according to the account of Tory nemesis Lt. David L. Kokernot. He claimed to have seen a gang of twenty to thirty mounted men on "Tory Hill" on the east bank of the San Jacinto River on the eve of battle. According to a powerful local tradition (and supported by the research of some careful historians), this band dispersed when it saw the Texas forces prepared for battle. Kokernot also maintained that the victors found a list of Tories among Santa Anna's baggage, but about all that remains are a few Texas arrest orders and other pieces of evidence. Historian Margaret Henson has compiled these fragments into an enumeration of suspected Tories. Of the twenty-seven men who have been so identified, about half came from only five different families, not counting those related by marriage. At least some of them or their kinsmen had been feuding with their "patriot" neighbors, including Kokernot, since the 1832 Anáhuac disturbances. Most of these 1836 Tories had been involved in that earlier conflict, also on the pro-centralist side. Generally married men and older than the typical Texas volunteer, their distinguishing comparative characteristic was length of residence, which averaged ten years. Many hailed from Louisiana, and several had crossed the border before emigrants became officially welcome. These origins suggest the possibility of Catholic religious roots and thus a tie that often bound people to the Mexican cause in Texas.[56]

However clannish these alleged Tories were in some respects, they do not appear to have acted in real concert in March and April of 1836. Their earlier leader, John A. Williams, left the area after March 3. Others set out more to protect their economic interests than to devote themselves to pro-Mexican activities. James Taylor White [born LeBlanc], placed his name on the roll of east Texas volunteers raised by Maj. Leander Smith in early April but did not actually serve. Instead, White conducted his annual cattle drive to Lake Charles during the last half of April. Another ex-Louisianan decided to convert part of his real property into a liquid asset. Jacob F. Winfree sold a half-league of improved land and left home on unspecified business before April 17. Area patriots came to believe that Winfree's business involved riding with the treasonous band of Tory hill fame, but others charged the suspected disloyalists with cattle rustling. In any case many of them left their residences during the latter part of April, for those who searched for Tories found instead only husbandless women and their children huddled together for protection.[57]

Other evidence further suggests that self-interested rather than genuine Tory behavior predominated. In mid-May President Burnet, a resident of the area, ordered the release of White and others because they had not committed an "overt act of treason." Several of the accused volunteered during the summer of 1836. These included members of two of the most frequently condemned families, the Barrows and the Winfrees. Such conduct demonstrates something other than strong commitment to Mexico; overall, the Liberty district produced a far shallower variety of Toryism than existed in western Texas.[58]

The potential for significant Tory activity receded with the retreat of Mexican military power after the San Jacinto battle; however, efforts to detect and punish collaborationists continued, first in east Texas and then in the western region. In late April and early May Kokernot led a small company which scoured the area from the battleground to the Trinity River. His expedition derived from Houston's orders to "drive all the horses and cattle back that you find to the east of this, except those that belong to honest citizens," but the manner of implementation created controversy. Kokernot first led the men to his house, where they captured not Tories or livestock but a sizable supply of whiskey. A member who joined the company there one morning after a brief separation found "'all hands and the cook' pretty tolerable tight, and . . . going it with a rush." In a few days, after "the whiskey gave out and the boys gave in with heavy *heads* [we] proceeded towards the Trinity."

This unheroic beginning set the tone for the rest of the campaign. The men detained one alleged Tory but soon released him. They rounded up some horses, but did not locate many genuine disloyalists. "The *gallant* Kokernot" did execute one charge, "putting to rout all the *wimmen folks*," but he and his men received a tongue-lashing sufficient to force their retreat. After episodes such as these the men concluded that their leader had acted out of "petty spite" for his neighbors and refused his further orders.[59] The authorities began to receive complaints from citizens who defended their behavior and condemned "this Scoundrel Kokernott" who "is desolating the homes of deserted families and grossly insulting women & children." According to this account, others who had fled the country during the military crisis "have now returned most flaming patriots." This "band of Lawless plunderers have been ransacking the neighborhood." Charges and countercharges of this nature continued well into June.[60]

Kokernot later claimed to have arrested or driven "every Tory out of Texas," but he did not deny that "we had no little sport in that expedition, chasing the cowards over the prairie." Neither the results nor the methods seemed to please his superiors. Houston verbally abused all those involved. Kokernot explained that upon his return, "[I] reported my acts to the commander in chief and got a hell of a cursing." He received orders twice from Burnet to redistribute the livestock to the owners. In mid-May another expedition arrested several Tories in the Liberty region, placing them in confinement on Galveston Island. The president quickly arranged for their release; he favored slower and less punitive civil action "unless they are guilty of some overt act of treason."[61]

Extralegal movements threatened others in east Texas who had avoided military service. Even political leadership of the Revolution did not win immunity from the wrath of anti-Tory crusaders. As H. H. Edwards explained in early May, a group of soldiers from Tenahaw municipality, headed by a Captain Braddy, "made use of Some very Rough measures." They "threatened to Burn & plunder Nacogdoches," which had been virtually depopulated in the Runaway Scrape, "under the plea that all the Inhabitants were Torries—& had combined with St. Anna." These soldiers announced intentions of killing several persons, including the head of the committee of safety, a course of action dissuaded only by community pressure and counterthreats of violence. Anti-Tory militance in east Texas died down after mid-May. Subsequently, Tory-baiting became a rhetorical device used by army agitators. These activities may have been unnecessary, but they seem to have quelled any lingering pro-Mexican sentiment in the southeastern area by early summer.[62]

In western Texas the depth of feelings and level of support for the centralists had been too significant to allow the Tories to recant or to submerge after the battle of San Jacinto. Their response to the Mexican defeat varied from one community to another. In Victoria "Tory" behavior had been more expedient than anything else. When Urrea's army returned in retreat in mid-May, only a few families from there fled southward with it. In contrast, the Mexican withdrawal caused great consternation in San Patricio. Loyalist leaders like the O'Daugherty family, as well as some of less ardent believers who had been treated mercifully by the Mexicans, accompanied the army all the way to Matamoros. In early June an advanced unit of Texans found only twenty families, many of them husbandless, in "St. Patricio." "The Tory party," reported a Texas officer, "have left this place with the Mexicans."[63] In the area stretching between San Patricio and Victoria, most of the non-Tejanos had fled eastward before or during Urrea's advance in March. Those remaining had just begun to reunite and rebuild under the rule of Santa Anna when first the armies of Urrea and Filisola and then the Texans under Rusk returned with their disturbing presence. Bonifacio Rodríguez may have exaggerated in recalling that "all" the area residents had rejoiced at "seeing themselves free of the [Anglo Texan] enemies who at every opportunity molested the people," but most did seen to be adjusting easily to the centralist order.[64]

Though many Mexican loyalists from Victoria to San Patricio fled with the retreating centralist forces to the Rio Grande and beyond, substantial numbers of Tejano Tories clung to their own lands or congregated at the Carlos de la Garza ranch in open defiance of the Texans. The Mexican generals felt obliged to engage in heated debate over responsibility for abandoning these loyal citizens to the vengeful Texan occupation force. While the exact number who fled to Mexico cannot be determined, it clearly was substantial, for the entire region suffered from noticeable depopulation during the early years of the Republic.[65]

In Béxar there had been less than a uniform Tory conversion. When Dr. J. H. Barnard, a survivor of the Goliad massacre, was brought by the Mexicans to Béxar to attend to the wounded, he received "respect and courtesy" from the people rather than animosity. Loyalties remained divided and difficult to assess from March through May. As preparations for the Mexican retreat began around May 20 "the citizens . . . that are hostile to Texas" also began "packing up and leaving," Barnard recorded in his journal. Meanwhile, he continued, "our friends, who are by no means few, are waiting with impatience for the Texan troops to come and take possession." Those who stayed expressed joy at the departure of the Mexican soldiers under Juan José Andrade on May 24. In fact, some, including erstwhile collaborator Angel Navarro, "broke out into transports that made them out quite ludicrously." This decision — to evacuate with the Mexican army or to remain in Béxar —

reflected deeper sentiments than simple reaction to maltreatment at the hands of one army or the other. According to Barnard, the Navarros "were all friendly to the Texas cause" but had not been "molested by the Mexican troops."[66]

This observer, unfamiliar as he was with prewar Béxar, gave a more optimistic accounting than was warranted. When Antonio Menchaca returned to his home in early June, he found the town "almost deserted." Many families, including his and Seguín's, had fled eastward in advance of Santa Anna's legions, and in Menchaca's opinion "a great many Mexican families who either from choice or compulsion espoused the Mexican cause went to Mexico."[67] Many others left the town for area ranches, preferring to risk attack by Comanches (emboldened by the wartime chaos) rather than to test the mood of the occupying Texas forces. According to reports that found their way to Mexico later in the summer, that mood turned out to be vengeful.

A company of twenty "Colonial partisans" under Seguín arrived on June 4 and allegedly instituted such shabby policies that townspeople soon abandoned their homes once more. The commander of this unit naturally viewed the situation differently. Finding that a majority of the residents "do not want to take up arms against" Mexico, Seguín believed his force inadequate in size if he should encounter "any resistance." "I am in danger," he wrote to General Rusk. The arrival of 240 Anglo-American reinforcements in mid-June provided Seguín with more security but, from the viewpoint of local citizens, also led to worsening insults and further property depredations. When Seguín's men evacuated on June 20 in order to join Rusk's army at Victoria, a Béxar refugee estimated that only forty families remained in town. The Texas forces left behind little but "sad memories in this place that was the city of Bejar," according to this account. José María Ortiz, who received this report from Músquiz, the former political chief, sent it on to Urrea with the postscripted conclusion that many families who had stayed behind wished to join the southward trek if their retirement could be given military protection. As late as September this general in Matamoros continued to concern himself with measures to protect the emigration of families from Béxar.[68]

As proof of Texan vindictiveness, Ortiz enclosed a copy of Seguín's parting proclamation to the people of Béxar. On behalf of what he still described as the "Federal Army of Texas," this officer ordered the remaining residents to abandon their homes and move eastward into the interior, driving their livestock with them to deny provisions to any expedition from Mexico. In urging compliance Seguín wrote that the Texas government was still in the process of determining the nature of Tejano loyalty. Voluntary implementation of the order, he wrote, would give the authorities

> proof of your attachment to the just cause, and the beloved liberty we are contending for. If on the contrary you fail to render this slight service, your disaffection will be manifest: and although a matter of regret to the supreme government, yet it can no longer treat you as Texians, but, perhaps as enemies. . . . your conduct on this day is going to decide your fate . . . If you maintain your post as mere lookers-on; . . . you will, without fail, be treated as true enemies and will suffer accordingly.

Seguín signed this proclamation as "Countryman and Friend" and insisted that he honestly conveyed prevailing Texas sentiment. Essentially, he warned that the opinions of Travis had become dominant: Tejano neutrality was being translated as Toryism. This attitude continued to hold sway well after the immediate crisis had passed. A visitor to San Antonio in 1837 noted that most of the genuine Mexican sympathizers had left the country with that army's retreat. "Although the great mass of the people are guilty of no over act [of support for Mexico], still their allegiance is held doubtful," he concluded.[69]

Tory activity from the outset of hostilities had centered in western Texas, where ethnic, religious, military, and political ties to Mexico combined to provide the centralists with a substantial reservoir of support. In the region of the Austin colonies all these ties were weak or nonexistent, and Santa Anna's cause received virtually no aid or comfort from the people. East Texas demonstrated Tory potential, but only among a minority further weakened by geographic isolation and thus unable to rally effective resistance to the rebellion. The Mexican retreat that followed San Jacinto forced most of the real or would-be Tories to recant or go silent in the east and to evacuate with the remnants of Santa Anna's army. This withdrawal, and the spirit of vengeance in the army that caused and supplemented it, left Texas largely unified in the cause of the Revolution, if still debating its proper meaning.

10. Los Tejanos

MEXICAN TEXANS IN THE REVOLUTION

The experience of Tejanos in the Texas Revolution, while distinctive from that of any other group, was not characterized by uniformity. Numbering over 4,000 on the eve of the conflict, the Texas Mexican population resided mostly in four communities. Except in Nacogdoches, with a Tejano population of over 600, they found themselves engulfed by the war. The approximately 450 De León colonists from in and around Victoria felt the effects less severely at first than did the 1,600 in the Béxar area and the 1,350 in the Goliad region, where the people suffered from living in the war zone.[1] Essentially, the Tejano experience centered around problems of military occupation, with the victorious side changing four times in less than a year. Almost any behavior, even that designed to protect themselves from the ravages of war, made the Tejanos seem like traitors from the perspective of one army, if not both, which in any case ravaged the people's food and other resources.

From October, 1835, until the end of March, 1836, the war took place in the Tejano homeland. The conflict not only ended the physical distance between Anglo and Mexican Texans but threw the two peoples together in an atmosphere of extreme tension. Initially, though they had not themselves begun the hostilities, Tejanos volunteered for the Texas side in substantial numbers, but enthusiasm for the war soon declined, and for significant reasons. The bitter experiences of living in occupied territory caused disillusionment. Political factors also led to growing doubts, as the cause changed from federalism within the

Mexican nation, which many Tejanos supported, to independence, which left them in a minority status. These influences evolved in different ways, depending on circumstances unique to each community.

Tejanos serving in the Texas cause came mostly from the town of San Antonio de Béxar in the fall of 1835. Names and numbers of volunteers cannot be determined with precision because of the absence of muster rolls for them for this period, but several sources indicate substantial recruitment early in the war. Years later San Antonio citizens claimed that 160 Tejanos had participated in the siege, service for which, as local resident Sam J. Smith wrote in 1874, "they got no pay or credit."[2] Juan Seguín, who commanded one of the native companies, identified the origins and numbers of the Tejano recruits of 1835: his company of thirty-seven men had entered at Salado Creek in October; Salvador Flores and Manuel Leal together raised forty-one volunteers from area ranches; fourteen (mostly Bexareños) deserted from Cos's forces in the city. Plácido Benavides brought a company of twenty-eight from Victoria, and an additional Tejano detachment of about twenty from the forces at Goliad later arrived along with a similar number of isolated enlistments from there.

From a variety of other sources, most especially bounty and donation grant records, the names of ninety-one Tejanos who served in the fall of 1835 have been ascertained. Biographical information on these men reveals the following profile: most were young, the average age being 27.5 (25 when measured by the median figure), about four to six years younger, in fact, than the Anglo volunteers of this period. Nevertheless, a majority of them had already married. Native-born Texans (85 percent) naturally dominated the ranks, and the few who had come north to settle from Mexico had done so seven to fifteen years earlier. The place of residence of these volunteers becomes even more difficult to establish; however, Bexareños clearly outnumbered any other group. Only fifteen of those who saw service in 1835 can be identified as from outside of the Béxar municipality, and the census records suggest that town residents were twice as numerous as those from the ranches. As Seguín recalled, his company was the largest, and it "was made up of men from this city [San Antonio]."[3]

Bexareño soldiers made contributions commensurate with their numbers. From his initial meeting with General Austin at Camp Salado on October 22, Captain Seguín energetically executed a number of varied responsibilities. Recruitment continued up to the storming of the city on December 5, but the unit became active from its inception.

As the commander in chief wrote on November 24, the company of "native Mexicans . . . was very efficient in the cause." On the fourteenth of that month Austin dispatched a unit under Salvador Flores on an "important" mission away from the scene of the siege. Primarily sent to scout for centralist reinforcements south of the Nueces River, its orders also involved capturing horses and burning the grasslands to inhibit enemy movement. The Tejanos seemed especially adept in this kind of service, no doubt because of their knowledge of the countryside. Austin praised them for capturing expresses directed to the centralist forces in Béxar, but he also made it clear that "Cap. Seguín and his men were at all times ready and willing to go on any service they were ordered. They uniformly acquited themselves to their credit as patriots and soldiers."[4]

This service included participation in battle. Seguín's men saw action with Bowie at missions San José and Concepción in November, and Tejanos answered the call for volunteers to storm the city on December 5. Antonio Cruz, of the Béxar company, so distinguished himself in the fighting at the Veramendi house as to attract commendation by no less of an anti-Mexican than Travis. Nonsoldiers also got into the action as the conflict came literally into their homes. Among these María Jesusa de García stood out, because, in the words of an act subsequently passed by the Texas Congress, she "was wounded and permanently disabled in rendering extraordinary services to the army of Texas at San Antonio." García had attempted to carry water to the Texans on December 5 in spite of the heavy Mexican barrage. These acts of individual valor gained particular recognition, but one veteran of the campaign extended the plaudits to the community as a whole. "Our army owe[s] many thanks to the brave inhabitants" of the city, he wrote on Christmas day, for they "ranked themselves on the side of liberty, and fought bravely with the Texan forces. Were all the Mexicans such ardent lovers of liberty, as the citizens of San Antonio, we should not now be left to fight our battles alone."[5]

That a sizable force of Bexareños turned out for the Texas cause came as no great surprise to the leaders of the rebellion, for the city had acquired a reputation of opposition to the military-centralist party. The more remarkable feature of the high level of volunteering was that those from town found sufficient opportunity to participate despite a form of martial law imposed by General Cos. On October 15, a full week before the Texas army arrived at Salado Creek near the town, he ordered Political Chief Angel Navarro to devise and administer a passport system. Essentially, this edict forbid anyone from leaving without a pass from either Cos or Navarro. The civil authority complied, periodically supplying a list of persons who had been given exit permits, but the commander expressed dissatisfaction with enforcement. The system had been in place but a few days when local resident Zeferino Ruiz boldly left town with no pass and even more brazenly returned with a note from one of the rebel leaders. According to further correspondence from Cos, only "a few inhabitants among this population have heeded the policy"; therefore, he informed Navarro, beginning November 18 and "without exception" anyone caught violating the passport rule would be sentenced to forced labor. This level of non-compliance occurred in the face of a strong night patrol, staffed by both infantry and cavalry.[6]

The Texas forces expected to benefit from the enemy's problems in controlling the town population. Before the army had even arrived one observer predicted that the number of Cos's troops required "to keep down the citizens" would be a significant advantage. In fact, several residents managed to leave town to join the Texas cause. Austin indicated that these included both "deserters" from the Mexican army and "inhabitants who have connected with us." Movement between Béxar and the rebel lines seems to have occurred almost constantly. Macedonio Arocha, one of the recruits, recalled later that he went back and forth at night from town to Seguín's company several times, to visit his family and to obtain extra provisions. Friendly Bexareños even helped the Texas artillery overcome its ammunition shortage by returning used cannon balls. Perhaps most importantly, the people of the city provided information on the centralist army and through intermediaries like rancher José María Solmas sent out confidential communications.[7]

Those who left the town brought complaints about the military rule of General Cos. According to reports made to Bowie and Fannin at Espada mission on October 22, "a large number of the citizens of Bexar and of this place, are now *laying out,* to prevent being forced to perform the most servile duties." Erasmo Seguín "and others of the most respectable citizens" were reputedly to be made "to sweep the public square, and in case [Cos] whiped [*sic*] us, to make their Ladies, grind tortias for his soldiers." The general eventually forced the elder Seguín to walk to his son's ranch, leaving behind the remainder of the family to endure the Texas barrage for the rest of the siege. Cos also impressed mules and drivers and perhaps other property, and he reportedly razed houses on the outskirts of town to provide a more favorable field of fire in case of a rebel assault.[8]

Hearing these reports, the Texas leaders came to expect more support from the Bexareños. Following a month of loosely conducted siege warfare, Austin issued a "Proclamation to the Inhabitants of Bexar" that amounted to an invitation for them somehow to make peace. This document enumerated an eight-point set of terms, half of which concerned capitulation and withdrawal, matters more appropriately directed to Cos or his superiors. Remaining provisions promised fair representation for Béxar and a kind of amnesty: "No Citizen will be persecuted nor molested in any way in either their persons or property on account of their political opinions." Finally, Austin indicated that all who sought the protection of his plan should present themselves to the army of Texas.[9] After this pronouncement the besieging forces increasingly considered the remaining residents to be enemies and suspected those who moved back and forth between the town and the Texan lines as potential spies rather than useful informants.[10] Naturally, this changing opinion led to increased tensions between Béxar civilians and the Texans.

Relations also worsened because of the army's growing demands for supplies. Actually, from the date of their arrival in October the Texas forces had but a meager commissary and little cash with which to make purchases. Even officers who attempted to respect private property had difficulty in establishing ownership of the corn, beans, and beef they needed; further they could not always determine the genuine needs of the local population, some of whom they suspected of intending to withhold from the Texans in order to sell to the centralists in town. As late as November 16 Austin had to explain to Antonio de la Garza why he would not be permitted to transport his maize and beans to the plaza while it remained in enemy hands. The commander assured his correspondent that war's end would bring restoration of civil authority and payment for properties confiscated from patriotic citizens (not enemies).[11]

Soon after their arrival in the nieghborhood it became obvious that, lacking the money with which to make purchases, the Texans would resort to impressment. Responding to queries regarding dealings with the recalcitrant *mayordomo* of Espada mission, Austin ordered Bowie and Fannin to use persuasion, give certificates of credit, and keep an accurate accounting: "In the event this arrangement will not satisfy him there is no resource left but to follow the Law of necessity, and take what you want." However oppressive this policy might have been, in these matters Austin showed more patience and restraint than did most other members of the army. One of the first assignments given Seguín was contracting with area ranch owners for corn and beans to be paid for in bank bills or on public credit. On November 17 Austin ordered Quartermaster Patrick C. Jack to organize a food-gathering expedition. This officer received authority to take charge of all wagons and oxen, employ loyal teamsters, and oversee the harvesting of the grain. Austin also attempted to prevent soldiers from killing beef and to exempt certain fields from being ravaged by the army.[12]

Despite these efforts, the Texas commander obviously knew that much property had been taken without attention to any form of payment. A week after his resignation Austin reminded the provisional government of its responsibility "to ascertain the amount of property thus [by compulsion] made use of, and to provide for a Just compensation." Nevertheless, over four years later Josefa Jiménez still had not settled the account for the corn "that during the storming of Bexar was taken from her by the volunteer army of Texas," as her claim read. These contributions burdened both poor and affluent. In 1840 a congressional resolution awarded Erasmo Seguín $3,004 for the oxen, mules, corn, beans, beef, and other supplies he had furnished in 1835.[13]

Had it not been for the moderating presence of Austin the impact of the war on the Tejano population of Béxar might well have been far worse. Many other officers like Fannin favored a more concerted scorched earth policy. On November 5 the general wrote his thoughts on military strategy to the Consultation. While he agreed basically that circumstances of war had undercut the middle ground, Austin opposed "laying waste the country round Bexar. I think [that] too hard on the inhabitants who are our friends." For some time this issue was a source of internal disaffection in the Texas army, but the general continued to order his subordinates to discriminate between friend and foe in raiding area ranches.[14]

These divisions on treatment of civilians still existed among the soldiers as they stormed the city and battled house-to-house between December 5 and 10. Consequently, one unit shot a boy who tried to escape from a captured dwelling and arrested three women and a priest. Another company stormed a stone house and shot inside until it heard the "screams of women & children" and then paroled the men who laid down their arms, allowing all of them to flee to an area away from the fighting. In making peace General Edward Burleson agreed to restore private property "to its proper owners," to protect the citizens of Béxar "in their persons," and not to molest civilian or soldier "on account of his political opinions hitherto expresed."[15]

The question of the war's impact on civilian life in Béxar had not greatly distracted either of the armies as they pursued the laws of necessity and confiscated, consumed, or destroyed property. The people of Béxar endured a battle that literally reached into their homes. The Texas tactics of turning houses into strongholds involved forced entries, tearing holes out of walls and ceilings, and reinforcing doors and windows with dirt and furniture. These methods left the city marked by heaps of ruins. Further, the siege created shortages for civilians trapped in the town; even those in farming areas controlled by Texans found that the army used up staples at an alarming rate. At the time of arrival in the outskirts of Béxar no less qualified an observer than West Point–trained Fannin described the provisions as virtually inexhaustible. Yet, less than a month later he reported to Austin, "We have nearly consumed all the corn &c near here."[16] These shortages translated into privation for Tejano civilians. Their sacrifices of liberty and property were substantial if only because the armies were large and more stationary than at any other time in the war.

The people of the Goliad area also experienced the traumas of military rule in the fall of 1835. The size and character of the occupation differed from that of Béxar in that the Texans triumphed there very early in the war, on October 9, and held the post with a garrison that seldom exceeded one hundred men. However, commander Dimitt asserted absolute control over both resources and the civil authorities, resulting in a form of domination at least equal to that suffered by the Bexareños. By late in the year, as Texas forces gathered in and around Goliad for a projected assault against Matamoros, the Tejanos of this region had to endure the pressure of a large, hostile army in their midst. In early spring, 1836, centralist troops arrived and added the hardships of battle to the sufferings of the people.

Not all these problems could have been predicted. The entire region acquired a reputation for lukewarmness toward the Texas cause; yet, Tejanos from both Victoria and Goliad volunteered initially in support of the rebellion. When Texans from Matagorda arrived at the de León colony on their way to conquer the Mexican fortress, Alcalde Juan Antonio Padilla, who considered it "disgraceful to live under the military yoke," joined the expedition. He brought into the ranks other prominent Victorians, including the empresario's son Silvestre de León and son-in-law Plácido Benavides. Austin described Padilla as "a true friend to Texas and to Liberty." Miguel Galán, from Goliad, volunteered on October 10, the day after the fort capitulated, to be joined soon by Paulino de la Garza, Agustín Bernal, and some of the men who had been serving in the Mexican garrison. Controversy soon developed, as Col. Benjamin Fort Smith wrote to his friend Austin, over what to do with "the Mexican Volunteers." "We know Not as yet how far they may be relied upon," he opined. Dimitt resolved the issue by sending Padilla "with a Small detachment of creole troops" under Benavides to Béxar for Austin to deal with personally. This company of about thirty men remained for the duration of the siege and participated with distinction in some of the fiercest fighting in December. [17]

What Dimitt apparently intended, and clearly achieved, amounted to a purging of Mexicans from his force. Although rancher Miguel Aldrete remained affiliated with this unit, even signing the controversial declaration of December 22, and men like Tomás Amador served the Texans as a messenger, Anglo and Irish colonists dominated the Goliad command for the remainder of 1835. Lacking the potentially moderating influence of "native" troops, the Texans became an army of occupation pitted against the people of the region. Perhaps the commander did not believe that he needed a Tejano perspective because, as one veteran later wrote, Dimitt "had a Mexican wife and was, for all practical purposes, a Mexican." Undoubtedly, the people of Goliad would not have concurred in this conclusion.

Even though a sizable body of centralist supplies fell into Texas hands with the capitulation of the fort, Dimitt immediately began to impress the property of local citizens. On October 10 he seized "into the public service" $120 worth of beef belonging to C. [J.] E. Vasquez. A few days later Domingo Falcón and A. Volors forcibly surrendered some of their cattle to the Texas army, and other residents of the vicinity furnished twenty horses for the use of the soldiers. Through the month of November the people continued to make more forced contributions—animals, corn, wagon wheels, a rifle, a string of ponies, even a crowbar—nothing seemed to escape the army's clutches. Dimitt's grasp reached one hundred miles north to the ranch of Erasmo Seguín, who lost five hundred dollars worth of mules to impressment. [18]

The garrison's most insatiable need seemed not to be food but transportation. In order to move Irish colonists out of the war zone and send provisions to Béxar, Dimitt seized both carts and teamsters. On November 13 Alcalde Galán enumerated the sufferings of the Goliad residents in a letter to Austin: "[The soldiers are] breaking into houses, ravaging the corn without the consent of property owners, killing cows randomnly without making an effort to know who they belong to, impressing servants without the consent of their masters, and then letting them loose without supervision . . . [or] paying them for their labor." The commander also made the people work on fortifying the plaza and perform other forms of manual labor.[19]

The citizens of Goliad responded in several ways. As Dimitt himself explained, "immediately after the place was taken," they began to seek refuge in the countryside. Some fled from the section altogether. On October 25 he continued to affect surprise at this reaction, claiming "I have done, and have said, every thing which I could do, or say, to pacify and inspire them with confidence." Dimitt attributed the people's conduct to awe of the military display earlier made by the centralists. Other observers assigned responsibility to the policies of the Texas military in general and its local leader in particular. John J. Linn complained to Austin of the many "acts of tireney" of Dimitt, "a great enimey of the Mexicans." All but twenty had left town; "the people are afraid to come [back] as they do not want to be made hewers of wood and Drawers of water."[20]

Having left their homes in search of security, in early November the Tejanos sought to rectify their situation through politics. Many enthusiastically welcomed the arrival of Governor Viesca, who came with an armed guard on November 11 in his flight from the centralists; as a legally constituted federalist leader, he must have seemed a potential deliverer. But Dimitt's refusal to receive the governor "in an official capacity" incited what the Texas officer called "insubordination, . . . discontent, and . . . a spirit of opposition, both in and out of the fort." Tejanos held a public meeting on the twelfth and protested military usurpation of democratically elected civil authority. All but one of the thirty-two who signed this document were Tejanos, but they gained some support among soldiers.[21]

Dimitt promptly declared martial law. His order proclaimed: "All persons manifesting an opposition dangerous to the cause espoused by the People of Texas—All who oppose, or threaten to oppose, the observance of order, of discipline, and subordination, or who endeavour to excite discontent wither in the Fortress, or within the Town, will be regarded as public enemies, arrested as such, and dealt with accordingly." Specifically, no one could arrive or leave without reporting and obtaining a passport. This policy brought on an additional set of protests, mostly directed to Austin and seeking replacement of the Goliad commander. Thomas G. Western, who had as the post's adjutant opposed Dimitt on the Viesca matter, explained that the inhabitants had not only "flown to the country for Security . . . [but also] prepared hiding places to which to escape at the very sound of the name Dimitt." The alcalde catalogued the various infringements on popular liberty and pointed out the irony of these being committed in the name of the liberal cause. Austin promptly ordered Dimitt's ouster and informed Galán that the replacement would respect civil authority; however, the Goliad garrison kept Dimitt in power. A public meeting at Texana renewed the Tejanos' request for protection by the provisional government,[22] but by then their fate more than ever rested with the increasingly powerful and antagonistic Texas army. Many area Tejanos continued to hide.

These inherited tensions, combined with newer aggravations, poisoned Tejano-military relations during that period. Considerable underground support existed for the centralists, and the U.S. volunteers and other troops who swelled in numbers between December and February held militantly anti-Mexican attitudes. Fannin reported from the fort in February that "no aid need be expected from Mexicans." Recruits from the United States likewise expressed skepticism about Tejano trustworthiness. As one wrote, the citizens of La Bahía "professed to be hearty in the cause of the revolution" but actually fled from town in order to hedge their fate. This perceived vacillation, which the people attributed to a desire to escape the unruly behavior of the Texas troops, led the soldier to doubt both words and deeds of support. He did admit that "the absconded citizens of Goliad . . . received us kindly, and treated us with hospitality, professed the warmest hospitality to our cause, and denied having any communication with the Mexican army."[23]

Residents of this region provided several kinds of service to Texas. Juan A. Zambrano went to Matamoros as a spy for Austin and fell prisoner to Urrea. Plácido Benavides, shortly after leading a company in the storming of Béxar, likewise set out on an intelligence-gathering mission to centralist-held territory near the Rio Grande. In early February he returned with news of an impending invasion, information that Fannin ignored, to his later grief. Other Tejanos made less spectacular contributions. Miguel Benítez, also a veteran of the siege, along with other drivers carried ammunition and other stores from the coast. Victor Loupy probably filled as many roles as any Texan in the Revolution.

He volunteered for the army at Goliad on October 9 and subsequently acted as soldier, interpreter, and contractor, supplying Fannin's troops with more than four hundred head of cattle. The centralists captured and imprisoned him; after the Revolution a Texas secretary of war endorsed Loupy's application for back pay with a commendation for his "long and meritorious service."[24]

One mercantile enterprise involving Tejanos from this region resulted in a substantial loss of property. José María Carbajal and his brother-in-law Fernando de León, of Victoria, chartered the *Hannah Elizabeth* in November to carry arms and other goods from New Orleans to the Texas forces. The vessel and proprietors fell prey to a centralist ship operating near the coast in December; their goods ended up in the hands of a group of Matagordans who had commissioned a coastal raider that recaptured the *Hannah*. Despite their vigorous protest, the Victorianos received none of the proceeds from the auction of the salvaged supplies. Nevertheless, Acting Governor Robinson appointed de León as aide-de-camp to organize the militia of Victoria, "believing that you are willing to serve your country in any way that you can be useful."[25]

The Tejano masses lost their property in the conflict not through business dealings but by the continuing impressment policies of the Texas army. Once again in early 1836 as in the previous year the most sought-after of their possessions were draft animals. To some extent earlier and then especially during the attempted retreat in March, A. C. Horton and other press gangs rounded up every yoke of oxen, team of mules, or stray horse they could find. Leg-weary infantrymen also attempted spur-of-the-moment appropriations from Tejano corrals, but they sometimes found the mounts too wild to be handled.

Most of the people of La Bahía stayed in their rural sanctuaries. Troops new to the town found little but "empty streets," as one wrote. "All of the inhabitants had kept indoors, and only a few aged Mexicans deigned to look at us from the small air-holes which form the windows of their cabins." For Tejanos even flight to ranches no longer provided protection from the more numerous and disorderly recruits who conducted frequent forays in search of provisions and enemies.[26]

When hostilities came to this region in February and March, more Tejanos fought on for the invaders than for Fannin. The wonder is that any sided with Texas at all, given the state of military-civilian relations. About ten Mexican Texans saw action in the Nueces River area, of whom two were killed and the others captured. As the action came closer to Refugio, Tejano participation on the side of the Revolution dwindled, although Mariano Carbajal and one other perished at Goliad. Either from simple charity or in support of the Texas cause, several Tejanas aided the few soldiers who had managed to escape the fate of Fannin and his men. These acts of mercy included tips about the locations of Urrea's soldiers as well as provisions of food and clothing.[27]

Whether they welcomed the invasion or opposed it, the coming of the war into their homeland devastated the lives of many Tejanos. Some who considered themselves noncombatants died in the guerrilla-like fighting around Refugio from March 11–13. They also lost equipment, horses, cattle, and other property; especially devastated were those who resided in the town, which rebel forces under William Ward burned on March 13. That same fate befell La Bahía, as Fannin set it ablaze just before beginning his tardy retreat. Santa Anna later used the fact that the Texas brand of warfare had "reduced [the Tejanos] to the most dreadful situation" to justify the vengeful treatment of Urrea's captives. At Victoria, which of all the Mexican-dominated communities of this area had shown the greatest loyalty to the Texas cause, the authorities had reserved twenty yoke of oxen to assist civilian evacuation in case of a centralist victory. Fannin impressed these at the last minute, depriving the people of the means of flight.[28] Ironically, the Texas army later used their failures to evacuate as evidence of Tory sentiment.

However harsh his policies toward the enemy, Urrea promised not "'to molest the inhabitants of the country who remained at their homes and took no part in the war.'" Yet, according to an official who carried this message, "'the general would depend on the citizens for much subsistence.'" This included a measure of cooperation as well as material support. Urrea forced the principal leaders of Victoria to report and perform certain duties. Fernando de León had to turn over hidden contraband goods. His brother-in-law Manuel Escalera served under compulsion as a courier for Urrea.[29]

In this period between December and April, 1836, the community of Béxar had as before lent more voluntary support to the Texas cause than had the areas to the south. Still, many of the problems experienced by Goliad also characterized the situation in the departmental capital. In the fall hostilities had been more intense and thus destruction greater in Béxar, and the people continued to supply an army of occupation after the surrender of Cos. For the entire period from December to April this community continued to feel in innumerable ways the burden of war.

Like other Texans, a majority of the Tejano soldiers returned to civilian life as soon after the December 5 victory over the centralists as possible, and most of those who served in 1835 did not join the army again in the spring of 1836. Instead, Anglo and Tejano veterans alike looked first to the care of their families in the belief that those who had not yet gone to war should do so. Though few at the time saw this retirement as anything but natural, some critics subsequently cited it as evidence of a lack of patriotic zeal. A substantial number of Bexareños in fact remained militarily active, albeit in a somewhat irregular fashion. Captain Seguín led a body of cavalry which tracked the movement of Cos's forces to scout their threatened return from south of the Rio Grande. Company commander Salvador Flores and a few others risked themselves in "spy" work north of that river to detect centralist troop movement, but throughout most of early 1836 the military authorities did not actually seek Tejano participation.[30]

During the month of December Tejanos of the town and the surrounding area still lived under military rule, as General Ed Burleson's successor, Francis W. Johnson, made no attempt to reestablish civil authority. The masses of people, though "greatly impoverished" in Neill's words, had to share their provisions with the military. Much of the burden of feeding the army of occupation still rested on area farmers. One such group living near San José mission resisted impressment of six wagon loads of corn with such "pitiful pleas" that the press gang leader consulted his superiors about returning the grain. Eventually, he decided that the farmers had been deceitful in claiming that this "was their only food until the next harvest" because they had actually intended to sell part of their holdings in town. The profit motive and dislike of Americans, not "dread of famine kept them from sharing their surplus with us." It seems not to have occurred to him that the impressed corn comprised the people's only asset in acquiring other goods from town because most of the farmers received certificates of credit, not negotiable currency, for the commodities taken by Seguín, Johnson, and other officers in December and January.[31]

By contrast to what he considered the grim behavior of the rural people, Herman Ehrenberg perceived a more light-hearted spirit in town. Residents who had fled during the siege returned soon after the peace of December 11 so that "bustle and animation again filled the streets, where Texans and Mexicans walked about their business without fear or resentment." Most of the native people seemed content to pursue their traditional pleasures and welcomed as "guests" the American volunteers who made up the bulk of the local garrison. Without the displays of protest that had occurred at the mission, merchants like Francisco A. Ruiz and José A. Navarro sold on credit a variety of supplies ranging from beef, corn, and other food to horses, mules, and cooking utensils. Nevertheless, the burden of having supplied armies since October had exhausted the area economy by January. Neill reported that even the ubiquitous cattle had come into short supply, and he received authorization to employ vaqueros at twenty dollars per month to drive in beef from the range. This promise of employment on credit hardly improved the economy. According to the acting governor, "the unfortunate inhabitants [were] reduced by the war, from opulence and ease, to penury and want."[32]

This material suffering did not lead to overwhelming disaffection by the people, as seen by a consensus of the military leaders stationed in Béxar. Only Travis seemed to fear Tejano treachery. In contrast, Neill wrote emphatically to Houston on January 14, "I can say to you with Confidence, that we can rely on great aid from the citizens of this town, in case of an attack." He cited the voluntary contribution of supplies by Gaspar Flores and Luciano Navarro as evidence of this genuine support. Within the next two weeks Bowie and G. B. Jameson confirmed Neill's assessment, with the latter giving praise to Seguín and others of "the most wealthy and influential citizens." This account also noted the problem of "loose [military] discipline" that led to soldier-civilian tensions.[33]

Neill had restored civil authority when he became head of the post at the end of 1835, but disorder associated with the struggle to succeed him threatened to undo the amicable relations he had created. The elevation of Bowie over Travis in this contest in February, as the latter wrote, made "everything topsy turvey." Bowie began interfering with private property, preventing citizens from carting their goods to the country, and in effect he abrogated civil government by releasing prisoners from jail. This act brought on conflict. Judge Seguín angrily resigned in protest, and Bowie retaliated by calling an armed parade of the Alamo troops, all of whom acted in what the post adjutant described as "a tumultously and disorderly manner," attributable to the drunkenness of the Texas forces.[34]

Part of these tensions grew out of the awareness of many Bexareños of the impending centralist invasion and their reaction to this threat. As the above episode revealed, a large number of citizens had been fleeing the town since mid-January. Knowledge of centralist plans did not indicate treason; rather, the local population simply took seriously the reports of those who had been dispatched to the Laredo area to gather intelligence. The Texas commanders also had access to this information but refused to retreat from the Alamo fortress.[35]

When Santa Anna's men began arriving on February 22, they found the town reduced in population but not entirely abandoned. Some of the people stayed at home in support of the invading force, but more often they had hopes of maintaining an undeclared neutrality. In part this waning of support for Texas may have been the result of the growing tensions between civilians and the Texas army; however, the most significant influence on local Tejano behavior was the failure of the military to prevent the centralist reoccupation. Like many Anglo colonists, Bexareños who supported the cause often chose to provide for the welfare of their families first before joining or reenrolling in the service. In fact, when the ranks of the Alamo defenders are defined to include all those who served under Neill in early February as well as Travis and Bowie later in the month, the number of Tejanos becomes nineteen rather than the three cited by Travis. Mostly from Béxar, this Tejano contingent of defenders ranked next to Gonzales in number of recruits and represented nearly twenty percent of the Texans who served in the army at San Antonio in the first two months of 1836. Many of the Bexareños received discharges from commander Neill and left to help evacuate their families, or like Seguín became messengers in one of the many last-ditch efforts to bring reinforcements to the fortress. Some, as historian Walter Lord suggests, may also have chosen to retire from what obviously had become a losing cause. The list of those who braved the assault in the Alamo should also include four or five Bexareñas and nine dependent children who had accompanied their husband-father-protectors into the fort.[36]

Generally, Santa Anna seemed determined to demonstrate restraint in his relations with the local population. A few Béxar homeowners had to quarter Mexican officers, and the Mexican president eventually confiscated and auctioned property belonging to "colonists" in the town, but his army apparently paid for more commodities than did the impressment-prone Texans, who once again had herded local cattle and seized corn and other property in their hasty flight into the fortress. Townspeople had considerable freedom of movement, some even managing to wander into and out of the fort after the siege had begun. In battle, too, most of the destruction of local property emanated from the Texans—Travis's men burned many houses in La Villita in an attempt to reduce the cover of the attackers.[37]

The day after the final assault the victorious general ordered Bexareños to return home where they would be protected in their domestic life. Actually, they did not easily or quickly resume normal routines. Alcalde Francisco Antonio Ruiz led a delegation of citizens forced to identify corpses, cart off Mexican bodies for burial, and prepare the funeral pyre for the defenders. Other leaders, including political chief Ramón Músquiz, established hospitals and attended the wounded before and after the battle. For the next two months civilians and soldiers suffered from scarcity of food and high prices. Nevertheless, the people endured these sufferings and still managed to display courtesy and kindheartedness, according to an American physician stationed there in April and May.[38]

A large number of Béxar residents fled before the invading force came onto the scene. Having placed their families in some rural sanctuary or on the road to the east and presumed safety, many of the men rallied to one of the military units forming in the vicinity of the Colorado River. Seguín, after failing to stir movement from Fannin, went to the neighborhood of Gonzales and organized some of these recruits into a company. Houston used this command as a rear guard during the long retreat and proposed similar duty for it at San Jacinto. At the insistence of its leader and men like Antonio Menchaca the Tejano company engaged in the battle as part of the left wing of the Texas army and behaved with suitable gallantry. Most estimates give the number in this unit at twenty-two to twenty-four (Seguín's recollection placed the figure at forty-six, including those who served in the rear baggage detail); adding those from Nacogdoches and other parts of Texas, thirty-two Tejanos can be identified by name as having served at this decisive battle. Most of them were young, averaging but twenty-five years in age, and 60 percent were single, characteristics that reflected the fact that family men had been diverted from service by the need to provide for their dependents. Thirteen others besides Seguín had also served in the Béxar siege of the previous fall.[39] Far more Bexareños had turned out for the Texas cause in the spring of 1836 than served in the battle of San Jacinto. Among those who gathered at Gonzales in early March, General Houston sent a company of twenty-five to forty under the command of Salvador Flores to defend families that had remained on their farms. Another body of about thirty soldiers escorted civilians from Béxar to Nacogdoches.[40]

Whichever destination they decided on, the fleeing civilians confronted substantial risks. Siege veteran Agustín Bernal took his family forty miles from town to the ranch of Tía Calvilla on the San Antonio River. He "was obliged to remain at that place," as he recalled years later, "to protect his wife and young child against the Indians and some parties of Mexican outlaws." Some of the women and children set off to the east with neither protectors nor adequate equipment. The Tejana wife of Erastus (Deaf) Smith loaded her two sets of twins and personal possessions in a bulky cart but had no draft animals. She borrowed a team from her fellow refugees on her one-leg-at-a-time journey. The more affluent Seguín family attempted to save three thousand sheep and a herd of cattle by driving them past the Colorado River, in the common but mistaken notion that Texas forces would stop Santa Anna's advance at that point. Slowed by their possessions and by the snarl of other families on the miserable roads, most of the Seguín animals fell to the pursuing division of General Joaquín Ramírez y Sesma. The family members managed to get away to San Augustine and then to Nacogdoches, but without their assets they had to sell personal property, including even clothing, just to avoid starving. Illness as well as poverty beset the Seguíns during their brief stay in east Texas.[41]

Their experience may have been particularly unpleasant because they entered an isolated and suspect Tejano community in Nacogdoches, where the Revolution engaged the Hispanic people politically — invariably in opposition — but not militarily and had less impact socially than elsewhere. Leaders of the Texas cause had attempted at the outset "to try and Rase the Maxacans" as a group, in the words of George A. Nixon, but repeatedly failed. Tejano militiamen did agree to serve as a home guard unit; however, this same official later wrote, "they Seeme Not to under Stand the Busi[-]ness."[42] This ruse of feigned ignorance allowed the masses to stay at home, but individuals made contributions to the war effort. In early November the Nacogdoches vigilance committee head informed Thomas J. Rusk that "the most wealthy" of the Tejanos have "furnished horses and money for the equipment" of a company of U.S. volunteers that came through town on the way to Béxar. These contributors included Miguel Cortines, "one of the few Mexicans whose energies have been used in our cause," Rusk later wrote. The supplies included a horse and four rifles valued at $210. In December Bernard Pantallion provided nearly one thousand eight hundred pounds of beef and pork to another of these companies, and others gave horses or worked as cooks, couriers, or servants.[43]

Although the Tejanos of east Texas refused to form into a single body and march to the front as a unit, individually they did join the army,

Anglo-American criticisms notwithstanding. Most of this volunteering occurred in fall of 1835, before the cause had become independence, when at least six "natives" from the region served in the siege of Béxar. Squire Cruse enlisted at Jasper on October 14; the remainder were from Nacogdoches. They came from a variety of personal circumstances, some of them being young and single, while Esteban Mora, forty-eight years old, had a wife and four children living at home. Juan José Ybarbo, another married man in his forties, received an honorable discharge that testified also to his bravery and his financial contributions to the Texas forces. Casimiro García fell prisoner to General Cos during the siege while serving in Rusk's company.[44]

Despite these examples of individual participation, the Tejanos as a whole remained a separate community in Nacogdoches. When newcomer William F. Gray arrived there in early February, he observed that "there is no social intercourse between them [Anglo Americans] and the Mexicans." The latter impressed him as "a quiet, orderly, and cheerful people, . . . unthrifty and unambitious," though some seemed atypically "intelligent and respectable." His own experience indicated a less than absolute segregation, in that Anglos frequented the Tejano gambling houses, but a high degree of separation clearly characterized both political and social behavior.[45]

Anglo-Tejano tensions continued well beyond the battle of San Jacinto. In June military authorities still considered the issue of drafting Nacogdoches Tejanos, and the local vigilance group discussed using force to make them join the revolutionary cause. At the end of the month Houston wrote to the head of that committee urging him "not to adopt any harsh measures towards the Mexicans in the neighborhood of Nacogdoches. Treat them kindly and pass them as tho' there was no difficulty or differences of opinion. *By no means* treat them with *violence.*" Though the General's advice apparently forestalled an immediate conflict, his argument rested on a flimsy public relations reasoning: "The world would damn our cause if we shed blood at home" before defeating the invader decisively. Thus, the future boded ill for the Tejanos as a group, and individually they began to suffer loss of liberty even during the summer of 1836. Local Mexicans found themselves detained illegally by private citizens, and the courts sentenced a Tejano to a whipping and a term of forced labor for a six-dollar fraud case.[46]

Residents of the other Tejano communities continued to face the problems of living in occupied Texas during the entire summer of 1836.

Though centralist armies retreated to the Rio Grande in May, all of the west remained an insecure area for several months. Many Tories evacuated southward with the army as it left Béxar on May 25. "The remaining citizens," as a U.S. soldier-physician there reported in his journal, "seem to be much relieved at the departure of the troops, with which they have been oppressed for three months. Some of them broke out into transports that made them out quite ludicrously. . . . Navarro was seen capering about the streets like a boy in perfect ecstasy of glee. He said that now he should recover his health; that nothing but the impure air occasioned by the residence of the Mexican troops had made him sick." Unfortunately, this celebration proved to be premature both for Navarro, who died two weeks later, and for the community as a whole, which continued to experience the difficulties of wartime occupation. Worries about reinvasion kept refugees in east Texas or in their rural hideaways, leaving the town depopulated. Some of the people of the municipality faced dire enough conditions that they set out to plunder the retreating army of Vicente Filisola as it retreated beyond the Nueces. Seguín arrived in Béxar in early June with such a small company that he felt insecure from a potential attack by Tories and from marauding Indians who threatened to rob, murder, and otherwise ravage the entire area.[47]

These various forces of disorder meant that the Bexareños would live under military rule for the remainder of the year, and army measures were often harsh. Initially, at least, the commander operated from a vision of restraint. Rusk specifically ordered Col. James Smith, head of a force dispatched to relieve Seguín at Béxar on June 8, that "you will be careful on going to San Antonio to prevent any unnecessary interruption to the citizens there. Such conduct as entering their homes and taking their property you will certainly forbid [as] improper" in that the people who remained in town had demonstrated friendship toward the Texas cause. Unfortunately, according to reports that reached Mexico that summer, the soldiers did exactly what the General had forbidden. Perhaps in response to this treatment, several townspeople joined those who had earlier given themselves over to centralist protection. This resumed flight renewed army fears of Toryism. Further, some of the people evidently drove their cattle southward with them, thus exacerbating fears of a reinvasion force being fed by Texas beef. Army-civilian relations had become a vicious cycle.[48]

When Seguín departed the town on June 21, he ordered the people of the region to herd their animals eastward, out of potential enemy use, as evidence of loyalty to Texas. Their subsequent conduct failed to satisfy the military leaders. A month later Rusk wrote, "I wish in a few days to give Bejar a shake."[49] This general's earlier goal of a civilian-army accord had largely vanished by August. Residents protested about their treatment, but Rusk could only express "eternal regret . . . that the distress of War should fall upon families of women and children." He promised that "in no case will they be injured by our Troops." His letter to Miguel Arciniega held out little hope for relief: "Bejar being the frontier however must be for some time the Theatre of War and as such will be exposed to many hardships & inconvenience."[50] At the end of August he ordered Col. Francisco Ruiz to visit the town and use his knowledge to ferret our disloyal persons. To the friends of Texas the general offered scant relief: personal protection and promises to pay for the articles they furnished to the army. Property that the military claimed to be public would be repossessed from private hands; those who drove off their cattle toward the Rio Grande would be treated as enemies. Even in the early fall a harsh regimen continued to dominate the community. On September 17 Seguín received orders to recruit a full brigade and a militia force to replace the small regular company previously stationed in the town. His instructions allowed use of military justice to preserve order "provided that sever[e] punishment does not extend to loss of life or limb."[51]

Refugees hiding in the east fared hardly better than the Bexareños remaining closer to home. Seguín and Antonio Menchaca did not gain leave to retrieve their families from Nacogdoches until mid-July. The effects of a fever epidemic still lingered a month later when they set out for home on what proved a traumatic journey. For much of the time only Menchaca felt well enough either to lead the wagon train or attend to the sick. They arrived home to find the town still largely deserted and, "to crown their misfortunes," as Seguín recalled years later, "their fields laid waste, and their cattle destroyed or dispersed." His own ranch had been "despoiled" either "by the retreating enemy, [or] had been wasted by our own army; ruin and misery met me on my return."[52]

The devastation may have seemed like a sudden transformation to the refugees, but it had in fact begun months earlier and affected all property owners whether they stayed home or fled. Seguín should not have been much surprised, for he had issued receipts for goods offered to or impressed by the army from other affluent Tejanos like the Navarros and José Antonio de la Garza. Life and property continued to be in danger as late as mid-October 1836 when a raiding party from Mexico entered San Antonio in search of plunder and perhaps revenge. Seguín, then a Colonel, still offered the local population little in the way of security other than the lame advice of driving their cattle out of the war zone. Those who clung to their homes in contravention of this policy were even regarded as "pretended friends" of Texas by the leading newspaper of the Republic.[53]

In the communities of Victoria, Goliad, and Refugio, the people experienced problems similar to those of the Bexareños but made worse by several factors. When the centralists troops arrived in the spring of 1836, most of the Mexican residents had stayed at home and made their peace with the new order. Since Urrea sought to win support from the local population and left but a small force of occupation behind as he marched east, the inhabitants lived under a relatively light-handed rule through the late spring. In contrast to the situation in Béxar, few of the natives celebrated the retreat of the centralist army in the second half of May. The withdrawal occurred in two phases, first by the division under Filisola, followed closely by that of Urrea.

These generals agreed that the retreat left the people in desperate position but launched into a protracted debate about who should be held responsible. Urrea blamed Filisola for ordering the evacuation and leaving the locals behind in a state of such depravity that no army could possibly subsist there, much less offer protection. Filisola claimed that he had attempted to prepare Goliad as a base for operations, a policy that Urrea had undermined by spreading panic as he passed through on the road to Matamoros. Further, the latter general allegedly had impressed so many draft animals and carts that the people had no means of fulfilling his advice to accompany the centralist army in retreat. However vigorously they debated the matter of blame, the two leaders agreed that many Tejanos had fled with the Mexican army and that those who stayed behind had been left defenseless to cope with a mean-spirited, vengeful Texas force. Neither general bothered to record popular responses, but one other officer did. The people, he wrote in his diary, expressed surprise at being compelled to abandon their property and retreat with the army: "The residents of Goliad, who had suffered much, became quite angry with us and insulted us, saying that we were fleeing as cowards from a handful of adventurers."[54]

Many of the area Tejanos remained on their homelands, either because they lacked the means to flee, chose to resist, or felt themselves safe because they had never voluntarily supported the centralist cause.

However, their previous loyalties counted for little in the summer of 1836. The doomsayers had been right; the Texas army arrived on the scene in a vindictive mood, already disposed to hate Mexicans. Their attitude worsened with the discovery of the grisly remains of the victims of the Goliad massacre.

Poor discipline added to the indiscriminate nature of army policies, as did the weakness of the commissary, which forced commanders to rely on local provisions. Limited in power at first by its small numbers, the army soon grew from four hundred to two thousand. An advanced unit under Col. Sidney Sherman camped near Victoria on May 23, looking for provisions and spies among the citizens, thus setting the tone for subsequent army policies. Rusk arrived there before the end of the month and extended the military influence to Goliad and San Patricio by sending out companies to forage for more supplies and probe for traitors. The commander of one such expedition reported on May 30 that he had found few arms and no documentary evidence to implicate the inhabitants of the ranches he had raided. Nevertheless, he impressed horses and intended to arrest enough family heads to serve as "examples" but not so many as to leave the women entirely defenseless.[55]

His and other groups of soldiers continued these forays in the next few days, reaching all the way to the Nueces River. On June 2 Captains H. Teal and H. W. Karnes reported an adverse response to these activities. Some "Mexicans citizens . . . stated that they was at there Ranch and some of our scouts came up and took them prisoner with some others and robed of there guns and there horses," threatening to remove them to Victoria. The officers protested these attacks for undermining support among the inhabitants, who had responded by fleeing with their cattle. The "rascooly" civilians had used army outrages to convince many of the "old settlers" that "they wood all be killed and they think that you are after them as hard as you can march."[56]

Many of these arrests, insults, and property confiscations resulted from the excesses of soldiers acting outside of army control. Several observers shared this conclusion. John J. Linn's account of the outrages against area Tejanos attributed them to soldiers, especially new recruits from the United States, who operated from a "creed [of] the total extermination of the Mexican race and the appropriation of their property to the individual use of the exterminators." He praised the commander for attempting to control these attacks against civilians and for offering "asylum" to Fernando de León. This head of the Victoria family that had lent so much support to the Texas cause suffered a bush-whacking while at army headquarters. A veteran of this period concurred in absolving Rusk of blame for these disgraceful attacks against the persons and property of the De Leones; he attributed the outrages to adventurers who excused their plundering by false allegations of their victims' unfriendliness. Yet, this account made it clear that the general had failed either to obtain a return of stolen goods or to control the band of army outlaws.[57]

Further, army leaders also seized civilian property in large quantities. Wealthier ranchers and merchants turned over not only cattle but also wagons, mules, oxen, rum, salt, and tobacco. The quartermaster, other officers, and even the commander himself issued some receipts for these goods, but much of what they took went undocumented and thus uncompensated. María Antonio de la Garza, of Victoria, surrendered around sixty head of cattle to the Texas army and received no certificate of impressment for over a year. Luckily, she managed to gain Rusk's endorsement of her claim, with an inscription that revealed much about the process. She had, in fact, "placed her cattle at the disposition of the army and many of them were used," wrote the general, "what number or quality I am unable to say."[58]

Rusk's policy may have been haphazard at first, but it soon became purposeful: throughout the western frontier the people would be removed and their land despoiled of its most valuable property, cattle. This strategy would provision the Texas army, deny support to a threatened enemy reinvasion, and remedy the irritant of civilian-military conflict. Tejanos, who comprised virtually all the people of this broad region, would suffer loss of their possessions, livelihood, and liberty so that the Revolution might be furthered. The Tory behavior of the area hardly served to excuse this oppressive policy, since a majority of that persuasion had already fled with the centralist forces or in response to attacks by the army of occupation in early summer. Most who remained and suffered from this forced evacuation had been loyal to the Texas Revolution. As in Béxar, Rusk's strategy was not implemented in a coherent fashion, but the army did compel substantial numbers to leave their homes.

On June 19 Rusk informed the secretary of war of the issuance of orders "to all the Families Mexicans and all to fall back at once and clear the Country." He offered residents of the entire region between the Guadalupe and Nueces rivers a grim choice — to flee either to Mexico or to a part of Texas out of the war zone, driving out their herds or surrendering them to the control of the army. In actuality, the Tejanos could not protect their properties because they lacked means or opportunity to remove possessions and must leave lands and homes to the mercy of the military. Feigning ignorance of the policy did not provide an effective shield. "Some of the Mexican families," in Rusk's words, "are pretending that they have no orders to remove," but he handled this ploy by reiterating his policy and sending cavalry units to enforce it. He paid particular attention to forcing the evacuation of the leading family of Victoria, the De Leones, by boarding them under guard onto vessels routed to New Orleans. The ranks of evacuees included Benavides, whose revolutionary service had most recently included fighting against Urrea, and José María Carbajal, also a staunch and early supporter of the federalist cause. The army loaded about eighty members of this extended family on the *Durango* at Matagorda Bay on June 26, bringing a large measure of success to Rusk's orders to "dispose of the Families."[59]

He intended to make a complete evacuation of all the Tejano-dominated areas, but enforcement became less rigorous away from Victoria. Carlos de la Garza gave no response to the soldiers who brought the removal orders to his ranch near Refugio and thus led his people into successful resistance. This act capped his thorough and consistent opposition to the Texas cause. In spite of this glaring exception, Rusk's otherwise ruthless policy allowed him to police the region more successfully for the remainder of the summer. Into the fall Texas authorities continued to issue orders to drive the livestock belonging to unfriendly citizens out of the valleys of the San Antonio and Nueces rivers.[60]

The ravages of the war and immediate postwar period left a permanent mark on the entire area. For years the De Leones remained in exile in Louisiana while their Anglo neighbors or newcomers to the area piled up legal claims to Tejano property. Expatriates Benavides and Carbajal never resettled in Texas; others in the family came back only after much of the land had been taken over by others and the cattle had been long-since lost. Poverty dogged this once-powerful clan both during and after their exile. The population centers of the region also underwent transformation. Victoria became what one historian has described as "a wild Anglo-American town, dominated by an army and many newcomers that distrusted and hated the Mexicans." Goliad and Refugio were largely destroyed during the fighting of the spring of 1836. Some of the Tejano residents were killed in the war, and many more became exiles south of the Rio Grande or exiles from their native land under the unrelenting pressure of the Texas army of occupation. Though exceptional ones like Carlos de la Garza remained to keep the Tejano heritage alive, the area as a whole suffered large-scale depopulation.[61]

Many Tejanos attempted to save their birthrights and perform their patriotic duties by volunteering for military service in the summer of 1836. Near the end of the year the *Telegraph and Texas Register* reported that "Col. Seguín, the untiring friend of Texas," commanded a force of about eighty "Americans" in the regular army and two hundred "Mexican citizen volunteers." Not nearly that number received the bounty grants due for service for the period May to December, 1836. Of those who did, about 40 percent had participated in earlier campaigns and tended to be young (in the mid-twenties, on the average) and single (62 percent). Virtually all of these veterans had followed Seguín into the army from the Béxar municipality. The Tejanos who joined for the first time in this period possessed as a group much less uniformity. Though the largest number volunteered in the Company "B" Cavalry of Bexareños led by Seguín's lieutenant, Manuel Flores, many served in one of the other units, usually some kind of mounted rangers, formed at various times and places in the summer and fall of 1836. Next to Béxar, Nacogdoches yielded the largest number; the region from Victoria to San Patricio, at that time being largely depopulated by Rusk, produced scarcely any soldiers. In personal characteristics these first-time volunteers showed more variety—they were older by an average of five years, some being in their fifties, and were more likely to be married than were the earlier Tejano recruits.[62] These attributes suggest a powerful and broad compulsion to demonstrate loyalty to Texas during this time of growing ethnic tensions.

Service of various kinds may have helped to advance the cause of the Tejanos individually or even as a community, as in the case of Béxar, but as a whole Texas policy toward citizens of Mexican descent had become capricious by the summer of 1836. Their problems stemmed mostly from living in a year-long war zone where they suffered from military policies of harsh material exploitation and ruthless denial of liberty. Well before the end of summer sweeping anti-Mexican prejudice had largely triumphed over restraint. Army-enforced deportations and property confiscations had become indiscriminate under General Rusk, with the burden falling as heavily on the patriotic Bexareños and Victorianos as on the defiant Tories of Refugio. For Tejanos the Revolution established a tradition of trouble and portended a future of overwhelming governmental discrimination and societal prejudice.

11. The Anglo Texans in Revolution and War

Like leaders of other revolutions and movements for national independence, Texas activists in 1835 and 1836 commonly depicted their cause as a popular one destined to attract widespread support. In various forms they conjured an image of the classes against the masses—more specifically, of priest-ridden military despots seeking to despoil the lives of unoffending but liberty-loving settlers. In Mexico dictatorial forces had snuffed out freedom through coercion or had purchased the loyalty of menials. In Texas, according to the prevailing scenario, the people would leave their plows and work benches to smite the would-be oppressors in a display of righteous solidarity.

During the early stages of the armed struggle some propagandists suggested that this vision of a democratic uprising had in fact been fulfilled. "We wish Santa Anna could witness the enthusiasm that prevails among all classes in regard to turning out for the war," the Brazoria *Texas Republican* boasted on October 11; "we believe if he did he would abandon the idea of subjugating Texas . . . & save him[self] the trouble of bringing his handcuffs." Its story of a youthful volunteer was echoed the following week by an account of *"Texas Patriotism"* in the *Telegraph and Texas Register*. It reported that the ladies, "bless their souls," had begun collecting lead scraps to mold into bullets, "and, if necessary, would enter the ranks and fight *manfully* for the rights of the country."[1]

As news of the coming of war spread eastward, so did evidence of pervasive support. Word of the capture of Goliad prompted a spontaneous demonstration in Nacogdoches which included a "general illumination," and morning bells pealed out the news of subsequent victories. The culturally-inclined there composed and performed a patriotic Texas song, fifty copies of which the committee of safety published along with hundreds of handbills and circulars. Nacogdoches joined other communities in designing flags to present to military companies at public ceremonies. The people who attended the barbecue of December 9 feasted on beef seasoned with cayenne pepper and a whole roasted black bear (whose skin served as the table centerpiece) plus potatoes, pickles, and currants, washed down with an ample supply of "muscat" wine, champagne, and gin, and topped off by cigars, all furnished at public expense by the local committee. Individual volunteers on their way to the front received invitations of lodging and entertainment from affluent families. During this initial flush of enthusiasm the young recruits seemed "genteel" and "full of enthusiasm for our Country" to observers like Susan Edwards Thorn.[2] In San Augustine she found the women possessing a "rough" appearance of field hands but admired their "cheerful" attitudes amidst wartime sacrifice. "The Ladies are so patriotic," she concluded, "that it is only those who have no relative engaged in the Glorious struggle that feel depressed."[3]

Even in the less zealous region of southeast Texas the war had a captivating effect, especially among the young. One schoolgirl later recalled that her male classmates quit studying, "talked war all the time and seemed to think that two or three hundred Texans could whip Mexico." News in December that something near to this youthful vision of glory had seemingly occurred at Béxar led to widespread rejoicing, buoyed by the jubilant return of the triumphant volunteers. This mood prevailed in part because most non-Hispanic Texans lived outside the war zone, even though some of the Refugio Irish and DeWitt colonists from Gonzales laid plans for or carried out evacuations and suffered property impressment by the Texas army.[4] During the fall of 1835 those who resided at or near the front felt the heaviest impact of the war. There the Revolution brought deepened internal divisions, displacement of civilians, destruction of property, and problems associated with housing and feeding the armies. To the east war-driven changes occurred in a less dramatic fashion: most communities experienced economic hardship, managing distribution of the burden in various ways.

In Nacogdoches, the political, trade, and transportation center of east Texas, civic leaders formed a committee of safety for the municipality even before the outbreak of war. As part of its responsibility for organizing revolutionary activity, this body on September 21, 1835, established a fund to supply arms, speed communications, and otherwise prepare for conflict. Seventeen subscribers from the area initially pledged $3,551, an amount that must have seemed abundant at first. Commanders of military companies raised near or passing through Nacogdoches either drew expenses directly from the fund or ran tabs with merchants, who in turn made periodic withdrawals. These semi-public disbursements went for all kinds of goods and services; not only did the volunteers arrive with ravenous appetites and thirsts, they also came unprepared for travel or battle. The committee even expended ten dollars on a "Tent cloth furnished Davy Crockett." Ordinary recruits also made a variety of purchases from the common to the exotic in food, clothing, and weapons. They acquired not only blankets, shirts, shoes, and boots, tin cups, kettles and pans, caps and hats, but also buckskin and thread, handkerchiefs, winter waistcoats, vests, and mittens. Their tastes in food and drink reflected the dominance of southern origins — mostly bread, coffee, corn, beef and pork, whiskey, and tobacco — but one unit also consumed a half-barrel of mackerel. Likewise, the volunteers armed themselves at public expense with all manner of weapons, ranging from rifles and other guns to butcher knives, whips, and an entire gross of tomahawks. The committee also supplied the volunteers with transportation in the form of horses, mules, wagons, and feed. These expenses exceeded all others — it required six hundred dollars for twenty-three saddles and bridles alone to mount Captain Breece's New Orleans volunteers on November 19, not counting the animals which, apparently, the company impressed from individuals.

Not surprisingly, the increasing demands made in October and November taxed the adequacy of local funds and supplies, but the arrival of Peyton Wyatt's company from Huntsville, Alabama, on December 5 must have shocked the committee. Over the course of the next week this one company ate and drank 1,300 pounds of beef, 482 pounds of pork, 760 pounds of sugar, and 100 pounds of coffee and ran up bills with almost every local merchant for such items as a drumhead. Altogether, these volunteers consumed goods and services valued at $465.59 in seven days. Nacogdoches leaders more or less bribed the Alabamians to move on. On December 13 Wyatt drew cash in the amount of $200; the committee also bought wagons, horses, and other gear, even hiring teamsters to haul the company's baggage to San Antonio. This cost an additional $712.50 but apparently seemed a prudent alternative to supplying the troops interminably. Altogether, this one unit ran up expenses of $1,378.09. Little wonder that the committee of safety reduced expenditures during the rest of December and in January but still declared itself "out of funds" on February 6.[5]

Though it fell short in the end, the organized effort of Nacogdoches had many advantages over the lackadaisical, piecemeal approach taken by most communities. San Felipe's committee actively procured soldier supplies. Brazoria also raised funds by subscription in early 1836, but before then citizens like Robert Mills, who contributed two horses to Cooke's company of New Orleans Greys, gave supplies individually as needs arose. Troops sometimes pressed animals into service formally by government authority, but on some occasions they simply took what they needed, by main force if necessary. Whether legal or not, the burden rested heavily and unevenly on the public, since military necessity did not recognize the principle of ability to pay. Frequently, single women such as Martha A. Reed, of Liberty municipality, furnished room, board, blankets, and horse feed to volunteers going to the war. She supplied food valued at $44.50 to a total of eighteen men on six separate occasions during a month-long period beginning October 27, but like many others she had to wait payment until after the war. Similarly, Mrs. A. B. Peyton, of San Felipe, provided $40.87 for troop expenses and rented out three yoke of oxen between October 12 and November 19; she never recovered two-thirds of these animals and had to hire a hand to track down the others. She claimed a $350 loss, not counting lost labor. The burden fell somewhat less heavily on individuals in places where contractors emerged to supply public needs, but merchants like John Lott, of Washington, complained in late December that without some repayment he could not continue to make "heavy advances" from his personal funds. Still, a month later he furnished accommodations and a horse to a small company headed by David Crockett. Soldiers from Texas also sacrificed their individual and familial interests by taking and sometimes even leaving horses, saddles, bridles, and wagons for public use.[6]

These losses in man-, horse-, and ox-power and the sacrifice of food and supplies to the army helped create hard times on the homefront from the very beginning of the war. Obviously, the poor who operated without slave labor had the most difficulty with the harvest. Women and children took to the fields picking cotton in greater than usual numbers, but the crop suffered what the *Telegraph and Texas Register* described as a "considerable loss" because of the departure of men who sacrificed "their own interest to the general good" by volunteering for military duty. Even before the first battles, the optimistic business climate of Texas collapsed. As the other newspaper explained, "the whole scene" had changed since summer. Emigration by settlers had ceased, farmers feared for their crops, and judicial proceedings halted, leading to a drastic fall in land values. Virtually "all business stagnated; and for peace and confidence, we had discord and disunion."[7] This journal expressed hope that the Consultation would restore order and thereby prosperity; nevertheless, war and political chaos continued into the winter. As a result, complaints of bad business could be heard from Nacogdoches to Gonzales. By mid-December Henry Austin, at Brazoria, sought help from his cousin to secure a loan in Philadelphia. Without money to pay family expenses "during the revolutionary Struggle," he wrote to Stephen F. Austin, "my best property" would have to be sacrificed. The desperate planter expressed a willingness to pay 20 to 25 percent interest.[8]

The depressed economy naturally effected the value of land, Texas's abundant asset, and created speculator controversies. Many, including according to one petition the "whole community of Nacogdoches," complained about the government's moratorium on land sales. In San Felipe Spencer H. Jack also campaigned for reopening the land offices in the name of the public good and popular rights. Though acting as agent for empresarios Austin and Williams, he argued that ordinary colonists, despairing of ever receiving their headrights, had lost confidence in the cause and sold depreciated titles. Thus, Jack maintained, the government had "put the honest but generally poor families in the hands of speculators" and deprived the masses of any "inducement to fight the battles of the country." Others agreed that speculators had begun to take advantage of perplexed colonists; certainly the number of agents and other buyers seemed to increase in early 1836. One of them, William F. Gray, met like-minded individuals almost everywhere he went in January and February as he meandered around looking for bargains from Nacogdoches to Galveston Bay to Washington-on-the-Brazos. Even during the Runaway Scrape later that spring, some minds turned to land speculation, believing with Henry Millard in the premise: "buy all you can at a low price now is the favorable time when the country is in such a panic." As late as May Texas remained too unstable for prices to begin to rebound.[9]

Many civilians suffered from social as well as economic disorder. In the Sabine district, with features of a border no-man's land, a loose band of armed men terrorized the country, stealing and "threatening the life of every one who opposes" them, according to one account penned in August, 1835. But at least one of these accused ruffians, Joseph Ferguson, left the area with the Texas volunteers in the autumn. Nevertheless, the rowdy elements remained powerful and bold enough to threaten the captain of a Mississippi military company which passed through the area the next spring.[10]

The absence of a political authority resulted in increased lawlessness. Assault victim Matthew Caldwell petitioned the provisional government for permission to take the law into his own hands to punish his assailant. Those who held back from vigilante-style justice faced the threat of long-term disorder. In Matagorda James Boyce, described by one citizen as "a man of no business or property, a curse and a nuisance to society," headed a "murdering, plundering, lawless band" which bullied the community from November, 1835, to February, 1836. One account attributed three murders and three serious assaults to this gang before its leader came to trial. Even after being judged guilty, Boyce managed to secure petitions for a new trial, reputedly by aligning himself with one of the local political factions. A similar set of events transpired in the municipality of Liberty in the cases of John M. and William M. Smith.[11] Citizens in San Felipe and Matagorda sought to organize patrols in the fall and winter of 1835; however, these bodies appear to have functioned only temporarily and ineffectively.[12]

Other factors also contributed to the decline of popular enthusiasm during the winter of 1835–36. To some extent lethargy resulted from poor communication and misinformation. According to the *Telegraph* "RUMORS OF DOOM" had circulated so frequently as to create skepticism among the people. The political chaos of December and January confused the public and eroded confidence. Localism remained a prevalent attitude. In Matagorda R. R. Royall discovered "some opposition" to participation in "common defense of our common country" as citizens concluded that they could not spare many men because their own community felt threatened.[13]

Various forms of race war — including challenges by several tribes of Indians — also undermined the security of many Texas communities. In east Texas, particularly in the Sabine and Nacogdoches areas, residents periodically pled fear of Indian uprisings in order to explain away their refusals to enlist. These concerns became especially serious in December and January and also existed in the region where the Comanches held sway throughout the war and with similar results. Army representatives who circulated along the frontier discovered, in the words of Silas Parker, much "indifference of the people as to the cause of Texas." They withheld horses, wagons, and their abundant foodstuffs from government agents and even from a company of rangers that had been serving there as protection from Indians. After only brief duty among the settlers of the region, one soldier complained: "it is discouraging to be with them." With little respite, the "savages" problem continued to weaken recruitment and to divert soldiers.[14]

By late winter few seemed to doubt that lethargy and personal concerns had triumphed over a national identity that demanded self-sacrifice. One U.S. volunteer who came intending to explore prospects for resettlement complained of the "want of society & government" in Texas, which "is fill up with people who are for their own emolument to the exclusion of others." In late February "A LADY OF TEXAS" wrote to the newspaper looking for support for a program to make clothing for the army, asking, "Have we not as much patriotism as our mothers and grandmothers?" Clearly, the decline of zeal was not a function of gender. What bothered officials most was the growing refusal to volunteer or accept even temporary enrollment in the militia, despite a state of emergency. The General Council described this behavior as "the unpardonable and almost criminal indifference of the people of Texas." The changing composition of the army at that time bore out the council's assertion.[15]

No matter how strong the desire to sit out the war, by February and March, 1836, the effects of the conflict seeped into the people's lives more fully than before. Word quickly spread that Santa Anna himself headed a sizable Mexican force with intentions of establishing the authority of the central government in Texas. His units began marching north from the Rio Grande before mid-February and won a series of engagements at the Alamo and (under Gen. José de Urrea) at Agua Dulce creek, San Patricio, Refugio, and Coleto. These armies then advanced eastward, meeting virtually no opposition for a month after Fannin surrendered on March 20. To Texans this foe seemed bent on ruthless policies — executing prisoners and fulfilling Santa Anna's legendary promise to lay waste the Texas countryside.

In fact, Mexican strategy did not operate from a clear-cut or uniform premise. On the one hand, official statements of policy repeatedly emphasized that "foreigners" and rebellious colonists would pay for the war with both their lives and property. At the same time Santa Anna ordered his soldiers to refrain from indiscriminate looting and burning. When Gen. Antonio Gaona marched toward Nacogdoches, his instructions required him to assure the "good inhabitants . . . of the paternalistic purposes of the supreme government, and that the force under your command will protect their rights and liberties."[16] After he encountered the ruins of Gonzales, burned a few days earlier by the army of Sam Houston, General Ramírez y Sesma observed that the Texans, rather than his men, had adopted a desperate, "barbaric" strategy. This Mexican general concluded that the incendiarism was designed to spread feelings of fanatical commitment to the Texas cause — those who had despoiled their own property would not allow the rest of their countrymen to make accommodations with the enemy. The Texas commander did not articulate any such revolutionary design; he bemoaned unnecessary waste of property. Yet, Houston refused to allow useful goods to fall into Mexican hands and inaugurated what became an almost routine tactic of destroying that which could not be carried by his army.[17]

This revolutionary war of the spring of 1836 posed new and greater challenges to the people of Texas. The winter military failures — in terms both of command disunity and low turnout — exposed the most populated districts to occupation or conquest. In the midst of the spring crisis many observers pointed out a disturbing irony: those who shirked military participation often had the most to protect in a material sense. The day before the Alamo fell the *Telegraph and Texas Register* gave a lengthy explanation of the regrettable "backwardness" of the people in volunteering for the war:

> We hear some complain, saying, they have already served longer, or contributed more, than some of their richer neighbors. . . . not unfrequently do we hear men say, they are ready to fight, but are not willing to turn out, while men possessed of lands and other property are staying at home to take care of their substance, the former not having a foot of land or little else to fight for. We acknowledge that the burthen of the present war has, thus far, fallen very unequally on our citizens.

With the stakes of the conflict now clearly being either victory or "expulsion or death," the paper expressed optimism that everyone would contribute.[18]

Instead, many responded to the crisis by removing themselves east of the war zone, to the despair of soldiers and government officials. Almost a month after the *Telegraph*'s frank analysis, Burnet complained that the "Lazy hounds" who had gathered at Harrisburg refused even to help gather steamboat wood. He expressed hope that these non-participants would turn back to fight once their families had been provided for, but a correspondent reported to the president that a group camped at nearby Spring Creek had responded to the latest call to arms by preparing to move even farther eastward. This April 8 estimate placed the number of eligible men east of the Brazos who refused military duty at one thousand. Even into the summer army leaders continued to assail the large landowners who at the time of crisis for Texas placed themselves out of danger rather than fighting.[19]

Analysis of individual and group behavior confirms this belief that a large number of wealthy and powerful men avoided armed service. Perhaps those most exposed to public scrutiny and potential ridicule were elected officials, especially the delegates to the Consultation and Convention. Advanced age excused at least a dozen of them. Five other former delegates discharged their public responsibilities by holding important positions in the cabinet or on diplomatic missions, though this seemed a decidedly lesser form of patriotism than taking up arms, at least to those who had volunteered.[20]

Others of these political leaders seemed to be more clearly culpable on the charge of failing the duty of defense of country. A few of them had been conservatives before March 2, but absence of sympathy with the course of the Revolution appears to have been but a minor factor in their avoidance of military service. "Old Three Hundred" settler Thomas Barnett, for example, had been elected to the Convention on a platform of defending the 1824 Mexican constitution, but he had signed both the Declaration of Independence and Texas Constitution. He did not join the army until July 1. Irish colonizers John McMullen and James Power also had risked a great deal in supporting the Texas cause, since retention of their landed estates would depend on the uncertain future of Texas politics, but in March and April they chose to flee to New Orleans rather than enroll in the army. Other representatives from this region also attempted to save themselves and to guard their families rather than to volunteer, establishing a pattern duplicated by many residents.[21]

Though the area that had been in the Department of the Brazos provided the bulk of the fighting forces in the spring of 1836, a considerable contingent of its top political leaders avoided military service, as they had the previous fall. A total of seventeen delegates from this region who were of conscriptable age (their average being forty) did not join the army. This conduct occurred more among ex-Consultation representatives than members of the Convention. The critics' characterization of large landholders as nonparticipants had some validity. William T. Millican and James Kerr were members of the "Old Three Hundred" of Austin's colony; John D. Newell and Samuel T. Allen had emigrated more recently but already possessed large holdings of real property. Yet, a more significant economic attribute was that a sizable number derived their income from nonagricultural pursuits; that is, they were lawyers, physicians, surveyors, or merchants. Further, they did not generally have a bigger stake in Texas by virtue of long residence — their average tenure (about five years) did not especially set them apart from those who volunteered.

Some of these political leaders attempted to conceal their nonparticipation with fancy, military-sounding titles: Samuel R. Fisher became Inspector General of the Army of the Reserve, a recruiting and provisioning position apparently similar to the one held by John G. W. Pierson, who styled himself aide-de-camp to former Governor Viesca. District of Washington representative Jesse Grimes received the appointment to organize his area's militia on March 25, but he apparently did nothing to that end and waited until summer to enroll himself. Others, such as John Fisher and William Menefee, fled eastward directly from the Convention to the border, where William F. Gray saw them on the eve of the battle of San Jacinto. If they excused their conduct at all they probably did so in the fashion of Edwin Waller and Samuel T. Allen, both of whom escorted families to safety with the declared intention of returning for military service.[22]

Analysis of how the elite of the Austin colonies conducted themselves during the months of revolutionary crisis rightly should include many who did not achieve election to either convention. Clearly, a substantial proportion of these other men of political and economic power also rebuffed the recruiters. Business partners Thomas F. McKinney and Samuel May Williams had both financial resources and a close association with the great empresario, but neither attracted substantial popular support. As a candidate of the so-called "Gentleman's party" the previous fall, McKinney received only seven votes. Though of appropriate age, they each departed to the United States without having performed military service. There they aided the financial interests of Texas, activities that received little acclaim in this heroic era. Other Austin cronies could cite age to explain their passivity during these days of crisis. Fifty-three-year-old Henry Austin persevered in Texas despite the economic doldrums until early March when with his relatives, the Perrys, he began to lay plans for family removal. By the end of the month he had arrived safely in New Orleans, where he spent part of his time writing letters critical of the "demagogues" and "wretched" rulers of Texas. Persons of wealth and influence may have suffered anxieties and financial troubles in common with the ordinary folk of their region, but they had sufficient resources to place themselves away from physical peril early and with relative ease.[23] Some of the politically active among the "Old Three Hundred" settlers were also old in years, but other younger men in this generally prosperous group dodged enlistment in the army and spent the wartime in circumspect, if not silent, fashion.

Individual cases of affluent public figures refusing enrollment in the army do not demonstrate uniformity of this behavior among the upper class. However, analysis of a unique document that enumerated the draft dodgers of the Austin district suggests a broad pattern of non-participation by the wealthy. On April 10, 1836, the conscription officer listed fifty residents who in his judgment had left the jurisdiction "without standing the draft." Several of these men stood falsely accused. Five, according to later notations on the document, should have been exempted as over-aged. Seven had, in fact, volunteered that spring and except in one case saw action at San Jacinto. Two had served in the siege of Béxar the previous fall and no doubt believed they should not have to go again until the non-combatants did their duty.

The remaining thirty-six—correctly identified as draft evaders—possessed several characteristics of affluence. Mostly married men (two-thirds of those whose status could be determined), they had resided in Texas long enough (about six years on the average) to acquire land and chattels and improve their properties. The Groce family, for example, had emigrated from Alabama in 1822 with a string of thorough-bred horses and ninety slaves, who carved "Bernardo" plantation out of the wilderness. The Groce's possessions, requiring fifty wagons to transport in the original trek, had grown to include a fine mansion, a cotton gin, and countless livestock. Their ample larder served as the basis for supplying the army of Texas as it camped on the estate from April 2–13. This contribution aside, the names Leonard and Jared Groce appeared on the enumeration of those who fled in evasion of the draft. Others of considerable wealth also gave their property but not their persons to the Texas cause. Since October James Cochran had supplied over $2,100 worth of cash and goods ranging from office supplies to shoes and food, but he did not join the ranks himself. G. E. Edward complied with Houston's order and gave up 150 bushels of corn to the army as it marched from the Colorado River toward Groce's place; yet, he refused the enrollment demand of the conscript officer. Other families in this region worked out their own informal compromises between duties to country and family. Fidellie Breeding went to the army while Fred Breeding remained to help care for a clan that included two over-aged men. James Price, a forty-six-year-old married man with six children, postponed his military career until the early summer.[24]

No enumeration of draft evaders exists for other districts, but lists of influential men in other communities can be constructed. Generally, this data reinforce the conclusion of widespread avoidance of military service by local leaders. In the Matagorda-Jackson districts about a dozen men who had been involved in committee work in the fall and winter never enrolled in the service. Some may have felt that other responsibilities took priority. Thomas Menefee, who had lived on the Arroyo Navidad since 1830, a widower in his mid-fifties, had seven children. On the other hand, Samuel B. Brigham, of Matagorda, did not serve despite his freedom from familial constraints. Twenty-eight-year-old merchant William L. Cazneau like others in his profession, left for the United States in early 1836.

Criticism for failure to volunteer naturally fell heaviest on those who had led Texas into the crisis and those who in economic terms had the most to lose. Yet, among the less publicized classes recruitment also fell far short of the near unanimity called for by revolutionary leaders. In fact, nowhere near a majority of the adult male populations enrolled in the army. Several petitions and similar documents from the Brazos department provide names and locations from which a rough estimate of participation rates may be drawn. The best of these, a petition circulated at Brazoria on August 9, 1835, received ninety-five signatures. Thirty-nine of these (about 40 percent) joined the army sometime before the San Jacinto battle; most of these soldiers (thirty-one) took the field during the spring of 1836. Those who stayed home more often than not had wives and children and exceeded the age of the typical Texas soldier. For other petitions circulated in this region, rates of participation of 35 percent and 36 percent occurred for the entire period of October, 1835, through April, 1836.[25] In general, the people who resided in the Colorado-to-Brazos-river region contentedly sat through the war in quiet anonymity until the arrival of Santa Anna's army brought the conflict literally to their homes.

Similar attitudes prevailed in eastern Texas. But the war never reached the doorsteps of most of these colonists, and they served at a much lower rate. Even more than elsewhere, major political leaders set a non-military example. More (twenty-six) army dodging representatives came from the Nacogdoches than the other departments; eleven of these men had attended the 1836 Convention. Overall, these east Texas delegates were somewhat younger (an average age of thirty-four) than their central Texas counterparts, but they were similar in terms of diversity of vocation and length of residence. Otherwise, no single pattern characterized their behavior, which instead reflected intensely localized situations.

In Nacogdoches, where deep political rifts had emerged, several one-time leaders opposed the direction taken by the Revolution, lost political favor, and steadfastly refused military service. Successful Convention candidate Charles S. Taylor found himself a reluctant signer of the Declaration of Independence but then returned home rather than to the army to fight in the conflict. The largest number of army-evading representatives from a single district (seven) came from Liberty municipality, an even more divided and complex area than Nacogdoches. Racked by internal conflict since 1832, southeast Texas contained a considerable pocket of pro-Mexican sentiment but also a large contingent of prorevolutionary militance. Its political leaders acquired a tendency for caution; in the end, they helped mold the Revolution but left the fighting to others. An even broader nonparticipation occurred to the north and east of Liberty in the Jasper district. Situated in relative security on the border and away from main-travelled roads, this municipality (earlier known as Bevil) had been apart from the mainstream of the Revolution from the first. Only half of its Consultation representatives bothered to attend; none of them saw fit to join the army. Two of Jasper's convention delegates returned home following adjournment and sat out the war.

Besides these representatives, other members of the elite in east Texas also displayed something less than sacrificial responses to the pressing need for manpower. In Liberty former alcalde and General Council member Hugh B. Johnson was among those avoiding military participation. Even in generally zealous San Augustine, six leaders of the vigilance committee stayed at home throughout the war. Sixty-one-year-old Elisha Roberts, at least, became noteworthy for his hospitality to passing soldiers. Land speculator Archibald Hotchkiss and former legislator William English lent little but rhetorical support to the cause, and that only in the fall before Texas adopted policies that potentially hurt their interests.

Nacogdoches had been the scene of bitter political upheaval on land and other issues. Not surprisingly, several of those who lost in these local and national power struggles sullenly sat out the military conflict. They included J. K. Allen, Richard Sparks, and former head of the land office George A. Nixon. This grand manipulator, who had filed personal claims to twenty-two leagues, fled the country in early March after attempting one last subterfuge. However, disenchantment with governmental policies and election outcomes was not the crucial factor in the decision on enlistment. Men who with word, pen, speech, money, and organizational energy had supported the Revolution failed to enroll in the army. Most notably, they included merchants Henry Raguet (a close friend of Houston), and brothers-in-law Frost Thorn and Haden Edwards, who quietly remained in their Nacogdoches abodes or found during this ungentle springtime good reasons to travel in the United States.[26]

With these neighbors as models, and living out of the war zone, the masses in eastern Texas served in smaller numbers in 1836 than the people of the Brazos region who confronted the invaders more directly. In some districts a dramatic decline in volunteering occurred. A variety of evidence indicates that the rates of participation in the Department of Nacogdoches fluctuated from one municipality to another but generally fell short of the levels reached in the Brazos region (about one-third of the adult male population). Censuses taken in 1835 provide data on the number of men of military age for four different municipalities, shown in Table 9.[27] These demonstrate an enrollment ratio pattern that varied enormously for the war as a whole—from a respectable 36 percent in the Jasper district to half that figure in the Sabine municipality. But during the crisis days of 1836 the disparity between municipalities flattened out as participation fell off dramatically everywhere, ranging from a low of 11 percent (Sabine) to a high of 18 percent (San Augustine). Another source corroborates the low participation rates in the Sabine district and provides the opportunity to describe the nonparticipants somewhat more fully. This second index is a militia roll made on April 25, 1835, which listed forty-nine men mustering for duty. Of these, eight (16 percent) joined the Texas army during the fighting stage of the Revolution, with only half that number serving in the spring of 1836. Those who failed to volunteer

Table 9. Rates of Military Participation:
Department of Nacogdoches

Municipality	No. Males, 16–50	Enrollment	
		Total*	Spring 1836
Jasper	141	51 (36%)	20 (14%)
Sabine	293	52 (18%)	33 (11%)
San Augustine	485	120 (25%)	85 (18%)
Shelby	161	50 (31%)	27 (17%)

*enrolled between October, 1835, and April, 1836

appear to have been overwhelmingly men of family; most had recently acquired title to their land and so displayed little evidence of exceptional wealth.[28]

In the central region, despite a larger army turnout, a majority fled their places of residence in panic at the approach of Santa Anna's army. This experience, which the people came to call sardonically the Runaway Scrape, eventually involved men, women, and children of every region, class, and condition. The able-bodied males who ran away received considerable ridicule but not the label of disloyalty; yet, their motivations — self-interest, protection of family, and the instinct for survival — resembled that of the Tories. Ironically, flight became a lesser form of patriotism, so common that it could not be popularly condemned or officially prosecuted, while those who stood by their places risked the charge of collaboration.

Texas patriots tacitly tolerated what seemed to be cowardly conduct because they knew that in many cases cruel choices had been forced on the people. Single men who fled faced opprobrium, but even Houston's army orders of March 21 acknowledged that "families moving for safety will be entitled to one armed man for their protection." As the army's eastward retreat exposed more of Texas to the enemy, soldiers like his assistant quartermaster informed the general that it had become "absolutely necessary" to take leave and alleviate his family's "helpless situation." Others left without such explanation but with full intention of returning. Then, given the great difficulty of locating any place that offered genuine security, they often failed their public responsibility. Those who rejoined the army sometimes did so in the face of family scorn. Mrs. George Sutherland gave more than a hint of the pressure she exerted on her soldier-husband. With three daughters and a brother she fled their frontier home after learning that the eldest son had perished at the Alamo. Mr. Sutherland accompanied them first to the Colorado River and then to the Brazos where, she explained to her sister, he "quit us and joined the army." The Sutherlands eventually made their way to the Sabine without the guidance of the head of family. Many Texans simply could not bring themselves to "quit" their families in this manner.[29]

Houston knew of these familial dynamics; nevertheless, he placed most of the responsibility for the panic on army "deserters." Some men volunteered, marched to Gonzales in early March, and then almost immediately fled on hearing of the Alamo disaster. They carried not only this news but a general sense of panic eastward with them. Only four days after his arrival, their commander began to bemoan the spread of "dismay and consternation among the people" by the "exaggerated reports" of ex-soldiers. In one community after another the mere appearance of these deserters seemed to spread an irrational sense of alarm, and Houston struggled unsuccessfully to stifle this problem.[30]

Governmental officials also grieved over what Burnet called the popular "influence of idle and groundless rumours." The interim president began issuing circulars to calm the people the day after his hasty inauguration, but the conduct of fellow politicians seemed to have more effect than his words. From Washington the Convention delegates dispersed "in all directions, with haste and in confusion," as one witness described the scene. He concluded that "a general panic seems to have seized them" and spread among the people of the Brazos region. Houston quickly chastised the poor example of this removal from the seat of government; the political leaders assigned blame to the general's inability to bring discipline to the army and his failure to make an early stand against the Mexicans.[31] Santa Anna later charged that the Texas army "forced" the people "to abandon their homes." The popular exodus was mostly spontaneous and usually hindered military movements, but public opinion did condemn as Tories those who stayed behind. Further, both civil and military authorities stepped up conscription efforts in early April with threats of property confiscation or other punishments. These policies had in some cases the opposite of the desired result, as men fled faster and farther eastward to avoid the draft.[32]

Reports of the suffering inflicted on the settlements in the western region also stimulated the Runaway Scrape in the rest of Texas. For weeks preceding the Mexican arrival, James W. Fannin and others in the Refugio area had informed their correspondents of Santa Anna's plans to "expel or exterminate every white man" and to rape "the *Fair daughters* of chaste *white women*." Acting out of this obsession, sharpened by the knowledge that his own impressment policies had deprived the people of transportation, the commander of the Goliad post delayed and fragmented his military response to General Urrea in a mostly vain effort at removing families from the war zone. The Irish colonists responded to the invasion slowly. A few San Patricians moved eastward, while those with Tory leanings naturally stayed in place. At Refugio little movement occurred before news arrived of the first battle, after which many women and children sought safety with units of the Texas army. Instead of conducting a prompt removal, Capt. A. B. King on March 11 concentrated these people at the mission church of Refugio, where Urrea besieged them three days later. Most of the nonmilitary personnel remained behind when the Texas force conducted an evacuation on March 15. They received mercy, although one or two women suffered wounds in the bombardment of the mission-fort. The Mexicans spared some of the captured men but executed others, depending on judgments about whether they had born arms and the success of relatives in pleading for clemency.[33]

Little if any accurate information on these events reached those who lived in central Texas. Rather, by word of mouth or pen people heard that settlements from Goliad to Victoria were "broken up"; the Irish "have abandoned their houses and are flocking into their colonies."[34] These reports intended to call men to arms, but instead the people largely imitated the described behavior and ran for their lives.

The popular response to the invasion was neither uniform nor entirely irrational. Behavior that some described as panic one day often seemed prudent with the passage of a little more time. Initial evacuations in the west took place under military supervision. On March 13, two days after receiving word of the fall of the Alamo, Houston burned Gonzales and began his retreat. He escorted families from this area, sometimes sending troops back for those left behind due to stubbornness, disability, or poor communications. These forces arrived at the Colorado River on March 17; fifty miles away that day Gray estimated that "thousands are moving off to the east. A constant stream of women and children and some men, with wagons, carts and pack mules, are rushing across the Brazos night and day." They fled, as he wrote, "to escape the anticipated storm of war." A day later from the Galveston Bay area, yet another ninety miles to the southeast, a merchant reported that people "are so alarmed—so panic struck that they are flying in every direction." They had bought up nearly all his provisions and except in a few cases refused military participation. He guessed that "nearly ⅚ of the inhabitants have left."[35]

While flight — even hysteria — occurred generally, some people in central Texas displayed far more calm. Two weeks after panic had seized Washington, one of Houston's subordinates reported that some Brazos bottom residents had stayed in their homes and would continue to do so if protected by the army. At the same time others loaded cotton at Groce's landing onto the steamboat *Yellow Stone.* Houston optimistically bragged that people on the east side of the Brazos had begun to plant corn in early April; others noted that the degree of alarm had also subsided in Harrisburg. Yet, a mass of refugees, their journeys slowed and made miserable by torrential rains, clogged the primitive Texas roads. Many had attempted to transport their possessions, even livestock, much of which they subsequently abandoned. The scene at Lynch's on the San Jacinto River reminded one observer of "a camp meeting" with its congregation of people and their tents, wagons, draft animals, and abundant baggage. This "flying multitude," as he described them, came to complete halts at crossings on the swollen rivers. The traffic jammed up — some reports estimated five thousand people at Lynch's at one time. The overburdened ferries frustrated nearly everyone, except perhaps a few light travelers who swam across, and helped renew the fears of those who worried about being trapped by Santa Anna. By April 12 the people of Harrisburg received word that this worst-case scenario appeared to have occurred — the Mexicans had the day before crossed the Brazos ahead of the Texas army and its apparently nonbelligerent commander.[36]

The people of central Texas, in the words of one army attendant, were "flying their homes for a place of security." A few assumed from the first that this meant the United States — these farsighted ones pushed on all the way to the Sabine. Others from all the coastal areas went by water to New Orleans; a boatload of forty Matagorda refugees continued on all the way to Mobile. Yet, many families from the Brazoria region, even some who fled on ocean-going vessels, landed in the Galveston Bay region. As the acting secretary of war complained to Houston, they "came here under the belief that they would be safe [but] are now exposed to the attack of the enemy." Rumors of Mexicans murdering women and children fed these anxieties, so in mid-April the panic renewed, this time in east Texas.[37]

Even geographically isolated Nacogdoches, hearing that a wing of the invading army under General Gaona had set off in its direction, joined in the Runaway Scrape. The mood there changed almost overnight. On April 10 a resident wrote to the president urging removal of the Texas government to the safety of Nacogdoches; the next day, amidst growing concern of a rising by local Indians and Tejanos, the committee of safety sought a U.S. commander for the local military company. When John A. Quitman arrived from Louisiana on the thirteenth at the head of a company of sixteen men, he found a minor debate over burning the town and about whether the home guard unit should make a stand or escort the defenseless to the Sabine. He concurred with local thinking in recommending the latter strategy. Two days later Quitman wrote to a comrade that "there is not a woman or child in the town of Nacogdoches. . . . there is no immediate danger to this section. The panic, however, has done its work. The houses are all deserted. There are several thousands of women and children on both sides of the Sabine, without supplies or money. Everything was left in flight—the corn in the crib, the meat in the smoke-house, their poultry, cattle, and furniture." He went on to report that "many" from San Augustine (only twenty-five miles from the border) had also taken to the road, and he noted having seen an estimated three hundred armed men heading east and away from the war. By April 17 a local officer wrote Houston that the situation had calmed somewhat, with concerns on the Indian-Tejano uprising diminishing and 220 men having been dispatched toward rather than away from the front. The commander's friend and chairman of the vigilance committee confirmed these facts and numbers but still complained, "the Authorities have found it utterly impossible to induce the men to abandon their flying families." He reported that every house on the road between the Trinity and the Sabine had been abandoned.[38]

This response in Nacogdoches and other communities and by individuals during the Runaway Scrape signified a breakdown in the national identity. Houston urged local leaders to place all recruits at his disposal as the best means "for the protection of the country, and families." His supporters had difficulty in selling this view. On April 16 after several days of attempting to enroll able-bodied refugees in east Texas, Ira Ingram admitted having failed to dispel the illusion that service there had more importance than in the main army. Other officers learned of the fragile nature of the commitments even to defend a particular locale. Buoyed by the presence of U.S. volunteers, Velasco-area residents wrote the commander "beseeching me *not to* remove the troops from here" and offering to help build fortifications. Three days later he reported that with the situation still desperate in San Antonio "the families are flying before the enemy, and have left their stock, their houses and crops to the mercy of the tyrant." Those few people remaining in the Velasco area refused to supply man- or horsepower to the fort.[39]

The fading spirit of self-sacrifice turned into a cycle that spelled national collapse: men refused early enrollment in the national army, which undermined defense; this led to a failure to fulfill the essential task of government—providing minimal security—and forced people to flee for their lives, further weakening the army. One officer who attempted unsuccessfully to rally the retreating civilians described perfectly the prevailing behavior. "[I] found," he wrote, "every man shifting for himself and helpless family." And, he could have noted, every woman, many of whom showed self-reliant spunk rather than fawning dependence. The grittiest of all, innkeeper Pamelia Mann, displayed also the prevailing spirit of individual over national interest. The last of her three yoke of oxen trudged in army service as she accompanied Houston's retreating army in April, 1836. Upon learning that the troops with her animals had taken the fork away from her intended destination, Mrs. Mann set out to retrieve them. She did so in a scene full of indelicate language, threats, and brandishing of pistols. As historian Fane Downs has shown, Texas women generally supported the war effort but also had to take charge of their own destiny, with survival itself at stake.[40]

Women's reminiscences generally show that individual or at best familial identities prevailed during the Runaway Scrape. People usually clung to their closest relatives as they took to the road. They occasionally sent aid to a desperate neighbor or joined together when situations required mutual aid. But after the crossing had been made or the climatic crisis weathered, these makeshift groups split up, and individuals or extended families went on their way, not to reunite until circumstance again dictated. As one participant wrote retrospectively, "all seemed to look out for themselves alone." A camp meeting atmosphere existed for some when traffic backed up, but the rule of self-interest and even widespread acrimony prevailed. Sharp dealings characterized their business relationships; for example, ferrymen faced charges of holding up the people with high fees. Noah Smithwick saw "men—or devils, rather—bent on plunder, galloping up behind the fugitives, telling them the Mexicans were just behind, thus causing the hapless victims to abandon what few valuables they had tried to save."[41]

The people in a few cases benefitted from a military escort, but these forces proved insufficient to prevent the reign of anarchy. When possible, some officers attempted to take charge of or destroy supplies of liquor. In the Brazos River bottom in early April James Collinsworth came upon "a scene of drunkenness & debauchery, when ladies of proud claims to decency and respectability were insulted in my presence." He poured out all the alcohol he could find amidst "many murmers & threats" but to the relief of others. Whether attributable to whiskey or not, Gray also witnessed "much squabbling and much injustice" among fugitives camped near the mouth of the Trinity. He marvelled at the militant conduct of those who had run from an unseen enemy and yet "are valiant in asserting their right to pass the river, and pistols shown and oaths sworn without stint." These men resisted even the chivalric proposal of transporting the women and children first. Gray concluded, "might here gives right."[42]

In response to the popular distress several observers joined Gail Borden, Jr., in calling on the government to provide "a fraternal care of the people." The Convention debated a general relief policy without adopting one, but by late March the cabinet had begun purchasing provisions to aid "the suffering women, and children of our country" as Secretary of State Samuel P. Carson wrote. Some of the people knew they needed more than piecemeal stopgap measures; a group of San Bernardo citizens pledged to submit themselves to martial law if the authorities would but act to restore order.[43] The government had moved more concertedly in all these directions by establishing a full-scale refugee camp on Galveston Island, a sparsely inhabited place deemed both accessible and secure.

Responsibility for this effort fell mainly to an area merchant (now colonel) James Morgan. He undertook to transport families to the island, and with other appointees to procure food and construct both housing and fortifications. He had the use of impressed slaves for labor and a small body of furloughed troops for a patrol, but with the number of refugees on the island reaching by one count one thousand, these resources quickly became inadequate. Many of the men proved once again unwilling to do much more than lounge around, a pursuit that in turn posed problems of discipline. On April 25, a week after he arrived on the island with his family and a few other cabinet members, Burnet ordered martial law on Galveston. Essentially this involved conscription of all white men and enrollment of all blacks into fatigue duty units.[44]

The government departed in a few days with news of the success of Texas arms, leaving Morgan to grapple with disgruntled and disorderly refugees. Though still empowered with martial law authority, the commander had difficulty controlling his subordinates, much less the civilians. Troops stationed elsewhere jealously complained of the luxuries afforded these refugees; the president ordered Morgan to ship sugar and coffee to the soldiers and retain only staples to feed the refugees. As late as July reports circulated of suffering experienced by the people at Galveston, occasioned in part by maldistribution of and speculation in public supplies. Problems of discipline also continued as the island commander apparently failed to control the availability of liquor. "I have ever considered the Suffering of the people as the peculiar object of the care of government," Burnet wrote to Morgan in early July. Despite this vision and a measure of success in staving off their starvation, the people viewed life on the island as but an extension of their Runaway Scrape tribulations. Slowly they left for home, although the camps still contained a few people in late July.[45]

That the refugees flocked to Galveston in such numbers offers proof not of the abundance it offered so much as of their desperation. "Suffering"—the word came to the lips of nearly everyone who underwent or witnessed their plight. The poorest among them seemed least prepared and most exposed. Families packed into an amazing variety of vehicles, from fine carriages to common wagons, carts, and even sleds. Many simply walked, and a few even went shoeless. They slept on soggy ground, often without tents, and with little bedding, especially after river crossings or some other travel crisis forced them to lighten their loads. Likewise, food shortages occurred periodically. Usually the refugees' initial provisions gave out because they miscalculated lengths of journeys or had to abandon livestock to increase their speed. And, of course, the rain, coming in apparently endless torrents, poured more misery onto their overburdened lives. These conditions led to a high incidence of disease, made more traumatic because infants frequently fell victim to one of the fevers that mystified the people of this era.[46]

In piecemeal fashion beginning in May and continuing through the summer refugees slowly ventured back to their homes. There they encountered yet another burden of the war—houses damaged if not destroyed, fences broken down, crops trampled, ravaged, or failing through neglect, livestock slaughtered or dispersed, and personal possessions ransacked. Unlike some of the other vicissitudes, property loss was generally a lasting consequence of the conflict. It resulted largely from the revolutionary policies adopted by the Texas army in the spring of 1836, which embraced desperate methods in order to deny provisions to the enemy. Houston's army burned Gonzales and San Felipe de Austin and Fannin's set fire to Refugio and La Bahía. Both in conformity to and in violation of official orders, Texas soldiers consumed or destroyed much of the property that stood in the path of its march. The Burnams later complained that their ferry, store, and residence on the Colorado River had been burned even though they lived outside the line of attack.

Where no Texas army passed through to do this grim work, Mexican commanders confiscated supplies, usually distributing food to their men and occasionally, as at Matagorda, hauling off cotton, tobacco, dry goods, and luxury items. Circumstances convinced some of the invaders that the settlers had destroyed their own houses; this made the soldiers hesitate little in smashing what had been left behind but could not be eaten or carried. Various Mexican units also torched farm houses as well as the small towns of Bastrop, Harrisburg, and New Washington.[47]

Once the war swung their way at San Jacinto, the Texans attempted to halt this devastation. They forced Santa Anna to order his successor to respect private property during his retreat, but this proved a difficult task as pillagers continued attacks in spite of official policy. Some of the depredations occurred at the hands of forces who recognized no authority. Before the army under Urrea arrived irregular bands had plundered Refugio, and these activities continued during the retreat of the Mexican army. Texas civilians also preyed on each other's property. L. A. McHenry, one of the victims, concluded that the thefts had been perpetrated "by plunderers, for the Mexicans were not in our neighborhood." One year later a visitor estimated that these irregular depredations had cost the people more than the destruction inflicted by Santa Anna's army.[48]

A few Texans managed to save some of their possessions by taking the risk of hiding out in their neighborhoods, giving them a head start in rounding up cattle once the invaders had retreated. Other settlers took time to bury property or even to erect religious symbols to promote respect. But many of the people saw their worst fears confirmed. As a Columbus resident wrote in mid-May after discovering the family home in ashes and its cattle driven off, "all was stillness round and the angel of gloom seemed to be hanging over the once lovely place. A shudder ran through our frames on beholding the change."[49]

For many Texans the experience of losing property to the war did not wait until they returned home following the Runaway Scrape. Their sacrifice occurred in a variety of times, places, and circumstances with the appearance of government purchasing or impressment agents. Only a fine line separated sale from forced confiscation, since both transactions rested on credit. At an early date in the conflict official policy had acknowledged that, when persuasion or threats failed to procure the necessary supplies, the goods would have to be pressed into service. In practice the army simply took what it needed, frequently with little regard for ownership. Even the citizen army of Texas developed a callous disregard for private possessions. This attitude caused Houston on April 3 to lecture on "the soldiers duty to protect the property of the Citizens & not to waste or destroy it," but this order provided no real means of ending abuses. Some civilians became convinced that troops actually went out of their way to inflict damages.[50]

During the spring of 1836 the war spread the economic burden to all regions and classes. Just before its adjournment the Convention specifically authorized impressment of privately held provisions, arms, wagons and teams in the Nacogdoches and San Augustine municipalities. In terms of total value the well-to-do supplied the most goods, with merchants contributing scarce items like tobacco, shoes, and clothing. Businessmen in western Texas seem to have been hit especially hard because of their proximity to the front, but traders in the Austin colony also turned over substantial quantities of supplies in late February and March.

Emergency conditions led to heated confrontations. R. R. Royall, of Matagorda, a vigorous leader of the Revolution, had given over a wide array of goods, both "pressed" and sold on credit, since the beginning of the war. He had also acted as a government agent in transferring material into public service, in some instances using his cash to purchase that which could not be obtained on credit. His sloop *Rattle Snake* had transported U.S. volunteers to Texas. In the end Royall held audited claims totalling more than $15,000. This included $500 for his sloop, which had been smashed by naval captain William Brown under the guise of keeping it out of enemy hands, even though the vessel's crew chief heatedly maintained that he could have easily sailed it to safety. Other wealthy citizens also turned over supplies to the government. Charles D. Sayre saw $940 worth of corn, molasses, ham, bacon, and dried fruit imported for his southeast Texas plantation taken instead to Galveston for use of the army in April, 1836, an experience he shared with other planters.[51]

Those with fewer possessions contributed less in monetary terms but perhaps more in the sense of vital sustenance. Their claims were generally for staple foods and transportation. Eliza Fares had her horse impressed by a company on the east side of the Brazos, still quite a distance from safety. Even farther to the west an army press gang took over Samuel Diamond's wagon on March 24 at the Colorado river, a full week after Houston had crossed it in retreat. When the military laid claim to the provisions of the common folk, it usually took plain fare—beef, pork, corn, and potatoes. Except in cases of the unusually persistent (like Pamelia Mann), army seizure of horses, mules, or other draft animals usually became permanent; payment, delayed until the fall of 1836, came in the form of some kind of depreciating government paper. The animals themselves seemed to disappear permanently, whether injured, stolen, or otherwise somehow "lost."[52]

Even under the most orderly of circumstances impressment would have been unpopular, but by April, 1836, government officials learned that the general anarchy of Texas had opened the way for special abuses. Essentially, two variations on the same scheme occurred—private citizens pretended to be press agents in order to steal, or legitimate members of the army impressed nonmilitary goods for their own gain. Burnet had first-hand experience with the problem; in early April one of these "scoundrels . . . on pretense of pressing for public service" made off with the president's own pistols and his neighbors' horses. Like this thief, several of these bogus agents headed for Louisiana or Arkansas to resell their plunder.[53]

Col. Sidney Sherman attributed this problem to poor military organization, "independent" companies being "permitted to roam about the country at pleasure. They do the country more damage than the common enemy." Another leader asserted that impressment abuses had demoralized the people and led to a form of war resistance. From San Augustine westward to Nashville in the frontier region, Sterling C. Robertson found that farmers had begun to hide away their horses at the first hint of the appearance of the press masters. Many refused military service out of fear that in their absence these agents "will strip his family of every thing that he might have for their support and comfort." Indeed, one war-impoverished civilian even lost the relief supplies given him by the government to soldiers who broke in and helped themselves. "Unprincipled and evil disposed men . . . fraudently taking possession of the private property of citizens" persisted and even increased after San Jacinto; finally, on July 12 Burnet handed down a proclamation limiting the number of army officers who could issue impressment orders. Nevertheless, both he and Houston continued into the late summer their piecemeal efforts to relieve the people of this abuse.[54]

The war's impact continued to be felt for the remainder of the year. Patriotic pressure remained strong enough to force many Texans to step up their contributions to the new nation. From throughout the young Republic, but especially in east Texas, men volunteered for the first time. Many of them had, of course, earlier fled in the face of the enemy; twenty-one former Consultation or Convention delegates headed the ranks of these new recruits who sought this chance to right themselves in the public eye. Some political leaders, including Stephen F. Austin who returned in late June, expressed confidence that the people of Texas had learned valuable lessons in unity, preparation, and sacrifice from the invasion experience.[55]

Other observers doubted whether public spiritedness actually improved. A number of the more affluent discharged their duty by buying off their obligation, hiring substitutes wherever they could be found. Several patterns existed in this form of enrollment. Many of the hirers appear to have been from east Texas, most of them had families, and often they did a brief stint in the army before seeking a paid stand-in. Rodney Anthony, from a family of eight, appears to have been representative of this group. He left San Augustine on a three-month hitch on the fourth of July but fulfilled only half his obligation before hiring a substitute. Demand quickly outreached supply, with the usual results. By midsummer substitutes commanded cash payments of between $45 and $100; Leonard M. Thorn, of Nacogdoches, had to pay $80 and a mule for transportation. Army leaders claimed that some substitutes suffered from illnesses or were already under other military obligations.[56]

The rush to find substitutes came in response to the more concerted efforts toward conscription during the summer of 1836. This in turn generated not only the usual excuse-making but also considerable resistance. In the Sabine district Edmund P. Gaines, son of a Convention delegate, headed the draft evaders, first by hiring a substitute who had already enrolled in the service and then by disputing the constitutionality of conscription in court. This case resulted in an increase in local "apathy and inertness" toward the recruitment process, according to a correspondent of Sam Houston. This lukewarm attitude and passive draft resistance prevailed in spite of renewed threats by the general and others to pursue property confiscation measures against those who refused to enroll when conscripted. The actual commander in the field complained that peace sentiment had also pervaded his army; Rusk estimated that three thousand men liable for service had refused enlistment.[57]

Recruitment might have been easier had the conditions of the people on the home front not remained so desperate. A disorderly state of affairs continued to prevail after the Texas victory. Attacks against private property came from a variety of sources. "Bush squatters" who had stayed behind when others joined in the Runaway Scrape destroyed or plundered their neighbors' farms in late April and May. Burnet described these thieves as "more destructive and abominable than the common foe." The army arrested some horse and cattle thieves, but it suffered from geographical and other limitations as a police force. Complaints about robberies could be heard from the Sabine to the Nueces throughout the summer of 1836. The Indians also became bolder and wider ranging in their raids.[58]

In spite of this general sense of insecurity, made worse by the threat of renewed invasion in midsummer, the masses had little choice but to go home and begin reconstructing their lives. The timing of their return depended on economic and familial circumstance, location in Texas, and individualized variables like personal nerve. In general, those with sufficient income or credit remained the longest away from home, until midsummer or later. East Texans had usually fled last and for the shortest distance and therefore returned first, but at least one Nacogdoches family prudently raised a corn crop on rented Louisiana land before venturing home. Other heads of family came back alone to produce food or income and repair damages before bringing their relatives. The Irish colonists of southwestern Texas, whose towns had been devastated, attempted to resettle during the summer, only to confront Rusk's policy of driving area livestock east of the Guadalupe river. This loss of a major source of food forced area residents generally to relocate; the region from Refugio to San Patricio remained depopulated for years. Most of the refugees from central Texas began the difficult trek home in late April.

Except for the absence of the sense of panic, they repeated some of their earlier experiences: once again river crossings became clogged with destitute families; they travelled slowly on foot or on broken-down horses and oxen that had been shunned by the press gangs; and they braved the obstacles of nature on the way. The refugees became increasingly anxious as they saw burned-out houses, broken-down fences, dispersed livestock, and trampled crops along the roads they travelled. At the end of the journey settlers from all regions found their farms and personal possessions in some state of destruction.[59]

Many came home in order to salvage what they could of their property. An even more basic drive—fear of hunger—stimulated others to risk an early trip back. Texas farmers knew well the demands of the season. On behalf of several of them James S. Montgomery inquired of General Houston on April 28 about the safety of the situation. They "wish to return and make corn," he told Houston. Soldiers soon left their units and rejoined their dependents in this consuming need to get their crops in the field. Some families went into partnership with each other in order to get the planting done in time. In the meantime shortages occurred from the Trinity to the Colorado, and prices inevitably rose during the summer for commodities that the settlers usually grew for themselves. The Texas cabinet, individual benefactors, and local governments all made efforts to distribute food to the needy, but piecemeal policies did not relieve the suffering. Fortunately, the spring rains that had been so miserable also made for good harvests where farmers succeeded in their planting. According to the *Telegraph*, east Texas expected abundant crops, and enough corn had been saved in the Brazos and Colorado to "produce a sufficiency for the consumption of the inhabitants." By fall it had revised downward this report of guarded optimism: less than half the residents west of the Brazos had returned early enough to make a crop; the army discharged men without providing them with the means to care for their families; and merchants also suffered from the "unsettled state" of the country.[60]

With their lives disrupted and business of all kind broken up, the people of Texas had to make many adjustments—both physical and psychological—in the summer of 1836. Some searched for new lines of work or pulled up stakes and moved once again. Innkeeper Angelina Peyton returned to San Felipe after the Runaway Scrape to find her "place barren of every thing—ruins all my things burnt up—crockery piles of cinders—ashes and incombustibles in heaps as left by the fire." She could stand to stay but a short time ("I was lonely—nobody came") before moving on to Columbia to open another tavern. Many people shared this mood of depression, but distance from Texas helped create a different perspective. Susan Thorn spent July of 1836 on a northbound

Mississippi River steamboat. In her boredom she yearned for her Nacogdoches home: "now if we were in Texas we would never want for excitement." She had become so accustomed to the revolutionary milieu "that all places" she visited on her journey "after a few days appear monotonous, and dull."[61]

Some Texans wanted to perpetuate the excitement of war, believing with Rusk that the lesson of the immediate past and the remembrance of starving women and children called for preventive strikes against Mexico. To this commander's chagrin, war weariness prevailed among the people. Feelings of despondency commonly occurred among refugees faced with rebuilding their lives. William Staffer, claiming that age, poor eyesight, and general infirmity exempted him from military service, had fled to the United States in April. He left his family there and returned to find his worst expectations fulfilled—nearly all his possessions had been "Laid wast" by the war. "You now nothing of my feeling," Staffer wrote to Austin, on seeing "14 years of the prime of My life gon from me in my old days." He began over, having "to raise A campt as I did when I first settled there" and to purchase even meal since his corn had been impressed. Doggedly, he went to work on a farm which had become "all groan up with weeds" and generally "maid the best of it all that I could." More tribulations came on the night of July 10 in the person of eight ruffians posing as patriotic avengers. These men swore to take Staffer "ded or alive" because of his alleged failure to support the war effort, a charge he disputed. He fled once again out of the country, raging against a society that tolerated "mobs and bands no better than Pyrets. . . . I did put my holl depenans in the declaration of the In dependans," he reflected bitterly, but now must "hunt a new Hom until a chang takes place" in the political order and social spirit.[62]

Others became equally weary of war but clung more tenaciously to what remained of their lives in Texas. Few had suffered more than Mrs. George Sutherland. She lost a son at the Alamo and then spent two months "wandering about" the countryside looking for a place of safety. With three little girls in tow she fled from their home west of the Colorado River to the Sabine, a journey of about two hundred miles made with little help from her soldier-husband. In mid-May the family became one of the first to return to the frontier region. There she "found nothing in the world worth speaking of." Houses and warehouses had all been burned in a destruction so complete as to leave "not one mouthful of anything to eat. God knows how we will make out," she acknowledged to her sister. "We are trying to raise something to eat but I fear we will miss it." Nevertheless, she concluded, "if we can have peace and can have preaching I wont care for the loss of what property is gone."[63] For Mrs. Sutherland and probably for most Texans, zeal for the war had vanished, worn down to a dogged determination to carry on.

12. The Black Texans and Slavery in Revolution and War

If language serves as a useful guide, the matter of slavery occupied an important place in the minds of the leaders of the Texas Revolution. Their rhetoric brimmed with imagery depicting a struggle between freedom and bondage. In their view Mexico sought to enslave the only people in the land who still dared to defend the cause of liberty. A group of volunteers in October, 1835, labeled Mexican rule as "worse than Egyptian bondage"; the following June Gen. Thomas J. Rusk sought to rally the people to the field against an enemy who intended "to make [them] the slaves of petty military commandants." The opposing soldiers thus became "menial slaves of military despotism. However appealing Texans found this vision of themselves as sufferers *"in the cause of Freedom and the Rights of Man,"* in candid moments they acknowledged that the conflict involved the issue of slavery in a manner far different from that portrayed in this propaganda.[1]

Wars for independence had invariably subjected the institution of slavery to profound tensions since the time of the American Revolution. Throughout the new world in the subsequent half-century a variety of forces shook the foundations of bondage and led to its overthrow, by a combination of black revolution and state action, in Haiti, the British West Indies, and the South American republics. In all these slave societies radical ideologies, accompanied by sudden shifts in political, economic, and military power, emerged during times of crisis to undermine the old order. Wars — international, internal, or both — accelerated these challenges to slavery and enabled many blacks to seize their freedom. Emancipation had not triumphed uniformly or without struggle even where the slaveholding classes had been weak, but revolutionary movements had left slavery isolated and threatened from outside and within.[2]

One external challenge came in the form of abolitionist agitation against Texas. A thoroughgoing denunciation, *The War in Texas,* by Benjamin Lundy, appeared in 1836 and attributed the Revolution to a proslavery conspiracy. This polemic presented the origins of the Revolution as exactly opposite to those identified in public pronouncements in Texas, which stressed liberty and human rights.[3] Lundy helped to make the antislavery movement explicitly anti-Texas, posing a threat to the otherwise favorable image that the Texas Revolution attained in United States public opinion. The abolitionists and their political supporters might have become a great factor had they managed to influence government policy toward a genuinely neutral stance. Yet, the Revolution enjoyed considerable popular support, and substantial aid from the United States went to Texas as the Jackson administration followed an unofficial stance of benign neglect regarding suppression of the flow of manpower, money, and supplies to the rebel forces.[4] These outside developments limited the threat to slavery, but the nature of the war itself meant that the Texas Revolution had a significant impact on both slaves and slaveholders. The struggle with Mexico raised before Anglos the specter of slave revolt, created for blacks other avenues to freedom besides rebellion, generated forces that weakened the hold of masters over bondsmen, and placed the very survival of the institution in Texas on the success of Texas arms.

As political tensions between Texans and the central government grew in the spring of 1835, the traditional Mexican restraint with regard to slavery appeared to be ending. Many leaders warned that military preparations in the interior would bring forcible emancipation and slave rebellion into Texas. General Cos hardly dispelled this anxiety when he warned that "the inevitable consequences of war will bear upon [the rebels] and their property."[5]

The renewed threat of imposed emancipation in case of war led some Texans to feelings of desperation. Fannin authorized the Consultation to sell his slaves in order to purchase munitions because "this property, and indeed any other, will not be worth owning, if we do not succeed."[6] Similarly, the Matagorda committee of safety and correspondence declared in October that, with a "merciless soldiery" advancing on Texas "to give liberty to our slaves, and to make slaves of ourselves; to let loose the blood hounds of savage war upon us, and deluge this beautiful country with the blood of her adopted children, we should be blind indeed to continue any longer inactive."[7] Preparedness was not the only course of action advocated by those fearful of war—others argued that the same considerations suggested the necessity of peace, to prevent an invasion by an army of liberation. Especially frightening was the prospect that the United States might enforce its prohibition of the international slave trade, preventing the transportation of bondsmen across the Sabine and leaving masters with no place to secure their property.[8]

The arrival of war was attended by more complaints about Mexican abolitionism and by heightened racial invective. A correspondent of the *Telegraph and Texas Register* pleaded for separation "from a people one half of whom are the most depraved of the different races of Indians, different in color" and inferior in character. From this it took but a short leap of imagination to transform the struggle into one between "Texian freemen" and slaves. "Will you now," John W. Hall asked the people of Texas, "suffer the *colored* hirelings of a cruel and faithless despot, to feast and revel, in your dearly purchased and cherished homes?" Lest any doubt remain about the racial and sexual nature of this reveling, Fannin called Texans to arms to prevent the prostitution of "the *Fair daughters* of chaste *white women*."[9] Given this view of the conflict as a race war, Anglo Texans naturally feared slave insurrection. With "war now pending," William H. Wharton compiled a list of evidence of Mexican hostility toward Texas: "1st With a sickly philanthropy worthy of the abolitionists of these United States, they have, contrary to justice, and to law, intermeddled with our slave population, and have even impotently threatened . . . to emancipate them, and induce them to turn their arms against their masters.[10] The military events that soon transpired led many to fear that Mexican abolitionism was far from "impotent."

As early as 1828 the Mexican government had considered the relation between slave revolt and Texas independence. Gen. Manuel de Mier y Terán, who believed that bondsmen experienced severe maltreatment and that they knew of the proemancipation intent of Mexican law, viewed the slaves as ripe for an uprising. But he argued against abolition, suggesting that the potential for a slave insurrection would restrain both the secession of Texas and the threat of invasion by the United States. Some subsequent officials believed that Mier y Terán had miscalculated. The government of Mexico dispatched Juan N.

Almonte to Texas in 1833–34 with secret instructions to inform the slaves of their liberty upon Mexican law and to promise them land as freedmen.[11]

In the summer of 1835 many Anglo Texans concluded that Mexico had acquired the will and power to implement an antislavery strategy. Reports circulated that Thomas M. Thompson, commander of the Mexican schooner of war *Correo,* had intended to impress and subsequently liberate "all the negro slaves in the country that he could get in his possession" when he sailed into Galveston Bay in late July. Even James H. C. Miller, a defender of the Mexican centralists because he had believed the government's goals to be pacific, wrote to warn of the Mexican invasion of Texas, which contemplated, among other evils, slave emancipation. More graphically, another Texan recently back from the interior of Mexico reported to the public that a large army had been dispatched. Its numerous oppressive policies included an intent to liberate the slaves and also to "let them loose upon their [the Anglo Texans'] families."[12] Benjamin R. Milam summarized the emerging consensus of opinion. He, too, warned that Mexican troops planned an unconventional warfare of recruiting Indians and attempting "if possible to get the slaves to revolt." Altogether these forces would "make a wilderness of Texas, and beggars of its inhabitants."[13]

The Anglo Texans knew, then, that the coming of war presented them with the task of preserving slavery amidst an atmosphere of crisis. The possibility of a slave insurrection placed an added burden on the embryonic Texas army, so initial responsibility for monitoring slave behavior rested with the multipurpose committees of safety organized by most communities. In the fall of 1835, for the first of two times, the fear of slave restlessness reached crisis levels in the region of the lower Brazos.

On September 22 a Brazoria committee announced the receipt of "information . . . clearly proving that much danger is to be apprehended from the slave population." It responded in a manner that befitted the southern heritage of its members, recommending organization of a "vigilant patrole [*sic*] . . . to keep the slave population in due subjection" and punishment of blacks caught away from their masters' premises. The following week a similar group in Matagorda echoed the call for "measures" to prevent "both alarm and danger."[14]

The alarm, however, did not subside. On October 6 two residents of nearby Columbia wrote Stephen F. Austin for confirmation of a reputed ascent up the river by Cos and two thousand soldiers. Both feared "great danger from the Negroes should a large Mexican force come so near" and sought to detain area troops to guard against these eventualities. This amphibious assault fell under the category of "false rumors," which one of the letters admitted were circulating; a few days later the *Telegraph* observed that people "have been alarmed at shadows." The military authorities thought enough of this threat that they kept Texas troops in the area.[15]

In mid-October residents of this region sought more substantial aid. Writing on October 17, B. J. White, at Goliad, informed Commander-in-Chief Austin of "unpleasant news" received from two individuals who had made the journey from Brazoria: "the negroes on Brazos made an attempt to rise." These rebels had an elaborate plan of redistributing the land, shipping cotton to New Orleans, and then making "the white men serve them in turn." The revolt had been vigorously suppressed, possibly with the aid of troops dispatched from Goliad under the command of a Major Sutherland. Of the nearly one hundred slaves "taken up," some had been hung and others "whipd nearly to death."[16]

Slave-related disturbances subsided until the spring of 1836. This relatively peaceful winter interval resulted from a series of circumstances: the brutal suppressions of October had perhaps quieted black unrest and reassured whites; and the military scene had shifted to the region around Béxar, where there were few slaves and where Texas arms temporarily prevailed. Nevertheless, patrols continued to function, and in December a proclamation warned the people of continued danger. In that document Sam Houston accused General Santa Anna of the unchivalric practice of distributing arms "to a portion of our population, for the purpose of creating in the midst of us a servile war." Those who lived near the coastal rivers continued after the first of the year to suspect that Mexican strategy included a plan to "send in troops by sea to excite the negroes."[17]

Changing military fortunes once again heightened the danger of slave insurrection. On March 5, 1836, Henry Austin advised James F. Perry to take his family eastward for safety. Predicting accurately that the front would come to the Colorado and Brazos region, the correspondent stated that there was danger from soldiers, plundering Indians, or a "possible rising of the negroes." Twelve days later a committee at Brazoria, alarmed by news of the fall of the Alamo, announced to the public that the advancing Mexican army sought "a general extermination" of the people, regardless of age or sex. The group claimed to have "been appraised" [*sic*] that the "treacherous and bloody enemy" intended to recruit Negroes "as instruments of his unholy and savage work, . . . thus lighting the torch of war, in the bosoms of our domestic circles." It proposed that measures be taken "for securing in a proper manner all negroes" and that a black work force be assembled to establish fortifications on the river. The committee's sensational rhetoric, plus this proposal of bringing together a large number of admittedly rebellion-prone slaves, may have contributed to the impending panic. Here as elsewhere in southwest Texas, most Anglos chose not to volunteer, organize, or fortify, but to flee.[18]

This panic turned into the Runaway Scrape, and about this same time black unrest erupted to the east. From Galveston Bay Col. James Morgan wrote his superiors with recommendations for protecting that area. "The Negroes high upon the Trinity, have manifested a disposition to become troublesome and in some instances *daring*," and he reported that they had sought a potentially dangerous alliance with the Coushatta Indians. The blacks apparently planned to "come down [to the south] and murder the inhabitants and join the Mexicans." Once again a combination of white reprisals (unnamed parties chased off one black rebel, whipped another, and killed a third) and an improved Texas military situation ended the threatened slave insurrection. These incidents weakened the Texans' military effort both by diverting attention from the enemy army and also by undermining recruitment. Even President Burnet acknowledged that some men had to be retained to protect their neighborhoods.[19]

None of these instances of slave unrest resulted in the actual shedding of white blood, but the Anglos' concern was prudent. Evidence of the reality of black rebelliousness came from many sources; in October and again in December the General Council took time to order the San Felipe patrol captain to arrest free blacks, one for making "violent threats" and another on a charge of "high crimes and misdemeanors." Furthermore, virtually all the preconditions for rebellion existed in Texas in 1835–36. As frontier residents, the slaves of this region had of necessity acquired skills with weapons that in this crisis could be turned against their masters. The slave ranks had recently grown in numbers with the importation of Africans, an element that frequently led uprisings throughout the Americas. The intellectual climate had filled with revolutionary rhetoric emphasizing freedom, rights, and liberty in the struggle against tyranny, despotism, and even slavery. Blacks had apparently acquired some familiarity with the emancipationist leanings of Mexico, which would have prepared them to embrace the invading force as an army of liberation. A Tory from Gonzales, writing in early 1836, quoted Brazoria slaveholders as saying that "their negroes, G— d—— 'em, were on the tip-toe of expectation, and rejoicing that the Mexicans were coming to make them free!" The internal divisions of the ruling authorities added to the opportunity for slave rebellion; only the whites' continued numerical superiority and success on the battlefield obstructed the chance for a more powerful black revolt.[20]

Mexico did not officially invite a slave rebellion. In fact, its army marched northward without a clear policy regarding slavery. As late as February, 1836, Santa Anna queried government officials in Mexico: "Shall we permit those wretches to moan in chains any longer in a country whose kind laws protect the liberty of man without distinction of cast or color?" At the end of the month F. M. Díaz Noriega replied that the contract system of Texas was an illegal pretext for slavery. In fact, those "unhappy people became free solely by the act of stepping into our territory," and he advised recruiting blacks for the army so they could discover and claim their own freedom. Such a policy, according to Noriega, had the added merit of preempting Texas complaints against unconstitutional appropriation of property.[21] Minister of War José María Tornel wrote Santa Anna on March 18, agreeing that the "philanthropy of the Mexican nation" had already freed Texas slaves. He advised the general to grant their "natural rights," including "the liberty to go to any point on the globe that appeals to them" or to remain in Texas or another part of Mexico, but the minister betrayed a concern that their area of residence be chosen so as to discourage future "disorder or upheaval." On April 9, 1836, Tornel published a congressional decree confiscating the property of those who promoted rebellion in Texas; however, it contained no specific reference to human chattels.[22]

Whatever hesitation may have been shown in published Mexican policy, the Mexican army had an actual disposition toward black freedom. The ranks of the first troops to arrive in Béxar even included some black infantrymen and servants. Until March the location of the fighting limited contact between Mexican soldiers and slaves, but the army's basic attitude became clear when Joe and Sam, black servants of the Alamo commanders, survived the slaughter at that fortress, the only Texas males to do so.[23] During the six-week interval that followed this victory, the Mexican army moved east of the Colorado and then the Brazos River and thus into the region where most bondsmen lived. These events put the people on the road and made managing slaves a problematical task. The commander had first-hand knowledge of this situation because of the troubles he had in caring for his slave Willis. On April 3 Houston dispatched his "boy" eastward to a friend's supervision, with instructions to "keep him strictly" in control. "He does me no earthly good, and only keeps me mixed [up] — almost to death," wrote the perturbed master. "Another thing," he continued, Willis "speaks Mexican," a skill that obviously would make it easier to succeed in fleeing to the invaders. "I wish him taken care of," Houston concluded, "You will have to flog him well."[24]

His personal experience may have influenced the general to attempt to secure the slave property of Texans who fled in the Runaway Scrape. The army did not always succeed in preventing blacks from "joining the enemy," as one observer described it. Slaves often seized the opportunity of running away, frequently in group ventures, and gained refuge with the invaders. Fourteen slaves and their families became free by fleeing to the command of General Urrea near Victoria on April 3, 1836. Even in retreat the Mexican forces attracted runaways: a Matagorda resident who returned to his home in early May discovered that at least thirteen blacks had "left my neighborhood" with the southbound army. He complained, too, that many cattle and eight wagons loaded with provisions, property that he valued at a total of $100,000, had been taken by the enemy. According to General Filisola, at least some of the plundered goods were taken by slaves who robbed houses in their flights for liberty.[25] The Mexicans found these fugitives often ready to serve as well as to seek protection. Blacks aided river crossings, acted as messengers, spies, or provocateurs, and performed other chores for their liberators.[26]

Enough slaves escaped to the Mexican army that the Texans provided for the return of these fugitives in the battlefield agreement forced on Santa Anna on April 22 (later confirmed in the Treaty of Velasco). The commanders left in charge of the Mexican army disagreed about whether and to what extent this provision should be implemented. General Filisola vacillated. Although he initially promised scrupulous conformity to the terms of the treaty, he put off the Texas commissioners; eventually he negotiated an armistice that admitted them to his camp, where they recovered prisoners and a few runaways. His fellow officers criticized Filisola's conduct as a violation of law, morality, and proper military procedure. Urrea refused to honor the Velasco agreements and later boasted that "all the slaves within my jurisdiction continued to enjoy their liberty. . . ." Capt. José Enrique de la Peña intervened personally in the cause of freedom when he disguised a soon-to-be-reenslaved black as a Mexican soldier and whisked him away from the Texas representatives at Goliad to Matamoros. Both sides charged the other with perfidy on this issue; a Mexican officer reported that the Texans had sold some prisoners of war into slavery. Frustration over the unfulfilled slavery provision of the Velasco treaty helped contribute to delays in the release of Santa Anna, but the Texans never regained more than a handful of the fugitives who found freedom with the Mexican army.[27]

Not all the slaves who escaped during the Texas Revolution sought or achieved protection from the Mexican forces, but the upheaval generated by the conflict increased the opportunities for running away. Mostly the slaves fled in groups, especially those who took advantage of the panic of the Runaway Scrape, and frequently they seized horses and weapons to ease and protect their journey. Some of the runaways had been previously conscripted to labor on military fortifications. The dislocation and breakdown of authority continued to protect escaped slaves long after the Texas-Mexican battles had ended; in November, 1836, a group of owners advertised for the return of "a number of African negroes" described as "wandering about the country" in the region of the Colorado River. Others fell into the hands of the authorities near Nacogdoches.[28]

The effects of the Revolution on the security of slave property lasted even into the year 1837. Some blacks fled in groups through the sparsely settled region west of the Colorado toward the Rio Grande, perhaps to join the colony of blacks already established in Matamoros. Most escaped bondsmen — in fact eight out of ten advertised as runaways or captives in 1837 — were Africans. Slave traders had taken advantage of weakened authority in Texas since 1834 and continued their illegal imports even during the war for independence. These unacculturated bondsmen proved especially recalcitrant and sometimes influenced American-born slaves to flee with them. Though sheriffs occasionally took them into custody, runaway Africans gained such a reputation for fierce resistance that they roamed around wilderness areas virtually without interference. Edwin Waller advertised for the return of Gumby and Zow for a year after his initial June 1837 notice before he gave up the effort. Brothers Leander H. and Pleasant D. McNeel, who also speculated heavily in African slaves, waited three months before calling public attention to their two runaways. During that period the heavily scarred twenty-five-year-old Arch was "taken up five or six times

. . . and made his escape every time," twice even breaking out of irons. The owner considered Arch "a great rascal," but admitted that both he and his companion were "smart, sensible negro[es]." The ranks of slave runaways changed abruptly in 1838, when only one of sixteen advertisements in the *Telegraph* sought the return of fugitives denoted as "Africans."[29]

While many blacks sought freedom through flight, others appear in the records as adherents on the Texas side. Though it is difficult to know how freely such service was given, some must have hoped to earn their liberty in this manner. Slaves provided aid to the cause in a variety of ways. Some contributed provisions, while others engaged in forms of military service. Capt. Josiah H. Bell dispatched his slaves Peter and Sam to help guard families near the front in April, 1836. Another slave named Peter, having previously obtained the privilege of hiring his own time as a teamster, transported provisions to the army in the fall of 1835. An enterprising bondsman named Cary "was of much service in carrying expresses" during the Revolution, according to a subsequent certificate written by his owner. These activities placed slaves in positions where they saw or heard valuable military information, especially since the invading soldiers commonly assumed that all blacks held pro-Mexican views. During the campaign that led to the battle of San Jacinto, slaves seemed to form an unofficial spying network that relayed the size, location, and disposition of Mexican forces, including their vulnerability on the afternoon of April 21. In spite of these efforts, the records reveal a total of only two emancipations recognized by Texas law.[30]

That there was no guarantee of reward became harshly apparent to Joe, a twenty-three-year-old slave who remained with his owner, Travis, during the battle for the Alamo. By his own account, conveyed according to one hearer "with much modesty [and] apparent candor," the servant fired at the attackers several times, received wounds but escaped the initial massacre by hiding in a building inside the fortress, narrowly avoided execution through an officer's intervention, and even spoke with Santa Anna concerning the Texas army. Joe evidently possessed considerable persuasive ability; a Mexican version of this episode explained that he obtained mercy by convincing his captors "that only force" had made him stay at the battle scene. However, his eloquence did not bring him freedom—Joe remained a slave in the Travis estate, living near Columbia for over a year after his great adventure. He apparently retained a sense of history, for he created his own method of celebrating the first anniversary of the battle of San Jacinto. Accompanied by a Mexican and taking two fully equipped horses, Joe chose that day to run away in search of the freedom that had eluded him.[31]

The free black population of Texas was small at the time of the Revolution, not exceeding 150 men, women and children by the largest estimate. Not all the men in this group had the opportunity to participate—some had gained their freedom by running away but had no legal papers to protect their status. Anglo suspicions about the threat of black insurrection also appear to have limited the involvement of this class of people. Robert Thompson, for one, stood for the draft but the authorities did not enroll him, though the Texans seldom rejected help from any quarter. Thompson ended up donating his gun and a horse, a form of contribution matched by others like Andrew Bell.

Nevertheless, the government did not display a consistent pattern of distrust, as shown by the contributions of several free blacks. William Goyens carried out sensitive diplomatic missions for the Texans. Many saw military service and compiled notable records. An 1835 emigrant to Jackson municipality, Samuel McCullough, Jr., joined with the volunteers who took the fortress at Goliad on October 9, where he became one of the first Texans to shed blood for the Revolution. Greenbury Logan, a free black serving with the Texas forces at Béxar, received crippling wounds in the storming of that place two months later. Hendrick Arnold appears to have played the most significant role, as the guide who led the assault into the city. The leaders valued Arnold's expertise so highly that they delayed the attack for a day so that he could participate. Free blacks also came to Texas as members of volunteer companies raised in the United States after the fighting began. One of them, Peter Allen, died in the Goliad massacre. Several other free blacks also joined the army either before or after the San Jacinto battle. In no way, then, did the war spare this segment of the Texas population. Logan's shoulder wounds left him unable to work in his blacksmith trade. Though Arnold continued to participate in the spy company led by his father-in-law, Erastus (Deaf) Smith, in January, 1836, he sought aid from the government on behalf of his family "who are in a state of destitution. . . . They have been reduced thereto by the present struggle for liberty," he pointed out.[32]

A greater number of blacks served the Texas cause involuntarily and with no prospect of reward. They labored as conscripts on the military fortifications at Galveston, prepared in late March and April of 1836 as a position from which to make a possible last stand. A few also helped cut steamboat wood or assisted on other smaller projects. Drafting slaves to work on fortifications obviously strengthened the Texas military position, but the idea also appealed to those who thought, in the words of the *Telegraph,* that removing bondsmen to army supervision "would leave greater security at home."[33]

Black workers came under military authority in a variety of ways. Some had been impressed; many accompanied their refugee owners to the island; others found themselves entrusted or hired to the army — for wages in a few cases but often only for board — by masters who had fled the country or who had despaired of providing them sustenance. The woodcutters were delivered by owners motivated by a stated sense of patriotic zeal, but slaves and masters both objected to the military regimen established at Galveston. On April 8, Colonel Morgan, in charge of preparing the island for defense, wrote to the secretary of war that he had arranged for approximately 140 bondsmen and women to work on the fort. Upon learning, however, that Burnet had authorized another officer "to *hire* hands . . . and to pay at the rate of $8 pr mo. and board," he had abandoned his plans. Eight days later Rusk provided orders to Morgan permitting him to impress certain slaves. While inspecting the island on April 25, Burnet issued a more sweeping proclamation giving the Galveston commander clear authority to muster "all the colored persons on the island" over age fourteen and to supervise their "fatigue duty." Efforts on the fort continued until toward the end of April, at which time the commanding officers went off in search of tools, leaving the project in charge of subordinates who neglected the duty. With the work unofficially at a halt, slaveowners began reclaiming their workers. James F. Perry paid twenty dollars in steamboat fares for transporting back to his home the four slaves who had been pressed into government service on Galveston Island.[34]

The war unsettled the normal routines of bondage and race relations. Emergency needs for labor arose; owners who went off to war sought special managerial arrangements for their work force; newspapers anticipated food crises and therefore urged corn rather than cotton production. The presence of hostile forces also disrupted work patterns. Masters attempted to shift their labor forces out of war zones and then back into their fields as the fortunes of war allowed, but they found this a difficult task of judgment and logistics. Some owners, with more concern for the security of their chattels than for the year's farming, ran their slaves eastward past the Trinity and Neches rivers all the way to the border. Those who took this precaution included the Groces, the largest slaveowners in Texas. A few planters removed their human property northward in rumored attempts to reach the Red River.

All this human motion weakened the bonds of slavery and rendered the institution very unstable. It also, of course, increased the danger that slaves would somehow manage to slip from the grasp of their masters. In times of crisis the arming of blacks may have been accepted as military necessity; afterwards, Anglo Texans worried about the dangers of this practice. On May 27, 1836, several Nacogdoches citizens petitioned the government to prevent "Negroes Carrying Arms" as a result of an incident the previous evening. Other slaves fell prey to Indian raids and physical perils in moving to and from the plantations; John, the slave of a San Antonio merchant, died in the fighting at the Alamo where he had been left, ironically, as a safety precaution.[35]

Threats to slavery posed by political change in Mexico, military efforts to impose this new order, and the upheavals generated by war — these challenges dominated the thoughts of defenders of the institution during 1835 and 1836. Slaveowners also recognized the dangers of a growing international antislavery movement. Authorities acted quickly to discourage a northern abolition society scheme to establish a free black colony in Texas in 1835, just as they had made their sentiments clear to Lundy on this matter two years earlier. "It is the opinion of all the *Texanos* with whom I have conversed on the subject," wrote an astute observer, "that the new government of Texas must sanction the holding of slaves as property."[36]

Buoyed by this proslavery and white supremacist consensus, Texas law and constitution makers in 1835 and 1836 moved to the task of protecting property, including the ownership of human beings, while also emphasizing doctrines of freedom. For a while Texas politicians struggled to hone their rhetoric of liberty and equality so as to pose no challenge to slavery, but the delegates to the constitutional convention coped with this problem more successfully.[37] They adopted a circumspect Declaration of Rights which began, "First. All men, when they form a special compact, have equal rights." These, including the privilege of bearing arms, were conferred not on "all men" or "people" but on "citizens." The Constitution then gave citizenship to "all persons (Africans, the descendants of Africans, and Indians excepted) who were residing in Texas on the day of the declaration of independence" and also to "all free white persons who shall emigrate to the republic."[38]

The Convention went much further than defining human rights in racial terms; it wrote into the framework of government a long list of positive guarantees of slavery. The appropriate section began by defining slave status: "All persons of color who were slaves for life previous to their emigration to Texas, and who are now held in bondage, shall remain in the like state of servitude: provided, the said slave shall be the bona fide property of the person so holding said slave." The Constitution also denied Congress any power to prevent U.S. emigrants "from bringing their slaves into the republic with them" or to emancipate slaves at some future time. Likewise, individuals could not free their bondsmen without gaining congressional consent and agreeing to send them out of the country. A milder version, which opened the possibility of continued residence for emancipated blacks "in cases of [their] meritorious conduct," was deleted from the final draft. This same fate befell a provision that specifically empowered Congress to "compel the owners of slaves to treat them with humanity." About the only issue on which slaveowners failed to gain complete defense of their interests was legislative apportionment; the Constitution provided for districting based on free population.[39]

Two additional aspects of the slavery question — the slave trade and free black issues — also confronted leaders of the Texas Revolution. Critics to the north and south charged that the Texas cause merely disguised the speculative effort to reopen importations from Africa and that Mexican "tyranny" actually sought to enforce laws against this and other nefarious practices.[40] The African slave traffic had accelerated in 1835 and 1836, when at least eight vessels, carrying about six hundred slaves from the West Indies, disembarked their cargoes at Gulf ports or river plantations. Until March, 1836, the Texas revolutionary governments largely ignored this issue. At the Constitutional Convention delegates debated the foreign slave trade as a problem of state; not one expressed a trace of genuine humanitarian feeling for the slaves. Nevertheless, in deference to world opinion and diplomatic positioning, the document prohibited importation of blacks from places other than the United States. The convention simply ignored the thorny question of the disposition of the Africans who might fall into government custody from captured slave ships. Burnet issued an April 3 proclamation against the illegal trade, but Texas had a poor reputation on this issue of international law and morality.[41]

The other racial question that drew the attention of the convention, the fate of free blacks, also grew out of concern for the protection of slavery. Texas masters believed that the presence of this class disrupted slave discipline and discouraged slaveholder migration. Reflecting this concept, the initial drafts of the March constitution in a straightforward manner forbid admission of all free blacks. Ultimately, the delegates, without recorded explanation, modified the language and thereby confused the issue. The relevant clause, by providing that "no free person of African descent . . . shall be permitted to reside permanently in the republic, without the consent of Congress," gave the government a free hand to control this group. However, three features of this wording worked to the advantage of free blacks — first, the constitution did not specifically forbid their emigration as had earlier drafts; second, it added the word "permanently," which by implication invited temporary residence; and third, it opened the possibility of congressional exemption. These potential benefits to free blacks apparently did not arise from a conscious intention of the delegates. By changing the focus from emigration to residence the constitution threatened the very existence of all free blacks, and unequivocally the document denied them citizenship. Texas thus entered nationhood with a constitution that defined human rights in racial terms and also provided a long list of positive guarantees of slavery.[42]

The Texas movement for independence had a dual character with respect to slavery and the black experience. The events of 1835 and 1836 had shaken slavery considerably, but in the end the Texas victory confirmed the institution. Black participation provided some increased opportunities for grasping freedom, but for the masses these were short-term or otherwise elusive. Ideologically, the Texans displayed generally reactionary impulses, despite frequent and fervent identifications with the Spirit of '76. The practical-minded Anglo Americans applied their version of liberty, equality, and democracy cautiously and only to themselves. This aspect of the Texas Revolution clearly owed a debt to the Great Reaction that swept the southern United States in the early 1830s. By then, radical worldwide abolitionism had also emerged, a development that fostered more reaction and thus reinforced the conservative emphasis on property, order, and white supremacy. However uncongenial in spirit toward black freedom, the Texas Revolution generated other forces — including armed conflict and internal dislocation — that temporarily challenged the slave-labor system and Anglo racial hegemony. Yet the brevity of the war and the sudden collapse of the Mexican invasion effort prevented the disintegration of slavery and allowed Texans three more decades to apply the doctrines of their southern heritage.

Conclusion

The political and social history of Texas in the years 1835–36 reveals an experience full of revolutionary dimensions. The movement's leaders established local committees of vigilance and safety to advance their cause and developed a popular ideology that emphasized the march of democracy in the Anglo-American tradition. But more challenging revolutionary developments also occurred — a variety of internal conflict flourished from the first. Texans entered their quarrel with Mexico as a fragmented people, individualistic, divided from one community to another by rivalries for land and other jealousies, bothered by ethnic and racial tensions, and lacking a consensus about the meaning of political changes in Mexico.

Beginning as a kind of regional separatist movement, the Texas rebellion had moved but a short distance before the requirements for wartime authority outpaced the capacities of its infant governments. Varied community interests grew into a myriad of disagreements which no political body had a sufficient combination of wisdom, will, leadership, and popular backing to resolve. The heads of the ever-changing interim governments found themselves suspected of inadequate zeal and failed to assert genuine control over their cause. A virtual state of anarchy existed for much of the struggle, and the requisite extra-constitutional measures were enforced haphazardly by the army. The military element in turn suffered from such democratic fragmentation that no coherent revolutionary purpose emerged to guide the Texas cause.

The army made essential contributions in pushing the regional movement to independence and enforcing material sacrifices. As the military zealots noted, war against the Mexican centralists unleashed new conflicts that had to be met if the Revolution were to succeed. A sizable body of Texans rallied to the opposing side, and the revolution stimulated other divisions: panic over slave rebellion, tensions between volunteers and the majority of Texans who refused military service, disagreements between soldiers and civilians over the impressment of supplies, anti-Tejano prejudices, and suspicions on vital issues such as land policy. Generally, the army had its way so fully that by the summer of 1836 it was swaggering toward a dismissal of constitutional restraint.

In social as well as political terms the Texans suffered from a kind of failed revolution. The social experience had many elements and by-products. For the masses of Texans the Revolution was a time of dislocation and grief, with morale descending to a threatening level. Blame for this response often fell on the public; however, the real source of the problem resided in the shortcomings of government. By failing to establish the central political authority necessary to direct the Revolution, the leaders of Texas had placed an impossible burden on the popular commitment. A cycle of suspicion and self-defense then gained an unbreakable grip on the people. What appeared as capricious seizures of property by the army made them defensive of their self-interests, and the inability of any central authority to compel equitable degrees of sacrifice and participation allowed jealousies to prevail.

This twisted cycle reached its zenith in the western region of Texas, the area of Tejano preponderance. The existence of considerable Tory behavior there gave the army a justification for enforcing militant policies. Texas Mexicans suffered grueling political, property, and status losses.

Inequitable distribution of the burdens of sacrifice and inadequate organization of resources — these were potentially fatal to the Revolution. Nevertheless, forces of geography, miscalculation by the enemy, aid from the United States, just enough volunteering, and incredible good fortune managed to carry Texas arms to a sudden triumph at San Jacinto. At least temporarily, this victory removed the burdens of war and occupation, but it did little to provide forceful government. In fact, political authority remained weaker than ever during the months that followed the Texas military triumph, and the army continued its de facto dominance.

From this context of flawed victory, in the late summer of 1836 the upheavals of revolution and war calmed sufficiently that thoughts began to turn to the future of Texas. Visions of distant grandeur did not occupy much of the public mind; rather, attention focused on more immediate prospects. Even romantic nationalist Mirabeau B. Lamar admitted that Texas stood "trembling as it were, upon the verge of anarchy, with too little credit abroad, and too much of the fiery elements of discord at home."[1] Thus, two questions confronted the new Republic: Could Texas face and resolve the divisions that had threatened it and begin to manage the Revolution? Could it bring enough order out of chaos to claim legitimate nationhood?

One observer attempted to reflect in a deep and dispassionate manner on these questions as a matter of his professional duty. Henry M. Morfit began making firsthand reports in August to his superior, U.S. Secretary of State John Forsyth. Recognition, the diplomatic issue of the day, rested on the potential of Texas for achieving stability. One of Morfit's early reports provided a demographic profile that, without emphasizing the point directly, noted divisions among the people. Like others, he estimated the Anglo population before the Revolution at just under forty thousand. Indians numbered about twelve thousand, blacks totaled around five thousand, and "native Mexicans" thirty-five hundred, leaving the Anglos numerically dominant but not united. The Texans he spoke to divided the population into "settlers" who had come before the revolution and volunteers who had emigrated since the outbreak of hostilities — seeking a good climate, revenge for Americans who had died in the war, or future wealth. This latter motive loomed most significant at the time and depended on securing claims to bounties of land.

Morfit also noted that the population had been dispersed and otherwise diminished by the war; he soon added that the economic forecast for Texas depended on an increase of the "industrious population" living "in a tranquil condition." Rich lands, abundant cattle, and favorable markets would amount to little unless the "pursuits of a settled people [were] properly organized by the restraints and protection of good laws." Whether Texas could develop these unattained "restraints" was obviously the most serious issue of the day, and in his initial analysis of these political prospects, the diplomat was cautious. He saw the government as reasonably "well administered" given its youth, lack of resources, and absence of harmony among the various branches. "It may still be considered a mere experiment upon independence," Morfit concluded, "which the loss of friends or of a single battle may disperse to the winds."[2]

At this same time the young Republic's only newspaper editorialized on the subject of government, as if to reply to the foreign representative and other Americans in Texas. It advised patience to the U.S. volunteers until the new nation could develop better public credit, speculation might ease, and land values could rise. The journal offered as well a comparative perspective on the difficulties of governing in a revolutionary setting. The United States in its infancy had experienced problems similar to and as severe as those currently faced by Texas. "Although we labor under great and apparently to some, insuperable difficulties, and disadvantages in systematizing and establishing an efficient government," wrote the editor, the American republic sixty years earlier had also faced "tumultuous movements" and other "vicissitudes" which "at times threatened [it] with even dissolution." These obstacles had been conquered only by "the good sense and perseverance of that people."[3]

The obvious questions in response were, did Texans have similar good sense, would they persevere, and, further, could they find the statesman to lead them through the tumultuous times? In its earlier stages, as one historian of the Texas Revolution has written, the struggle had been the product of the varied visions of competing personalities rather than "the design of a master planner." No single leader had emerged "displaying the qualities" necessary "to rise above the issues and win the sustained confidence and support of the whole public." The interim government had taken the necessary step toward political stability by providing for elections on the first Monday in September to ratify the March constitution and to elect the specified officials.[4] Those elevated to power by these contests would constitute the sixth set of leaders to attempt to rule Texas in twelve months. Voters and candidates alike approached the electoral process with great interest and seriousness, as if the outcome might be the last chance to make their Revolution work.

Burnet's election proclamation of July 23 attempted to provide for all the technicalities that might cast doubt on the outcome. In addition to ensuring the usual voting procedures, the rules allowed citizens absent from their homes in military service or as refugees to cast ballots. Nevertheless, the troubles of the recent past quickly engulfed the election. Critics charged that Burnet had timed the contest (set for the first Monday in September) in such a way as to promote the candidacy of his personal favorite. Old factional dynamics and emotion-laden issues reappeared. On August 11 from army headquarters Gen. Thomas J. Rusk described the source of his despair to Sam Houston:

> If we do not soon adopt some system and some rules of Law to gov-
> ern the angry passions of men we shall forfeit all our claims to the
> benefits of that kind providence to whom we owe our success so far
> corruption stalks abroad in this Land the still voice of reason and
> truth is suppressed and without a speedy change we shall feel the
> bitter effects of the informed system of slander distraction and abuse.
> . . . Lord have mercy on us save us from the enemy and from the
> mighty operations of our own Great Men.

Contentions threatened to make the election a source of disunity rather than one of accord.[5]

Congressional candidates attempted to outmaneuver each other by aligning themselves with the most popular issues and by emphasizing moderation on the most controversial ones. For example, William H. Jack in Brazoria and Mosely Baker in San Felipe both favored annexation to the United States, opposed leniency toward captured Mexican President Santa Anna, endorsed compensation to veterans, and urged defeat of measures that would in effect expropriate the holdings of large landowners from the Mexican colonizing period. Ex-captain Baker, in particular, also sought to identify himself with the Revolution and with populist positions. The individuals who composed the glorious "Texian band" that fought the war, he maintained, "were not the wealth of the land. They were in the main her poorest citizens, and entitled to receive at the hands of government a liberal and just compensation in land." He promised quick measures to put the veterans in posses-sion of their entitlements and to compensate the settlers of his region who had been impoverished by the late military campaign. Baker also joined the growing number who denounced the "old party violence and old party prejudice" that threatened again to "agitate the country— should the citizens of Texas again allow themselves to be divided . . . then will the day of destruction to Texas have arrived, and instead of a government of law, producing order and confidence and giving pros-perity and greatness, we shall have anarchy and violence and misrule."[6]

Baker and similar-minded candidates in effect proposed a postwar consensus that few dared to oppose directly. It involved boasting of the future of Texas while also endorsing annexation to the United States, evoking memories of past glories while denouncing revolutionary tur-moil, and promising fair compensation to all who had suffered in the cause of the Revolution without committing injustices against the old settlers who had helped to people the land. However popular this ide-ology, Texas faced one issue that threatened to block its elevation — the presidential election. Neither of the two initial candidates was able to rise above the bitter divisions of the immediate past.

Try as he might, Stephen F. Austin could not shake the prejudice that had grown in his absence. Though endorsed by prominent citizens, including former political enemy William H. Wharton, and emphasizing his credentials for accomplishing annexation, the great empresario found himself on the defensive. He had to deny affiliation with corrupt land speculators, involvement in the policy of saving the Mexican commander from his just fate, and identification as the favorite of the unpopular interim president. Zealots like Gen. Thomas J. Green reflected army distrust of Austin as a lukewarm politician who would "forever lay about and boot lick Santa Anna['s] royal feet" in order to prepare the way for a return to Mexican sovereignty that would guarantee large empresario holdings. Gossip circulated that Austin had already promised all the cabinet positions to cronies and vote brokers.[7]

Opposition to Austin also reflected the demographic and regional factors that had undermined stability in earlier stages of the Revolution. He aroused especially strong distrust in deep East Texas, among recent emigrants, and in the army—elements numerous enough to ensure his defeat. However, at first no suitable candidate emerged as an alternative. Rusk enjoyed a momentary boom, soon nipped by his refusal to make the race. Ex-governor Henry Smith agreed to run, but his well-deserved reputation for emotional excess made him unqualified for a position requiring post-revolutionary statesmanship.[8]

The prospects for bitter divisiveness in the presidential contest did not ebb until August 20, less than two weeks before the election, when Sam Houston at last officially entered the race. His timing was masterful—the short duration before the polling would allow him to dodge specific responses to the issues. Ever since his return from New Orleans, where he had gone for treatment of the wound suffered at San Jacinto, Houston had been receiving correspondence urging him to lead. Usually descriptions of what Rusk called "utmost confusion and disorder" under the existing cabinet prefaced these pleas, which concluded with words like "your popularity and influence is greatly needed to quiet the country and keep things straight." Though this letter argued for Houston's resumption of military command, others suggested that his entry into the presidential race would produce an easy victory. They generally emphasized the theme of national crisis: the army hungry, turbulent, and alienated from the political order; rampant suspicions of political corruption and speculative double-dealing; and the total unsuitability of the announced candidates. Houston learned, too, that Smith would gladly step aside in order to assure the defeat of Austin.[9]

While biding his time in declaring for office, the Hero of San Jacinto began announcing what amounted to a platform. It emphasized unity and offered more platitudes than policies. As he wrote to Rusk, the leaders "should pursue that course that will harmonize the feelings of citizens, insure the protection of individual rights, and honestly promote the true interests of their Country." He emphasized the need to set aside factionalism in order to begin the Republic unburdened of past bitterness. The ex-commander received overwhelming support from veterans and current members of the army. They believed, as one politicized woman wrote, that Houston "is in favor of making a more equal division" of the landed domain and "stands altogether the volunteer's friend."[10] He also prompted enthusiasm among those who held that the army needed a firmer command. Further, "many of the old settlers who are too blind to see or understand their interest" as Austin saw it, intended to vote for Houston, who would also carry East Texas. With an unbeatable coalition, the general won by a vote of 5,119 to 743 for Smith and 587 for Austin: the Revolution had produced a dramatic change in Texas leadership.[11]

A major question confronted the new government: Could it achieve and maintain the kind of consensus that had previously eluded Texas? The short duration of the Revolution favored the growth of constitutional restraint. While the processes that gripped Texas during the previous year clearly reflected revolutionary dynamics, the brevity of the experience limited the degree to which revolution had wrenched apart the political order and social fabric.

The government in late 1836 had another major advantage over the previous failures—a broadly popular and charismatic head of state. Houston also proved that he retained the political talent that he had shown earlier in Tennessee, and he had the advantage of making a fresh beginning. The elections demonstrated a consensus not only for the presidency but also in favor of the Constitution and the idea of annexation. They were conducted smoothly and "with much moderation," in the words of the encouraged U.S. diplomatic emissary. The first Congress, comprising men with a wide variety of personal and political backgrounds, began meeting in early October. It resolved a problem posed by the fact that the unpopular Burnet still held the presidency, burdened further by lame duck status. He left office on

October 22, agreeing to resign six weeks early under the threat of congressional removal. This act closed the Revolution on a fitting note of extra-constitutionality.[12]

Houston as president openly strived for legitimacy and consensus. He brought all major personalities and factions into the government — in addition to Vice-President Lamar, Houston nominated Austin for secretary of state and Smith for the treasury, the popular Rusk for the war post, and men of repute to the other positions.

The government responded to the most fundamental issues by attempting to balance conflicting interests. Land policy especially required delicate handling, even though the vastness of the public domain gave Texas a decided advantage in determining its distribution. Congress had to decide which set of claimants would have priority. It soon enacted laws providing that settlers with uncompleted headrights would file first, thus giving them the prime lands in established neighborhoods where they may have already been living as squatters. The policy expanded the number who would be eligible for land bounties for military service but delayed the date of this distribution for another year. Empresario claims that had been completed before the Revolution were protected like other valid titles of settlers, but grants that had not been previously fulfilled remained invalidated by the Constitution. Congress turned over other disputed empresario matters to the courts. Likewise, potential vengeance against allegedly unpatriotic residents was directed to the mercies of local citizenry. Another issue — establishing new institutions of justice and local government — was easily resolved by structures constructed in accordance with Anglo-American traditions.[13]

One major issue threatened this budding consensus: the militant and unruly army. All observers acknolwedged that the military had genuine causes for complaint. Even its adversary Burnet spoke to the Congress of past "privations" of the army and of the need to reward recent recruits. Into the early fall soldiers continued to complain of the inadequate quantity and quality of food and clothing, but the more serious problem appeared to be rampant disorder. Rather than enforcing discipline, the officers set bad examples — drinking, quarreling, fighting, and even killing each other. Further, as a body the army remained politicized and discontented, even while its composition shifted to a predominance of U.S. volunteers. Some efforts had been made by Austin and others to diminish the flow after the battle of San Jacinto, but the force grew to about two thousand men by late 1836, the largest since the outset of hostilities. Many of the junior grade officers gained extended furloughs, which they spent at the capitol in not-so-subtle lobbying activities. Some openly threatened legislators on issues relating to soldier interests, expressing particular disgruntlement when settler land interests received priority over veterans' claims. As a visitor to Texas explained, "This preference in favor of those who, it was said, shared none of the sufferings and privations of the war over others whose days and nights were spent in the tented field was pronounced unjust, ungrateful, and oppressive."[14]

President Houston recognized the magnitude of the army problem and had the credentials to resolve it. As the wounded ex-commander, he could not readily be charged with an anti-military attitude. In one of his first acts the new head of state issued a general order nullifying the furloughs of those officers he saw milling around Columbia in great numbers, urging cessation of these leaves, and threatening to arrest those away from their posts as deserters. Other actions also gave clear evidence that the president would not submit to military pressure. He vetoed the measure extending land bounties to recruits who had entered Texas service since July and steadily asserted civilian control with procedures designed to establish the authority of the War Department. Congress gave the president the power to organize the military according to U.S. army regulations.

Houston had a major setback when Secretary of War Albert Sidney Johnston, sent to assume command in December, suffered a serious wound in a duel with Felix Huston, the general he had been ordered to replace. The victor remained in command, as if by battle-right. The president resolved this intolerable situation in the spring of 1837 by subterfuge. Bringing General Huston to the capital for a strategy session, Houston secretly sent the secretary of war on a simultaneous mission to army headquarters. He offered immediate furloughs (revokable at any time) to the camp-weary volunteers, half of whom left the army and many the country as well. His army reduced in size and power, Felix Huston soon followed the others back to the United States. Texas defense then rested on a tiny regular army and quixotic citizen volunteers, but President Houston had set aside the specter of military dictation that had appeared to be a lasting legacy of the Revolution.[15]

What had been throughout 1836 a failed revolution, with a government lacking the will and power to tame the discordant elements of disorder, became within a few years a reasonably restrained constitutional system. Nevertheless, growth and progress amidst struggle and discontent characterized the entire political history of the Texas Republic. The feelings of harmony that swept Houston into office in 1836 and prevailed in his first few months as president soon dissipated; however, he brought a degree of popularity and restraint that had been entirely lacking in the Revolution. Extreme bitterness flared in electoral contests and over some specific issues — even the matter of locating the capital threatened to erupt into civil war — but ideological consensus also predominated. Executive power changed hands peaceably following each of the four elections. Threats to impeach Houston over his handling of Texas defense never materialized, and few dared even talk of *coup d'etat*. Undoubtedly, the preservation of civil authority came in part from the character of leadership rather than from an underpinning of political stability. The best historian of government in the Republic concludes, "If Houston desired to be a military strong man and to pose as the savior of the Republic, the opportunity was . . . at hand" following the Mexican invasions of 1842. The ex-general not only eschewed such an act but opposed governmental assumption of emergency powers out of respect for personal liberties and from fears of a cycle of revolution. At the same time, government did not provide the young nation with an adequate system of defense.

In short, Texas survived the internal and external threats to its existence without really resolving many of the underlying problems. However popular the Texas national identity became in retrospect, the Anglo masses always rallied to the cause of annexation to the United States, even after their "infant" Republic had been independent for almost a decade. The major appeal of that measure was invariably the amplified prospect for peace, order, and security. [16]

The outlook of improved fortunes through annexation had no appeal to the minorities of Texas. Sudden military success had nipped the radical tide as applied to Anglo Texans by limiting the needs and thus the potential of the Revolution. Opposition to the Texas cause had quickly dwindled, and the decline of Tory attitudes limited extremism. No reign of terror emerged in communities where the Anglo ethnic majorities prevailed. Yet minority elements in Texas felt the effects of the Revolution in a harsh and lasting manner.

Tejanos experienced a kind of revolutionary purge in the years 1835–36, their lives being filled by bitter and destructive conflict, harsh material exploitation, and ruthless denial of liberty. Despoliation and depopulation had been the major social consequence of the Revolution, results both of an extended presence by contending armies and of divided popular loyalties. The Texas army became larger than ever in the winter of 1836–37, and it preyed on local property from necessity or out of a misplaced sense of revenge. The military attempted to drive eastward what cattle it could not consume itself, transforming the area into a kind of buffer zone between centralist armies south of the Rio Grande and the heartland of Anglo habitation east of the Guadalupe. Those who survived a year of the ordeals of war and military occupation confronted a future with more of the same, hardened by sweeping anti-Mexican prejudice.

After 1836, the continued threat of invasion from Mexico retarded the peopling and economic growth of western Texas. Further, tensions between Mexico and Texas, while promoting "solidarity and patriotism at home" as one historian observes, also accelerated Anglo hostility toward Tejanos. Certainly anti-Mexican attitudes did not begin with the Revolution. As Arnoldo De León demonstrates, North Americans came to Texas with prejudices against people of darker color that soon developed into a fuller revulsion against Tejano culture.[17] Revolution, war, and independence energized these notions with the spark of revenge. At Béxar Col. Juan Seguín with difficulty managed to save his hometown from destruction in early 1837, but the pattern of property expropriation by occupying forces continued, made worse by a pattern of Anglo land grabbing.[18] As Andrés A. Tijerina has shown, except in the region south of the Nueces, the Tejano population of the Republic had difficulty patenting their land claims and thus remained in a state of decline from pre-Revolution levels.[19]

Tejanos responded to these continued antagonisms in several ways. Some continued the flight to the south; others persisted and hoped for improvement that did not come. Each passing year confirmed their minority status and waning political influence. A large portion of the Tejano community in Nacogdoches heeded the call for rebellion and for rallying to the standard of Mexico when raised by Vicente Córdova in 1838–39. Thereafter, suspicions abounded in western Texas concerning the complicity of Bexareños in support of projected or actual Mexican invasions that occurred in 1842. These affairs even ensnared Texas patriot Juan Seguín on charges of disloyalty. In fact, Tejanos remained divided between support of the two nations. Many lost their allegiance for the government of Texas, which continually preyed on their property and otherwise treated them as enemies. Tejano-Anglo thievery, violence, and mutual lawlessness remained the norm for the remaining years of the Republic.[20]

The black experience in the years 1835–36 had a dualism unlike that of any other group in Texas society. Breakdowns in authority induced by war and rebellion gave slaves improved opportunity to seize freedom. Preservation of such gains required that blacks leave Texas with the Mexican army, a path chosen eagerly by many. The sudden collapse of the Mexican invasion effort prevented the disintegration of slavery, and the presence of the Anglo-American political order stimulated rapid growth of the institution in the decade after the Revolution.

Slaves rose from a ratio of less than one in ten to more than one out of every four of the Texas population by 1847. Little had remained for the nation's lawmakers to do in the way of positive guarantees for slavery, given the thoroughness of the constitution-makers on that subject.[21] Few blacks managed to gain or maintain freedom by identifying with the Texas cause, for the practical-minded Anglo Americans applied their version of liberty, equality, and democracy cautiously and only to themselves. The Texas Constitution had been unintentionally ambiguous regarding the status of free blacks; vague wording opened a legal loophole by which a small free black class developed. Nearly all of this expansion resulted from migration; only two slaves received legal emancipation (with congressional approval) during the nation's entire history. Both gained their owner's endorsement and demonstrated records of significant service in the war for independence. An unstated policy of benign neglect regarding punitive measures before 1840 allowed some free black immigration to Texas, and remembrance of individual contributions to the cause during the Revolution helped sidetrack a threat to eradicate the entire population thereafter. Nevertheless, governmental policy had managed to retard the development of the free black community to one of the smallest in the Americas.[22]

No Anglo came forth in public to challenge the powerful consensus of racial opinion or to argue in favor of equality and democracy applied across racial lines, but free black military veteran Greenbury Logan spoke out for himself. Disabled by his war wounds, fearful of losing his property to back taxes, and having no "say in eny way," he recalled his loss of liberty bitterly in an 1841 petition to Congress: "I love the country and did stay because I felt myself mower a freeman then in the states . . . but now look at my situation. every privileg dear to a freeman is taken a way."[23] However much the Texans might boast of their revolutionary heritage, national policy on race followed the dictums of the South, itself in the grips of a reaction against human liberty.

In response to these racial policies, black Texans continued to identify with Mexico as a land and force of freedom. Mexican military ventures in Texas and around the Rio Grande attracted ex-slave participation. Runaways and other blacks fought in Tejano-led uprisings and Mexican invasions. Even without direct Mexican assistance, runaways, especially those who fled in groups, sought their liberty in Mexico during the period of the Republic as they had during the Revolution.[24]

For Texans of Hispanic and African descent the outcome of the Texas Revolution was a sudden reversal of fortunes. Powerful racial and ethnic antagonisms — expressed not only institutionally in slavery but also by custom in the form of endemic Tejano-Anglo hatred, suspicion, and conflict — became fixed in the Texas identity during its brief experience of nationhood.

Other habits of mind also received confirmation, according to the leading social historian of the Republic. These included an aggressive "fighting spirit" which, William R. Hogan concludes, became both a "national compulsion" and an "individual necessity" given the weakness of the state and the pervasive forces of disorder. A rough-and-tumble style of politics emanated from the restless individualism of a people generally impatient with social restraints and unconcerned about imbroglios of the past. Texas society tended to accept newcomers in a democratic spirit and give them the opportunity to plunge ahead in the competition for economic betterment. A decade of grim material realities followed independence. Yet optimism and stamina characterized the survivors, who continued to rally to calls for expansion and adventure even as failure dogged their steps. "The period of the Texas Revolution and the republic which emerged from it," Hogan concludes, "bred a temper peculiarly Texan."[25]

These distinctive traits naturally found ample cultural expression. Early folklore generally centered on the tall tale, and its central figures displayed the qualities that Texans admired most: hospitality offset by quick tempers; perennial willingness to fight, especially against Indians or Mexicans; struggles of the individual against the environment; and the hazards of a settled life. The brief Texas past provided usable materials for a national culture. People already displayed the selective memory that would transform such figures as Travis, Bowie, and Crockett into legends. The penchant for social drinking gave ample opportunity for toasting on Texas' very own national holidays. Theater-goers attended patriotic drama, and poets trumpeted the glories of the land. National symbols abounded: the Lone Star flag, the battleground at

San Jacinto, and even a sacred tomb (the Alamo). Orators also sounded the historic theme, or for variety, the futuristic one of "this young, rising, and interesting Republic."[26]

Even after Texas surrendered its independence so meekly, the sense of distinctiveness lived on in the popular mind, whether in or out of the state. Historical consciousness remained strong, and it centered on the Revolution. Holidays commemorated its events, the names of school buildings celebrated its heroes (even Fannin somehow acquired that status), proud descendants founded organizations to identify themselves with and to further its memory. In the process, the legend became *the* Revolution, but not *a* revolution, cleansed of its political turbulence, regional disharmonies, conflicts of interest, social turbulence, and racial or ethnic strife. Essentially, the Texas Revolution was transformed into little more than a staple for the swaggering boastfulness of the archetypal Texan.[27]

Appendix:
Political Experience of the Convention Delegates

REPRESENTATIVES TO THE CONSULTATION

Barrett, T.
Bower, J. W. [did not attend]
Byrom, J. S. D.
Coleman, R. M. [did not attend]
Everitt, S. H.
Grimes, J.
Hardin, A. B.
Houston, S.

Menefee, W.
Moore, J. W.
Parmer, M.
Power, J. [did not attend]
Rusk, T. J. [did not attend]
Waller, E.
West, C.
Woods, J. B.
Zavala, L.

MEMBERS OF THE CONVENTIONS OF 1832–33

Gazley, T. J.
Grimes, J.

Houston, S.
Lacey, W. D.
Menefee, W.

Taylor, C. S.
West, C.

MEMBERS OF THE COUNCIL OF
THE PROVISIONAL GOVERNMENT

Grimes, J.
Hardin, A. B.

Menefee, J. W.
Parmer, M.
Power, J.

Waller, E.
West, C.

OFFICEHOLDERS UNDER MEXICAN RULE

Barnett, T.	Alcalde	San Felipe de Austin
Brigham, A.	Alcalde	Brazoria
Gazley, T. J.	Ayuntamiento	San Felipe de Austin
Grimes, J.	Ayuntamiento	San Felipe de Austin
Moore, J. W.	Ayuntamiento	San Felipe de Austin
Navarro, J. A.	Congress of Mexico	
Ruiz, F.	Officer, Army of Mexico	
Taylor, C. S.	Alcalde	Nacogdoches
Waller, E.	Alcalde	Brazoria
Woods, J. B.	Alcalde	Liberty
Zavala, L.	Ambassador from Mexico to France	

COMMITTEES OF SAFETY AND OTHER REVOLUTIONARY BODIES

Briscoe, A.	Anáhuac pledge, June 1835
Bunton, J. W.	Committee of Safety, Bastrop, Dec. 1835
Collinsworth, J.	Brazoria public meeting, Aug. 1835
Fisher, J.	Committee of Safety, Gonzales, July 1835
Gaines, J.	Committee of Safety, Sabine, Dec. 1835
Houston, S.	Committee of Safety, San Augustine
Moore, J. W.	Anáhuac pledge, June 1835
Stewart, C. B.	Committee of Safety, Columbia, July 1835
Waller, E.	Committee of Safety, Columbia, July 1835
Woods, J. B.	Permanent Council, Oct. 1835
Zavala, L.	Committee of Safety, Harrisburg, Aug. 1835

Notes

Throughout the notes, Spanish orthography is modernized, abbreviations are expanded, and spelling has been standardized for clarity and easier reading. Otherwise, names are given in the notes in the same way they appear in the original sources.

INTRODUCTION.

1. Broadside, "To the People of Texas," Feb. 13, 1836, Andrew Jackson Houston Collection (hereafter cited as AJH), Texas State Archives, Austin (hereafter cited as TSA).

2. (San Felipe) *Telegraph and Texas Register,* Dec. 2, 1835; David G. Burnet, Inaugural Address, Mar. 17, 1836, in John H. Jenkins, ed., *The Papers of the Texas Revolution, 1835–1836* (Austin: Presidial Press, 1973) 5:101 (hereafter cited as PTR); "A True Mexican" to Messrs. Johnson, Baker and Givens, July 18, 1835, Samuel May Williams Papers, Rosenberg Library, Galveston; (Brazoria) *Texas Republican,* Sept. 19, 1835.

3. Quoted in Claude Elliott, "Alabama and the Texas Revolution," *Southwestern Historical Quarterly* 50 (Jan. 1947): 320 (hereafter cited as *SHQ*).

4. Haden Edwards to J. W. Robinson, Nov. 29, 1835, William Campbell Binkley, ed., *Official Correspondence of the Texas Revolution* (New York: D. Appleton-Century Co., 1936) 1:135 (hereafter cited as *OCTR*).

5. Daniel Cloud to brother, Dec. 28, 1835, quoted in Archie P. McDonald, "The Young Men of the Texas Revolution," *Texana* 3 (Winter 1965): 344.

6. David J. Weber, *The Mexican Frontier, 1821–1846: The American Southwest Under Mexico* (Albuquerque: University of New Mexico Press, 1982), p. 245.

7. [Benjamin Lundy], *The War in Texas; A Review of Facts and Circumstances* (1837; Upper Saddle River, N.J.: Gregg Press, 1970), pp. 3–7, 15, 20, 27, 33.

8. Howard R. Lamar, "Foreign Perceptions of the Texas Revolution" (lecture presented at the Texas State Historical Association, Austin, Mar. 7, 1986).

9. Quoted in Eugene C. Barker, *The Life of Stephen F. Austin Founder of Texas* (Nashville and Dallas: Cokesbury Press, 1925), p. 493.

10. Chester Newell, *History of the Revolution in Texas* (reprint ed., Austin: Steck, 1935), pp. 10, 23, 25, 26, 37, 43, 45; Henderson King Yoakum, *History of Texas from its First Settlement in 1685 to Its Annexation in 1846* (New York: Redfield, 1855), pp. 292–367. John Henry Brown emphasized conservatism somewhat less than other nineteenth century writers in *A History of Texas, 1685–1892* (St. Louis: L. E. Daniell, 1893), 1:279–80.

11. Paul Leo Hendrix, "An Historiographical Study of the Texas Revolution" (M. A. thesis, University of Houston, 1961), pp. 41–69. For the Jackson-Houston conspiracy thesis, see Richard R. Stenberg, "The Texas Schemes of Jackson and Houston, 1829–1836," *Southwest Social Science Quarterly* 15 (Dec., 1934): 229–50. The most persistent recent scholar to emphasize land speculators is Malcolm McLean, who asserts that the military advance into Texas in 1835 inadvertently sparked armed resistance, while intending only to round up land speculators who had corruptly manipulated the Coahuila and Texas legislature. See *Papers Concerning Robertson's Colony in Texas* (Arlington: UTA Press, 1974–1984) 10:57–80. Barker attempted to refute that theory in several places, most especially "Land Speculation as a Cause of the Texas Revolution," *Quarterly of the Texas State Historical Association* 10 (July, 1906): 76–95 (hereafter cited as *QTSHA*).

12. Eugene C. Barker, *Mexico and Texas 1821–1835* (Dallas: Turner Publishing Co., 1928), pp. v, 61, 91.

13. Ibid., 148–49.

14. Samuel Harmon Lowrie, *Culture Conflict in Texas 1821–1835* (New York: Co-

lumbia University Press, 1932), pp. 60–76, 173, 179–81; Carlos E. Castañeda, *Our Catholic Heritage in Texas, 1519–1936* (Austin: Von Boeckmann-Jones Co., 1939) 6:197–266.

15. Harbert Davenport, "The Men of Goliad," *SHQ* 43 (July, 1939): 6.

16. William C. Binkley, *The Texas Revolution* (Baton Rouge: Louisiana State University Press, 1952), pp. 1, 127, 132.

17. John H. Jenkins, "Available Resources Make Revolution Important Texas Research Topic," *Texas Libraries* 15 (Fall, 1979): 118; Stephen R. Niblo and Laurens B. Perry, "Recent Additions to Nineteenth Century Mexican Historiography," *Latin American Research Review* 13 (1978): 17.

18. David Weber, "Refighting the Alamo: Mythmaking and the Texas Revolution," in *Myth and the History of the Hispanic Southwest: Essays by David J. Weber* (Albuquerque: University of New Mexico Press). In Weber's *Mexican Frontier*, see especially chapters 9 and 12 for Texas subjects.

19. For a more lengthy review of recent scholarship see Paul D. Lack, "In the Long Shadow of Eugene C. Barker," in Walter Buenger and Robert Calvert, eds., *Texas through Time* (College Station: Texas A&M University Press, 1991).

20. One brief interpretive study that explored the revolutionary theme is McDonald, "Young Men of the Texas Revolution." Other scholars of the Texas experience have continued to interpret Texas independence as essentially conservative in origin which, as Joe B. Frantz wrote in his broad study of the Texas experience, "like all revolutions . . . progressed beyond its original aim" but then underwent a swift and orderly transition to nationhood (*Texas: A Bicentennial History* [New York: W. W. Norton, 1976], p. 61). In 1984 a contemporary European scholar, Andreas Reichstein, wrote in German a book on the Texas independence movement, recently translated and published as *Rise of the Lone Star: The Making of Texas* (College Station: Texas A&M University Press, 1989). Generally revisionist, this work deals mostly with questions regarding causation, emphasizing the role of land speculators and of U.S. expansionism. Reichstein downplays ethnic and regional influences and doubts the revolutionary dimensions of the Texas Revolution, seeing it instead as simply a separatist rebellion.

21. The works on revolution are legion; two useful studies that summarize and evaluate much of this scholarship are Thomas R. Green, *Comparative Revolutionary Movements* (Englewood Cliffs, N.J.: Prentice-Hall, 1974), and Mark N. Hagopian, *The Phenomenon of Revolution* (New York: Dodd, Mead, & Co., 1974).

22. Hagopian, *Phenomenon of Revolution,* p. 39, 71.

23. The most prominent of the popular historians of Texas, T. R. Fehrenbach, attributes immense consequences to the Texas Revolution. Much about the Revolution remains unclear, he writes in *Lone Star* (New York: Macmillan, 1968): "The results are clear, however. They can be measured on maps, and in population and power," (p. 175). As to the outcome of the battle of San Jacinto: "the balance of power in Texas had turned. The American west was won," (p. 233).

24. Hagopian, *Phenomenon of Revolution,* pp. 1–40, 97.

25. This basic theme in Crane Brinton, *The Anatomy of Revolution* (New York: Random House, 1965), has been confirmed by scholars of individual revolutions and those who adopt a comparative approach as well.

26. The thesis of Arno Mayer, *The Dynamics of Counterrevolution in Europe, 1870–1956: An Analytical Framework* (New York: Harper-Row, 1971), is summarized

and applied to the Southern Confederacy in the brilliant synthesis by James McPherson, *The Battle Cry of Freedom* (New York: Oxford University Press, 1988), p. 245. See also Emory Thomas, *The Confederacy as a Revolutionary Experience* (Englewood Cliffs, N.J.: Prentice-Hall, 1971).

27. Green, *Comparative Movements* (p. 8), and Hagopian, *Phenomenon of Revolution* (p. 1) serve as the major sources for this composite definition. This latter study poses a clear definition but one that cannot be adopted easily without also appropriating its social science jargon.

28. Brinton, *Anatomy*, pp. 237–61; Green, *Comparative Movements*, p. 11; Hagopian, *Phenomenon of Revolution*, pp. 194–250.

29. Green, *Comparative Movements*, pp. 49, 51–57, 65–71, 97; Hagopian, *Phenomenon of Revolution*, pp. 101, 194–250, 263–69, 271–80.

30. Amos Pollard to Henry Smith, January 16, 1836, General Correspondence, Adjutant General Army Papers (hereafter cited as AP).

CHAPTER 1.

1. Barker, *Mexico and Texas*, p. 86.

2. Paul D. Lack, "Slavery and the Texas Revolution," *SHQ* 89 (Oct., 1985): 183–85.

3. Ohland Morton, *Terán and Texas: A Chapter in Texas-Mexican Relations* (Austin: Texas State Historical Assn., 1948), pp. 95–136; Barker, *Mexico and Texas*, pp. 3–23, 32–61, 87–90; Weber, *The Mexican Frontier*, pp. 162–76.

4. Weber, *Mexican Frontier*, pp. 150–55, 156.

5. Barker, *Mexico and Texas*, pp. 91–99.

6. Gene Brack, "Mexican Opinion and the Texas Revolution," *SHQ* 72 (Oct., 1968): 170–82; Nettie Lee Benson, "Texas as Viewed from Mexico, 1820–1834," *SHQ* 90 (Jan., 1987): 219–91.

7. Margaret Swett Henson, *Juan Davis Bradburn: A Reappraisal of the Mexican Commander of Anahuac* (College Station: Texas A&M Press, 1982), pp. 46–110; Barker, *Austin*, pp. 374–403.

8. Barker, *Austin*, pp. 406–29; Benson, "Texas as Viewed from Mexico," p. 288; Jesús F. de la Teja and John Wheat, "Béxar: Profile of a Tejano Community, 1820–1832," *SHQ* 89 (July, 1985): 33.

9. Castañeda, *Catholic Heritage* 6:252; Binkley, *Texas Revolution*, pp. 16–21.

10. Austin quoted in Barker, *Austin*, 512; William R. Hogan, *The Texas Republic: A Social and Economic History* (Norman: University of Oklahoma Press, 1946), p. 229.

11. A. C. Allen to Sam Houston, Feb. 28, 1834, AJH; Thomas H. Borden to Moses Lapham, March 8, 1835, in Joe B. Frantz, ed., "Moses Lapham His Life and Some Selected Correspondence," *SHQ* 54 (Apr., 1951): 466.

12. (Brazoria) *Texas Republican*, July 5, 1834.

13. Stephen F. Austin to [James F. Perry], Mar. 10, 1835, *PTR* 1:35; Sterling C. Robertson to Mr. Hunt, Oct. 5, 1835, *PTR* 1:51.

14. Andrew Forest Muir, ed., *Texas in 1837: An Anonymous, Contemporary Narrative* (Austin: University of Texas Press, 1958), pp. 133–34.

15. Mark E. Nackman, "Anglo-American Migrants to the West: Men of Broken Fortunes? The Case of Texas, 1821–1845," *Western Historical Quarterly* 5 (Oct., 1974):

441–55; Gerald Ashford, "Jacksonian Liberalism and Spanish Law in Early Texas," *SHQ* 57 (July, 1953): 1–18, 34–36; Weber, *Mexican Frontier,* pp. 162–63.

16. J. P. Cole to M. B. Lamar, Sept. 3, 1835, *PTR* 1:413.

17. Castañeda, *Catholic Heritage* 6:220; Weber, *Mexican Frontier,* pp. 16–26, 108–10.

18. (San Felipe) *Advocate of the People's Rights,* Feb. 22, 1834; (Brazoria) *Texas Republican,* June 6, 1835; Binkley, *Texas Revolution,* p. 17.

19. Binkley, *Texas Revolution,* pp. 21–22.

20. William Fairfax Gray, *From Virginia to Texas, 1835* (reprint ed., Houston: Fletcher Young Publishing Co., 1965), p. 130; Binkley, *Texas Revolution,* pp. 21–33; Weber, *Mexican Frontier,* pp. 50–80; Lowrie, *Culture Conflict,* pp. 53–58; Barker, *Mexico and Texas,* pp. 63–72, 91–99; William Stuart Red, *The Texas Colonists and Religion 1821–1836* (Austin: E. L. Shettler, 1924), pp. 71–77; Fane Downs, "'Tryels and Trubbles': Women in Early Nineteenth-Century Texas," *SHQ* 90 (July, 1986): 42–44.

21. Lack, "Slavery and the Texas Revolution," pp. 186–87, 189.

22. J. P. Cole to M. B. Lamar, September 3, 1835, *PTR* 1:413 (quotations); Arnoldo De León, *They Called Them Greasers* (Austin: University of Texas Press, 1983), pp. 6–10; Lowrie, *Culture Conflict,* pp. 76–80; Mary Whatley Clarke, *Thomas J. Rusk, Soldier, Statesman, Jurist* (Austin: Jenkins Press, 1971), p. 26.

23. Austin quoted in Arnoldo De León, *The Tejano Community, 1836–1900* (Albuquerque: University of New Mexico Press, 1982), p. 12; Castañeda, *Catholic Heritage* 6:205; Weber, *Mexican Frontier,* pp. 164–65.

24. Hobart Huson, *Refugio; A Comprehensive History* (Woodsboro, Tex.: Rooke Foundation, Inc., 1953), 1:119, 123–28, 161–63.

25. Margaret S. Henson, *Samuel May Williams, Early Texas Entrepreneur* (College Station: Texas A&M University Press, 1976), pp. 45–61; McLean, ed., *Robertson's Colony* 10:25–80.

26. Nancy Boothe Parker, ed., "Mirabeau B. Lamar's Texas Journal," *SHQ* 84 (Oct., 1980): 321; Weber, *Mexican Frontier,* pp. 245–48; Henson, *Williams,* pp. 64–65; On the political factions see Margaret S. Henson, "Tory Sentiment in Anglo-Texan Public Opinion, 1832–1836," *SHQ* 90 (July, 1986): 2–9, 13; and Jodella Dorothea Kite, "The War and Peace Parties of Pre-Revolutionary Texas, 1832–1835" (M. A. thesis, Texas Tech University, 1986), p. 85.

27. (San Felipe) *Advocate of the People's Rights,* February 22, 1834.

CHAPTER 2.

1. Weber, *Mexican Frontier,* pp. 247–48; Binkley, *Texas Revolution,* pp. 39–41.

2. Binkley, *Texas Revolution,* pp. 42–43; Weber, *Mexican Frontier,* pp. 247–48; Llerna Beaufort Friend, "The Life of Thomas Jefferson Chambers" (M.A. thesis, University of Texas, 1928), pp. 45–60.

3. Barker, "Land Speculation," pp. 76–95; Barker, *Austin, Founder,* pp. 460–77; Henson, *Williams,* pp. 63–75; Edward A. Lukes, "The De Witt Colony of Texas" (Ph.D. diss., Loyola University, 1971), p. 226; Agustín Viesca to the editors of *El Cosmopolita Suplemento* (Monterrey), Jan. 7, 1837, reprinted in Hobart Huson, *Captain Phillip Dimmitt's Commandancy of Goliad* (Austin: Von Boeckman-Jones, 1974): unnumbered pages.

4. Castañeda, *Catholic Heritage* 6:261–62.

5. McLean, ed., *Robertson's Colony* 10:66–80. Elsewhere, Mexico carried out "a strong centralizing trend" in local government (W. H. Timmons, "The El Paso Area in the Mexican Period, 1821–1848," *SHQ* 84 [July, 1980]: 3).

6. Martín Perfecto de Cos to [José María Tornel], Apr. 6, 9, 1835, *PTR* 1:56–57, 60; Weber, *Mexican Frontier*, pp. 248–49.

7. Ugartechea to Antonio Tenorio, June 20, 1835, *PTR* 1:156; [Angel Navarro to Domingo de Ugartechea], May 15, 1835, Robert Bruce Blake Research Collection (hereafter cited as Blake), Barker Texas History Center, University of Texas at Austin (hereafter cited as BTHC) Supplement 10:367; Juan Zenteno to Domingo de Ugartechea, May 31, 1835, *PTR* 1:134–35.

8. Antonio Tenorio to the Military Commander of Coahuila & Texas, Apr. 9, 1835, *PTR* 1:61; José María Tornel to Martín Perfecto de Cos, Apr. 29, 1835, *PTR* 1:85; Martín Perfecto de Cos to [José María Tornel], May 28, 1835, *PTR* 1:131.

9. Marcial Borrego to the inhabitants of the State of Coahuila and Texas, Apr. 8, 1835, *PTR* 1:58–59; Agustín Viesca to the inhabitants of Coahuila and Texas, Apr. 15, 1835, *PTR* 1:73–75; Martín Perfecto de Cos to Domingo Ugartechea, May 30, 1835, Béxar Archives (Barker Texas History Center, University of Texas at Austin, microfilm), reel 165, frames 343–44 (hereafter cited as BA).

10. Martín Perfecto de Cos [to the Public], May 12, 1835, *PTR* 1:105–106; Martín Perfecto de Cos to [José María Tornel], Apr. 6, 1835, *PTR* 1:56–57.

11. W. Barrett Travis to David G. Burnet, Apr. 11, 1835, *PTR* 1:63 (first and third quotations); Travis to Burnet, May 21, 1835, *PTR* 1:122 (second quotation).

12. F. W. Johnson to Wm. Martin, May 6, 1835, *PTR* 1:100; Samuel M. Williams to Wyly Martin, May 3, 1835, *PTR* 1:88–89; Coahuiltexanus [to the people of Texas], May 4, 1835, Blake 14:57–61.

13. Henry Austin to J. F. Perry, May 5, 1835, *PTR* 1:93–94; T. J. Chambers to [J. H. C. Miller], June 30, 1835, *PTR* 1:173–74.

14. Commander of Coahuila and Texas to the Political Chief of Béxar, May 16, 1835, Blake 14:104, 107; Domingo de Ugartechea to [Angel Navarro], May 16, 1835, *PTR* 1:109; Angel Navarro to the Secretary of State of Coahuila and Texas, May 18, 1835, *PTR* 1:112–15; [Ugartechea] to the Political Chief, May 17, 1835, BA, reel 165, frame 173.

15. Juan N. Seguín, *Personal Memoirs* (San Antonio: Ledger Book and Job Office, 1858), [p. 5]; Agustín Viesca to the editors, Jan. 7, 1837, in Huson, *Dimmitt's Goliad*, unpaged; Agustín Viesca order, May 20, 1835, BA, reel 1, frame 522.

16. (Brazoria) *Texas Republican*, June 27, 1835; J. B. Miller to [the Public], June 21, 1835, *PTR* 1:157–58; the Ayuntamiento of the Jurisdiction of Austin to the inhabitants of the sd. jurisdiction, June 20, 25, 1835, Blake 14:168–71; James H. C. Miller to Phillip Smith, July 4, 1835, Blake 9:383.

17. Address of R. M. Williamson, July 4, 1835, *PTR* 1:195, 199; [Minutes of the San Felipe meeting], June 22, 1835, General Correspondence, Thomas Jefferson Rusk Papers (hereafter cited as Rusk Papers), BTHC; Weber, *Mexican Frontier*, pp. 243–44.

18. Henry Austin to J. F. Perry, June 24, 1835, *PTR* 1:164; (Brazoria) *Texas Republican*, June 27, 1835.

19. (Brazoria) *Texas Republican*, June 27, 1835; Resolutions, Columbia Public Meeting, June 28, 1835, *PTR* 1:170–71.

20. Travis to D. G. Burnet, May 21, 1835, *PTR* 1:132–33; Ro. Wilson to Wm. B. Travis, May 13, 1835, *PTR* 1:108.

21. Domingo de Ugartechea to Martín Perfecto de Cos, May 1, 1835, *PTR* 1:86; Antonio Tenorio to Domingo de Ugartechea, June 25, 1835, *PTR* 1:167.

22. [Anáhuac petition], May 5, 1835, *PTR* 1:92–93; Ayuntamiento of Liberty to [the public], June 1, 1835, *PTR* 1:136.

23. Jno. A. Williams to [Henry Rueg], July 3, 1835, *PTR* 1:185; [A. Briscoe statement], June 4, 1835, *PTR* 1:143–44; [San Felipe Pledge], June 22, 1835, *PRT* 1:161–62; Binkley, *Texas Revolution*, pp. 48–49; Antonio Tenorio to Comandante Principal of the States of Coahuila and Texas, July 7, 1835, Blake Supplement 2:394–95.

24. Binkley, *Texas Revolution*, p. 127.

25. Mina Resolutions, July 4, 1835, *PTR* 1:191–94.

26. [Edward Gritten] to Domingo de Ugartechea, July 5, 1835, *PTR* 1:204; [Gonzales meeting], July 7, 1835, *PTR* 1:214–16.

27. [Domingo de Ugartechea] to Manuel Sabariego, July 29, 1835, BA, reel 166, frame 117; José M. Valdéz and the Ayuntamiento to the Public, Aug. 20, 1835, BA, reel 166, frame 388; José M. Valdéz to Angel Navarro, Aug. 21, 1835, BA, reel 166, frame 398.

28. Asa Brigham, Circular, July 11, 1835, *PTR* 1:230–31; Asa Brigham to San Felipe meeting, July 14, 1835, *PTR* 1:240; Committee of Columbia to citizens, July 15, 1835, *PTR* 1:242.

29. William Menefee to W. Martin, July 17, 1835, *PTR* 1:251–52; Lydia Ann [McHenry to John Hardin McHenry], July 4, 1835, in George R. Nielsen, ed., "Lydia Ann McHenry and Revolutionary Texas," *SHQ* 74 (July, 1971): 398–400.

30. Eduardo Gritten to Domingo de Ugartechea, July 5, 1835, *PTR* 1:204; [Domingo de Ugartechea] to [Martín Perfecto de Cos], July 25, 1835, *PTR* 1:276.

31. José María Tornel to Martín Perfecto de Cos, Aug. 3, 1835, *PTR* 1:305; Martín Perfecto de Cos to [Domingo de Ugartechea], June 22, 1835, Blake Supplement 9: 377–78.

32. Martín Perfecto de Cos to [the Public], July 5, 1835, *PTR* 1:203; Thomas M. Thompson to the Citizens of Anáhuac, July 26, 1835, *PTR* 1:279; (Brazoria) *Texas Republican*, July 25, August 22, 1835; Minister of Relations to President of the Meeting held at the Municipality of Gonzales, Aug. 12, 1835, Austin Papers, Transcriptions Series IV, BTHC (hereafter cited as APT).

33. [Angel Navarro] to Martín Perfecto de Cos, Aug. 1, Sept. 1, 1835, BA, reel 166, frames 202–03, 551–52; Martín Perfecto de Cos to Political Chief of the Department of Brazos, July 7, Aug. 1, 9, 1835, *PTR* 1:212–13, 297–98, 326.

34. J. B. Miller to [Domingo de Ugartechea], July 16, 1835, *PTR* 1:247; (Brazoria) *Texas Republican*, Aug. 8, 1835.

35. [James H. C. Miller to J. W. Smith, July 25, 1835], *PTR* 1:274; Wyly Martin to Domingo de Ugartechea, Aug. 16, 25, 1835, in McLean, ed., *Robertson's Colony* 11:303, 354.

36. Martín Perfecto de Cos to the Political Chief, Nacogdoches, Aug. 17, 1835, BA, reel 166, frame 377; Henry Rueg to the Political Chief of the Department of Brazos, July 28, 1835, Provisional Government Letterbook (hereafter cited as PGL), TSA; H. Rueg to Ayuntamiento of San Augustine, August 9, 1835, Alcalde Papers 2, BTHC; H. Rueg to the Ayuntamiento of Liberty, Aug. 22, 1835, Alcalde Papers 2.

37. Antonio Menchaca to the Governor of the State, Aug. 23, 1835, BA, reel 166, frame 432; [Domingo de Ugartechea] to Pedro E. Bean, July 30, 1835, BA, reel 166, frame 135.

38. [W. B.] Travis to [Henry] Smith, July 6, 1835, *PTR* 1:209; [W. B.] Travis to James Bowie, July 30, 1835, *PTR* 1:239; (Brazoria) *Texas Republican,* July 18, 1835.

39. (Brazoria) *Texas Republican,* July 18, 25, August 8, 22, 1835; James H. C. Miller to John W. Smith, July 25, 1835, *PTR* 1:290.

40. Sam Wolfenberger to J. S. Lester, July 28, 1835, *PTR* 1:283; (Brazoria) *Texas Republican,* July 18, 1835.

41. John J. Linn to James Kerr, July 30, 1835, *PTR* 1:288; John J. Linn to James Kerr, Aug. 1, 1835, PGL.

42. William J. Fisher to Committee of Safety for Mina, July 4, 1835, *PTR* 1:188–89 (quotation); Mina Resolutions, July 4, 5, 9, 1835, *PTR* 1:191–94; (Brazoria) *Texas Republican,* July 18, 1835.

43. James Kerr to Ira B. Lewis, Aug. 3, 1835, *PTR* 1:303.

44. William H. Wharton to [the Public], July 25, 1835, *PTR* 1:277.

45. (Brazoria) *Texas Republican,* July 25, August 8, 22, 1835; [Brazoria meeting], Aug. 9, 1835, *PTR* 1:323–25; W. B. Travis to [Henry Smith], Aug. 5, 1835, *PTR* 1:412–13; Benja. F. Smith to Jas. F. Perry, Aug. 15, 1835, *PTR* 1:346–47.

46. Resolutions, Nacogdoches Public Meeting, [Aug. 15, 1835], *PTR* 1:343–45; Lois Foster Blount, "The Nacogdoches Committee of Vigilance and Safety, 1835–1836," Blake 66:190–95; Minutes of the Ayuntamiento, Sept. 5, 1835, Blake 22:246–48.

47. W. B. Travis to Henry Smith, Aug. 24, 1835, *PTR* 1:368; B. T. Archer to fellow citizens, Aug. 20, 1835, *PTR* 1:355–58; Resolutions, San Felipe Public Meeting, Aug. 26, 1835, *PTR* 1:370–71; Resolutions, Liberty Public Meeting, Aug. 30, 1835, Records of Citizens Meetings (hereafter cited as RCM), Secretary of State Records of Legislative and Executive Bodies Prior to the Republic, TSA.

48. W. B. Travis to [Andrew Briscoe], Aug. 31, 1835, *PTR* 1:379; W. B. Travis to D. G. Burnet, Aug. 31, 1835, *PTR* 1:380.

49. Stephen F. Austin to Mary Austin Holley, Aug. 21, 1835, Eugene C. Barker, ed., *The Austin Papers* (Austin: University of Texas Press, 1926), 3:102; Barker, *Austin,* pp. 449–59; Stephen F. Austin to Samuel M. Williams, Aug. 22, 1835, *PTR* 1:363–64.

50. [F. W. Johnson] to S. F. Austin, Sept. 5, 1835, *PTR* 1:417; John R. Jones, Jr. to [Moses Austin Bryan], Sept. 1, 1835, *PTR* 1:383–84.

51. S. F. Austin [speech], Sept. 8, 1835, *PTR* 1:427; S. F. Austin to T. F. McKinney, Sept. 26, 1835, *PTR* 1:491.

52. [Henry Austin] to M. A. Holley, Sept. 10, 1835, *PTR* 1:431; Moses Austin Bryan to [William F. Hunter], Sept. 15, 1835, Gerald S. Pierce, ed., "Some Early Letters of Moses Austin Bryan," *SHQ* 70 (Jan., 1967): 469; Binkley, *Texas Revolution,* pp. 34–35.

53. Edwd. Gritten to D. C. Barrett, Sept. 8, 1835, *PTR* 1:428; J. W. Fannin to David Mills, Sept. 18, 1835, *PTR* 1:457; Edward Gritten to the Alcalde, Ayuntamiento, and People of Gonzales, Oct. 4, 1835, APT; Ecay Músquiz to Political Chief, Sept. 12, 1835, Nacogdoches Archives Transcripts (hereafter cited as NA) 87:51–53, TSA.

54. (Brazoria) *Texas Republican,* Sept. 19, 1835; Resolutions, San Felipe Meeting, Sept. 12, 1835, *PTR* 1:441–44; Wm. Barrett Travis to [Henry Smith, Sept. 15, 1835], *PTR* 1:448; Committee of Safety of the Jurisdiction of Austin, Circular, Sept. 18, 1835, *PTR* 1:455.

55. Resolution, Committee of Safety for the Jurisdiction of Columbia, Sept. 22, 1835, *PTR* 1:478; Philip H. Sublett to Austin Committee of Safety, Sept. 22, 1835, *PTR* 1:480; E. M. Pease to D. C. Barrett, Sept. 15, 1835, *PTR* 1:447–48; Resolutions, Meeting of Citizens of Matagorda, Sept. 26, 1835, *PTR* 1:489–90.

56. Wm. P. Harris and John W. Moore to Stephen F. Austin, Sept. 23, 1835, *PTR* 1:484–85; E. Bailey to ———, Sept. 26, 1835, *PTR* 1:492; R. R. Royall to Stephen F. Austin, Sept. 30, 1835, *PTR* 1:510–12; B. T. Archer to Stephen F. Austin, Sept. 25, 1835, PGL; Thomas J. Rusk to Radford Berry, Sept. 11, 1835, NA 82:252.

57. [San Jacinto Resolutions], Aug. 8, 1835, (Brazoria) *Texas Republican*, Aug. 19, 1835; Resolutions, Liberty Meeting, Aug. 30, 1835, RCM; [Lorenzo de Zavala to colonists, ca. Aug. 7, 1835], *PTR* 1:314.

58. ——— to ———, Sept. 8, 1835, *PTR* 1:429; Stephen F. Austin, speech at Brazoria, Sept. 8, 1835, *PTR* 1:423–27; (Brazoria) *Texas Republican*, Sept. 26, 1835.

59. W. H. Jack to the people of Texas, [ca. Aug. 9, 1835], *PTR* 1:329; Stephen F. Austin to T. F. McKinney, Sept. 26, 1835, *PTR* 1:491.

60. Horatio Allsberry to the People of Texas, in (Brazoria) *Texas Republican*, Aug. 29, 1835; James H. C. Miller to the People of Texas [Sept., 1835] *PTR* 1:517.

61. Branch T. Archer to the people of the jurisdiction of Columbia, [ca. Sept. 20, 1835], *PTR* 1:467–69.

CHAPTER 3.

1. Stephen F. Austin to the Committee of Matagorda, Oct. 2, 1835, *PTR* 2:14.

2. Stephen F. Austin to [D. C. Barrett], Oct. 5, 1835, *PTR* 2:42; Stephen F. Austin to [Committee of Vigilance and Safety, San Augustine], Oct. 13, 1835, *PTR* 2:43.

3. (Brazoria) *Texas Republican*, Oct. 11, 1835; the Council to the Committees of Safety & Volunteers Eastward, Oct. 10, 1835, Communications Sent, Records of the Consultation, TSA; (San Felipe) *Telegraph and Texas Register*, Oct. 17, 1835; B. T. Archer to the People of the jurisdiction of Columbia, [ca. Sept. 20, 1835], *PTR* 1:467.

4. Alwyn Barr, *Texans in Revolt: The Battle for San Antonio, 1835* (Austin: University of Texas Press, 1990), pp. 15–59.

5. Austin quoted in Barker, *Austin*, p. 493; Henry Smith to the Council, Dec. 18, 1835, *PTR* 3:248.

6. [Lorenzo de Zavala] to Stephen F. Austin, Sept. 17, 1835, *PTR* 1:453–55.

7. (San Felipe) *Telegraph and Texas Register*, Oct. 17, 1835; [Minutes] of the Committee of Safety meeting, Liberty municipality, Oct. 6, 1835, RCM; Circular from the Committee of Safety of the jurisdiction of Austin, Oct. 3, 1835, *PTR* 2:17–21; [Sabine District Meeting], Nov. 7, 1835, *PTR* 2:350–51.

8. Gail Borden to the Committee of Safety, Columbia, [ca. Oct. 8, 1835], *PTR* 2:74.

9. Journal of the Proceedings of the General Council (hereafter cited as GCJnl), Oct. 11, 1835, Records of the General Council of the Provisional Government (hereafter cited as GC), TSA; P. W. Grayson to Stephen F. Austin, Oct. 11, 1835, *PTR* 2:94.

10. For a list of delegates at the October council see Circular to the People, Oct. 18, 1835, *PTR* 2:157.

11. R. R. Royall to the Committee of Safety, Columbia, Oct. 9, 1835, Communications Sent, Records of the Permanent Council, (hereafter cited as PC Comm. Sent),

TSA; R. R. Royall to Stephen F. Austin, Oct. 14, 1835, *PTR* 2:130; S. F. Austin to [Council], Oct. 25, 1835, *PTR* 2:215–16.

12. R. R. Royall to S. F. Austin, Oct. 21, 1835, *PTR* 2:184–85; Circular from the Council of Texas to the People Generally, Oct. 18, 1835, *PTR* 2:157.

13. R. R. Royall to the Citizens of the United States of the North, Oct. 26, 1835, *PTR* 2:225–26; R. R. Royall to the Committees of Safety and Volunteers Eastward, Oct. 10, 1835, *PTR* 2:89–90.

14. Circular from the Council of Texas to the People Generally, Oct. 18, 1835, *PTR* 2:160; R. R. Royall to the People of Texas, Oct. 23, 1835, PC Comm. Sent.

15. R. R. Royall to S. F. Austin, [Oct.] 16, 1835, *PTR* 2:140–41; [Resolution of the Permanent Council, Oct. 28, 1835], *PTR* 2:252.

16. GCJnl, Oct. 14, 1835; R. R. Royall to S. F. Austin, Oct. 21, 1835, *PTR* 2:184–85.

17. R. R. Royall to Stephen F. Austin, Oct. 18, 1835, *PTR* 2:155; Thomas F. McKinney to Richard R. Royall, Oct. 28, 1835, PC Comm. Sent; Resolution, Oct. 27, 1835, Resolutions, Records of the Permanent Council.

18. M. A. Bryan to James F. Perry, Oct. 26, 1835, *PTR* 2:222.

19. Not counting the presiding officer, 56 delegates signed the November 7 Declaration to the People, 53 voted in the gubernatorial election on the twelfth, and 54 approved the provisional government on the thirteenth. The membership list was compiled from the Journals of the Consultation, in *PTR* 9:256–75; past partisan affiliations of the delegates were determined by the biographical sketches in Walter P. Webb, et al., eds., *The Handbook of Texas* (Austin: Texas State Historical Assn., 1952–1976); correspondence in Eugene C. Barker, ed., *The Austin Papers;* references in Barker, *Life of Austin;* and internal evidence from the records of the Consultation.

20. Records of the committees of safety and public meetings supplied lists of participants in those bodies; past political activity was determined from the biographical data in Webb, et al., eds., *Handbook* and *Biographical Directory of the Texas Conventions and Congresses, 1832–1845* (Austin, Tex.: n.p. 1941).

21. Minister of Relations [of Mexico] to President of the Meeting held at Gonzales, Aug. 12, 1835, APT; Martín Perfecto de Cos to the Ayuntamiento of Brazoria, July 12, 1835, (Brazoria) *Texas Republican,* August 22, 1835.

22. Lists of the individuals who made up these various groups were derived from the records of the committees of safety, signatures to the pledges made at Harrisburg on June 4 and San Felipe on June 22, Records of the Consultation (TSA), and the list of delegates in *Biographical Directory* (See *PTR* 1:143–44, 161–62, 9:243–86). Age and residence data came from *Biographical Directory;* Webb, et al., eds., *Handbook;* Gifford White, *1830 Citizens of Texas* (Austin, Tex.: Eakin Press, 1983); and Sam Houston Dixon and Louis W. Kemp, *The Heroes of San Jacinto* (Houston, Tex.: Anson Jones Press, 1932).

23. Data on previous political activity was derived from the *Biographical Directory* and Webb, et al., eds., *Handbook.*

24. Others of the Monclova speculators who dropped from the public eye included John Durst, Robert Peebles, Mosely Baker, and Francis W. Johnson, though Baker plotted a coup, and he and Johnson entered the military. For the McKinney election controversy, see (Brazoria) *Texas Republican,* Sept. 26, Oct. 3, 10, 1835. See also Thos. F. McKinney to James F. Perry, Oct. 4, 1835, APT; Wm. H. Wharton to the Public, Oct. 5, 1835, *PTR* 2:56.

25. These fallen leaders included William J. Fisher, Thomas J. Gazley, and Henry P. Hill, of the Mina Committee of Safety; B. D. McClure, Eli Mitchell, James H. C. Miller, and John Fisher, officers of the July 7 Gonzales public meeting.

26. Only two (George M. Patrick, of Liberty, and John W. Moore, of Harrisburg) had formerly been with the "war party" that signed the Anáhuac pledge or pursued peaceful accommodation (Political Chief Wyly Martin and Mina committee of safety president D. C. Barrett). The matter of factional identity and leadership roles was subject to much confusion and disagreement even at the time that events were unfolding.

27. Jostus [pseudonym], "Union," in McLean, ed., *Robertson's Colony* 9:336.

28. See note 19 above on the sources used for determining partisan loyalties.

29. Address of Branch T. Archer, Nov. 3, 1835, *PTR* 2:248–50; G. Borden, Jr., to S. F. Austin, Nov. 5, 1835, *PTR* 2:323.

30. Archer, Barrett, Houston, and Zavala all exercised considerable influence, but no single member dominated the proceedings in the way that some biographers have suggested. See for example, Raymond Estep, "The Life of Lorenzo de Zavala" (Ph.D. diss., University of Texas, 1942), pp. 354–55.

31. Philip A. Sublett et al. to the committee of safety for the jurisdiction of Austin, Sept. 22, 1835, *PTR* 1:480; (San Felipe) *Telegraph and Texas Register*, Nov. 7, 1835.

32. Resolutions, Nov. 3, 4, 1835, Acts of the Consultation, Records of the Consultation (hereafter cited as Acts Cons.), TSA; G. Borden, Jr. to S. F. Austin, Nov. 5, 1835, *PTR* 2:322.

33. Journal of the Consultation, Nov. 9, 1835, *PTR* 9:265; S. F. Austin to the Committee of Safety, San Felipe, Oct. 13, 1835, *PTR* 2:107–08; D. C. Barrett to [the Consultation], Nov. 4, 1835, *PTR* 2:312–13; Resolution, Nov. 6, 1835, Acts Cons.; Barker, *Austin*, p. 490.

34. Resolution, Nov. 6, 1835, Proceedings [of the Consultation], Nov. 3–14, 1835, Records of the Consultation, TSA; Declaration of the People of Texas, In General Convention Assembled, Nov. 7, 1835, *PTR* 2:346–48.

35. Weber, *Mexican Frontier*, p. 245; [S. F. Austin] to [Provisional Government], Dec. 2, 1835, *PTR* 3:71–72.

36. "Organic Law" or Plan for Provisional Government of Texas, Nov. 13, 1835, Acts Cons.

37. Journal of the Consultation, *PTR* 9:266–69; S. F. Austin to [the Consultation], Nov. 5, 1835, Letters Received, Records of the Consultation, TSA.

38. [Provisional Constitution of Texas], see especially Articles III and IV, *PTR* 9:277–81.

39. Ibid., 9:272. Herbert P. Gambrell, *Mirabeau Buonaparte Lamar, Troubadour and Crusader* (Dallas: Southwest Press, 1934), p. 63, attributes Smith's election solely to Houston's animus toward Austin.

40. [Provisional Constitution of Texas], especially articles XIV, XV, and XVIII, *PTR* 9:280–81; Journal of the Consultation, *PTR* 9:266.

41. Journal of the Consultation, *PTR* 9:249; "Of the Military," Nov. 14, 1835, Acts. Cons.

42. Journal of the Consultation, *PTR* 9:274–75; J. W. Robinson to T. J. Rusk, Nov. 13, 1835, *PTR* 2:400; Committee on the state of the army, report, Nov. 15, 1835, Ordinances, Decrees, and Resolutions, GC.

43. Resolution, Nov. 14, 1835, Acts Cons.

CHAPTER 4.

1. S. F. Austin to Sam Houston, Nov. 14, 1835, *PTR* 2:407.

2. Henry Smith to the Legislative Council of Texas, Nov. 16, 1835, *PTR* 2:439; Smith to Council, Dec. 18, 1835, *PTR* 3:248; An Ordinance . . . to administer oaths, Dec. 1, 1835, PGL, p. 27.

3. B. B. Goodrich to Legislative Council, Dec. 20, 1835, AP; Committee Report, Jan. 6, 1836, Committee Reports, GC; Resolution Providing for the troops at Bejar, Jan. 17, 1836, GC.

4. S. F. Austin to Henry Smith, Jan. 10, 1836, *PTR* 3:462–64.

5. Henry Smith to the Commander in Chief of the Army of the people, Nov. 13, 1835, *PTR* 2:401–402; Resolution, Nov. 30, 1835, Ordinances, Decrees, and Resolutions, GC.

6. Ordinances for organizing the Militia, a regular army, and an Auxiliary Volunteer Corps, Nov. 24, 25, Dec. 8, 1835, Ordinances, Decrees, and Resolutions, GC; Committee Report, Dec. 6, 14, 1835, Committee Reports, GC; Sam Houston to D. C. Barrett, Dec. 9, 1835, Don Carlos Barrett Papers, BTHC.

7. Committee Report, Jan. 29, 1836, Committee Reports, GC.

8. General Council to the Mexican People, Dec. 11, 1835, *PTR* 3:167; [S. F. Austin to the Provisional Government], Dec. 2, 1835, *PTR* 3:71; Henry Smith to Edward Burleson, Dec. 9, 1835, *PTR* 3:127–28; El Ciudadano José María Gonzales . . . á sus Conciudadanos, Dec. 10, 1835, Broadside Collection, TSA.

9. S. F. Austin to Thomas F. McKinney, Dec. 16, 1835, *PTR* 3:210; James W. Robinson to Thomas F. McKinney, Dec. 17, 1835, *PTR* 3:234; C. Alan Hutchinson, "General José Antonio Mexía and His Texas Interests," *SHQ* 82 (Oct., 1978): 140–41.

10. Goliad Declaration, Dec. 22, 1835, Committee Reports, GC; Committee of State and Judiciary Report, Jan. 3, 1836, Committee Reports, GC.

11. A Resolution for Calling a Convention, Dec. 10, 1835, Ordinances, Decrees, and Resolutions, GC.

12. Thomas F. McKinney to S. F. Austin, Dec. 17, 1835, *PTR* 3:228; Thomas F. McKinney to Thomas J. Rusk, Dec. 25, 1835, Rusk Papers.

13. S. F. Austin to F. W. Johnson, Dec. 22, 1835, *PTR* 3:282–83 (quotations); S. F. Austin to Provisional Government of Texas, Dec. 22, 1835, *PTR* 3:284–86; S. F. Austin to Henry [Austin], January 7, 1836, *PTR* 3:429–30.

14. S. F. Austin to T. J. Rusk, Dec. 25, 1835, Rusk Papers.

15. S. F. Austin to Thos. J. Rusk, Jan. 7, 1836, Rusk Papers; James Kerr to the People of Texas, Jan. 4, 1836, *PTR* 3:415–21.

16. Sam Houston to Henry Smith, Jan. 6, 1836, *PTR* 3:425–26; John Sowers Brooks to A. H. Brooks, Jan. 20, 1836, John Sowers Brooks Papers, BTHC; Jas. Gaines to J. W. Robinson, Jan. 9, 1836, *PTR* 3:455.

17. Goliad Declaration, Dec. 22, 1835, GC.

18. Of the original council members only Henry Millard from the Wharton-Smith faction stayed active after November. The least experienced members included J. D. Clements, W. P. Harris, and Claiborne West, of the original council, and new members Alexander Thompson, E. Collard, and Jesse Burnham, all of whom also voted for or later approved of impeachment along with Barrett, Royall, Malone, Jones, McMullen, Kerr, Linn, Hanks, Daniel Parker, and even Millard. For sources of data

on partisanship, see note 19 from chapter 3. The most complete published account of the governor-council split is Ralph W. Steen, "Analysis of the Work of the General Council, Provisional Government of Texas, 1835–1836," *SHQ* 42 (July, 1938): 32–45.

19. Henry Smith [to the Council, Dec. 17, 1835], *PTR* 3:237–39; Henry Smith to the Council, Dec. 27, 1835, AJH.

20. Henry Smith to Sam Houston, Dec. 3, 1835, AJH.

21. Henry Smith to [William Ward, Jan. 6, 1836], *PTR* 3:428.

22. Henry Smith to J. W. Groce, Jan. 18, 1836, *PTR* 4:63; Henry Smith to J. W. Robinson, Jan. 10, 1836, *PTR* 3:468.

23. Henry Smith to the President and Members of the Council, Jan. 9, 1836, *PTR* 3:458–60.

24. Committee Reports, Jan. 11, 12, 1836, Committee Reports, GC; Committee to Henry Smith, [Jan. 12, 1836], Committee Reports, GC; Henry Smith to the Legislative Council, [Jan. 12, 1836], *PTR* 3:499.

25. J. W. Robinson, Governor's Message to the General Council, Jan. 14, 1836, *PTR* 4:17, 18 (quotations), 19–25; Council to THE PEOPLE OF TEXAS, Jan. 11, 1836, *PTR* 3:470–75.

26. James W. Robinson to John H. Money, Jan. 20, 21, 1836, *PTR* 4:91, 117–18; Henry Smith to Thomas R. Jackson, Feb. 2, 1836, *PTR* 4:244; Ordinance, Jan. 17, 1836, PGL, p. 117.

27. R. R. Royall to the Council, Jan. 27, 1836, *PTR* 4:161; Wyatt Hanks to the Governor and Council, Feb. 2, 1836, *PTR* 4:240–41; Thomas F. McKinney to the president of the Council, Jan. 14, 1836, *PTR* 4:12; J. W. Fannin to James W. Robinson, Jan. 21, 1836, *PTR* 4:104–105; Major ——— Moody to the President and Members of the General Council, Jan. [———, 1836], AJH.

28. [Citizens and Soldiers Meeting] to editor, *Brazoria Gazette*, Jan. 26, 1836, *PTR* 4:153–55; Amos Pollard to [Henry Smith], Jan. 27, 1836, AP.

29. J. C. Neill to Executive Council of Texas, Jan. 27, 1836, *PTR* 4:159; W. Barrett Travis to Henry Smith, Jan. 28, 1836, *PTR* 4:176–77.

30. Henry Smith to S. F. Austin, Jan. 30, 1836, *PTR* 4:204; Henry Smith to J. W. Robinson, Jan. 18, 1836, *PTR* 4:68–69; James W. Robinson to Henry Smith, Jan. 21, 1836, *PTR* 4:108.

31. Advisory Committee to [J. W. Robinson], Jan. 31, 1836, *PTR* 4:205–206; Alexr. Thomson and J. D. Clements to Henry Smith, Feb. 11, 1836, AJH.

32. James W. Robinson, Proclamation, Feb. 12, 1836, *PTR* 4:308–12.

33. Pedro Ellis Bean to the Military Commander at Béxar, July 28, Aug. 18, 1835, *PTR* 1:280 (quotation), 352–53; [Minutes, meeting at Nacogdoches, Aug. 15, 1835], *PTR* 1:343–45.

34. Moseley Baker and F. W. Johnson to the Chairman of the General Council of Texas, Oct. 23, 1835, *PTR* 2:199 (quotation), 200; Jorge Ant. Nixon to S. F. Austin, Oct. 10, 1835, *PTR* 2:88.

35. [Minutes and Resolutions], Sept. ———, Dec. 10, 1835, Nacogdoches Committee of Vigilance and Safety Records, TSA.

36. Mosely Baker and F. W. Johnson to the Chairman of the General Council of Texas, Oct. 23, 1835, *PTR* 2:199–201; Nacogdoches Committee of Vigilance and Safety resolution, Oct. 21, 1835, Blake 26:65.

37. [Resolutions of Public Meeting in Nacogdoches], Nov. 27, 1835, *PTR* 3:9–11;

S. H. Everitt to J. W. Robinson, Nov. 29, 1835, *PTR* 3:25; W. Richardson to Sam Houston, Nov. 28, 1835, AJH.

38. S. H. Everitt to Jas. W. Robinson, Dec. 19, 1835, *PTR* 3:255–56; Henry Raguet to [Sam Houston], Dec. 3, 1835, AJH.

39. John Forbes to James W. Robinson, Jan. 12, 1836, *PTR* 3:496–97; Jas. Gaines to J. W. Robinson, Jan. 9, [1836], *PTR* 3:454; Forbes to Robinson, Jan. 22, 1836, *PTR* 4:114.Radford Berry was procurador and sometimes acting alcalde; Jorge Antonio (George) Nixon served as *síndico;* Hoffman was the alcalde beginning in January, 1835; Allen had served on Houston's staff.

40. Henry Smith to the General Council, Dec. 26, 1835, *PTR* 2:333; H. S. Kimble to John Forbes, Jan. 14, 1836, *PTR* 4:11; Committee report, Dec. 8, 1835, Committee Reports, GC; Council resolution, Dec. 4, 1835, Blake 26:80–82; Henry Rueg to Alcalde, Jan. 10, 1836, Blake 14:351.

41. Jas. Gaines to J. W. Robinson, Jan. 9, [1836], *PTR* 3:454; Address of Jonas Harrison of the Committee of Vigilance and Safety San Augustine, Dec. 22, 1835, *PTR* 3:287–92; S. H. Everitt to Jas. W. Robinson, Dec. 13, 1835, *PTR* 3:178.

42. [Committee of Safety of Liberty] to Branch T. Archer, Nov. 9, 1835, *PTR* 2: 366–67; Liberty Committee of Safety [address], Oct. 24, 1835, in (San Felipe) *Telegraph and Texas Register,* Nov. 7, 1835.

43. R. R. Royall to S. F. Austin, Oct. 16, 1835, *PTR* 2:140–41; [Resolution of the Permanent Council, Oct. 28, 1835], *PTR* 2:252.

44. Wm. G. Harris to Judge Harris, Jan. 19, 1836, Don Carlos Barrett Papers.

45. Charles Willson to R. R. Royall, Dec. 24, 1835, PGL, 109–10; R. R. Royall to S. F. Austin, Sept. 30, Oct. 12, 1835, *PTR* 1:510–12, 2:106; Henry Smith to the Legislative Council, Dec. 16, 1835, *PTR* 3:215–16.

46. Angel Navarro to Alcalde of Goliad, Sept. 21, 1835, BA, reel 166, frames 784–85; Guadalupe de los Santos to Angel Navarro, Sept. 25, 1835, BA, reel 166, frame 808. As late as February residents of San Patricio still hoped to function under the prerevolution framework of government (Memorial [to the Convention], Feb. 1, 1836, Memorials, Records of the Convention of 1836, TSA).

47. Geo. M. Collinsworth et al., resolution, Oct. 9, 1835, *PTR* 2:76–77; P. Dimmitt to S. F. Austin, Oct. 15, 1835, *PTR* 2:134–35.

48. S. F. Austin to Benjn. Smith, Oct. 12, 1835, *PTR* 2:102–103; P. Dimmitt to S. F. Austin, Oct. 17, 1835, *PTR* 2:145–47; P. Dimitt to the Inhabitants of Texas, Nov. 16, 1835, AP; F. W. Johnson to Governor, Dec. 17, 1835, Governor's Correspondence, Records of the Provisional Government (hereafter cited as Gov. Corr.), TSA.

49. P. Dimitt, General Order, Nov. 12, 1835, *PTR* 2:382; P. Dimitt to S. F. Austin, Nov. 13, 1835, *PTR* 2:389–92.

50. Thomas G. Western to S. F. Austin, Nov. 13, 1835, *PTR* 2:402–403; [Goliad Volunteers] to S. F. Austin, Nov. 21, 1835, *PTR* 2:480–84.

51. P. Dimitt to Henry Smith, Jan. 10, 1836, AP; Proceedings of a General Meeting at Texana, Dec. 30, 1835, Communications Received, GC.

52. J. C. Neill to Governor and Council, Jan. 6, 1836, Communications Received, GC; Amos Pollard to Henry Smith, Jan. 16, 1836, AP.

53. Jas. P. Caldwell to S. F. Austin, Dec. 8, 1835, *PTR* 3:115; Sterling C. Robertson to Council, Dec. 18, 1835, *PTR* 3:246–47; Thomas F. McKinney to provisional govern-

ment of Texas, Dec. 25, 1835, *PTR* 3:312–13; (San Felipe) *Telegraph and Texas Register,* Nov. 21, 1835.

54. Henry Smith to the Legislative Council, Nov. 25, 1835, *PTR* 9:150–51.

55. James W. Robinson to Thos. J. Rusk, Dec. 19, 1835, Rusk Papers; S. F. Austin to T. F. McKinney, Jan. 17, 1836, *PTR* 4:39; Henry Smith to Leonard Groce, Dec. 24, 1835, *PTR* 3:308–309; Daniel Parker to Barrett, Jan. 8, 1836, *PTR* 3:447.

56. Henry Millard to D. C. Barrett, Dec. 29, 1835, *PTR* 3:365–66; Sam Houston to D. C. Barrett, Jan. 2, 1836, *PTR* 3:405; Sam Houston to John Forbes, Jan. 7, 1836, *PTR* 3:436–37.

57. Mrs. P. Mann to S. Houston, Feb. 3, 1836, *PTR* 4:248; James W. Robinson to Sam Houston, Jan. 18, 1836, AJH.

58. See Webb, et al., eds., *Handbook of Texas* 1:326, 525, 601, 2:195, 218, 368–69, for brief sketches of these figures: T. Jefferson Chambers, John Fisher, Eli Mitchell, J. B. Miller, William Duncan, Willian Pettus, and Wyly Martin.

59. E. M. Pease to Wyatt Hanks, Feb. 8, 1836, *PTR* 4:289; Wyatt Hanks to J. W. Robinson, Feb. 6, 1836, *PTR* 4:274; D. C. Barrett to [J. W. Robinson], Feb. 10, 1836, *PTR* 4:299.

60. (San Felipe) *Telegraph and Texas Register,* Jan. 30, Feb. 20, 1836; James W. Robinson to Sam Houston, Feb. 14, 26, 1836, AJH; Geo. W. Poe to Henry Smith, Feb. 12, 1836, AP.

61. (San Felipe) *Telegraph and Texas Register,* Feb. 27, 1836.

CHAPTER 5.

1. Henry [Austin] to Mary Austin Holley, Mar. 29, 1836, *PTR* 5:222.

2. R. R. Royall to Sam Houston, Feb. 8, 1836, AJH.

3. A Resolution for Calling a Convention, Dec. 10, 1835, *Ordinances and Decrees of the Consultation . . . and the Convention, PTR* 9:446.

4. S. H. Everett to D. C. Barrett, Jan. 17, 1835, *PTR* 4:44; (San Felipe) *Telegraph and Texas Register,* Jan. 23, 30, Feb. 20, 1836; Geo. W. Poe to Henry Smith, Feb. 2, 1836, *PTR* 4:242; Mrs. P. Mann to S. Houston, Feb. 3, 1836, *PTR* 4:248; Meeting of the Citizens of the Municipality of Jackson, n.d., RCM.

5. (San Felipe) *Telegraph and Texas Register,* Jan. 16, 1836; "A Resolution for Calling a Convention," *PTR* 9:447.

6. Memorial of the Volunteers [of Refugio] . . . to the Convention, Feb. ——, 1836, *PTR* 4:473–74; S. Rhoads Fisher to —— Baker, Feb. 22, 1836, *PTR* 4:401–402; [Journals of] the General Convention at Washington, March 1–17, 1836, *PTR* 9:307–309; Hermann Ehrenberg, *With Milam and Fannin* (Dallas: Tardy Publishing Co., 1935), pp. 136–37.

7. Meeting of the Citizens of the Municipality of Jackson convened at Texana, n.d., RCM; E. Rains to [Henry] Smith, Jan. 20, 1836, Gov. Corr.; Thomas H. Borden to the Voters of the Municipality of Austin, Jan. 19, 1836, APT.

8. M. Hawkins [to J. W. Robinson], Jan. 24, 1836, *PTR* 4:137; Memorial of Bexar officers [Feb. 5, 1836], *PTR* 4:264.

9. Memorial of Bexar officers [Feb. 5, 1836], *PTR* 4:264; J. C. Neill to Henry Smith, Jan. 23, 1836, Gov. Corr.; Edward Gritten to James W. Robinson, Feb. 2, 1836, Gov. Corr.

10. G. B. Jameson to Henry Smith, Feb. 11, 1836, Gov. Corr.; Amos Pollard to Henry Smith, Feb. 13, 1836, AP. In the regular election seventeen candidates received votes, but Antonio Navarro received 65, Francisco Ruiz 61, Erasmo Seguín 60, and Gaspar Flores 59 while José María Salinas gained the next highest number with only 8. None of the four soldiers named in this balloting received more than 3 ([Election returns], Municipality of Béxar, Feb. 1, 1836, BA, reel 166; frame 496).

11. Gray, *From Virginia to Texas*, p. 92; John Forbes to J. W. Robinson, Jan. 22, 1836, *PTR* 4:114–15.

12. Gray, *Virginia to Texas*, p. 89; Narrative of Thomas J. Walling, quoted in Dixon and Kemp, *Heroes of San Jacinto*, p. 352.

13. Wyatt Hanks to Govr & Council, Feb. 2, 1836, *PTR* 4:240–41; Gray, *Virginia to Texas*, pp. 89–90.

14. Gray, *Virginia to Texas*, p. 91.

15. Ibid., pp. 92, 100 (quotation); Citizens of Nacogdoches to Governor and Council, Mar. 12, 1836, Nacogdoches Committee of Vigilance and Safety Records.

16. S. F. A[ustin] to T. F. McKinney, Jan. 21, 1836, *PTR* 4:95–96.

17. Henry Smith to William Bryan, Feb. 5, 1836, *PTR* 4:268; James W. Robinson to J. W. Fannin, Mar. 6, 1836, PGL.

18. Joseph E. Field, *Three Years in Texas* (p p d), p. 33; Resolution, [March 3, 1836], Acts of the Convention, Records of the Convention, TSA.

19. Past political activity and most other biographical data came from *Biographical Directory of Texas Conventions* and Webb, et al., eds., *Handbook of Texas*. Records of the committees of safety and public meetings supplied lists of participants in earlier political activity. See Appendix: Political Backgrounds of the Convention Delegates, for a listing by delegate.

20. The representation of Jasper (Bevil), Brazoria (Columbia), Austin, Liberty, and Washington lost one place each. There were two more delegates (59) at the Convention than at the Consultation (57). Those who repeated as delegates to both bodies are listed in Appendix A.

21. The figure 37.4 was the mean; the median age was 36. This compares to a mean of 39.3 and median of 38 for the Consultation delegates. Convention delegates had resided in Texas for an average of 4.68 years, the median date of emigration being 1832; for Consultation delegates the average length of residence was 7.07 years, with the median date of emigration being 1830.

22. The delegates' service records came from Webb, et al., eds., *Handbook of Texas* and Thomas Lloyd Miller, *Bounty and Donation Land Grants of Texas, 1835–1888* (Austin: University of Texas Press, 1967).

23. Gray, *Virginia to Texas*, p. 130.

24. Estep, "Zavala," p. 361; James Kerr to the People of Texas, Jan. 4, 1836, *PTR* 3:415–21. Zavala, according to his biographer, was "forced to deviate" from defending the 1824 constitution by "the preponderance of the desire for complete independence." Other delegates stayed away rather than surrender their opposition to independence.

25. Committee of State & Judiciary Report, Jan. 3, 1836, Committee Reports, GC; Ordinance, n. d., Committee Reports, GC; A Resolution for Calling a Convention, Dec. 10, 1835, Committee Reports, GC.

26. (San Felipe) *Telegraph and Texas Register*, Dec. 2, 1835, Feb. 20, 27 (quota-

tion), 1836; James W. Robinson to Sam Houston, Jan. 18, 1836, AJH; S. F. Austin to Henry [Austin], Jan. 7, 1836, *PTR* 3:429–30.

27. Sam Houston to Citizens, [Jan. 15, 1836], *PTR* 4:29–30; David G. Burnet to Henry Clay, Mar. 30, 1836, *PTR* 5:238–39.

28. George C. Childress to Sam Houston, Feb. 13, 1836, AJH; James K. Greer, "The Committee on the Texas Declaration of Independence," *SHQ* (Apr., 1927): 243.

29. [Journals of] the Convention, *PTR* 9:493–96.

30. Gray, *Virginia to Texas*, pp. 120, 121, 124 (quotation); Clarke, *Rusk*, p. 32.

31. Gray, *Virginia to Texas*, pp. 125–26, 128–30.

32. [Journals of] the Convention, *PTR* 9:289; Rupert N. Richardson, "Framing the Constitution of the Republic of Texas," *SHQ* 31 (Jan., 1932): 209; "The Constitution of the Republic of Texas," *Handbook of Texas* (revised edition, publication pending by the Texas State Historical Association).

33. [Journals of] the Convention, *PTR* 9:326, 328, 349–50; Gray, *Virginia to Texas*, p. 130.

34. See the Declaration of Rights, first, second, thirteenth, and fourteenth sections, Article VI, Section 8, *PTR* 5:116 (first and second quotations), 117 (third quotation), 113 (fourth quotation); J. E. Ericson, "Origins of the Texas Bill of Rights," *SHQ* 62 (Apr., 1959): 457–58.

35. See chapter 12 on blacks in the Texas Revolution for an extended discussion of the constitutional and legislative enactments on the status of free blacks and slaves.

36. Gray, *Virginia to Texas*, p. 128; [Journals of] the Convention, *PTR* 9:323.

37. Gray, *Virginia to Texas*, p. 95; S. H. Everitt to David G. Burnet, Mar. 17, 1836, *PTR* 5:120–21; Andrew Forest Muir, ed., "The Union Company in Anahuac, 1831–1833," *SHQ* 70 (Oct., 1966): 256. According to delegate Collinsworth, the "land speculator" faction included Ellis, Potter, Childress, Robertson, and Robert Hamilton. Those who generally aligned themselves with Collinsworth or opposed the previously named group in land debates were Menefee, Hardeman, Thomas, Houston, Rusk, Everitt, Gazley, Menard, and G. W. Smyth (James Collinsworth to [M. B. Lamar], n.d., *PTR* 4:475–76).

38. See Section 10 in General Provisions of the Constitution, *PTR* 5:113, 114 (quotation), 115; Richardson, "Constitution," 205–207. At least two of the delegates, Carson and Houston, had previously been involved in the John T. Mason land dealings invalidated by the Convention, but there is no record of this having been made an issue in the debates (Llerena Friend, *Sam Houston, the Great Designer* [Austin: University of Texas Press, 1954], pp. 45, 69, 70).

39. Gray, *Virginia to Texas*, p. 130; [Journals of] the Convention, *PTR* 9:323, 342–43, 360–61, 367, 370; Eugene C. Barker, "The Texas Revolutionary Army," *QTSHA* 9 (Apr., 1906): 256; Thomas L. Miller, "Texas Bounty Land Grants, 1835–1888," *SHQ* 66 (Oct., 1962): 222–25.

40. [Journals of] the Convention, *PTR* 9:320–21.

41. Resolution, [Mar. 4, 1836], Acts of the Convention.

42. James W. Robinson to Sam Houston, Feb. 14, 1836, AJH; (San Felipe) *Telegraph and Texas Register*, Mar. 5, 1836.

43. Ordinance to Organize the Militia of the Republic of Texas, Mar. 12, 1836, *PTR* 5:58 (quotation), 59–62.

44. Ibid., 5:59; [Journals of] the Convention, *PTR* 9:354; Resolution, Mar. 12, 1836, Acts of the Convention.

45. W. B. Travis to the President of the Convention, Mar. 12, 1836, *PTR* 4:504; Jas. Collinsworth to J. L. Bennett, Mar. 12, 1836, *PTR* 5:57; [Journals of] the Convention, *PTR* 9:356, 367–68.

CHAPTER 6.

1. [Journals of] the Convention, *PTR* 9:363; Schedule Sec. 1, 4, 8 of the Constitution of the Republic of Texas, *PTR* 5:111, 112; Executive Ordinance, Mar. 16, 1836, PGL.

2. *Biographical Directory,* pp. 63, 165, 197–98; Richardson, "Constitution," p. 195; Friend, *Sam Houston,* pp. 45, 69, 70; Webb, et al., eds., *Handbook of Texas* 1:301, 766, 2:401, 771; David G. Burnet to Sam Houston, Nov. 26, 1835, *PTR* 2:511; David G. Burnet to James Morgan, May 28, 1836, *PTR* 6:494; Judge [James] Collinsworth to [M. B. Lamar], n. d., *PTR* 4:475–76.

3. Gray, *From Virginia to Texas,* pp. 126, 128, 131, 133, 147, 162; [Journals of] the Convention, *PTR* 9:339; David G. Burnet to Thomas Toby, May 25, 1836, *PTR* 6:369–70.

4. David G. Burnet, Inaugural Address, Mar. 17, 1836, *PTR* 5:101. He concluded with an appeal to end partisanship.

5. [Burnet order, Mar. 25, 1836], *PTR* 5:186–88; [David G. Burnet] to Wm. Hardin, Mar. 25, 1836, *PTR* 5:185.

6. David G. Burnet, Proclamation, Mar. 29, 1836, *PTR* 5:226–28; Robt. Potter to Thomas B. Bell, Mar. 31, 1836, *PTR* 5:242; David G. Burnet to the citizens of Texas, Apr. 6, 1836, *PTR* 5:340–41; Thos. J. Rusk to the people of Texas, Apr. 13, 1836, AJH.

7. John Carrington [certificate], Apr. 10, 1836, AP.

8. David Thomas to Sam Houston, Apr. 6, 1836, AJH. Attorney General Thomas briefly held the war post when Rusk took a field command.

9. Committee of Vigilance and Safety [of Nacogdoches to John T. Mason], Apr. 11, 1836, *PTR* 5:432–33; Jas. Grimes [to David G. Burnet], Mar. 28, 1836, *PTR* 5:215; Public Notice of a Meeting of the Citizens [of Nacogdoches, Mar. 1836], *PTR* 5:267.

10. [Minutes of a Public Meeting at San Augustine, June 15, 1836], *PTR* 7:158; Sydney O. Penington to [David G. Burnet], May 15, 1836, *PTR* 6:300.

11. See chapter 11 on Anglo civilian life for an analysis of popular behavior in the days of the Runaway Scrape and chapter 9 for a discussion of army impressment policies.

12. Henry Millard to T. B. Huling, Apr. 7, 1836, Thomas Byers Huling Papers, BTHC; Jas. Gaines to [D. G. Burnet], Mar. 28, 1836, *PTR* 5:215.

13. D. G. Burnet to James Morgan, May 16, 1836, *PTR* 5:308–309; Sam Houston, Army Orders, Apr. 5, 8, 1836, AJH; S. C. Robertson to Thomas J. Rusk, May 27, 1836, *PTR* 5:392–93.

14. David G. Burnet to *Citizens of Texas,* June 20, 1836, *PTR* 7:211–13; David G. Burnet to Peter W. Grayson and James Collinsworth, June 20, 1836, *PTR* 7:206–207; Mirabeau B. Lamar to ——— Chenoweth, July 8, 1836, *PTR* 7:396–97; Henry Raguet to Sam Houston, June 27, 1836, AJH; [Sam Houston] to the Citizens of Texas West of the Red River, July 2, 1836, AJH; [Sam Houston] to Willis H. Landrum, Aug. 1, 1836, AJH.

15. Sam Houston, Orders, Aug. 11, 1836, AJH; Sam P. Carson to John H. Millin, Mar. 29, 1836, Executive Record Book, Correspondence of the President and State Department, TSA; David G. Burnet, Proclamation, July 12, 1836, *PTR* 7:427.

16. D. G. Burnet to Wm. Hardin, Sept. 5, 1836, *PTR* 8:391–92.

17. Thos. J. Rusk to David G. Burnet, June 12, 1836, *PTR* 7:138; Thomas J. Rusk to [David G. Burnet], June 11, 1836, *PTR* 7:124.

18. Wm. H. Wharton to P. P. Rea, June 12, 1836, *PTR* 7:131; Memucan Hunt to M. B. Lamar, June 14, 1836, *PTR* 7:151.

19. Sam Houston to Thomas J. Rusk, Mar. 23, 1836, *PTR* 5:168–70; W. B. Dewees to [Clara Cardello], May 15, 1836, *PTR* 6:282–83; Jno. R. Jones to [Samuel P. Carson], Mar. 25, 1836, Executive Record Book. Members of the army exaggerated the lack of martial display by the political leaders. Twelve delegates besides those who had already been in the army served in the six months after March 17, bringing to 36 (61 percent) the number who volunteered during the course of the war.

20. Estep, "Zavala," pp. 364–65; Thomas J. Rusk, Bailey Hardeman, and Lorenzo de Zavala to [David G. Burnet], May 1, 1836, Executive Record Book; Thomas F. McKinney to Thomas J. Rusk, May 20, 1836, Rusk Papers; David G. Burnet to Samuel P. Carson, May 23, 1836, *PTR* 6:357.

21. David G. Burnet to A. Briscoe, May 21, 1836, *PTR* 6:348; David G. Burnet to the People of Texas, [Sept. 6, 1836], *PTR* 8:398–401; Estep, "Zavala," pp. 371–77; Ramón Martínez Caro, *A True Account of the First Texas Campaign,* in Carlos Castañeda, trans., *The Mexican Side of the Texas Revolution* (Dallas, Tex.: P. L. Turner Co., 1928), p. 131.

22. David G. Burnet to Peter W. Grayson and James Collinsworth, June 20, 1836, *PTR* 7:207; Citizens of Municipalities of Austin & Harrisburg to Cabinet of Texas, June 7, 1836, *PTR* 7:50; [Resolutions of] the citizens of the Red Land, June 15, 1836, *PTR* 7:157.

23. Memucan Hunt to the President and Cabinet, June 3, 1836, *PTR* 6:512; Lamar quoted in Gambrell, *Lamar,* p. 109.

24. A. C. Allen to fellow citizens in arms and the Volunteers from the United States, July 23, 1836, *PTR* 8:11–12; Henry M. Morfit to John Forsyth, Aug. 23, 1836, *PTR* 8:302–303. See chapter 9 on the army's perspective on this episode.

25. David G. Burnet to the People of Texas [Sept. 27, 1836], *PTR* 9:15; Mary Whatley Clarke, *David G. Burnet* (Austin: Pemberton Press, 1969), pp. 97, 108–17, 124–27; Binkley, *Texas Revolution,* pp. 110–16. Originally Zavala, Collinsworth, Hardeman, and Grayson supported the ideas embodied in the Velasco treaty.

26. Lorenzo de Zavala to [David G. Burnet], June 3, 1836, *PTR* 6:515; Zavala quoted in Raymond Estep, "Lorenzo de Zavala and the Texas Revolution," *SHQ* 57 (Jan., 1954): 331.

27. L. A. McHenry to [John Hardin McHenry], June 17, 1836, in Nielsen, ed., "Lydia Ann McHenry," p. 402; Geo. A. Nixon to Sam Houston, Aug. 10, 1836, AJH; Estep, "Zavala and Texas Revolution," 339; F. A. Sawyer to [James] Morgan, June 6, 1836, *PTR* 7:46. Members of the cabinet—Secretary of State: Samuel P. Carson, James Collinsworth, W. H. Jack; Secretary of War: T. J. Rusk, W. D. C. Hall, M. B. Lamar, Alexander Somervell, Frank A. Sawyer, J. A. Wharton; Secretary of the Navy: Robert Potter, on leave after April 20, the post going unfilled with the secretary of war signing the necessary documents; Secretary of the Treasury: Bailey Hardeman; Attorney Gen-

eral: David Thomas, P. W. Grayson (unfilled after May 26). After the second week of June no more than four were active in cabinet affairs.

28. David G. Burnet to the People of Texas No. 4, [Sept. 27, 1836], *PTR* 9:15; David G. Burnet to James Morgan, May 28, 1836, *PTR* 6:394; David G. Burnet to M. B. Lamar, July 8, 1836, *PTR* 7:392; Charges and Specifications [against David G. Burnet], July 14, 1836, John Forbes Papers, BTHC.

29. S. F. Austin to Henry Austin, June 27, 1836, *PTR* 7:278–79.

30. E. M. Pease to [Lorrain Thompson Pease], Jan. 8, 1837, Katherine Hart and Elizabeth Kemp, eds., "E. M. Pease's Account of the Texas Revolution," *SHQ* 68 (July, 1964): 88; Thomas J. Rusk to Sam Houston, July 2, 1836, *PTR* 8:343.

31. Jas. Collinsworth to T. Rusk, May 31, 1836, Rusk Papers; Sam Houston to H. Raguet, July 9, 1836, AJH.

32. [Lorenzo de Zavala to Gen. Mexia, May 26, 1836], *PTR* 6:384; S. F. Austin to [James] Collinsworth and [Peter] Grayson, July 9, 1836, *PTR* 7:401.

33. M. B. Lamar to [David G.] Burnet, July 17, 1836, *PTR* 7:472; Thomas J. Rusk to Gail Borden, Aug. 8, 1836, *PTR* 8:164.

34. David G. Burnet to the People of Texas No. 2, [Sept. 13, 1836], *PTR* 8:464; (Columbia) *Telegraph and Texas Register,* Sept. 6, 1836.

35. Edward J. Wilson and G. L. Postlewhaite to the Public, Sept. 10, 1836, *PTR* 8:434–35, 436–37; T. J. Chambers to the Public, Oct., 1836, *PTR* 8:122.

CHAPTER 7.

1. William H. Wharton [to the public, Oct., 1835], *PTR* 2:55; Circular from the Committee of Safety of Austin to the Committee of Nacogdoches and San Augustine, Oct. 4, 1835, *PTR* 2:32; Haden Edwards to J. W. Robinson, Nov. 29, 1835, *OCTR* 1:135.

2. Jac. F. Fowler to Sam Houston, Oct. 26, 1835, AJH.

3. Geo. M. Collingsworth, et al., [agreement at Guadalupe Victoria], Oct. 9, 1835, *PTR* 2:76–77.

4. One of the men stationed at Goliad estimated the Texas force at 180 men (P. W. Grayson to S. F. Austin, Oct. 11, 1835, *PTR* 2:94). However, Huson's study, *Captain Phillip Dimmitt's Commandancy of Goliad,* p. 29, places its strength at no more than 120. See also pp. 35–36, 133, 178.

5. Noah Smithwick, *The Evolution of a State: or Recollections of Old Texas Days* (Austin: University of Texas Press, 1985), p. 73.

6. David M. Vigness, *The Revolutionary Decades, 1810–1836* (Austin, Tex.: Steck-Vaughn, 1965), p. 160; Barker, *Austin,* p. 485; Lukes, "DeWitt Colony," p. 244.

7. S. F. Austin, General Orders, Oct. 14, 1835, *PTR* 2:123–24 (quotation); [S. F. Austin] Order No. 1, Oct. 11, 1835, *PTR* 2:93.

8. Thos. J. Rusk to Sam Houston, Nov. 14, 1835, *PTR* 2:413.

9. S. F. Austin, [order], Nov. 24, 1835, *PTR* 2:495–96; Barr, *Texans in Revolt,* pp. 27–59, 67–68.

10. The number of Tejanos in the siege of Béxar and at other places in the fall of 1835, according to the memory of Juan Seguín, was 160 (Juan N. Seguín et al. to Stephen H. Darden, Jan. 12, 1875, *Texana* 5 [Spring, 1967]: 81–82).

11. The number of recruits who can be definitely identified as U.S. volunteers who

came to Texas after the fighting began was 142; using this ratio of United States to Texas soldiers for those whose origins have not been identified, a fair estimate of the total number of U.S. volunteers in the force in 1835 would be 192.

12. Benj. F. Smith to [S. F. Austin], Oct. 13, 14, 1835, *PTR* 2:121, 131, 132 (first quotation); P. Dimitt to S. F. Austin, Oct. 15, 30, 1835, *PTR* 2:134-35, 266 (second quotation); W. H. Jack to Stephen F. Austin, Oct. 13, 1835, *PTR* 2:114-15; Benj. J. White to S. Houston, Nov. 13, 1835, AJH.

13. [Goliad volunteers] to Stephen F. Austin, Nov. 21, 1835, *PTR* 2:480-84.

14. S. F. Austin to the President of the Consultation of Texas, Nov. 3, 1835, *PTR* 2:305; Henry Smith to Sam Houston, Nov. 14, 1835, *PTR* 2:415-16; Of the Military [Nov. 14, 1835], Acts Cons.

15. *Journals of the Consultation,* Nov. 13, 1835, *PTR* 9:274-75; James W. Robinson to Thos. J. Rusk, Nov. 15, 1835, *PTR* 2:428; Henry Smith to the Commander in Chief of the Army of the People, Nov. 13, 1835, *PTR* 2:401-402.

16. Report of Committee . . . on the army in the field, Nov. 28, 1835, Committee Reports, GC; Robert C. Morris to Sam Houston, Nov. 29, 1835, AJH; J. W. Fannin to Sam Houston, Nov. 18, 1835, AP; Sam Houston to Wyly Martin, Nov. 24, 1835, AJH; Sam Houston to Henry Smith, Dec. 6, 1835, AJH.

17. Barker, "Texas Revolutionary Army," pp. 230-35; H. Smith to William Ward, [Jan. 6, 1836], *PTR* 3:428.

18. Fellow Citizens and Friends to Edward Burleson et al., Dec. 15, 1835, *PTR* 3:200; Resolution [on enlistment oaths], Dec. 27, 1835, PGL. A random sampling of about 10 percent of the military claims records reveals twelve discharges from the Béxar forces between December 5 and the end of the year, mostly (two-thirds) between December 9 and 14 (Audited Military Claims, Comptroller of Public Accounts [hereafter cited as AMC], TSA).

19. S. F. Austin to the Provisional Government of Texas, Dec. 22, 1835, *PTR* 3:285; James Gillespie to T. J. Rusk, May 29, 1836, Rusk Papers; Sam Houston to [Henry Smith], Dec. 26, 1835, AJH; Hobart Huson, ed., *Dr. J. H. Barnard's Journal* ([Refugio, Tex.]: n.p., 1950), p. 6; Barker, "Texas Army," pp. 230-31.

20. Thos. Llewellyn et al. to F. W. Johnson, Dec. 25, 1835, *PTR* 3:313-14; J. C. Neill to Sam Houston, Jan. 14, 1836, Communications Received, GC; ——— Carey to ——— Carey, Jan. 12, 1836, *PTR* 3:491-92; F. W. Johnson to James W. Robinson, Dec. 25, 1835, *PTR* 3:327.

21. W. Barrett Travis to Henry Smith, Feb. 13, 1836, *PTR* 4:327-28; J. J. Baugh to Henry Smith, Feb. 13, 1836, AP.

22. Henry Smith to [William Ward, Jan. 6, 1836], *PTR* 3:428; Barker, "Texas Army," p. 255; Sam Houston to Henry Smith, Jan. 6, 1836, Madge Hearne Collection, TSA; Committee Reports, Dec. 25, 27, 1835, GC; [Council] TO THE PEOPLE OF TEXAS, Jan. 11, 1836, *PTR* 3:470-75.

23. Sam Houston to Henry Smith, Jan. 17, 1836, *PTR,* 4:46-47; Committee Report, Jan. 29, 1836, GC; F. W. Johnson to the Provisional Governor, Dec. 17, 1835, Gov. Corr.; P. Dimitt to Henry Smith, Jan. 10, 1836, AP; Ehrenberg, *With Milam and Fannin,* p. 123.

24. Geo. W. Poe to Sam Houston, Feb. 2, 1836, *PTR* 4:241; James W. Robinson to Sam Houston, Feb. 14, 1836, AJH; William T. Riviere, "Sam Houston's Retreat," *SHQ* 46 (July, 1942): 11; Ira Westover to Sam Houston, Feb. 7, 1836, AJH.

25. All but 15 of these 245 can be identified in terms of residence or some kind of biographical detail. As a whole these recruits were younger (the average age was 28) than those who served the previous year, and 57 percent were single. The birthplace of 140 is known, with 22 percent being born outside the U. S., 14 percent hailing from the northern states, 19 percent from the lower South, and 45 percent from the upper South. The Texas ranks were dominated by the last-hour influx of 51 volunteers from Gonzales, representing over one-third of all the Texas residents who served at Béxar or the Alamo in 1836. Other parts of the Brazos department supplied 30 percent of the Texas troops, with the Béxar and Nacogdoches departments providing about 18 percent each.

26. Although 672 is the total number who served in the Goliad region between January and the end of March, Fannin never commanded nearly that many. According to Hobart Huson, the "total paper strength" of this army was just over five hundred in late February, about two hundred being at Refugio with William Ward or A. B. King and otherwise absent. The arrival of some militia and cavalry under Hugh M. Fraser and A. C. Horton at the end of the second week in March still left Fannin with well under 350 effectives (Huson, *Refugio; A Comprehensive History* 1:322-23).

27. Captain John Chenoweth formed one company of Béxar veterans in January; Samuel O. Pettus took over command of a company of San Antonio Greys previously led by William G. Cooke; and David Burke led a third company that had served at Béxar, sometimes called the Mobile Greys. The Georgia Battalion consisted of four companies captained by William Wadsworth, W. J. Bullock, James C. Winn, and Isaac Ticknor; the last named of these units arrived in Texas on January 19, with the others having debarked in December. The Alabama companies of Burr H. Duval and Jack Shackelford both came in January, whereas Amon B. King's Paducah (Kentucky) volunteers and Peyton Wyatt's Huntsville volunteers had been in Texas since Christmas. The three remaining companies of U.S. recruits were J. M. Allen's survivors of the Tampico misadventure and small squads formed in February on Texas soil and officered by Thomas K. Pearson and Samuel Sprague. The Texas companies were led by Ira Westover (forty-five men plus six transfers from other companies), Thomas Llewellyn (thirty men), A. C. Horton (forty-two men), and H. M. Fraser (eleven men). Harbert Davenport, in "Notes from an Unfinished Study of Fannin and His Men," (typescript, TSA) pp. 30-84, details the movement of individual soldiers from company to company, the nature and date of the military action, and the fate of each man. His subsequent pages give additional biographical details on these soldiers.

28. About 38 percent of the Texans (as opposed to U.S. recruits) who served at the Alamo or with Fannin between January and March, 1836, were veterans of the 1835 campaigns (98 of 261). For the entire force of this period the number of 1835 veterans was 19 percent (171 of 917).

29. Resolution, [Mar. 4, 1836], Acts of the Convention.

30. Resolution, Mar. 12, 1836, ibid.; (San Felipe) *Telegraph and Texas Register,* Feb. 20, Mar. 5, 1836; Ordinance to Organize the Militia of the Republic of Texas, Mar. 12, 1836, *PTR* 5:58-62; [David G. Burnet] to Wm. Hardin et al., Mar. 25, 1836, *PTR* 5:185; Public Notice of a Meeting of the Citizens of Nacogdoches, [Mar. 19, 1836], *PTR* 5:267.

31. David Thomas to Sam Houston, Apr. 6, 1836, AJH; Sam Houston to Henry Raguet, Apr. 19, 1836, *PTR* 5:504; David G. Burnet to the citizens of Texas, Apr. 6,

1836, *PTR* 5:340–41; Thos. J. Rusk to the People of Texas, Apr. 13, 1836, AJH; John Carrington, Certificate, Apr. 10, 1836, AP.

32. David G. Burnet, Proclamation, Mar. 29, 1836, *PTR* 5:226–28; Thomas J. Rusk to David G. Burnet, Apr. 6, 1836, AP; Binkley, *Texas Revolution,* pp. 107–108; Eugene C. Barker, "The San Jacinto Campaign," *QTSHA* 4 (Apr., 1901): 300, 312–13, 317.

33. Sam Houston, "The Campaign of 1836," in James M. Day, comp., *The Texas Almanac 1857–1873: A Compendium of Texas History* (Waco: Texian Press, 1967), pp. 270–73; Barker, "San Jacinto Campaign," pp. 276, 309, 335; Webb, et al., eds., *Handbook of Texas* 2:554.

34. Barker, "Texas Army," p. 260. Binkley, *Texas Revolution,* added specificity to Barker's conclusions, stating that "more than two thirds of the men who fought under Houston at San Jacinto were old residents" (p. 110).

35. Rosa Kleberg, "Some of My Early Experiences in Texas," *QTSHA* 1 (Apr., 1898): 300. One of the few histories to note the regional dimension of the army that fought at San Jacinto is "Compendium of the History of Texas [1860]," Day, comp., *Texas Almanac,* pp. 314–15, 324.

36. Scarcely any Tejanos received credit for service in the spring of 1836 except those under Seguín at San Jacinto; nevertheless, he later claimed that from fifty to seventy other Hispanics had enrolled in units that were assigned duty escorting families that fled toward Nacogdoches or acted as frontier guards (Juan Seguín to the Comptroller of Texas, Dec. 5, 1874, José Almeda [Almeida] folder, AMC; Seguín et al., to Darden, *Texana* 5:82–84).

37. Miller, *Bounty and Donation Grants* (p. 827), points out that donation laws entitled a veteran of both the Béxar siege and San Jacinto battle to only one certificate of that kind and that this source thus underestimates the number who served in two campaigns. However, multiple service was also reflected in bounty warrants and by muster rolls, so the comparison shown between Tables 6 and 7 reflects a broadly accurate if not an exact profile.

38. James W. Pohl and Stephen L. Hardin, "The Military History of the Texas Revolution: An Overview," *SHQ* 89 (Jan., 1986): 271. Comparison with participation rates in other wars is difficult, even if only the Texas experience is considered. The Texas war for independence lasted a shorter time and also stimulated a lower rate of participation by Texans than did the Civil War twenty-five years later. The best estimate of the number of Texans in the Confederate army at the end of 1861 (a period of time comparable to that which is being measured for the Texas Revolution) is twenty-five thousand, a rate of service that is approximately the same as for the Texas Revolution measured against total population and somewhat greater measured against free population (Ralph A. Wooster and Robert Wooster, "'Rarin for a Fight': Texans in the Confederate Army," *SHQ* 84 [Apr., 1981]: 392). The population figures for 1860 for computing the rate of participation came from Randolph B. Campbell, *An Empire for Slavery: The Peculiar Institution in Texas, 1821–1865* (Baton Rouge: Louisiana State University Press, 1989), p. 143.

39. Thos. J. Rusk to David G. Burnet, June 20, 1836, *PTR* 7:215; Thomas J. Rusk to [Sam Houston], July 20, 1836, AJH; Thomas J. Green to A. Sommerville, July 25, 1836, *PTR* 8:33. The size and composition of the Texas army in July and August derives from Binkley, *Texas Revolution,* p. 112, and Joseph M. Nance, *After San Jacinto* (Austin: University of Texas Press, 1963), pp. 18–19. According to Nance, this Texas

army had 2,503 officers and men organized into 53 companies, with 39 companies being comprised "chiefly" of 1,813 U.S. volunteers who had come to Texas after the San Jacinto battle.

40. Smithwick, *Evolution of a State*, p. 107; Clarke, *Thomas J. Rusk*, pp. 71–81; S. Sherman to T. J. Rusk, May 23, 1836, Rusk Papers.

41. Thomas J. Rusk to David G. Burnet, June 11, 12, 1836, *PTR* 7:124, 136–38; David G. Burnet to *Citizens of Texas*, June 20, 1836, *PTR* 7:212–13; Sam Houston to W. E. Harris, July 9, 1836, *PTR* 7:404–405. A sampling of Audited Military Claims records suggests an influx of substitutes into the army in June.

42. David G. Burnet to Messrs. Collinsworth and Grayson, July 8, 1836, *PTR* 7:388; William P. Miller to Sam Houston, July 7, 1836, AJH; Thomas J. Green to T. J. Rusk, July 16, 1838, *PTR* 7:464–65; T. J. Rusk to David G. Burnet, July 4, 1836, *PTR* 7:363.

43. M. B. Lamar to D. G. Burnet, July 17, 1836, *PTR* 7:471–73; Thomas J. Green to Sam Houston, July 18, 1836, AJH; Felix Huston to Sam Houston, Aug. ———, 1836, AJH; R. R. Royall to M. B. Lamar, July 13, 1836, *PTR* 7:443; F[airfax] C[atelet] to Editor, July 20, 1836, *PTR* 7:495.

CHAPTER 8.

1. S. F. Austin, General Orders, Oct. 14, 1835, *PTR* 2:123–24.

2. Thomas G. Western to S. F. Austin, Nov. 13, 1835, *PTR* 2:402–403.

3. M. A. Bryan to James F. Perry, Nov. 7, [1835], *PTR* 3:345; S. F. Austin to Henry Austin, June 27, 1836, *PTR* 7:278.

4. S. F. Austin to [J. F. Perry], Nov. 22, 1835, *PTR* 2:487; Philip A. Sublett to S. F. Austin, Nov. 21, 1835, *PTR* 2:486.

5. A. H. Jones to Wm. E. Jones, Jan. 15, 1836, *PTR* 4:31; Barr, *Texans in Revolt*, pp. 52–53, 66, 84. Barr points out that other factors (information from spies) besides the quixotic temperament of the troops contributed to indecisions regarding the assault.

6. Huson, ed., *Barnard's Journal*, p. 12; Sam Houston to Thomas J. Rusk, Mar. 29, 1836, *PTR* 5:234–35; J. H. Bostick to [family], Apr. 14, 1836, *PTR* 5:466; Barker, "The San Jacinto Campaign," pp. 258, 284, 336; J. C. Duval, *Early Times in Texas* (Austin: H. P. N. Gammell, 1892), p. 45; Andrew Forest Muir, "The Mystery of San Jacinto," *Southwest Review* 36 (Spring, 1951): 80.

7. S. F. Austin [General Order], Nov. 12, 1835, *PTR* 2:381; Sam Houston, Army Orders, Apr. 3, 1836, AJH.

8. J. W. Fannin to J. W. Robinson, Feb. 16, 1836, *PTR* 4:351; Address of Branch T. Archer, Nov. 3, 1835, *PTR* 3:249; James H. Pohl and Stephen L. Hardin, "The Military History of the Texas Revolution: An Overview" *SHQ* 89 (Jan., 1986): 274–75.

9. Sam Houston to [the troops], May 11, 1836, *PTR* 6:220; John B. Allison to T. J. Rusk, June 14, 1836, *PTR* 7:143; J. H. McLendon, "John A. Quitman in the Texas Revolution," *SHQ* 52 (July, 1948): 176–77.

10. Jas. P. Caldwell to S. F. Austin, Dec. 8, 1835, *PTR* 3:115; Benj. J. White to S. Houston, Nov. 13, 1835, AJH.

11. Smithwick, *Evolution of a State*, p. 75; Pohl and Hardin, "Military History" (pp. 282–83), suggest that the poverty of the recruits accounts for the number who came without weapons.

12. Sam Houston to A. Hutchinson, Nov. 30, 1835, *PTR* 3:48; Taylor quoted in Mark E. Nackman, "The Making of the Texan Citizen Soldier, 1835–1860," *SHQ* 78 (Jan., 1975): 239.

13. Henry Smith to the Legislative Council of Texas, Nov. 16, 1835, *PTR* 2:439; David G. Burnet to James Morgan, May 28, 1836, *PTR* 6:393; Moses Lapham to Amos Lapham, Nov. 21, 1836, in Frantz, ed., "Moses Lapham," p. 469.

14. John Sowers Brooks to "My dear father," Dec. 23, 1835, *PTR* 3:296; John Sowers Brooks to "dear sister," Mar. 4, 1836, *PTR* 4:508; Gray, *From Virginia to Texas*, p. 118.

15. Smithwick, *Evolution of a State*, pp. 102–103; Ehrenberg, *With Milam and Fannin*, p. 183.

16. R. R. Royal to Sam Houston, Dec. 28, 1835, AJH.

17. Davenport, "The Men of Goliad," p. 18; J. W. Fannin to Genl. Mexia, Mar. 11, 1836, *PTR* 5:47; D. G. Burnet to Antonio López de Santa Anna, May 17, 1836, *PTR* 6:311–12.

18. Ralph W. Steen, ed., "A Letter from San Antonio de Béxar in 1836," *SHQ* 52 (Apr., 1959): 513–18; Walter Lord, *A Time to Stand* (New York: n.p., 1961), p. 55.

19. Sam Houston to David Thomas, Apr. 13, 1836, *PTR* 5:407; J. Hazard Perry to Robert Potter, Apr. 9, 1836, *PTR* 5:406; Sam Houston [Pardon], Apr. 9, [1836], AJH; G. W. H[ockley] to T. J. Rusk, Apr. 17, 1836, AJH.

20. Smithwick, *Evolution of a State*, p. 81; Affidavit of Ignacio Espinosa, Aug. 17, 1859, Agapito Texado folder, Court of Claims Collection, Archives Division, General Land Office, Austin (hereafter cited as GLO); Barker, "Texas Revolutionary Army," p. 249n1.

21. Barker, "San Jacinto Campaign," p. 243; Barker, "Texas Army," p. 259; Dixon and Kemp, *Heroes of San Jacinto*, pp. 235–37; Sam Houston to J. Collinsworth, Mar. 15, 1836; Sam Houston, Army Orders, Apr. 5, 8, 1836, AJH; Sam Houston to Nat Robbins, Apr. 15, 1836, AJH.

22. Thos. J. Rusk to M. B. Lamar, May 12, 15, 17, 1836, *PTR* 6:249 (first quotation), 301 (second quotation), 314; Thos. J. Rusk to J. W. E. Wallace, July 16, 1836, *PTR* 7:466.

23. Barker, "Texas Army," p. 249; Ehrenberg, *With Milam and Fannin*, pp. 44–45; Gambrell, *Lamar*, pp. 80–81; Sam Houston to Thomas J. Rusk, Mar. 23, 1836, *PTR* 5:168–70.

24. S. F. Austin, General Orders, Oct. 14, 1835, *PTR* 2:124; B. H. Duval to Sm. P. Duval, Mar. 9, 1836, *PTR* 5:34, 35; [Pedro Delgado], "Mexican Account of the Battle of San Jacinto," in Day, comp., *Texas Almanac*, p. 625; Marilyn McAdams Sibley, ed., "Letters From the Texas Army, Autumn, 1836: Leon Dyer to Thomas J. Green," *SHQ* 72 (Jan., 1969), 376, 378.

25. Lord, *A Time to Stand*, p. 40; Thos. J. Rusk to M. B. Lamar, May 17, 1836, *PTR* 6:314–15; *The Narrative of Robert Hancock Hunter* (Austin: Encino Press, 1966), p. 16.

26. Huson, ed., *Barnard's Journal*, p. 6; J. J. Baugh to Henry Smith, Feb. 13, 1836, AP.

27. Austin quoted in Barker, *Austin*, p. 73; *Narrative of Hunter*, p. 13; Thomas J. Rusk to Pinkney Caldwell, June 28, 1836, Rusk Papers; ———— Allen to ———— Lurlock, July 5, 1836, AJH; Sam Houston order, Apr. 7, 1836, *PTR* 5:362; J. Hazard Perry to Robert Potter, Apr. 9, 1836, *PTR* 5:406–408; Ordinance, Feb. 19, 1836, Proceedings of the Ayuntamiento, Subgroup Series 5, Subseries D, Nacogdoches Archives (microfilm, Genealogical Collection, TSA).

28. L. Smithers to S. F. Austin, Nov. 4, 1835, *PTR* 2:318–19; John F[isher] to Stephen F. Austin, Nov. 3, 1835, *PTR* 2:304–305.

29. (San Felipe) *Telegraph and Texas Register*, Dec. 2, 1835; Sam Houston et al. to the officers of the Army of the People, Nov. 13, 1835, Rusk Papers.

30. James Bowie and J. W. Fannin to Austin, Oct. 23, 1835, *PTR* 2:202; S. F. Austin to James Bowie and Fannin, Oct. 24, 1835, *PTR* 2:203; Barker, *Austin*, p. 485; Smithwick, *Evolution of a State*, p. 74; Barker, "Texas Army," p. 241.

31. Wm. H. Wharton to B. T. Archer, Nov. 26, 1835, *PTR* 2:520; Journals of the Consultation, Nov. 9, 1835, *PTR* 9:266; Thos. J. Rusk to James W. Robinson, Nov. 25, 1835, AP.

32. John S. Rutland to John W. Moore, Nov. 26, 1835, AP; B. B. Goodrich to the Legislative Council, Dec. 20, 1835, AP.

33. J. C. Neill to Sam Houston, Jan. 14, 1836, Private Correspondence of [the] General Council, GC; D. P. Cummings to Father, Jan. 20, 1836, *PTR* 4:86–87; Resolution Providing for the troops at Bejar, Jan. 17, 1836, PGL; J. W. Robinson to P. Dimitt, Jan. 18, 1836, AP.

34. J. C. Neill to Henry Smith, Jan. 27, 1836, AP; G. B. Jameson to Henry Smith, Feb. 11, 1836, Gov. Corr.

35. Jno R. Jones [to the Secretary of State], Mar. 25, 1836, Executive Record Book; Dixon and Kemp, *San Jacinto*, p. 240; Dilue Rose Harris, "Reminiscences of Dilue Harris," *QTSHA* 4 (Jan., 1901): 174–75.

36. D. G. Burnet to James Morgan, May 18, 1836, *PTR* 6:324; Wm. Atwell to T. J. Rusk, June 10, 1836, Rusk Papers.

37. Officers of the army to David G. Burnet, May 26, 1836, *PTR* 6:380; D. G. Burnet to M. B. Lamar, July 8, 1836, *PTR* 7:390; A. Huston to Secy of War, July 15, 1836, *PTR* 7:458–59.

38. Goliad Declaration, Dec. 20, 1835 [date of adoption, signed Dec. 22], Communications Received, GC.

39. [Resolution of] the Army of the People now Before Bejar, n. d., Rusk Papers; B. J. White to S. Houston, Nov. 13, 1835, AJH.

40. Goliad Declaration, Dec. 20, 1835; J. C. Neill to Henry Smith, Jan. 23, 1836, Gov. Corr.

41. F. W. Johnson to Wyatt Hanks and J. D. Clements, Dec. 24, 1835, *PTR* 3:305–308; M. Hawkins to Henry Smith, Jan. 20, 1836, *PTR* 4:88; Citizens' and Soldiers' Meeting to editor, *Brazoria Gazette*, Jan. 26, 1836, *PTR* 4:153–55.

42. Officers of the army to David G. Burnett [*sic*], May 26, 1836, *PTR* 6:379–82.

43. Thomas J. Rusk to David G. Burnet, June 11, 12, 1836, *PTR* 6:123–25, 136–37, 138 (quotation).

44. Thomas J. Rusk to Marabeau [*sic*] B. Lamar, June 1, 1836, *PTR* 6:486–87; Samuel Dexter, Report, June 4, 1836, *PTR* 7:19; [Rusk order], June 25, 1836, *PTR* 7:257.

45. Tho. J. Rusk to M. B. Lamar, May 29, 1836, *PTR* 6:410–11; H. A. Hubbell to ———, June 4, 1836, *PTR* 7:16; F. A. Sawyer to ——— Morgan, June 6, 1836, *PTR* 7:46; Arthur Henrie to T. Rusk, May 17, 1836, Rusk Papers.

46. David G. Burnet, Address to the Army of Texas, June 11, 1836, *PTR* 7:118; David G. Burnet to M. B. Lamar, July 8, 1836, *PTR* 7:393.

47. Charges and Specifications preferred against David G. Burnet Esquire a Citi-

zen of Texas by E. L. R. Whelock, July 14, 1836, *PTR* 7:446–48; Henry Millard, orders to A. Turner, July [16], 1836, Rusk Papers.

48. (Columbia) *Telegraph and Texas Register,* Aug. 16, 1836; David G. Burnet to T. J. Rusk, Aug. 5, 1836, *PTR* 8:127–28; David G. Burnet to James Collinsworth and Peter W. Grayson, Aug. 10, 1836, *PTR* 8:186; A. Huston to Thos. J. Rusk, July 19, 1836, Rusk Papers.

49. Thomas J. Rusk to A. Sommerville, July 25, 1836, *PTR* 8:32–33; Sam Houston to the General Commanding the Army, July 26, 1836, AP; Thos. J. Rusk to [Sam Houston], July 20, 1836, AJH.

50. T. J. Green to S. Houston, July 18, 1836, AJH.

51. Edward J. Wilson and G. L. Postlewhaite to the Public, Sept. 10, 1836, *PTR* 8:433–38; T. Jefferson Chambers to the Public, Oct. 24, 1836, *PTR* 9:113–16, 119, 122.

CHAPTER 9.

1. See Tables 2–8, chapter 7, on military participation. The best estimate of San Patricio's population is 600 in 1834, a figure that suggests that the Texas Revolution attracted scarcely any support in this Irish colony (Rachel B. Hébert, *The Forgotten Colony: San Patricio de Hibernia* [Burnet, Tex.: Eakin Press, 1981], p. 29).

2. Ibid., pp. 35, 357–61.

3. P. Dimitt to S. F. Austin, Oct. 17, 19, 1835, *PTR* 2:146, 165–67; Martín Perfecto de Cos to [José María Tornel], Nov. 2, 1835, *PTR* 2:299.

4. A. H. Jones to J. W. Fannin, Nov. 12, 1835, *PTR* 2:384; P. Dimitt to Stephen F. Austin, Nov. 13, 1835, *PTR* 2:391; Ira Westover to Saml Houston, Nov. 15, 1835, *PTR* 2:431–32; Hébert, *Forgotten Colony,* pp. 36, 123–25.

5. P. Dimitt to the Inhabitants east of the Guadalupe, Nov. 16, 1835, AP; Hébert, *Forgotten Colony,* p. 184.

6. Jno. Turner to P. Dimitt, Nov. 30, 1835, *PTR* 3:51; P. Dimitt to Henry Smith, Dec. 2, 1835, *PTR* 3:75; James McGloin to Lewis Ayers, Dec. 27, 1835, in Charles H. Ayers, "Lewis Ayers," *SHQ* 9 (Apr., 1906): 279.

7. José Enrique de la Peña, *With Santa Anna in Texas,* trans. Carmen Perry (College Station: Texas A&M University Press, 1975), pp. 82–85; Committee on State and Judiciary Report to the General Council, Jan. 15, 1836, Committee Reports, GC; Hébert, *Forgotten Colony,* pp. 25–26, 45n, 95, 116, 119, 120, 154, 175–76, 283–85, 429, 430, 432; R. R. Brown, "Expedition under Johnson and Grant," in Day, comp., *Texas Almanac,* p. 222.

8. The present account emphasizes the importance of local dynamics and of defending self-interest for all Texans of this period, regardless of ethnicity. A more definitive judgment about motivations and causation behind Tejano loyalties — for or against centralism — awaits additional research on the Mexican period of 1821–36. Clearly, no single, simple factor determined Tejano behavior. (Arnoldo De León, "Tejanos and the Texas War for Independence: Historiography's Judgment," *New Mexico Historical Review* 61 (Apr., 1986): 137–46; Gilberto M. Hinojosa and Gerald E. Poyo, "Mexican Texans in the Revolution," [paper read at the Texas State Historical Association meeting, March 5, 1986]).

9. Address of the Council to the Mexican People, quoted in Ralph W. Steen,

"Analysis of the Work of the General Council, Provisional Government of Texas, 1835–1836," *SHQ* 42 (July, 1938): 323; Thomas F. McKinney to the provisional Govt. of Texas, Dec. 22, 1835, *PTR* 3:293–94. Historians of Texas racial attitudes toward Mexicans disagree on the strength of Anglo prejudices and the role of this factor in determining policy in the Revolution. Arnoldo De León, *They Called Them Greasers* pp. 1–23, emphasizes the origins of racism in color prejudice and its pervasiveness even among moderates like Stephen F. Austin. James Ernest Crisp, "Anglo Texan Attitudes Toward the Mexican, 1821–1845" (Ph.D. diss., Yale University, 1976), pp. 7–194, views Anglo prejudices as slower to develop and less significant.

10. Steen, "General Council," p. 340; "El Ciudadano José María Gonzalez . . . á sus Concuidadonos," Dec. 10, 1835, Broadside Collection, TSA.

11. [Military Affairs Report, Dec. 6, 1835], *PTR* 3:102.

12. Address of Jonas Harrison, Dec. 22, 1835, *PTR* 3:290.

13. [Sam Houston] to Comrades, Citizens of Texas!, [Jan. 15, 1836], *PTR* 4:29–30.

14. Henry Smith to the Council, Dec. 12, 1835, *PTR* 3:174.

15. [Sam Houston] to Comrades, Citizens of Texas!, [Jan. 15, 1836], *PTR* 4:29–30.

16. Table 2 in chapter 7 quantifies the background of those who served in the fall of 1835. Twenty-two men, mostly Irish, came from the municipality of Refugio.

17. Roberto Galán to Esteban Austin, Nov. 13, 1835, APT; [Goliad public meeting record, Nov. 12, 1835] Proceedings, RCM.

18. Quoted in Davenport, "Men of Goliad," p. 12; Huson, *Refugio* 1:215.

19. Huson, *Refugio* 1:214, 217, 221, 223; Mtn. Perft° de Cós to [José María Tornel], Apr. 6, 1835, *PTR* 1:56–57.

20. Ehrenberg, *With Milam and Fannin*, p. 119; Duval, *Early Times*, p. 29.

21. [James W. Fannin to James W. Robinson, Feb. 21, 1836], *PTR* 4:392.

22. Huson, *Refugio* 1:160–61; Downs, "Mexicans in Texas," pp. 242–43; Harbert Davenport, "Captain Jesus Cuellar, Texas Cavalry, Otherwise 'Comanche'," *SHQ* 30 (July, 1926): 56–62; Receipts by P. Dimitt, Nov. 28, 1835, Feb. 2, 1836, by J. W. Fannin, Jr., Feb. 20, 1836, Carlos de la Garza folder, AMC.

23. José de Urrea, *Diary*, in Castañeda, trans., *Mexican Side*, pp. 215 (quotation), 231.

24. Ibid., p. 218; Lewis Ayres to "Father Sister and Brother," Dec. 26, 1836, in Ayers, "Ayers," 272–75; Huson, *Refugio* 1:288, 293–96; Duval, *Early Times*, p. 36; Webb, et al., eds., *Handbook of Texas* 1:702, 2:456; Field, *Three Years in Texas*, p. 29.

25. De la Teja and Wheat, "Béxar," p. 34; De León, "Historiography," 10.

26. Downs, "Mexicans in Texas," pp. 232–35; Joseph Martin Dawson, *José Antonio Navarro Co-Creator of Texas* (Waco, Tex.: Baylor University Press, 1969), p. 52n.

27. Angel Navarro to the Secretary of State of Coahuila and Texas, May 18, 1835, *PTR* 1:112–15; Angel Navarro, Chief of Internal police of the Department of Bejar to all its Inhabitants, Oct. 14, 1835, *PTR* 2:128–29; ——— to Juan Zenteno, Oct. 8, 1835, BA, reel 167, frame 160.

28. Martín Perfecto de Cos [address to the troops], Oct. 14, 1835, BA, reel 167, frame 231; Martín Perfecto de Cos to Angel Navarro, Oct. 15, 17, 1835, BA, reel 167, frames 236, 251–53; Reports on the condition of the army, Aug. 1, 31, 1835, Oct. 1, 1835, BA, reel 166, frames 199, 200, 521, reel 167, frame 70; Angel Navarro to [José María Flores], Oct. 18, 1835, BA, reel 167, frames 29–62; Angel Navarro to [Martín Perfecto de Cos], Oct. 20, 1835, BA, reel 167, frames 370–71. The Béxar cavalry com-

pany had between 87 and 93 men (mounted on 119 horses) between August and October, 1835; some of these were listed as stationed elsewhere, reducing the effective force by one-half. Some of them appear to have been given duty to guard the plaza, which would have kept them in Béxar. This presidial company thus had about eighty men when hostilities commenced in October, though some of them changed sides in response to federalist appeals of the besieging forces.

29. Martín Perfecto de Cos to [Angel Navarro], Oct. 23, 1835, BA, reel 167, frames 376–77; Martín Perfecto de Cos to Jefe Político de ese Departamento, Nov. 17, 1835, BA, reel 167, frame 411; S. F. Austin to Inhabitants of Béxar, Nov. 18, 1835, *PTR* 2:452–53.

30. Ehrenberg, *With Milam and Fannin,* pp. 82, 98 (quotation), 101–102, 112–15; Mag Siffs, account of Taking of San Antone, n. d., *PTR* 3:391.

31. W. B. Travis, [affidavit], Feb. 22, 1836, Antonio Cruz folder, AMC; Thomas H. Borden to the Voters of the Municipality of Austin, Jan. 19, 1836, APT.

32. James Presley, "Santa Anna in Texas," *SHQ* 62 (Apr., 1959): 492; De León, "Historiography," p. 7; Lord, *Time to Stand,* pp. 67, 80, 83, 92, 113–14.

33. W. Barrett Travis to the President of the Convention, Mar. 3, 1836, *PTR* 4:504.

34. Juan José Andrade to ———, Apr. 20, 1836, *PTR* 5:506; Richard G. Santos, *Santa Anna's Campaign Against Texas, 1835–1836* (Salisbury, N.C.: Documentary Publications, 1982), pp. 69, 83n; Election Returns, Apr. 6, 1836, BA, reel 167, frame 543.

35. Geo. W. Poe to the Permanent Council, Dec. 9, 1835, Communications Received, GC; de la Peña, *With Santa Anna,* p. 111.

36. Pedro Ellis Bean to [Domingo de Ugartechea], Aug. 18, 1835, *PTR* 1:352–53; Election poll book, town of Nacogdoches, Dec. 13, 1835, NA 85:5–28.

37. Vicente Córdova to the Alcalde of this village, Aug. 30, 1835, NA 83:231; Vicente Córdova, address to the Militia Co. of Nacogdoches, Aug. 31, 1835, Blake, 53:251.

38. Radford Berry to Vicente Córdova, Oct. 15, 1835, NAT 84:50; [Ayuntamiento minutes, 1835], NA 85:36; Vicente Córdova to the Alcalde of this village, Oct. 23, 1835, NA 84:59.

39. John M. Dor to Sam Houston, Nov. 29, 1835, *PTR* 3:22; Vicente Córdova to the citizen alcalde of this village, Oct. 20, Nov. 10, 1835, NA 84:57, 69.

40. Report of Committee . . . , Dec. 10, 1835, Raguet Family Papers, in Lois Foster Blount Papers, Ralph W. Steen Library, Special Collections, Stephen F. Austin University, Nacogdoches, Texas (hereafter cited as SFA). Arthur Henrie to Henry Smith, Jan. 3, 1836, *PTR* 3:412; Jas. Gaines to J. W. Robinson, Jan. 9, 1836, *PTR* 3:454–55.

41. Vicente Córdova to Manuel Flores, July 19, 1835, *PTR* 1:256; J. Bonnell to E. P. Gaines, June 4, 7, 1836, *PTR* 7:9–10, 47; Deposition of Juan Francisco Basques [Vásquez], Parish of Natchitoches, Sept. 7, 1836, *PTR* 8:409; [Affadavit of Miguel Cortines], July 10, 1836, Blake 3:258–60.

42. D. A. Hoffman, Notice Given at my office in the Town of Nacogdoches, Apr. 9, 1836, AJH.

43. R. A. Irion to Sam Houston, Apr. 17, 1836, AJH; Henry Raguet to Saml Houston, Apr. 17, 1836, AJH.

44. Vicente Córdova to R. A. Irion, Apr. 14, 1836, AJH.

45. R. A. Irion to V. Córdova, Apr. 14 [two different letters on this day], Apr. 15, 1836, AJH.

46. Henry Raguet to Saml Houston, Apr. 17, 1836, AJH; R. A. Irion to Sam Houston, Apr. 17, 1836, AJH; Sam Houston, "Campaign of 1836," in Day, comp., *Texas*

Almanac, pp. 275; Sam Houston to Henry Raguet, July 4, 1836, Nacogdoches Committee of Vigilance and Safety Records.

47. Sam Houston to Wylie Martin, Apr. 2, 1836, *PTR* 5:294; José Urrea to [Benjamin Harrison], *PTR* 5:428.

48. José Urrea to Antonio López de Santa Anna, Apr. 22, 1836, *PTR* 6:18–20; Antonio López de Santa Anna, *Manifesto . . . ,* in Castañeda, *Mexican Side,* pp. 22–23; Urrea, *Diary,* pp. 241–42; Henson, "Tory Sentiment," p. 25.

49. Sam Houston to T. J. Rusk, Mar. 29, 1836, *PTR* 5:234–35; Eugene C. Barker, "James H. C. Miller and Edward Gritten," *QTSHA* 13:149–53; Barker, "Don Carlos Barrett," p. 144; Gray, *From Virginia to Texas,* p. 151.

50. J. Gaines [to D. G. Burnet, Mar. 28, 1836], *PTR* 5:215; J. Morgan [to David G. Burnet], Apr. 10, 1836, 424–25.

51. Webb, et al., eds., *Handbook,* 1:129, 2:513–14. Charges of refusal to surrender their political authority that derived from the Mexican constitution were levelled against Shelby judges E. Rainey and James English, Jr., and Nacogdoches land official Radford Berry (Sydney O. Perrington to David G. Burnet, May 15, 1836, *PTR* 6:300; S. H. Everitt to David G. Burnet, Mar. 17, 1836, *PTR* 5:120–21). On the case of Pedro [Peter] E. Bean, see Sam Houston to David A. Hoffman, Apr. 13, 1836, AJH; Santos, *Santa Anna Campaign,* p. 43; John Sprowl, Certificate as to the conduct of Ellis Bean, NA 85:59.

52. Thos. J. Rusk to Pres. Burnet, Apr. 10, 1836, AP; R. R. Royall to S. F. Austin, [October] 16, 1835, *PTR* 2:140–41. Historians disagree about the strength and genuineness of Tory sentiment in the Liberty-Anáhuac area. Andrew Forest Muir, "Tories in Texas, 1836," *Texana* 4 (Summer, 1964): 81–94, dismisses much of the rumors of Toryism as part of a gossiping oral tradition, while other scholars document and explain the conduct of those who supported Mexico out of economic interest and loyalty (Henson, "Tory Sentiment," pp. 27, 31; Kent Gardien, "Kokernot and His Tory," *Texana* 8 [1970]: 271, 277–78; W. B. Scates, "Early History of Anahuac," in Day, comp., *Texas Almanac,* pp. 681–82).

53. Gray, *Virginia to Texas,* p. 166; Gardien, "Kokernot," pp. 269–70.

54. Hervey Whiting to James Morgan, May 3, 1836, *PTR* 6:157–58. Other witnesses charged that Whiting had served as a courier for the Mexican army to carry Santa Anna's proclamation. Henson, "Tory Sentiment," pp. 25, 28, includes him on her list of Liberty-area Tories. Muir devotes several pages to exonerating Whiting ("Tories in Texas," pp. 87–93).

55. Muir, "Tories in Texas," pp. 87, 93–94; H. Whiting to J. Morgan, May 8, 1836, *PTR* 4:157; James Reed to J. Morgan, June 8, 1836, *PTR* 7:71; Tom Turner to Dearest Mother, Sept. 8, 1836, *PTR* 8:415. Tom Turner may have served as a messenger to other east Texans for Santa Anna, though Muir asserts that the man referred to as Turner by various accounts was a slave of James Morgan.

56. Gardien, "Kokernot," p. 276. Henson, "Tory Sentiment," pp. 11, 19, 27, 32–34, provides the names of twenty-seven Tory suspects for the period March–May, 1836. Other sources included in compiling the group biographical profile include Webb, et al., eds. *Handbook,* 1:525, 2:894; White, *1830 Citizens of Texas,* pp. 137, 146, 149, 160, 170, 176, 194, 195, 196, 197, 225; Mary McMillan Osborn, "The Atascosita Census of 1826," *Texana* 1 (Fall, 1963): 305, 307, 308; Muir, "Texas Tories," pp. 87, 92; Gardien, "Kokernot," pp. 280–84.

57. Williams signed a petition but was not heard from after that ([Petition], Mar. 3,

1836, *PTR* 4:50–56). On Winfree, see Henson, "Tory Sentiment," pp. 32–34; Gardien, "Kokernot," pp. 280–84; Gray, *Virginia to Texas*, pp. 281–83.

58. Henson, "Tory Sentiment," pp. 11, 32–34; Miller, *Bounty and Donation Grants*, pp. 92, 452, 696. On the arrest of Winfree and others see E. F. Stanley to James Morgan, May 15, 1836, *PTR* 6:299.

59. Gardien, "Kokernot," pp. 270–72, reproduces Houston's order as genuine, though the original document is not extant.

60. Hervey Whiting to James Morgan, May 3, 1836, *PTR* 6:157–58.

61. Gardien, "Kokernot," p. 269; [Endorsement at the end of the letter] Sam Houston to D. L. Kokernot, Apr. 30, 1836, *PTR* 6:129; D. G. Burnet to James Morgan, May 16, 1836, *PTR* 6:308; Chas. Hawkins to C. Gallegher, May 15, 1836, *PTR* 6:293; Wm. Scott to Genl. Rusk, May 17, 1836, Rusk Papers.

62. H. H. Edwards to Thos J. Rusk, May 11, 1836, *PTR* 6:222; Thos. J. Green to editor, Aug. 6, 1836, *PTR* 8:139–40.

63. Jesse Turner to [T. J.] Rusk, June 11, 1836, Rusk Papers; Urrea, *Diary*, p. 231; de la Peña, *With Santa Anna*, pp. 172–73, 185; [Vicente Filisola], *Evacuation of Texas* (Waco: Texian Press, 1965), pp. 21–22; Andrew A. Boyle, "Reminiscences of the Texas Revolution," *QTSHA* 13 (Apr., 1910): 290; Hébert, *Forgotten Colony*, p. 190.

64. Bonifacio Rodríguez to José de Urrea, Oct. 6, 1836, *PTR* 9:64; Antonio López de Santa Anna to José de Urrea, Mar. 29, 1836, in Umberto Daniel Filisola, ed., "Correspondence of Santa Anna during the Texas Campaign, 1835–1836" (M.A. thesis, University of Texas, 1939), pp. 76–77; Downs, "Mexicans in Texas," pp. 243–44.

65. Duval, *Early Times*, p. 29; Downs, "Mexicans in Texas," p. 247.

66. Huson, ed., *Barnard's Journal*, pp. 30–33, 34.

67. Quoted in Downs, "Mexicans in Texas," p. 246.

68. José María Ortiz to the Senior Govr of the Department of Coahuila and Texas, August, 1836, Guerra y Marina, Archivo General de Mexico, BTHC, pp. 51–53; Juna N. Seguín to Thomas J. Rusk, [June 7, 1836], Rusk Papers; José Urréa to Mtro. de la Guerra y Marina, Sept. 2, 1836, Rusk Papers.

69. Juan Nepomuceno Seguín to the inhabitants of Béxar, June 21, 1836, *PTR* 7:224; Muir, ed., *Texas in 1837*, p. 107.

CHAPTER 10.

1. Tijerina, "Tejanos and Texas," pp. 18, 35.

2. Sam J. Smith to Edward Miles, Sept. 21, 1874, José Almeda folder, Republic Pension Applications (hereafter cited as RPA), Comptroller of Public Accounts, TSA; Juan Seguín to the Comptroller of the State, Dec. 5, 1874, ibid. Smith validated his assessment by his knowledge of the claimants, the fact that other veterans did not come forth to expose false claims, and the fact that Sam A. Maverick, a participant in the storming of December 5–10 "always in his lifetime recognized them all as fellow soldiers." Juan Seguín recalled that "no muster rolls were made while we were besieging Bexar," but an unsigned statement in the muster roll files described the roll of the Mexicans as "being misplaced" (Adjutant General Military Rolls, Texas Revolution, 1835–1836, TSA). See also Downs, "Mexicans in Texas," pp. 233–34.

3. Juan Seguín to the Comptroller of the State, Dec. 5, 1874, José Almeda folder,

RPA; Seguín et al. to Darden, Jan. 12, 1875, pp. 81–82. Downs, "Mexicans in Texas," pp. 233–34, attributes the fact that small numbers received bounty or donation grants to several factors, especially growing ethnic tensions, poor communications, and migration out of Texas. Two sources supplied the Spanish surnames on which all the group profiles of military service by Tejanos are based. Most names and dates of service came from Miller, *Bounty and Donation Grants*, while a few came from a search of Spanish surnames in Republic Pension Applications, Audited Military Claims, and Unpaid Claims Files, TSA. These archival sources also supplied some biographical materials, supplementing the data in Gifford White, *1830 Citizens of Texas*.

4. S. F. Austin to James Bowie and Capt. Fannin, Oct. 24, 1835, *PTR* 2:149; S. F. Austin to J. W. Fannin, Nov. 14, 1835, *PTR* 2:406; S. F. Austin to Salvador Flores, Nov. 14, 1835, *PTR* 2:407; S. F. Austin [certificate on Juan Seguín], Nov. 24, 1835, BA, reel 167, frame 412.

5. An Act for the relief of María Jesusa García, Feb. 1, 1844, María Jesusa García folder, Audited Civil Service Records, TSA; DeWees, *Letters from an Early Texas Settler to a Friend*, p. 159; Seguín, *Memoirs*, pp. 7–8; W. B. Travis, [certificate], Feb. 22, 1836, Antonio Cruz folder, AMC.

6. Cos to Navarro, Nov. 17, 1835, BA, reel 167, frame 411; John W. Smith [to Thomas W. Chambers], Sept. 2, 1835, *PTR* 1:407–408; P. Dimitt to S. F. Austin, Oct. 20, 1835, *PTR* 2:172; Martín Perfecto de Cos to Angel Navarro, Oct. 15, 1835, BA, reel 167, frame 236–38; Cos to Navarro, Oct. 23, 1835, BA, reel 167, frame 375; Angel Navarro to [Martín Perfecto de Cos], Oct. 20, 1835, BA, reel 167, frame 370; Navarro to Cos, Oct. 25, 1835, BA, reel 167, frame 381.

7. David B. Macomb to ———, [Oct. 5, 1835], *PTR* 2:50; [S. F. Austin] to José María Gonzales, Nov. 18, 1835, *PTR* 2:450; J. W. Fannin, Jr. to Stephen F. Austin, Nov. 18, 1835, *PTR* 2:457; Macedonio Arocha folder, RPA; Field, *Three Years in Texas*, pp. 18–19.

8. James Bowie and J. W. Fannin, Jr. to [Stephen F.] Austin, Oct. 22, 1835, *PTR* 2:190–91; S. F. Austin to James Bowie, Oct. 27, 1835, *PTR* 2:230; Seguín, *Memoirs*, pp. 16–17; Martín Perfecto de Cos to [Angel Navarro], Oct. 23, 1835, BA, reel 167, frames 376–77.

9. [S. F. Austin, Proclamation to the Inhabitants of Béxar, ca. Nov. 18, 1835], *PTR* 2:452–54.

10. F. W. Johnson et al. [to S. F. Austin], Nov. 6, 1835, *PTR* 2:338–39; Military Affairs Committee Report, Dec. 6, 1835, *PTR* 3:102–104.

11. James Bowie and J. W. Fannin, Jr., to [Stephen F.] Austin, Oct. 22, 23, 1835, *PTR* 2:190–91, 202–203; Stephen F. Austin to Antonio de la Garza, Nov. 16, 1835, *PTR* 2:433.

12. S. F. Austin to James Bowie and Capt. Fannin, Oct. 24, 1835, *PTR* 2:206; [Receipt by Esteban F. Austin], Nov. 11, 1835, Luis Gonzales folder, AMC; [Receipt by Juan N. Seguín], Feb. 4, 1837, José María Arocha folder, AMC; S. F. Austin to Juan Seguín, Oct. 24, 1835, *PTR* 2:208; S. F. Austin to Patrick C. Jack, Nov. 17, 1835, *PTR* 2:444–45.

13. S. F. Austin to the Provisional Government of Texas, Nov. 30, 1835, *PTR* 3:42; [Power of attorney by Josefa Jimenez], Antonio Cruz folder, AMC; Receipts, Erasmo Seguín folder, AMC.

14. S. F. Austin, ["confidential" letter to the Consultation], Nov. 5, 1835, Letters Received, Records of the Consultation; R. B. Irvine to [Sam Houston], Nov. 7, 1835,

AJH; S. F. Austin to Edwd. Burleson, Nov. 15, 1835, *PTR* 2:417–19; J. W. Fannin to [Sam Houston], Nov. 18, 1835, *PTR* 2:459.

15. Mag Siffs, account of Taking of San Antone, n.d., *PTR* 3:391; Ehrenberg, *With Milam and Fannin*, p. 82; [Cos Capitulation], Dec. 11, 1835, *PTR* 3:157. Other civilian casualties occurred as a result of firing from the centralist side (M. L. Cummins, ed., "The Storming of San Antonio de Bexar in 1835," *West Texas Historical Association Yearbook* 22 [1946]: 114).

16. J. W. Fannin to [Sam Houston], Nov. 18, 1835, *PTR* 2:459; Barr, *Texans in Revolt*, pp. 68–71, 76–80, 83.

17. J. Antonio Padilla to Lorenzo Zavala, Oct. 8, 1835, *PTR* 2:72; Austin [to the Council] Nov. 3, 1835, PGL; Benj. F. Smith to [S. F. Austin], Oct. 13, 1835, *PTR* 2:121; P. Dimitt to S. F. Austin, Oct. 15, 1835, *PTR* 2:134; [Certificate by Thomas G. Western], June 8, 1836, Miguel Galán folder, [Affidavit, n. d.], Tomás Amador folder, AMC; [Unsigned certificate], Agustín Bernal folder, RPA; [Affidavit, n. d.], Paulino de la Garza folder, Court of Claims Collection, GLO.

18. Smithwick, *Evolution of a State*, p. 18; Receipt by P. Dimitt, Oct. 10, 1835, C. E. Vásquez folder, AMC; Receipt by P. Dimitt, Oct. 15, 1835, Domingo Falcón folder, AMC; Receipt by P. Dimitt, Nov. 26, 1835, Antonio Vásquez folder; AMC; Receipt by P. Dimitt, Nov. 28, 1835, Carlos de la Garza folder, AMC; Receipt by P. Dimitt, Nov. 29, 1835, Gertrudio Méndez folder, AMC; Receipt by P. Dimitt, Dec. 4, 1835, Ignacio Cantú folder, AMC; Receipt by P. W. Humphries, Oct. 17, 1837, Erasmo Seguín folder, AMC; Bartolome Pagés to the Council of the Provisional Government, Dec. 2, 1835, *PTR* 3:80–81.

19. P. Dimitt to S. F. Austin, Oct. 27, 1835, *PTR* 2:233; Certificate by P. Dimitt, Nov. 26, 1835, Andrés Guzmán folder, AMC; Roberto Galán to Stephen Austin, Nov. 13, 1835, APT.

20. P. Dimitt to S. F. Austin, Oct. 17, 25, 1835, *PTR* 2:146, 217; John J. Linn to Austin, Nov. 11, 1835, *PTR* 2:379.

21. P. Dimitt to Stephen F. Austin, Nov. 13, 1835, *PTR* 2:390–91; A. H. Jones to J. W. Fannin, Nov. 12, 1835, *PTR* 2:384–85; A Record of the public meeting held in Goliad on Nov. 12, 1835, RCM.

22. P. Dimitt, General Order, Nov. 12, 1835, *PTR* 2:382; Thomas G. Western to S. F. Austin, Nov. 13, 1835, *PTR* 2:402; Roberto Galán to Esteban Austin, Nov. 13, 1835, AP; Proceedings of a Public Meeting at Texana, Dec. 30, 1835, Communications Received, GC.

23. J. W. Fannin to J. W. Robinson, Feb. 16, 1836, *PTR* 4:351; Huson, ed., *Barnard's Journal*, pp. 8, 13.

24. Certificate by Bernard A. Bee, Oct. 23, 1837, Juan A. Zambrano folder, AMC; Affidavits by J. Bennett, Nov. 30, 1837, J. Snively, n. d. (quotation), Ed Patterson, Dec. 31, 1838, Victor Loupy folder, AMC; affidavit by Miguel Benítez, Dec. 5, 1874, Miguel Benítez folder, RPA; Robert Morris to [James W. Fannin], Feb. 6, 1836, *PTR* 4:274–75.

25. James W. Robinson to Fernando de León, Feb. 14, 1836, quoted in A. B. J. Hammett, *The Empresario Don Martín De León* (Waco: Texian Press), pp. 136–37; Ernest C. Shearer, "The Caravajal Disturbances," *SHQ* 55 (Oct., 1951): 202; J. W. Fannin, Jr. to Henry Smith, Dec. 11, 1835, *PTR* 3:158–60; S. Rhoads Fisher to the Provisional Government of Texas, Dec. 17, 1835, *PTR* 3:219–21.

26. Ehrenberg, *With Milam and Fannin,* pp. 119–20; Receipt by A. C. Horton, Mar. 14, 1836, José María Hernández folder, AMC; Certificate by A. C. Horton, Sept. 17, 1836, Manuel Zepeda folder, AMC; Receipt by Thos. K. Pearson, Dec. 5, 1835, M. López folder, AMC; Affidavit of Esteban Cisneros, Oct. 9, 1857, Esteban Cisneros folder, Unpaid Claims, Comptroller of Public Accounts Collection, TSA.

27. Duval, *Early Times,* p. 60; Downs, "Mexicans in Texas," pp. 242–43; Antonio López de Santa Anna to [José de] Urrea, Mar. 3, 1836, *PTR* 4:501; Samuel G. Hardaway to Robert Collins, June 6, 1836, *PTR* 7:41; Affidavit by P. Dimitt, Apr. 20, 1836, Mariano Carabajal folder, AMC. Francisco García and other members of A. C. Horton's company escaped after the battle of Coleto (Pay Certificate, Francisco García folder, AMC).

28. Antonio López de Santa Anna to David G. Burnet, May 23, 1836, *PTR* 6:361; John Joseph Linn, *Reminiscences of Fifty Years in Texas* (New York: D & J Sadlier, 1883), pp. 125–26.

29. Quoted in Linn, *Reminiscences,* pp. 249, 284; Downs, "Mexicans in Texas," pp. 243–44; Hammett, *De León,* p. 48.

30. Affidavit of Macedonio Arocha, n. d., Macedonio Arocha folder, RPA; Downs, "Mexicans in Texas," p. 234.

31. J. C. Neill to the Governor and Council, Jan. 6, 1836, Communications Received, GC; Ehrenberg, *With Milam and Fannin,* pp. 112–14; Receipts by F. W. Johnson, Dec. 16, 25, 1835, Juan José Casillas folder, Higinio Cuéllar folder, AMC; Receipt by Juan N. Seguín, Feb. 12, 1836, María Jesusa de Treviño folder, AMC; Certificate by Juan Nepomuceno Seguín, n.d., Antonio Cruz folder, AMC.

32. Ehrenberg, *With Milam and Fannin,* p. 98; James W. Robinson, Message to the Council, Jan. 14, 1836, *PTR* 4:25; Resolution providing for the troops at Bejar, Jan. 16, 1836, PGL; Receipt by F. W. Johnson, Dec. 26, 1835, Receipt by Robt. Morris, Jan. 1, 1836, José Antonio Navarro folder, AMC; Certificate of payment, Dec. 13, 1836, Francisco Antonio Ruiz folder, AMC; Lord, *Time to Stand,* p. 57.

33. J. C. Neill to Sam Houston, Jan. 14, 1836, Communications Received, GC; G. B. Jameson to Sam Houston, Jan. 18, 1836, *PTR* 4:59; James Bowie to H. Smith, Feb. 2, 1836, *PTR* 4:238.

34. W. Barrett Travis to Henry Smith, Feb. 13, 1836, *PTR* 4:328; J. J. Baugh to H. Smith, Feb. 13, 1836, General Correspondence, AP.

35. Downs, "Mexicans in Texas," pp. 235–37; J. C. Neill to the Governor and Council, Jan. 14, 1836, *PTR* 4:15; D. P. Cummings to Father, Jan. 20, 1836, *PTR* 4:87; Lord, *Time to Stand,* p. 69.

36. Lord, *Time to Stand,* pp. 113–14; Downs, "Mexicans in Texas," pp. 237–38; Santos, *Santa Anna's Campaign,* p. 70.

37. Lord, *Time to Stand,* pp. 83–84; Ben Proctor, *The Battle of the Alamo* (Austin: Texas State Historical Association, 1986), pp. 23, 26; Antonio López de Santa Anna to José de Urrea, Mar. 3, 1836, *PTR* 4:501; José Reyes López to Antonio López de Santa Anna, Apr. 5, 1837, in Castañeda, trans., *Mexican Side,* p. 53.

38. Antonio López de Santa Anna to the Inhabitants of Texas, Mar. 7, 1836, *PTR* 5:20–21; Juan José Andrade to ———, Apr. 20, 1836, *PTR* 5:506; Francis Antonio Ruiz, "Fall of the Alamo," in Day, comp., *Texas Almanac,* pp. 356–57; de la Peña, *With Santa Anna,* p. 59.

39. Seguín, *Memoirs,* pp. 7–12; José Antonio Menchaca, Reminiscences, 1807–1836,

Typescript, Part I, p. 7, Part II, pp. 3–4, BTHC. The identities of Tejanos who served at San Jacinto derived from several sources: Sixteen names (with different spellings) appear on both donation lists and muster rolls and are given brief biographical sketches in Dixon and Kemp, *Heroes of San Jacinto.* These authors added five other names. Three more came from donation warrants. Those who do research for the San Jacinto foundation have recently added two names; another came from the rolls of the company raised by Haden Arnold at Nacogdoches, which fought at San Jacinto. Seguín much later presented affidavits of five more soldiers who were also in his company at San Jacinto.

40. One source gave the size of Flores company as twenty-five (Affidavit by Domingo Díaz, Dec. 22, 1858, Clemente García folder, Court of Claims Records, GLO). Seguín estimated this unit at "more than forty men" (Juan Seguín to the Comptroller of the State, Dec. 5, 1874, José Almeda folder, RPA). In another letter a few days later Seguín placed the number who served in the spring of 1836 at seventy-one (not counting the forty-six in his command with Houston). These included twenty-eight under Flores and forty-three with Deaf Smith and others escorting Anglo families or in similar duty (Juan Seguín et al to Stephen H. Darden, Jan. 12, 1875, *Texana* 5:82–84).

41. Agustín Bernal affidavit, Nov. 28, 1874, Agustín Bernal folder, RPA; Downs, "Mexicans in Texas," p. 246; Seguín, *Memoirs,* p. 17.

42. George A. Nixon to Stephen F. Austin, Oct. 10, 20, 1835, *PTR* 2:88, 168; Enrique Rueg to the Constitutional Alcalde of this village of Nacogdoches, Oct. 20, 1835, *PTR* 2:170.

43. Henry Rueg to Thomas J. Rusk, Nov. 9, 1835, *PTR* 2:371; Certificates by Thos. J. Rusk and Henry Raguet, May 1, 1837, Miguel Cortines folder, AMC.

44. The service of these Tejanos was identified from bounty warrants or donation certificates or from their claims records. See Miller, *Bounty and Donation Grants,* pp. 89, 723, 818, 837; Juan J. Ybarbo folder, Public Debt Papers, Comptroller of Public Accounts Collection, TSA; Squire Cruse folder, Unpaid Claims; Casimiro García folder, AMC.

45. Gray, *From Virginia to Texas,* pp. 92–96.

46. Sam Houston to H. Raguet, June 30, 1836, AJH; Sterling C. Robertson to T. J. Rusk, June 18, 1836, *PTR* 7:198; Records of the Office of Alcalde, Blake.

47. Huson, ed., *Barnard's Journal,* p. 34; Edwd. Burleson to T. J. Rusk, May 5, 1836; Juan N. Seguín to Thomas J. Rusk [June 7, 1836], General Correspondence, Rusk Papers; [Filisola], *Evacuation of Texas,* p. 48; James Smith to T. J. Rusk, June 8, 1836, *PTR* 7:75–76.

48. Thos. J. Rusk to James Smith, June 8, 1836, *PTR* 7:74; José María Ortiz to the Senior Governor of the Department of Coahuila and Texas, August ——, 1836, Guerra y Marina, Archivo General.

49. Thomas J. Rusk to [Sam Houston], July 20, 1836, *PTR* 7:505; Juan Seguín "TO THE INHABITANTS OF BEXAR," June 21, 1836, *PTR* 7:224.

50. T. J. Rusk to Miguel Arciniega, Aug. 5, 1836, *PTR* 8:133.

51. Order No. 1, John A. Wharton to Juan N. Seguín, Sept. 17, 1836, Juan N. Seguín folder, AMC; Thos. J. Rusk to Col. Ruiz, Aug. 29, 1836, *PTR* 8:346–47.

52. Seguín, *Memoirs,* p. 18; Menchaca, Reminiscences, Part III, p. 22.

53. Lord, *Time to Stand,* p. 92; Dawson, *Navarro,* pp. 62–63; Receipt by Juan N. Seguín, Feb. 20, 1837, José Antonio Navarro folder, AMC; Receipt by Juan N. Seguín,

Apr. 2, 1837, Luciano Navarro folder, AMC; Receipts by Juan Seguín, June 20, 1836, Feb. 24, 1837, José Antonio de la Garza folder, AMC; (Columbia) *Telegraph and Texas Register,* Nov. 9, 1836.

54. De la Peña, *With Santa Anna,* p. 185; José Urrea to the Secretary of War and Navy, June 1, 15, 1836, *PTR* 6:493–96, 7:160–61; Vicente Filisola, *Representation,* in Castañeda, *Mexican Side,* p. 185.

55. S. Sherman to Rusk, May 23, 1836, Rusk Papers; Tho. J. Rusk to M. B. Lamar, May 17, 1836, *PTR* 6:314–15; J. M. Burton to Thos. J. Rusk, May 30, 1836, *PTR* 6:414.

56. H. Teal and H. W. Karnes to Thos. J. Rusk, June 2, [1836], *PTR* 6:502.

57. Robert W. Shook, ed., "A Letter from John J. Linn," *SHQ* 72 (Oct., 1968): 240; Linn, *Reminiscences,* p. 200; Smithwick, *Evolution of a State,* p. 102.

58. Certificate by T. J. Rusk, Nov. 23, 1837, María Antonia de la Garza folder, AMC; Juan N. Seguín, Certificate, June 15, 1836, Luciano Navarro folder, AMC; P. Caldwell, Receipt, June 22, 1836, Plácido Benavides folder, AMC; Receipts by Thos. J. Rusk, May 30, 1836, Thos. J. Green, Oct. 30, 1836, Miguel Alderete folder, AMC.

59. Thomas J. Rusk to A. Somerville, June 19, 1836, *PTR* 7:203; John Forbes to T. J. Rusk, June 25, 1836, *PTR* 7:254; F[airfax] C[atelet] to Editor, July 20, 1836, *PTR* 7:495; Thomas J. Rusk to P. Dimitt, June 22, 1836, Rusk Papers; Thomas J. Rusk to Pinkney Caldwell, June 28, 1836, Rusk Papers.

60. Huson, *Refugio* 1:398; Henry W. Barton, "The Problem of Command in the Army of the Republic of Texas," *SHQ* 62 (Jan., 1959): 304; Thos. J. Rusk to J. W. E. Wallace, July 16, 1836, *PTR* 7:466.

61. Hammett, *De León,* p. 70; Huson, *Refugio,* 1:402.

62. (Columbia) *Telegraph and Texas Register,* Dec. 17, 1836; Discharge papers by Secretary of War William J. Fisher, May 15, 1837, Martín Flores folder, AMC.

CHAPTER II.

1. (Brazoria) *Texas Republican,* Oct. 11, 1835; (San Felipe) *Telegraph and Texas Register,* Oct. 17, 1835.

2. Susan Wroe Edwards Thorn Journal, 1835–1836, SFA, pp. 46, 48; F. Thorn to the Committee of Vigilance and Safety, Oct. 20, 1835, *PTR* 2:169; Committee of Vigilance & Safety Records, Nacogdoches, Nov. 7, 9, 10, 1835, Dec. 9, 1835, Raguet Family Papers, SFA; Karl Wilson Baker, "Following the New Orleans Greys" *Southwest Review* 22 (Apr., 1937): 222–23.

3. Thorn Journal, pp. 4 (quotation), 48.

4. Ibid., p. 5; Harris, "Reminiscences," 126; William H. Oberste, *Texas Irish Empresarios and Their Colonies* (Austin: n.p., 1953), p. 153; Receipts by Matthew Caldwell, Dec. 8, 18, 1835, Horace Eggleton folder, AMC.

5. Nacogdoches Committee of Safety Records, Raguet Papers.

6. Journal of the Proceedings of the Council, Oct. 14, 1835; B. B. Goodrich to the Council, Dec. 12, 1835, AP; Receipt by D. Crockett, Jan. 23, 1836, John Lott folder, AMC; Receipt by J. D. McLeod, James Martin folder, AMC; Affidavit by James F. Perry, Robert Mills folder, AMC; Receipts by Henry Millard, Dec. 27, 1835, and Wm. Pettus, Jan. 19, 1836, Mrs. A. B. Peyton folder, AMC; Ledger of Martha A. Reed, Martha A. Reed folder, AMC; Receipt by J. G. Read, Nov. 28, 1835, AMC.

7. (San Felipe) *Telegraph and Texas Register,* Oct. 26, 1835; (Brazoria) *Texas Republican,* Sept. 26, 1835.

8. H. Austin to S. F. Austin, Dec. 15, 1835, *PTR* 3:196; Wm. K. English to Editor, Oct. 16, 1835, *PTR* 2:139; Albert Martin to [Don Carlos] Barrett, Dec. 19, 1835, *PTR* 3:261.

9. Haden Edwards to the Council, Nov. 26, 1835, *PTR* 2:516; Spencer H. Jack to the Council, Jan. 9, 1836, *PTR* 3:456–57; Henry Millard to T. B. Huling, Apr. 7, 1836, Thomas Byers Huling Papers, BTHC; John Forbes to James W. Robinson, Dec. 23, 1835, *PTR* 3:298–99; Gray, *From Virginia to Texas, 1835,* pp. 88, 93, 107; Samuel T. Allen to Caleb J. Miller, May 18, 1836, Marc S. Simmons, ed., "Samuel T. Allen and the Texas Revolution," *SHQ* 68 (Apr., 1965): 484.

10. C. H. Sims to Radford Berry, Aug. 24, 1835, NA 83:217; McLendon, "Quitman," p. 170.

11. J. S. Robertson to [D. C.] Barrett, Feb. 8, 1836, *PTR* 4:290–91; Report of the Committee on State and Judiciary, Jan. 3, 1836, Committee Reports, GC; David G. Burnet et al., to James W. Robinson, Feb. 28, 1836, *PTR* 4:452–53; Saml. Williams et al., to James W. Robinson, Mar. 3, 1836, *PTR* 4:505–506.

12. (San Felipe) *Telegraph and Texas Register,* Oct. 17, 1835; Charles Wilson to R. R. Royall, Dec. 24, 1835, PGL, 109–10.

13. (San Felipe) *Telegraph and Texas Register,* Oct. 10, 1835; R. R. Royall to Stephen F. Austin, Sept. 30, 1835, *PTR* 1:510; Wm. G. Harris to Judge Hanks et al., Jan. 19, 1836, Don Carlos Barrett Papers; Thorn Journal, 1, 4, 48; [Harriet A. Ames], "The History of H. Ames," BTHC, p. 15.

14. Silas M. Parker to the General Council, Dec. 17, 1835. *PTR* 3:230; John S. Rutland to John W. Moore, Nov. 26, 1835, AP; Thorn Journal, p. 5; [Sam Houston] to the Citizens of Texas West of the Red River, July 2, 1836, AJH; (San Felipe) *Telegraph and Texas Register,* Oct. 17, 1835.

15. J. G. Ferguson to A. J. Ferguson, Mar. 2, 1836, *PTR* 4:489; (San Felipe) *Telegraph and Texas Register,* Feb. 20 (third quotation), 27 (second quotation), 1836. See Table 3 in chapter 7 for analysis of the army make-up in the winter of 1835–36.

16. Antonio López de Santa Anna to Antonio Gaona, Mar. 22, 1836, *PTR* 5:163; José María Tornel to the Public, Apr. 9, 1836, *Texas as Province and Republic 1795–1845, the Bibliography by Thomas W. Streeter* (microfilm; hereafter cited as *Streeter*), BTHC; Antonio López de Santa Anna to Vicente Filisola, Jan. 22, 1836, Filisola, ed., "Correspondence of Santa Anna During the Texas Campaign, 1835–1836," p. 48.

17. Ant° Lopez de Santa Anna to [José María Tornel], Mar. 18, 1836, Guerra y Marina, Archivo General; Joaquín Ramírez y Sesma to Antonio López de Santa Anna, Mar. 15, 1836, *PTR* 5:85; [Sam Houston] to Wylie Martin, Apr. 9, 1836, Wylie Martin Correspondence, Blount Papers.

18. (San Felipe) *Telegraph and Texas Register,* Mar. 5, 1836.

19. D. G. Burnet [to James Morgan], Apr. 3, 1836, *PTR* 5:304; A. Roberts to D. G. Burnet, Apr. 8, 1836, *PTR* 5:388; Thos. J. Green to Sam Houston, July 18, 1836, AJH.

20. [James Collinsworth to Sam Houston, Apr. 8, 1836], *PTR* 5:372.

21. On the activities of the political leaders mentioned above, see Webb, et al., eds., *Handbook of Texas* 1:112, 2:122, 403–404; Miller, *Bounty and Donation Grants,* pp. 91, 534–35, 647. These same two sources were used in all the composite profiles of the Texas elite groups in this chapter. For the group in this citation, see also Huson, *Refugio* 1:291, 306; (San Felipe) *Telegraph and Texas Register,* Jan. 23, 1836.

22. Fifteen of these seventeen nonparticipants had been selected to the Consultation; two served only at the Convention, while five attended both gatherings. Gray, *Virginia to Texas*, p. 167; Samuel Rhoads Fisher file, AMC; Samuel T. Allen to Thomas J. Allen, May 18, 1836, Simmons, ed., "Allen," p. 486.

23. Henson, *Williams*, pp. 82–84; Josiah H. Bell folder, AMC; Henry Austin to Mary Austin Holley, Mar. 29, 1836, *PTR* 5:221–22.

24. Certificate of John Carrington, Apr. 10, 1836, AP. Additional composite biographical data come from research on individuals in White, *1830 Citizens of Texas*, and Character Certificates, Spanish Collection, Archives Division, GLO. For the individuals described above, see also G. E. Edward, Jared Groce, Leonard Groce, and James Cochrane folders, AMC; Elizabeth Silverthorne, *Plantation Life in Texas* (College Station: Texas A&M University Press, 1986), pp. 12–13.

25. Other documents that might help indicate rates of participation are less place specific, but they do not significantly contradict the pattern shown for Brazoria.

26. Webb, et al., eds., *Handbook*, 2:429, 776; John Forbes to James W. Robinson, Jan. 22, 1836, *PTR* 4:115; S. H. Everitt to David G. Burnet, Mar. 17, 1836, *PTR* 5:120–21; Gray, *Virginia to Texas*, p. 95.

27. Enrollment figures are taken from Tables 3, 4, 5, and 8. The numbers for male population, 16–50, derive from Marion Day Mullins, *The First Census of Texas, 1829–1836* (Washington, D.C.: National Genealogical Society Publications, 1959), pp. 6–13, for Shelby [previously Tenaha], 21–27 for Jasper [Bevil], and 36–43, 95–100 for Sabine and for San Augustine, Robert Bruce Blake Collection, Supplement, Vol. 14, SFA.

28. List of the Sabine Company, Apr. 24, 1835, *PTR* 1:82–83. Mullins, *First Census*, pp. 29–41, contains names and ages as shown by the Sabine District census taker. Other data for this composite profile came from White, *1830 Citizens of Texas*, and Character Certificates, GLO.

29. [Mrs. George Sutherland to her sister], June 5, 1836, *PTR* 7:25; Sam Houston, Army Orders, Mar. 21, 1836, *PTR* 5:154; D. Pittman to Sam Houston, Apr. 3, 1836, *PTR* 5:312.

30. Sam Houston to James Collingsworth, Mar. 15, 1836, AJH; Sam Houston, Army Orders, Apr. 5, 1836, AJH; Sam Houston to Nat Robbins, Apr. 15, 1836, AJH.

31. David G. Burnet to the Citizens of Texas, Mar. 18, 1836, *PTR* 5:126–27; Gray, *Virginia to Texas*, p. 134; Sam Houston to Thomas J. Rusk, Mar. 23, 1836, *PTR* 5:169.

32. Santa Anna, *Manifesto*, in Castañeda, trans., *Mexican Side*, p. 25; de la Peña, *With Santa Anna*, p. 111; David Thomas to Sam Houston, Apr. 6, 1836, AJH.

33. J. W. Fannin to J. W. Robinson, Feb. 7, [1836], *PTR* 4:280; E. N. Hill, "Siege of the Mission of Refugio," in Day, comp., *Texas Almanac*, pp. 341–42; Huson, *Refugio* 1:293–309.

34. F. W. Johnson to the Convention, Mar. 8, 1836, *PTR* 5:27; San Felipe Committee to Citizens of Texas, [ca. Mar. 3, 1836], *PTR* 4:500.

35. Gray, *Virginia to Texas*, p. 134; J. Morgan to ———, Mar. 24, 1836, *PTR* 5:181. Sam Houston, "Campaign of 1836 . . . ," in Day, comp., *Texas Almanac*, pp. 270–71.

36. Gray, *Virginia to Texas*, pp. 142–43, 150, 151; Gwen Vincent, "The Runaway Scrape of the Texas Revolution: The Return and Effect on the Participants" (M.A. thesis, Hardin-Simmons University, 1976), pp. 34–37, 39–40, 43–45, 51; Valentine Bennett to Sam Houston, Apr. 1, 1836, AJH; M. W. Smith to Sam Houston, Apr. 1, 1836,

AJH; Sam Houston to T. J. Rusk, Apr. 3, 1836, AJH; Sam Houston to Ira Ingram, Apr. 5, 1836, AJH.

37. E. Morehouse to Sam Houston, Apr. 6, 1836, AJH; Jesse Benton to Thos. J. Rusk, Apr. 3, 1836, Rusk Papers; Gray, *Virginia to Texas*, p. 154; Vincent, "Runaway Scrape," p. 31; Elliott, "Alabama and the Texas Revolution," p. 321.

38. John A. Quitman to Sam Houston, Apr. 15, 1836, *PTR* 5:484–85; Henry Raguet to Sam Houston, Apr. 17, 1836, AJH; Vincent, "Runaway Scrape," pp. 59–62; J. Darrington to David G. Burnet, Apr. 10, 1836, AJH; J. A. Quitman to the Officers in Command at Nacogdoches, Apr. 13, 1836, AJH.

39. Sam Houston to R. R. Royall, Mar. 24, 1836, *PTR* 5:180; Geo. W. Poe to Henry Smith, Mar. 3, 1836, AP; Geo. W. Poe to the editor of the *Mobile Register,* Mar. 6, 1836, *PTR* 5:9; Ira Ingram to Sam Houston, Apr. 16, 1836, AJH.

40. Benj. J. White to the Committee of Brazoria, Mar. 22, 1836, *PTR* 5:164; Downs, "Women," pp. 46–48.

41. De Wees, *Letters,* p. 204; Smithwick, *Evolution of a State,* p. 90; Kleberg, "Early Experiences," pp. 300–301; Harris, "Reminiscences," pp. 160–67; Vincent, "Runaway Scrape," p. 58.

42. [James Collingsworth to Sam Houston, Apr. 8, 1836], *PTR* 5:373; Gray, *Virginia to Texas,* p. 164; D. Thomas to Sam Houston, Apr. 4, 1836, AJH; R. A. Irion to Captains Smith, Radcliffe and Chester, Apr. 14, 1836, AJH.

43. Sam P. Carson to John H. Mullin [McMullin], Mar. 29, 1836, Executive Record Book, TSA; G. Borden, Jr. to David G. Burnet, Mar. 25, 1836, *PTR* 5:184; [Resolution, Mar. 13, 1836], Acts of the Convention; [Petition of San Bernardo residents] to W. D. C. Hall, Mar. 30, 1836, AP.

44. David G. Burnet to Stephen Richardson, Apr. 7, 1836, *PTR* 5:357–58; David G. Burnet [Proclamations], Apr. 9, 1836, *PTR* 5:399; David Thomas to Sam Houston, Apr. 14, 1836, AJH.

45. D. G. Burnet to J. Morgan, June 20, July 7, 1836, *PTR* 7:208–209, 377; David G. Burnet to officers of the Army of Texas, June 4, 1836, *PTR* 7:12–13; W. Lawrence to James Morgan, July 27, 1836, *PTR* 8:46; Kleberg, "Early Experiences," p. 302.

46. Vincent, "Runaway Scrape," pp. 52–59; Downs, "Women," pp. 51–53; John Holmes Jenkins, ed., *Recollections of Early Texas: the Memoirs of John Holland Jenkins,* pp. 41–43; Elizabeth Beeson to [David G. Burnet], Apr. 10, 1836, *PTR* 5:416.

47. Barker, "San Jacinto Campaign," pp. 243, 247, 248, 312; Huson, *Refugio* 1:302; *Narrative of Hunter,* pp. 11–13; de la Peña, *With Santa Anna,* pp. 22, 97, 99, 102; Vincent, "Runaway Scrape," pp. 48, 49.

48. L. A. McHenry to [John Hardin McHenry], July 17, 1836, in Nielsen, ed., "Lydia Ann McHenry," p. 402; Huson, *Refugio* 1:288; Antonio López de Santa Anna to Vicente Filisola, Apr. 22, 1836, AJH; Vicente Filisola to Antonio López de Santa Anna, Apr. 28, 1836, *PTR* 6:105–106; Muir, ed., *Texas in 1837,* p. 61.

49. W. B. Dewees to [Clara Cardello], May 15, 1836, *PTR* 6:287; Caroline von Hinueber, "Life of German Pioneers in Early Texas," *QTSHA* 2 (Jan., 1899) 230–32; Jenkins, ed., *Recollections,* pp. 41–44.

50. Sam Houston, Army Orders, Apr. 3, 1836, AJH; R. R. Royall to Wm. Hall, Oct. 14, 1835, GC Jnl; Smithwick, *Evolution of a State,* p. 74; Receipt by T. J. Rusk, n. d., John C. Clark folder, AMC.

51. [Journals of] the Convention, *PTR* 9:367–68. The folder of R. R. Royall contains documents relating to claims between September, 1835, and the end of 1836. For the case of the *Rattle Snake,* see the certificate of William Brown, Aug. 8, 1836, and the affidavit of Eli Thompson, Nov. 14, 1836. Sayre's claim was based on his own affidavit, July 2, 1836. For other individual cases of impressment see the AMC folders of Horace Eggleston, J. C. Neill, Joshua Fletcher, J. Urban, William O. Huff, James F. Perry, and William Newland.

52. This profile of property impressment is based on AMC files under the following names: Paulina Anglier, John Beacham, John Bowman, Octavius Cook, William Cooper, Samuel Diamond, John Eden, Eliza S. Faris, Elisha Flack, Robert Grimes, John A. Gurley, Eliza Hardeman, Thomas J. Hughes, and Nathaniel Robbins. See also David G. Burnet to J. W. Moore and De Witt Clinton Harris, Aug. 13, 1836, *PTR* 8:220.

53. David G. Burnet to Wm. Hardin, Apr. 3, 1836, *PTR* 5:303; James S. Montgomery to S. Houston, Apr. 27, 1836, *PTR* 6:99–100; De Wees, *Letters,* pp. 207–208.

54. S. Sherman to [T. J.] Rusk, May 17, 1836, Rusk Papers; Sterling C. Robertson to T. J. Rusk, June 18, 1836, *PTR* 7:197–98; David G. Burnet, Proclamation, July 12, 1836, *PTR* 7:427.

55. S. F. Austin to Henry Austin, June 27, 1836, *PTR* 7:278–79.

56. This profile is based on a random sampling of about 15 percent of the AMC folders and evidence of military service in scattered other sources, including Miller, *Bounty and Donation Grants.* See also Articles of Agreement, Charles Smith and Leonard Mortimer Thorn, July 3, 1836, AP; Joseph Rowe to [Alpha Anthony], Aug. 6, 1836, *PTR* 8:142–43.

57. Thos J. Rusk to M. B. Lamar, May 12, 1836, *PTR* 6:249; Sterling C. Robertson to Thomas J. Rusk, May 27, 1836, *PTR* 6:392–93; Thomas J. Rusk to A. Sommerville, July 25, 1836, *PTR* 8:32–33; Benjamin Bryant to Sam Houston, Aug. 13, 1836, AJH.

58. D. G. Burnet TO THE PEOPLE OF TEXAS, [ca. Sept. 20, 1836], *PTR* 8:496; John Turner and John Chenowith to M. B. Lamar, July 6, 1836, *PTR* 7:374; W. M. Birch to [T. J.] Rusk, June 15, 1836, Rusk Papers; Sam Houston to A. Horton, Aug. 10, 1836, AJH.

59. Vincent, "Runaway Scrape," pp. 65–67, 73–74; Harris, "Reminiscences," pp. 169–79; Thomas H. Brenan to [D. G. Burnet], June 4, 1836, *PTR* 7:11; Ira Ingram to William Parker, June 30, 1836, *PTR* 7:316–17; Clarke Beach to David G. Burnet, May 9, 1836, *PTR* 6:190; Receipt by C. T. Carr, Aug. 6, 1836, Ebeneazor Frazer folder, AMC.

60. James S. Montgomery to S. H[o]uston, Apr. 28, 1836, *PTR* 6:110; (Columbia) *Telegraph and Texas Register,* Aug. 16, Nov. 9, 1836; T. J. Rusk to M. B. Lamar, May 15, 1836, *PTR* 6:301; Resolutions, Sept. 20, 21, 1836, Nacogdoches Committee of Safety, Raguet Papers; Vincent, "Runaway Scrape," pp. 84, 89; Kleberg, "Early Experiences," p. 170; *Narrative of Hunter,* pp. 21–22; Harris, "Reminiscences," p. 179.

61. Peyton quoted in Downs, "Women," p. 55; Thorn Journal, p. 20; E. M. Pease to Dear Father, May 26, 1836, *PTR* 6:382; James Small to David G. Burnet, June 28, 1836, *PTR* 7:306.

62. William Staffer to Stephen F. Austin, Sept. 28, 1836, APT. Thos. J. Rusk to David G. Burnet, June 15, 1836, *PTR* 7:138.

63. [Mrs. George Sutherland to Sister], June 5, 1836, *PTR* 7:24–26.

CHAPTER 12.

1. (Brazoria) *Texas Republican,* Oct. 10, 1835; Thomas J. Rusk to the People of Texas, June 27, 1836, *PTR* 6:287; Haden Edwards to James W. Robinson, Nov. 29, 1835, *OCTR* 1:135; Council to the People of Texas, Feb. 13, 1836, *OCTR* 1:419.

2. David Brion Davis, *The Problem of Slavery in the Age of Revolution, 1770–1823* (Ithaca, N.Y.: Cornell University Press, 1975), pp. 255–342.

3. Merton L. Dillon, "Benjamin Lundy in Texas," *SHQ* 63 (July, 1959): 60; [Benjamin Lundy], *The War in Texas.*

4. Eugene C. Barker, "The United States and Mexico, 1835–1837," *Mississippi Valley Historical Review* 1 (June, 1914): 3–30.

5. Martín Perfecto de Cos to the Public, July 5, 1835, *PTR* 1:203. See chapters 1–2 for discussions of the antislavery threat of the centralists as a factor in bringing on the Revolution.

6. James W. Fannin to the president of the Convention of Texas, Nov. 6, 1835, *PTR* 2:337.

7. (San Felipe) *Telegraph and Texas Register,* Oct. 17, 1835.

8. Linn, *Reminiscences,* p. 115.

9. (San Felipe) *Telegraph and Texas Register,* Feb. 27 (first quotation), Mar. 5 (second quotation) 1836; (Nacogdoches) *Texan and Emigrant's Guide,* Dec. 26, 1835; Fannin to Robinson and General Council, Feb. 7, 1836, *PTR* 4:280.

10. [William H. Wharton], *Texas: A Brief Account, PTR* 9:240.

11. Wendell G. Addington, "Slave Insurrections in Texas," *Journal of Negro History* 35 (Oct., 1950): 411; Morton, *Terán and Texas,* pp. 106, 117–19; Vigness, pp. 101–102, 139.

12. Andrew J. Yates et al. [affidavit], Aug. 29, 1835, *PTR* 1:378; James H. C. Miller to the People of Texas [Sept., 1835?], *PTR* 1:517; Horatio Allsberry to the Public, Aug. 28, 1835, *Austin Papers* 3:108.

13. B. R. Milam to Johnson, July 5, 1835, *Austin Papers* 3:82–83.

14. Resolutions of the Committee of Safety of the Jurisdiction of Columbia, Sept. 22, 1835, in (Brazoria) *Texas Republican,* Sept. 26, 1835; Resolutions of the Committee of Safety for Matagorda, Sept. 30, 1835, *Austin Papers* 3:144.

15. Thomas J. Pilgrim to S. F. Austin, Oct. 6, 1835, *Austin Papers* 3:162 (quotations); (San Felipe) *Telegraph and Texas Register,* Oct. 10, 1835; Josiah H. Bell to S. F. Austin or Peter W. Grayson, Oct. 6, 1835, *PTR* 2:57; Richard R. Royall to S. F. Austin, Oct. 10, 1835, *PTR* 2:89.

16. B. J. White to S. F. Austin, Oct. 17, 1835, *Austin Papers* 3:190; [Ames], "H. Ames," p. 12.

17. Houston to Citizens, Dec. 12, 1835, *PTR* 3:171; Williams to Don Carlos Barrett, Jan. 2, 1836, *PTR* 3:407.

18. Henry Austin to James F. Perry, Mar. 5, 1836, *Austin Papers* 3:318; Brazoria meeting, [Mar. 17, 1836], *PTR* 5:98–99.

19. James Morgan to [Sam P. Carson], Mar. 24, 1836, Executive Record Book; Kenneth Wiggins Porter, *The Negro on the American Frontier* (New York: Arno Press, 1971), pp. 381–82; Burnet Proclamation, Mar. 29, 1836, *OCTR* 2:557–58.

20. Harold Schoen, "The Free Negro in the Republic of Texas," *SHQ* 40 (Jan., 1937): 172 (first and second quotations); David Barnet Edward, *The History of Texas,*

or the Emigrant's Guide (reprint ed., Austin: Pemberton Press, 1967), p. 248; GC Jnl, Oct. 16, 1835, TSA; Lester G. Bugbee, "Slavery in Early Texas," *Political Science Quarterly* 13 (Dec., 1898): 663; Eugene D. Genovese, *From Rebellion to Revolution: Afro-American Slave Revolts in the Making of the Modern World* (Baton Rouge: Louisiana State University Press, 1979), pp. 1–50.

21. Santa Anna, *Manifesto Relative to the Texas Campaign and His Capture,* in Castañeda, trans., *Mexican Side,* p. 65; F. M. Díaz Noriega to Antonio López de Santa Anna, Feb. 29, 1836, Guerra y Marina, Archivo General, pp. 24–35.

22. José María Tornel y Mendívil to Santa Anna, Mar. 18, 1836, *PTR* 5:136 (quotations); José María Tornel to the Public, Apr. 9, 1836, *Streeter.*

23. John W. Smith to [Thomas J. Chambers], Sept. 2, 1835, *PTR* 1:406; de la Peña, *With Santa Anna,* p. 44; Newell, *History of the Revolution in Texas,* pp. 88–89; "Joe," entry in the revised *Handbook of Texas,* Texas State Historical Association, publication pending.

24. Sam Houston to S. P. Carson, Apr. 3, 1836, *PTR* 5:308.

25. William Parker to Editor of the *Free Trader,* Apr. 29, 1836, *PTR* 6:123; [José de Urrea], *Diary,* in Castañeda, trans., *Mexican Side,* p. 238; R. R. Royall to T. J. Rusk, May 14, 1836, Rusk Papers; Vicente Filisola to Comandante de las fuersas de Texas, May 22, 1836, Rusk Papers.

26. Eugene C. Barker, "The Influence of the Slave Trade in the Colonization of Texas," *SHQ* 28 (July, 1924): 32–33; de la Peña, *With Santa Anna,* p. 104; Hervey Whiting to Morgan, May 3, 1836, *OCTR* 2:654; Holley, *The Texas Diary,* p. 45; "Reminiscences of Ann Raney Thomas Coleman, 1810–1877," Ann Raney Thomas Coleman Papers typescript, Part 1, p. 160, BTHC; Samuel E. Asbury, ed., "The Private Journal of Juan Nepomuceno Almonte, February 1–April 16, 1836," *SHQ* 48 (July, 1944): 32.

27. Urrea, *Diary,* pp. 269–70; de la Peña, *With Santa Anna,* pp. 170, 179; Caro, *First Texas Campaign,* in Castañeda, trans., *Mexican Side,* p. 126; Treaty of Velasco, May 14, 1836, *PTR* 6:274; Rusk to Mirabeau B. Lamar, May 17, 1836, *PTR* 6:315; Filisola to Santa Anna, May 25, 1836, *PTR* 7:371; Filisola to ———, June 3, 1836, *PTR* 6:508; Manuel de Micheltorena to Tornel, June 8, 1836, *PTR* 7:67–69.

28. (Columbia) *Telegraph and Texas Register,* Nov. 9, 1836; (Brazoria) *Texas Republican,* July 18, 1835; Barker, "Slave Trade," pp. 152–53; Gray, *From Virginia to Texas,* p. 168; Thomas B. Bell to Robert Potter, Apr. 12, 1836, *OCTR* 2:633; G. Pollitt to Richard Sparks, Aug. 19, 1836, Blake 15:101.

29. (Columbia/Houston) *Telegraph and Texas Register,* Nov. 9, 1836, June 8, July 1, 29, Aug. 5 (quotations), Sept. 16, 1837; DeWees, *Letters,* p. 211; *Matagorda Bulletin,* Sept. 27, 1837; Clarke Beach to D. G. Burnet, May 9, 1836, *PTR* 6:190; Schoen, "Free Negro," 39:33, 40:173.

30. Certificate [addressed to Cary], Nov. 11, 1839, Williams Papers; de la Peña, *With Santa Anna,* p. 131; (San Felipe) *Telegraph and Texas Register,* Mar. 5, 1836; Wyly Martin to Sam Houston, Apr. 7, 1836, *PTR* 5:362; David Thomas to Houston, Apr. 14, 1836, *PTR* 5:475; Schoen, "Free Negro," 40:113; Peter Bell and Sam Bell folders, RPA.

31. Gray, *Virginia to Texas,* pp. 136–37; de la Peña, *With Santa Anna,* p. 44; (Houston) *Telegraph and Texas Register,* May 26, 1837.

32. Hendrick Arnold to the General Council, Jan. 4, 1836, *PTR* 3:414; Victor H. Treat, "William Goyens: Free Negro Entrepreneur," in Alwyn Barr and Robert A. Calvert, eds., *Black Leaders: Texans for Their Times* (Austin: Texas State Historical Association, 1981), pp. 19–47; Schoen, "Free Negro," 39:299, 302, 40:27–34, 92, 269, 41:84–85, 98, 102 n31.

33. (San Felipe) *Telegraph and Texas Register,* Mar. 12, 1836.

34. Morgan to Rusk, Apr. 8, 1836, *OCTR* 2:611; Burnet Proclamation, Apr. 25, 1836, *PTR* 6:52; Morgan to [Carson], Mar. 24, 1836, Executive Record Book; J. F. Perry to Emily Perry, Apr. 26, 1836, James Franklin and Stephen Samuel Perry Collection, Papers and Manuscripts, Series A: Correspondence, Vol. IV, BTHC; José de Urrea to Santa Anna, Apr. 22, 1836, *PTR* 6:18–19; George P. Digges to Houston, Apr. 23, 1836, *PTR* 6:27; James F. Perry folder, AMC.

35. Gray, *Virginia to Texas,* pp. 151, 166–67, 169–70; (San Felipe/Columbia) *Telegraph and Texas Register,* Mar. 12, Dec. 27, 1836; Ben Milam to J. W. Fannin, Nov. 15, 1835, *PTR* 2:428; H. Austin to J. F. Perry, Mar. 5, 1836, *PTR* 4:515; Houston to Ira Ingram, Apr. 5, 1836, *PTR* 5:331; DeWees, *Letters,* p. 205; Petition to the Ayuntamiento of the Municipality of Nacogdoches, May 27, 1836, Memorials and Petitions; Amelia Williams, "A Critical Study of the Siege of the Alamo," *SHQ* 37 (Apr., 1934): 285; Dixon and Kemp, *Heroes of San Jacinto,* p. 420.

36. Beaumont Committee to Henry Millard, Dec. 2, 1835, *PTR* 3:73; Dillon, "Lundy," 47–53, 60; Gray, *Virginia to Texas,* p. 68; Ordinance to Prevent the Importation of Free Negroes," Jan. 5, 1836, H. P. N. Gammel, comp., *The Laws of Texas, 1822–1897* (Austin, Tex.: Gammel Book Co., 1898), 1:1,024.

37. For earlier rhetoric, see [Williamson to Consultation], Nov. 6, 1835, *PTR* 2:341; A Resolution for calling a Convention, Dec. 10, 1835, *PTR* 9:446; (San Felipe) *Telegraph and Texas Register,* Mar. 12, 1836.

38. Constitution of Texas, Declaration of Rights and General Provisions, Sections 6 and 10, *PTR* 5:113, 116.

39. For the relevant portions of the Constitution of the Republic see Article I, Section 7, General Provisions, Section 6, 9, and 10, *PTR* 5:104, 113. For the earlier draft of the constitutional provisions regarding slavery, see [Journals of] the General Convention, *PTR* 9:338.

40. James E. Winston, "New York and the Independence of Texas," *SHQ* 18 (Apr., 1915): 369; Martín Perfecto de Cos to the Commander at Anahuac, May 26, 1835, *PTR* 1:215.

41. Holley, *Diary,* p. 29; Barker, "Slave Trade," p. 152; Fannin to Major Belton, Aug. 27, 1835, *PTR* 1:373; William P. Harris to "Friend Hanks," Jan. 19, 1836, *PTR* 4:72; William S. Fisher to Henry Smith, Mar. 2, 1836, *PTR* 4:490; [Journals of] the Constitutional Convention, *PTR* 9:340, 362; Constitution of the Republic of Texas, General Provisions, Section 9, *PTR* 5:113; John Forbes to Bailey Hardeman, Apr. 6, 1836, Executive Record Book; Ethel Zivley Rather, "Recognition of the Republic of Texas by the United States," *QTSHA* 13 (Jan., 1910): 231–32.

42. Constitution of Texas, General Provisions, Sections 9 and 10, *PTR* 5:113; Ephrain Douglass Adams, ed., "Correspondence from the British Archives Concerning Texas, 1837–1846," *QTSHA* 17 (Oct., 1913): 199–200; Schoen, "Free Negro," 41:104–105; [Journals of] the Constitutional Convention, *PTR* 9:490–91.

CONCLUSION

1. Quoted in Mark E. Nackman, *A Nation within a Nation: The Rise of Texas Nationalism* (Port Washington, N.Y.: Kennikat Press, 1975), pp. 71–72.

2. Henry M. Morfit to John Forsyth, Aug. 27, Sept. 14, 1836, *PTR* 8:335–38, 475–76 (quotations).

3. (Columbia) *Telegraph and Texas Register,* Sept. 6, 1836.

4. Binkley, *Texas Revolution,* pp. 126–27.

5. Thos. J. Rusk [to Sam Houston], Aug. 11, 1836, *PTR* 8:205–206; David G. Burnet [Election Proclamation], July 23, 1836, *PTR* 8:15–17.

6. (Columbia) *Telegraph and Texas Register,* Aug. 9, 16, 1836.

7. Thos. J. Green to Sam Houston, Aug. 1, 1836, AJH; S. F. Austin to T. J. Rusk, Aug. 9, 1836, *PTR* 8:165–68; Henry Millard to Thos. B. Huling, Aug. 23, 1836, *PTR* 8:300–301.

8. Henry Millard to Thos. B. Huling, Aug. 23, 24, 1836, *PTR* 8:104–105, 300–301; Stanley Siegel, *A Political History of the Texas Republic, 1836–1845* (Austin: University of Texas Press, 1956), p. 54.

9. Thos. J. Rusk [to Sam Houston], July 25, 1836, AJH; R. M. Coleman to S. Houston, July 30, 1836, AJH; Nibbs to Sam Houston, Aug. 1, 1836, AJH; T. J. Green to Sam Houston, July 30, 1836, *PTR* 8:69.

10. Sam Houston [to T. J. Rusk], Aug. 8, 1836, *PTR* 8:160; [L. A. McHenry to J. H. McHenry], Aug. 25, 1836, in Nielsen, ed., "Lydia Ann McHenry," p. 405; Barker, *Austin,* p. 513.

11. A. Huston to Sam Houston, Aug. ———, 1836, AJH; S. F. Austin to James F. Perry, Sept. 2, 1836, *PTR* 8:370; Siegel, *Political History,* pp. 47–54.

12. Henry M. Morfit to John Forsyth, Sept. 12, 1836, *PTR* 8:450; Binkley, *Texas Revolution,* pp. 116–18; Clarke, *Burnet,* pp. 158–59.

13. Miller, *Public Lands of Texas,* pp. 27–32, 45–48.

14. Muir, ed., *Texas in 1837,* p. 148; David G. Burnet, Message to the First Congress, Oct. 4, 1836, *PTR* 9:45–50; Leon Dyer to Thomas J. Green, Sept. 21, 25, Oct. 9, 1836, in Sibley, ed., "Letters from the Texas Army," pp. 376, 378, 382; Henry W. Barton, "The Problem of Command in the Army of the Republic of Texas," *SHQ* 62 (July, 1952): 299.

15. Sam Houston, General Orders, Oct. 24, 1836, AJH; Miller, *Public Lands,* pp. 45–46, 48; Clarke, *Rusk,* pp. 94–95; Barton, "Command," pp. 304–307; Siegel, *Political History,* pp. 66–67.

16. Siegel, *Political History,* pp. 189–98, 199 (quotation), 200–206, 210–11, 222, 250–55.

17. Nackman, *Nation within a Nation,* p. 92; Arnoldo De León, *They Called Them Greasers,* pp. 1–23.

18. Seguín, *Memoirs,* pp. 15–16, 18.

19. Tijerina, "Tejanos and Texas," pp. 319–25.

20. Downs, "Mexicans in Texas," pp. 258–65.

21. Campbell, *Empire for Slavery,* pp. 55, 134, 144–45.

22. Schoen, "The Free Negro," 40:94–98, 103–108, 169–99, 271–72, 273–85.

23. Ibid., 41:83 (first quotation), 84n (second quotation).

24. Porter, *Negro on the American Frontier,* p. 382; Andrew Jackson Sowell, *Rangers and Pioneers of Texas,* (New York: Argosyn Antiquarian, 1964), pp. 187–89; Nance, *After San Jacinto,* p. 308; *Civilian and Galveston Gazette,* June 11, 1843, June 8, 1844.

25. Hogan, *Texas Republic,* pp. 291–94, 297 (quotations).

26. Ibid., pp. 114, 124, 159–62, 172–78, 190 (quotation), 223, 267–69; Nackman, *Nation within a Nation,* p. 83.

27. Nackman, *Nation within a Nation,* pp. 129–33.

Essay on Sources

Although this book owes a significant debt to historians who have written on this period before, the present focus, perspective, and conclusions are substantially different. Those interested in a more extended historiographical analysis are advised to consult my essay, "In the Long Shadow of Eugene C. Barker," in Robert Calvert and Walter Buenger, eds., *Texas through Time* (College Station: Texas A&M University Press, 1991). The essay below focuses on primary rather than secondary sources.

Research in primary documents naturally begins in the most accessible materials. Scholars interested in Texas for the period 1835–36 have a tremendous advantage in that so much has been compiled and published. Important editorial contributions began years ago with collections by Eugene C. Barker, ed., *The Austin Papers* (3 vols., Austin: University of Texas Press, 1926); and William Campbell Binkley, ed., *Official Correspondence of the Texas Revolution* (2 vols., New York: D. Appleton-Century Company, 1936). Several important diaries and memoirs have been in and out of print for some time (with the most recent editions listed below); of these the classics are William Fairfax Gray, *From Virginia to Texas, 1835* (Reprint edition, Houston: Fletcher Young Publishing Co., 1965), which is currently out of print and soon-to-be edited and re-released by T. Thomas Taylor Publishers; Mary Austin Holley, *The Texas Diary, 1835–1838*, J. P. Bryan, ed. (Austin: University of Texas Press, 1965); Andrew Forest Muir, ed., *Texas in 1837: An Anonymous, Contemporary Narrative* (Austin: University of Texas Press, 1958); and Noah Smithwick, *The Evolution of a State: or Recollections of Old Texas Days* (Austin: University of Texas Press, 1985). Nancy Boothe Parker, ed., "Mirabeau B. Lamar's Texas Journal," *South-*

western Historical Quarterly 84 (Oct., 1980): 197–220, (Jan., 1981): 309–30; and Katherine Hart and Elizabeth Kemp, eds., "E. M. Pease's Account of the Texas Revolution," *Southwestern Historical Quarterly* 68 (July, 1964): 79–89; are shorter but important. Also useful but more difficult to find (and thus inviting new editions) are Hermann Ehrenberg, *With Milam and Fannin* (Dallas, Tex.: Tardy Publishing Co., 1935); Hobart Huson, ed., *Dr. J. H. Barnard's Journal* ([Refugio, Tex.]: n. p., 1950); and especially Juan N. Seguín, *Personal Memoirs* (San Antonio, Tex.: Ledger Book and Job Office, 1858).

Somewhat tedious but necessary reading for showing the experiences of women are the following memoirs: Dilue Rose Harris, "Reminiscences of Dilue Harris," *Quarterly of the Texas State Historical Association* 4 (Jan., 1901): 155–89; and Rosa Kleberg, "Some of My Early Experiences in Texas," *Quarterly of the Texas State Historical Association* 1 (Apr., 1898): 297–302. For the Mexican participants see Carlos Castañeda, trans., *The Mexican Side of the Texas Revolution* (Dallas, Tex.: P. L. Turner Company, 1928); José Enrique de la Peña, *With Santa Anna in Texas,* trans. Carmen Perry (College Station: Texas A&M University Press, 1975); and Samuel E. Asbury, ed., "The Private Journal of Juan Nepomuceno Almonte, February 1–April 16, 1836," *Southwestern Historical Quarterly* 48 (July, 1944): 10–32.

Published collections of letters that proved to be especially rewarding include Joe B. Frantz, ed., "Moses Lapham His Life and Some Selected Correspondence," *Southwestern Historical Quarterly* 54 (Apr., 1951): 462–75; George R. Nielsen, ed., "Lydia Ann McHenry and Revolutionary Texas," *Southwestern Historical Quarterly* 74 (July, 1971): 393–408; Gerald S. Pierce, ed., "Some Early Letters of Moses Austin Bryan," *Southwestern Historical Quarterly* 70 (Jan., 1967): 461–71; and Marilyn McAdams Sibley, "Letters From the Texas Army, Autumn, 1836: Leon Dyer to Thomas J. Green," *Southwestern Historical Quarterly* 72 (Jan., 1969): 371–84.

Important as the works cited above may be, nothing comes close to the nine five-hundred-page volumes edited by John H. Jenkins under the title *The Papers of the Texas Revolution, 1835–1836* (Austin, Tex.: Presidial Press, 1973). A tenth volume contains a reliable, if not exhaustive, index. Materials collected in this series include letters, reports of government bodies (including various committees of correspondence), proclamations, army orders, and other miscellaneous items. Often these "papers" have been previously published, usually in the works cited above, but Jenkins also combed through archival holdings as well. The chronological arrangement facilitates research, and the listing of the source or location of the documents at the end of each volume provides those who are interested with leads for further research. A fair number of the letters are in Spanish, so Jenkins' collection is of interest to those exploring Mexican or Tejano subjects. This remarkable editorial achievement undoubtedly brought forward documents that would otherwise have escaped attention and made it possible to focus time in the archives in a more efficient and profitable manner.

However fundamental Jenkins's *Papers* and other published primary sources might be, work in manuscript collections is still at the core of this study and must be investigated by serious students of this time period. Though Jenkins made use of the Béxar Archives, his early volumes went to press with only brief summaries of many documents. These archives are at the Barker Texas History Center at the University of Texas at Austin and are also on microfilm, and can now be used with much greater ease and reliability because of the monumental name guide by Adán Benavides. The Béxar Archives are indispensable to understanding of the political situation (and to a lesser extent the social scene) in the Department of Béxar through the year 1835 but dwindle in volume in 1836 as Mexican authority crumbled. By contrast, the Nacogdoches Archives contain correspondence and other sources for East Texas and are available as "transcripts" in 86 volumes of typescript in the Archives Division of the Texas State Library in Austin and other places. This material is somewhat richer for other locations in Texas than the name would imply because of the number of letters originating from other places in the province. Some of the documents from the Nacogdoches Archives are also printed in the Robert Bruce Blake Research Collection (ninety-three volumes), which contains a wide variety of materials for a broader period of East Texas history. It is available at the Texas State Archives, the Special Collections room of the Ralph W. Steen Library, Stephen F. Austin University, Nacogdoches, and the Barker Center, which also has a card file index that aids name identification and other kinds of searches.

The Special Collections division at the Steen Library also has available in typescript several valuable sets of papers, especially the Lois Foster Blount Papers (which also contains the Wylie Martin Correspondence, the Raguet Family Papers, and the exceptional journal of Susan Wroe Edwards Thorn, who observed closely and wrote astutely). The largest collection of family papers and correspondence is of course at the Barker Center. I found that the following papers were especially interesting for the politics of the 1835–36 period: the Don Carlos Barrett Papers; the Alcalde Papers (a two-volume typescript); and the Nacogdoches Committee of Vigilance and Safety Records, 1835–37. A few documents are in the Stephen F. Austin Papers, Transcriptions that did not make it into Barker's publication.

Three collections in the Barker Center are indispensable because they contain valuable material not published by Jenkins or any other edition of documents on the Texas Revolution. The Thomas Jefferson Rusk Papers contain correspondence from many different places and parties. The Guerra y Marina section of the Archivo General de Mexico is available as a typescript and provides copies of orders and other correspondence emanating from Mexico. José Antonio Menchaca's Reminiscences, 1807–1836, also a typescript, is an underutilized Tejano document.

The bulk of the research for this project took place in the Texas State Archives. The most valuable set of papers there is the Andrew Jackson Houston Collection, which contains an abundance of documents from Houston and his varied correspondents that have never been printed. Any researcher interested in this period should mine this collection rather than make the mistake of assuming that all its contents have been made available elsewhere. The Madge Hearne Collection is also valuable if not so deep. The Adjutant General Army Papers (General Correspondence) has documents valuable for political and social as well as military history and likewise has not all been made available in any printed edition. Several other collections in the Texas State Archives were also very rewarding; these include the Broadside Collection, the Petitions and Memorials Collection (with a name index rather than chronological organization), the Executive Record Book of Correspondence of the President and State Department; and the Provisional Government Letterbook.

Most official records of the various entities that served governmental purposes during the time of the Texas Revolution are organized under the rubric of the Secretary of State Pre-Republic Legislative and Executive Bodies. The Records of the Permanent Council, the Consultation, the Convention of 1836, and the Provisional Government contain subunits of Acts, Communications Sent, Letters Received, Proceedings, Memorials, Resolutions, Committee Reports, Ordinances, and Decrees.

For the social history of the period of the Texas Revolution and the Republic, perhaps the most valuable source is a collection of materials that few serious scholars have examined in a systematic manner. These are various claims records filed by individuals to government entities in an effort to recoup payment for property and services rendered to the state. As such they contain invaluable evidence of the impact of war and revolution on the lives of the people of Texas. Specifically, these claims records are in the Comptroller of Public Accounts collection under the following titles: Audited Civil Service Records, Audited Military Claims, Public Debt Papers, Republic Pension Applications, and Unpaid Claims. They are so massive that all the folders could not be consulted; my approach was to examine all the folders with Hispanic or female names and randomly about 15 percent of the remaining folders. These materials are at the core of the research for this book.

Identifying members of the Texas army of the period October, 1835, through April 21, 1836, required special kinds of research and thus needs a separate explanation. A variety of sources were required, both published and manuscript materials. Thomas Lloyd Miller, *Bounty and Donation Land Grants 1835–1888* (Austin and London: University of Texas Press, 1967), is a compilation of all the extant records of application by veterans or their heirs for donation grants (for the siege of Béxar [1835], the battles of the Alamo and San Jacinto, and service under J. W. Fannin in 1836) and bounty claims (given according to length and date of service). This source was used to construct files of all those who served at the Béxar siege or battle of San Jacinto and those who enrolled between October 1, 1835, and April 21, 1836, without specific place of service being designated.

The list of men who served with Fannin was derived from Harbert Davenport, "Notes from an Unfinished Study of Fannin and His Men," (typescript, Harbert Davenport Collection, Archives Division, Texas State Library). This work contains meticulously reconstructed rolls of Fannin's men, arranged by company, though overlapping has to be eliminated since Davenport repeated the names when men transferred from one unit to another. Thomas L. Miller, "Fannin's Men: Some Additions to Earlier Rosters," *Southwestern Historical Quarterly* 61 (Apr., 1958), 522–32, supplied a few other names, as did Daughters of the Republic of Texas, *Muster Rolls of the Texas Revolution* (Austin, Tex.: DRT, Inc., 1986), 28–40. This volume also was used as a source for the files of those who served in the army under Sam Houston in 1836 and various units of volunteers in 1835 and 1836.

The names of the soldiers stationed at San Antonio de Béxar in February and March, 1836, came principally from Amelia Williams, "A Critical Study of the Siege of the Alamo," *Southwestern Historical*

Quarterly 36 (Apr., 1933): 251–87, 37 (July, 1933): 1–44, (Oct., 1933): 79–115, (Jan., 1934): 157–84, (Apr., 1934): 237–312, supplemented and corrected by Walter Lord, *A Time to Stand* (New York, 1961), 160–78, and Thomas L. Miller, "The Roll of the Alamo" *Texana* 2 (Spring, 1964), 454–64. The data on Béxar/Alamo veterans include men who served there on the Texas side in February and March, not just those who died in the engagement. Some of these soldiers left in February before the arrival of the Mexican forces; many of these names were supplied by Colonel J. C. Neill's muster roll of February 12, 1835, General Land Office Muster Roll Book (Archives Division, Texas State Library). A few more veterans of this and other campaigns were discovered in sampling the Audited Military Claims, Comptroller of Public Accounts (Archives Division, Texas State Library).

Muster rolls for units formed in 1835 provided names of many additional soldiers who did not file bounty or donation claims. These were "List of those engaged in Storming of Bexar A. D. 1835," "Reports of the names of the volunteers who stormed Bexar on December 5th," and "Capt. P. Dimitt's Muster Roll [Goliad], 1835" (Adjutant General Military Rolls. Texas Revolution, 1835–1836, Archives Division, Texas State Archives). The muster lists for Béxar service in the Archives and Records Division, General Land Office, mostly duplicate the Adjutant General rolls but also supplied a few additional names of 1835 soldiers. Service for 1835 was also documented from the Goliad Declaration, December 22, 1835, Records of the General Council, Secretary of State Record Group (Archives, Texas State Library); and Captain George M. Collinsworth, et al., Agreement, Guadalupe Victoria and Goliad, October 9, 1835, John H. Jenkins, ed., *Papers of the Texas Revolution* (Austin, 1973) 2:76–77.

Both the GLO list and those reproduced in the DRT *Muster Rolls* were researched in compiling files of veterans of the San Jacinto engagement. The muster roll book in the General Land Office Archives provided names of men who enrolled in "ranging" companies, as well as units raised in Washington, Jasper, Lynchburgh, and San Augustine in 1835 and 1836 (Muster Roll Book, Archives Division, General Land Office), 46–48, 199–202, 216. The roll of the Nacogdoches Mounted Volunteers in the Adjutant General Military Rolls (Archives, Texas State Library) was also used.

Several explanations are in order regarding the completeness and the reliability of the data in Tables 2–8. The number who engaged in military service, 3,685 as shown in Table 8, represents an unduplicated total; i.e., names were counted and biographical detail incorporated only once, even when the men served in two or more units or campaigns at different times. Therefore, the sum of those enumerated in Tables 2–5 exceeds the figure shown in Table 8 because some men served in more than one place, time, or engagement, as shown by Table 6. Further, the numbers shown in each table represent only those who can be identified by name and thus underestimates somewhat the total who participated in the army. Specifically, some men joined but did not stay long enough to receive bounty or donation grants or served in units for which no muster rolls are extant. Clearly, Tejanos are underrepresented in these numbers (see Chapter 10).

Some biographical data were discovered for just over 90 percent (all but 364) of the soldiers as the basis for this group profile. The figures shown parenthetically in the tables represent the number of cases for each entry and used in computing percentages. No conscious sampling was performed; rather, an effort was made to find all possible information on each soldier. The parenthetical numbers are given in order to indicate the possible reliability of the data in each category for each table.

Many sources were examined in the search for biographical detail. The profile derives from research on each soldier in the file. Several secondary sources supplied useful information: *Biographical Directory of Texas Conventions;* Harbert Davenport, "Notes from an Unfinished Study of Fannin and His Men" (Typescript, Archives Division, Texas State Library); Sam Houston Dixon and Louis W. Kemp. *The Heroes of San Jacinto* (Houston, Tex.: Anson Jones Press, 1932); Hobart Huson, *Refugio; A Comprehensive History* (Woodsboro, Tex.: Rooke Foundation, 1953); Walter Lord, *A Time to Stand;* Walter P. Webb, et al., eds., *The Handbook of Texas;* and Williams, "Siege of the Alamo." A number of published compilations of primary materials also proved to be especially useful. Carolyn Reeves Ericson, *Nacogdoches — Gateway to Texas. A Biographical Directory, 1777–1849* (Ft. Worth, Tex.: Arrow/Curtis Printing Co., 1974); Malcolm McLean, ed., *Papers Concerning Robertson's Colony in Texas* (Arlington, Tex.: UTA Press, 1974–1984), Vols. 1–11; Marion Day Mullins, *The First Census of Texas, 1829–1836* (Washington, D.C.: National Genealogical Society Publications, 1959); Mary McMillan Osburn, ed., "The Atascosita Census of 1826," *Texana* 1 (Fall, 1963): 299–321; the San Augustine census of 1835, in Blake, Vol. 4 (SFA); and especially Gifford White, *1830 Citizens of Texas* (Austin, Tex.: Eakin Press, 1983) and *Character Certificates in the General Land Office of Texas* (St. Louis: Ingmire Publications, 1985).

Ultimately, the research depended on work in archival sources. Most useful were the well-arranged materials in the Archives and Records Division of the General Land Office. One typescript finding aid, "Index to Field Notes Plots, Spanish Archives," helped speed research by providing names of land grantees, date of title, amount (from which marital status could be ascertained), and colony and/or county. This source thus curtailed the need to examine all manuscript documents. Mostly, though, biographical information was discovered on character certificates contained in land grant files. These are arranged by land district but indexed individually by name of grantee. First class headright grants (issued to those who arrived in Texas prior to March 2, 1836) depended on certificates issued to the grantee in the county of his residence at the time of Texas independence. Normally, these documents indicated amount of land to which the applicant was entitled (or marital status), date of emigration to Texas (though sometimes the documents listed only "before May 2, 1835" or "prior to the Declaration of Independence"), and occasionally origin outside of Texas. These documents also provided place of residence because of the requirement that certificates be issued by officials in those counties rather than by officials in counties where land claims were being located. White used these certificates and other land records in compiling his "census," but only for those who came prior to 1831. Appeals made to the Court of Claims were also included in the Republic and State Land Grant Index; these records also provided some biographical information, though not in as uniform a manner as the certificates of character. When the index indicated that an applicant had been awarded a second class headright, this provided evidence that the grantee had emigrated after independence.

A few of those who could not be identified and described on the basis of the above sources were located in Pension Applications and Audited Military Claims, Comptroller of Public Accounts Records (Archives Division, Texas State Library). These records also served to correct a few errors in dates of service given in other sources.

Occasionally, place of origin was deduced from the name of the unit in which the soldier served. At the siege of Béxar, October to December, 1835, Thomas H. Breece and William G. Cooke commanded companies of "Greys" recruited in New Orleans. The origin of the few (fifty) whose residences could not be determined in the Béxar siege companies commanded by John York, James Chesshire, M. B. Lewis, William H. Patton, George English, and James Swisher were distributed according to county place ratios of the other men in their respective companies. This procedure could not be used for subsequent armies like the one of Sam Houston that fought at San Jacinto because their companies did not have the same degree of geographic autonomy; however, Fannin's command had clearly delineated geographic units. My research indicated that only twenty-three Texas residents (their number is indicated parenthetically below) served in the companies of U.S. volunteers led by David M. Burke (3), John Chenoweth (2), Thomas K. Pearson (4), Samuel O. Pettus (5), William A. O. Wadsworth (1), Peyton S. Wyatt (3), John M. Allen (1), Burr H. Duval (2), Jack Shackelford (1), and Samuel Sprague (1). Eighteen other Texas residents served on Fannin's staff or in unknown companies, while the bulk of the Texans were in companies commanded by Ira Westover, Thomas Llewellyn, A. C. Horton, and Hugh M. Frazer (containing a total of 76 Texans, 27 U.S. volunteers, and 9 whose date of emigration could not be identified). This data made it possible to proceed on the assumption that those in the companies of U.S. volunteers who could not be identified as having Texas residences had in fact left their homes in the United States to fight in Texas after the outbreak of hostilities in October, 1835.

Residence origin of the men who served in the units not associated with any military action in the spring of 1836 (Table 5) likewise could not be determined by the name of their company (when known), even though several of these units were recruited at and associated with a particular place. Of the seventy-three men enrolled in Captain James Smith's Nacogdoches Mounted Volunteers, only thirteen could be identified as hailing from Nacogdoches county. The others came from eight different counties or were recent emigrants from the U.S. Most of those who served in the Jasper Volunteers, raised by James Chesshire on March 23, 1836, could not be identified. The San Augustine volunteers of W. D. Ratliff came from 11 counties and the United States besides local sources. Only John A. Quitman's company, which arrived at Nacogdoches from Mississippi on April 12, 1836, had a discrete identity by place.

Seymour V. Connor's "The Evolution of County Government in the Republic of Texas," *Southwestern Historical Quarterly* 55 (Oct., 1951): 187–90, helped make it possible to identify the 1835–36 equivalents of places and political units named in the land claims of the General Land Office (frequently even first class headright claims were not filed until 1837 or 1838 after boundaries had been changed).

Index

Moore, John W., 44
Mora, Esteban, 200
Morfit, Henry M., 255
Morgan, James, 228–29, 243, 249
Moya, Agustín, 161, 163
Moya, Juan, 161, 163
Músquiz, Ramón, 181, 198

Nacogdoches: army provisioning at,
210–11; ayuntamiento of, 29, 65, 146;
citizens meetings in, 30, 32, 65; committee of safety at, 40, 64–66, 199,
209–10; conscription efforts in, 100–
102; and Convention elections, 79–81;
department of, 11, 19; and economy,
212; military preparations in, 35; opposition to government in, 175; and
race, 213–14; and runaway slaves, 246;
support in, for revolution, 64–66, 208–
11; Tejanos in, 13, 29–30, 64, 199–200;
Tories from, 169–73
Nacogdoches, municipality (county) of,
115, 123, 127, 129–31, 133, 220–22
Nacogdoches Mounted Volunteers, 128
Navarro, Angel, 26, 161; and Coahuila
state government, 21–22; and Mexican
army, 180, 201; and passport system,
185; as political chief, 28; as Tory, 165–
66
Navarro, José Antonio, 83–84, 88, 165,
196
Navarro, Luciano, 196
Neill, J. C., 62, 196; and command at
Béxar, 71, 119, 142, 145; and Conven-
tion elections, 79; seeks supplies, 148,
196
Newell, Chester, xv–xvi
Newell, John D., 217
New Orleans, 148
New Orleans Greys, 144, 210–11
Newport (Virginia) Rifle Company, 140
New Washington, Tex., 230
Nixon, George A., 64–65, 199, 221
Noriega, F. M. Díaz, 244

O'Docherty (O'Daugherty), William,
157–58
O'Docherty, Sussanah, 157–58, 180
Old Three Hundred, 216–21
Organic Law, 50–51
Ortiz, José María, 181

Padilla, Juan A., 59, 69, 189
Page, Benjamin, 177
Pantallion, Bernard, 199
Parker, Silas, 128, 214
Payton, Angelina, 235
peace party, 15, 30
Pease, E. M., 74, 107
Peck, S. R., 100
Peebles, Robert, 19
Penington, Sydney, 100
Permanent Council, 40–43
Perry, J. F., 25, 46, 242, 249
Perry, James Hazard, 143
Pettus, William, 41, 72–73
Peyton, Mrs. A. B., 211
Pierson, John G. W., 217
Poe, George W., 120
political chiefs, 11
Pollard, Amos, 79
popular disturbances of 1832, 6
Potter, Robert: and Convention, 80–81,
84, 88; and militia enrollment, 99; as
secretary of navy, 97; and Velasco treaty,
105–106
Power, James, 14, 90, 159, 216
provisional government, 53, 73. *See also*
Council

Quitman, John A., 171–72, 226

race war, 213, 226
Raguet, Henry, 66, 172, 221
Ramírez y Sesma, Joaquín, 199, 215
Ratliff, W. D., 128
Rattle Snake, 231
Red River, municipality (county) of, 84–
85, 115, 123, 127, 129–31, 133
Red Rover company, 145
Reed, Martha A., 211
Refugio: 14, 26; and Convention elec-
tions, 78; fighting at, 194, 223; im-
pressment at, 209; war aftermath in,
203–207
Refugio, municipality (county) of, 115,
123, 127, 129–31, 133
regionalism, 10, 64
religion, 12
revolution: defined, xix–xxi; models of,
xx–xxii
Roberts, Elisha, 220
Roberts, John S., 81, 84

CPSIA information can be obtained
at www.ICGtesting.com
Printed in the USA
BVHW032059041219
565577BV00001BA/12/P

9 780890 967218